The Economics of Art Museums

A National Bureau
of Economic Research
Conference Report

The Economics of
Art Museums

Edited and with an Introduction by

Martin Feldstein

 The University of Chicago Press

Chicago and London

MARTIN FELDSTEIN is the George F. Baker Professor of Economics at Harvard University, and is president and chief executive officer of the National Bureau of Economic Research.

The University of Chicago Press, Chicago 60637
The University of Chicago Press, Ltd., London
© 1991 by the National Bureau of Economic Research
All rights reserved. Published 1991
Printed in the United States of America
00 99 98 97 96 95 94 93 92 91   5 4 3 2 1

ISBN (cloth): 0-226-24073-8

Library of Congress Cataloging-in-Publication Data

The Economics of art museums / edited and with an introduction by Martin Feldstein.
    p.   cm. —(A National Bureau of Economic Research conference report)
    Includes bibliographical references and index.
    1. Art museums—Economic aspects—United States. I. Feldstein, Martin S.   II. National Bureau of Economic Research.   III. Series: Conference report (National Bureau of Economic Research)
N510.E27   1991
338.4'770813—dc20   91-27088
                                                          CIP

Contents

Preface

The National Bureau of Economic Research organized a project to explore the economic issues facing the major art museums of the United States. For this purpose we defined economics broadly to include not only the financial situation of the museums but also the management and growth of museum collections, the museums' relationship with the public, and the role of the government in supporting art museums.

This volume brings together nontechnical essays on these issues by economists associated with the National Bureau of Economic Research and personal statements by leaders of our major national art museums and related foundations. I hope that it will be read not only by economists but also by museum officials and trustees. Museum directors generally come to their responsibilities with a background in art history and curatorial work but without experience in thinking about the management and public policy aspects of museum administration. Trustees who serve on museum boards generally have a background in business or law but have not previously tried to apply their experience to the unusual economic problems of museums. I hope that the background papers, the panelists' remarks, and the summary of the discussion will help them to approach their responsibilities with a better understanding of the problems and possibilities of the museum.

A small group of NBER economists met in 1989 to examine these issues informally and to plan the specific research. We benefited from the participation of several officials of leading museums and of the Association of Art Museum Directors (AAMD). In organizing this project I also had very helpful personal discussions about these issues with Neil Rudenstine, then of the Mellon Foundation, and Alan Shestack of the Museum of Fine Arts, Boston.

The Association of Art Museum Directors conducts an annual statistical survey of its members to obtain information on finances and attendance. We are grateful to the AAMD and in particular to Bruce H. Evans, Director of the

Dayton Art Institute, who supervises the annual survey, for their cooperation in providing these data. An analysis of several aspects of these data is presented by Professor Richard N. Rosett in the first background paper of this volume. Several other researchers in the project also used these data for their work.

In December 1989 the project culminated in a two-day conference at which the NBER economists who prepared the background papers met with directors and curators from principal American museums and other leaders of the museum community. The small size of the group allowed for a lively discussion that, in my view, successfully bridged the two cultures. Our meeting was organized into five sessions: (1) The Museum's Collection, (2) The Museum and the Public, (3) Museum Finances, (4) The Museum and the Government, and (5) a final overview session aimed at integrating these separate issues.

Each session was launched by three or four personal statements. The full texts of these remarks are presented in the first part of this volume together with summaries of each discussion. The background papers appear in the second part of this volume. I am grateful to all of the participants for their contributions to the project and for their participation in the conference. I also want to thank Professor Douglas Elmendorf of Harvard University and the NBER for preparing the summary of the discussion and for his general help with editing this volume.

Financial support for this project came from the J. Paul Getty Foundation, the Mellon Foundation, the New York Times Foundation, and Mr. David Rockefeller. I am grateful to all of them for their generosity.

I am also pleased to thank several members of the NBER staff for their assistance in the planning and execution of the meetings and in the preparation of this volume, particularly Kirsten Foss Davis, Ilana Hardesty, Mark Fitz-Patrick, Kathi Smith, and Candace Morrissey.

Martin Feldstein

Introduction

Martin Feldstein

Museums are fundamentally different from other institutions in our economy and society. Like universities and symphony orchestras, they play a central role not only in the current cultural life of the nation but also as conveyors of our cultural heritage from one generation to the next. But unlike universities and orchestras, they are literally the preservers of the objects of culture themselves.

Although art museums are a vital part of our culture, financially they are relatively neglected stepchildren of our affluent economy. As nonprofit institutions, they lack both the ability to raise financial resources in the ways that profit-making businesses can and the substantial public funding of government activities. The largesse that can flow to universities from loyal alumni is not available to museums.

The sharp rise in the value of paintings and other forms of art during the past decade has made museums both remarkably rich and at the same time remarkably poor. They are rich if measured by the value of their collections at current market prices but poor because the sharp rise in the relative price of art severely limits their ability to acquire additional works of art.

Museums that are so rich in art are also poor when judged by the operating budgets available for the preservation, protection, restoration, display, and education associated with that art. There is a distressing contrast between the cultural importance and artistic treasures of our nation's leading museums and their very modest operating budgets. The 150 largest art museums have a combined annual operating budget of less than $1 billion, not even one percent of national spending on higher education and only about as much as Americans spend each year on fishing tackle or golf equipment.

The federal government's annual support through the National Endowment for the Arts is less than $15 million. The total direct support to nongovernmental art museums from all levels of government totals only about $70 million a year, about the federal government's daily spending on farm subsidies.

The budget stringency of museums reflects not only their status as private nonprofit organizations but also their mission to preserve art and to display it to a broad public. The mission of displaying art to the public restricts revenue by limiting the appropriate admission charges. Although a for-profit organization with a collection of Rembrandts or Renoirs might be able to earn substantial income by charging very high admission fees, a nonprofit museum would not follow such a policy because the resulting substantial decline in attendance would be contrary to the museum's basic mission.

The character of museums restricts their financial ability in another important way. Additions to a museum's collection, as well as the restoration and preservation of the existing collection, are analogous to the investment in plant and equipment by a manufacturing business. But unlike a for-profit business, a museum cannot finance these investment activities by issuing equity. And while the art collections themselves are very valuable assets, the purpose of the museum as a curator and public displayer of art means that the collections cannot be treated like financial assets or like the assets of an ordinary business that can be sold whenever funds are needed.

This introductory essay, as well as several of the background papers and personal statements, discusses some of the practical issues that museums face in dealing with the inherent conflict of being rich in art and poor in operating budgets. I came to the subject of this volume as someone without any specialized knowledge about the economics of art museums but with an interest in nonprofit organizations more generally and in the effects of government policies, particularly tax policies, on the private sector. I learned a good deal from the economic background papers and from the comments of the museum experts at the conference reported in this volume. My comments here are an attempt to summarize some of the key conclusions that I believe emerged from the research and the discussions as well as some personal ideas about the economic problems facing our leading museums.

It is convenient to organize these comments in three parts dealing with the uses of funds, the sources of funds, and the necessary trade-offs among conflicting goals that museums must face.

Uses of Funds

Consider first the three major uses of museum funds: operating costs, art acquisitions, and the construction of new facilities.

Operating costs are primarily personnel costs, including the professional staff of curators and conservationists and the support staff of office employees, maintenance workers, guards, and so on. Because of the nature of museum activities, there is little or no scope for the type of technical progress that reduces labor inputs in manufacturing businesses, financial enterprises, and the like. Operating costs are therefore likely to rise indefinitely at about the same rate as wages and therefore at a rate that is about two percentage points greater than the rate of increase of the general price level. This has important implications for endowment management to which I return below.

Acquisitions of new works of art will depend primarily on gifts and bequests of those works of art. The current tax rules (particularly the rules subjecting the appreciation in the value of gifts of appreciated property to the alternative minimum tax) are clearly a major barrier to the museums' ability to attract gifts of important works of art. Unless the tax rules are modified, expensive works of art are likely to lie beyond the reach of all but a very few American museums.[1] Although museums will continue to purchase some works of art, the heavy burden of operating expenses will absorb most of the unrestricted funds and the high prices of major works of art will make purchases very difficult. The most likely source of funds for the purchase of art will be from "deaccessioning" (to use the term that museum officials prefer to "selling" in the same way that politicians prefer "revenue enhancements" to taxes) some items from the collection in order to strengthen or diversify the collection in other ways. The subject of deaccessioning is also one to which I return below.

Finally there is spending on the construction of new buildings or the expansion of old ones. Because museums generally have much more art than they have the space to exhibit, there is always pressure to expand the size of the museum itself. As in other nonprofit organizations, it is often far easier to raise funds for a major building than for operating expenses. But as Neil Rudenstine warns in his comments in this volume, buildings are not only expensive per se but also lead to increases in the overall level of operating budgets. Limitations on operating budgets as well as on construction funds mean that museums that are eager to display more of their total collection will have to develop creative ways of showing a larger portion of their collection in a limited amount of space, even if that means a less-than-ideal presentation of some of the material.

Sources of Funds

Except for the Washington, D.C. museums that are supported by the federal government and those museums that are supported primarily by state and local governments (as discussed in the background papers by Richard N. Rosett and Charles T. Clotfelter), most of our major art museums are private nonprofit organizations that must depend for their funds on admission charges, charitable gifts, the limited profits that are generated by museum shops and restau-

---

1. After the completion of this project, Congress passed legislation excluding gifts of art to museums in 1991 only from the alternative minimum tax with an understanding that an extension of that new rule might be enacted during 1991.

rants, a relatively small amount of endowment income, and an even smaller amount of funds from the government.

In practice, revenues from admissions provide only about 5 percent of the total income of the largest 150 art museums. Traditional economic analysis provides a reason for concluding that an art museum should in principle not be funded through admission charges. Although the analysis is familiar to economists, it is worth reviewing here for the noneconomist readers of the volume. A fundamental idea in economics is that a nation's resources are used in the best way when each economic activity is expanded to the point where the benefit to consumers of any further expansion is just balanced by the cost of providing one more unit of that activity. Thus the production of bread should be increased until the value of the last loaf (as measured by a consumer's willingness to pay for it) is equal to the cost of producing it. If there is another consumer who would value an additional loaf of bread more than the cost of producing it, it would be good to produce the extra bread. But if the last loaf cannot be sold for what it costs to produce, too much bread is being made.

When applied to art museums, this implies that as long as an extra visitor to the museum imposes no additional costs on the museum or on other visitors, the ideal admission policy is to have no charge at all. Even a modest admission charge might deny someone who wished to see the collection the opportunity to do so even though his or her seeing it would impose no cost. It would be wrong to restrict attendance in this way just as it would be wrong not to produce a loaf of bread when there is a buyer willing to pay more than the incremental cost of production.[2]

Some charge could be justified for visitors to particularly popular exhibitions or whenever the galleries are crowded, because the existence of crowds reduces the enjoyment of other visitors and thereby imposes a kind of nonmonetary cost on them. But these "congestion-based" admission charges would not be able to cover the total cost of the museum's activities (including conservation) at the appropriate level of intensity.[3]

The conservation activities of the museum do not benefit only those who currently visit the museum. Future generations of visitors will benefit from the collection as well. Moreover, the reproduction of works of art in books

2. In the language of economics, it is appropriate to have no admission charge because museum attendance is a "public good," that is, the museum's collection can be enjoyed by an additional person without increasing the total cost of production. In contrast, it is appropriate to charge for bread because bread is a "private good," that is, the total cost of bread production must rise if an additional loaf of bread is to be consumed.

3. The appropriate level of intensity of museum activities is easier to define conceptually than to assess in practice. The appropriate level of spending by the museum is the highest level of spending at which any increase in spending does not produce current and future benefits to the museum's audience that are as large as the additional cost. Any reduction in the level of spending would reduce the benefits to the museum's audience by more than the reduction in costs.

and videotapes extends the group that benefits from the museum's collection beyond those who can actually visit the museum. Although it is obviously appropriate to charge for the cost of producing such books or videotapes, adding a royalty charge to the price would discourage some people from seeing the art even though they could do so without imposing any additional cost on the museum.

The case against charging admission fees and publication royalties is fully persuasive only when there is enough support from private contributions and government funds to maintain the appropriate level of museum activities. When these other sources of funds are inadequate, higher admission fees may be better than lower levels of spending. The possibility that admission charges could appropriately be a more important source of funds than they are today is discussed in the last section of this chapter.

Cash gifts from individuals and corporations account for about one-third of the annual operating budgets of the major 150 museums, with about four-fifths of those funds coming from individuals. As Don Fullerton's background paper indicates, the tax deductibility of charitable gifts significantly increases the total dollar amount of such giving, and the increase in giving induced in this way is substantially more important than all direct government support for art museums.

The 1986 reduction in individual marginal tax rates and the unfavorable treatment of gifts of securities under the alternative minimum tax rules have substantially reduced the value of gifts of cash and securities to museums (as well as the gifts of art). Although such financial gifts will undoubtedly increase in the future as incomes rise, the relative size of such giving will be depressed unless there is a change in tax rules with respect to charitable giving.

Although charitable contributions are an important source of museum finance, the voluntary nature of charitable giving means that these funds are likely to be less than enough to support the appropriate level of museum activities. The key reason is that any individual can enjoy the museum's services without being a contributor. Although each contributor also enjoys the satisfaction of giving, as well as the benefits of enhanced museum services, most of the benefit of an extra dollar in the museum's treasury goes to the large number of other museum visitors. Even with the reduction in the cost of giving implied by the tax rules, individuals will not be motivated to contribute enough to support the appropriate level of museum activities. Even individuals with the highest marginal tax rate must forego roughly 65 cents of alternative spending to give a dollar to a museum, while that dollar will benefit literally hundreds or thousands of museum visitors.

Because our museums are such a great national treasure, it is tempting to hope that Washington will provide greater support in the future. But whatever the merits of the case for increased federal funding—and the traditional "public goods" analysis indicates that they are considerable—direct federal support now accounts for less than 2 percent of the total operating budgets of the nation's private art museums, and the remarks of Andrew Oliver of the National Endowment for the Arts in this volume confirm that there seems little prospect of a significant increase. Our political tradition makes additional support from local governments and through the federal tax system more likely than increased direct funding from Washington, but the financial pressures on states and localities at the present time make significant increases in funding for the arts unlikely.

Income from endowments now contributes about one-sixth of the museums' total operating budgets. Richard N. Rosett's background paper reports that museums have used an average payout rate of 6.4 percent in calculating the amount of their endowment that they spend. About three-fourths of this income is spent on current operations and the rest on acquisitions.

Some simple calculations show that this current practice represents an unsustainably high rate of spending of endowment funds in most museums. If the endowment income is not to decline over time as a fraction of total spending, the size of the total endowment must increase over time at the same rate as the operating budget. Since operating expenses rise with the level of wages, which have increased over the long term at about 2 percent a year more than prices, the growth of the endowment must exceed the rise in the general price level by about 2 percent a year. Major universities with well-managed endowments invested in a combination of debt and equity securities calculate that over long periods of time the real inflation-adjusted return on endowments averages only about 4 percent. Even if a museum's endowment is judged to be large enough in relation to current expenditures that the endowment need only grow at 2 percent a year in real terms, the spending financed by the endowment should be limited to 2 percent plus the value of gifts and bequests to the endowment. Very few museums have the flow of endowment gifts and bequests that would justify spending as much as the 6.4 percent average payout rate that museums as a whole are now taking.

As I listened to the discussion at the meeting and talked with museum officials, I concluded that while museums are doing a great deal to expand annual operating gifts from individuals and corporations, they are doing less to increase major bequests and gifts to the endowment fund. By contrast, universities appear to do much more to attract very large gifts and bequests to be added to endowment capital. One reason for the difference is that major universities are financially much larger than major museums and can justify the specialized professional staff needed to solicit major gifts and bequests. The only way for museums to know if they could be successful in seeking such capital funds is to regard such a fund-raising project as an investment with an uncertain payoff, devoting funds to the project for several years to see if it repays the effort and expenditure.

Quantifying Trade-Offs

Museums quite rightly have a multiplicity of missions including not only the display of the collection but the preservation and restoration of the works of art, scholarly research, and public education. Understandably, the staff and trustees of the museums might generally believe that more of these activities would be better than less.

The desire to expand services is characteristic of those who are responsible for all types of nonprofit organizations, including education, health-care, welfare services, and religious organizations as well as museums. From society's perspective, however, the expansion of each type of activity must be balanced against the real costs. If we step away from the nonprofit sector for a moment, for most of the vast array of ordinary goods and services produced in our economy, the basic forces of supply and demand do a very good job of balancing the values of various products and services with their costs of production.

But in the nonprofit sector, the market cannot be counted on to achieve the correct level of spending on different types of activities. The mechanisms that society has created to supplement the market in support of nonprofit organizations are also far from perfect in balancing the costs and benefits of different activities. In some activities, too few resources are available (in the sense that additional spending would create benefits that exceed their costs), while in other areas, the method of financing causes the volume of resources to be excessive. Because of the "public good" character of museums, the total level of spending is almost certainly less than optimal, while the financing of hospital care through tax-subsidized private and public insurance probably causes the level of spending on hospital care to be excessive.

Those who are responsible for the governance and management of museums must therefore recognize that they are unlikely ever to have enough funds to operate their institutions at the level of activity that could be justified in an ideal world. Instead they must make difficult choices of what to do with the limited funds available.

As J. Carter Brown, Director of the National Gallery of Art, correctly notes in his comments, economists emphasize the need to recognize trade-offs in every type of activity. A museum cannot do more of everything, but faces trade-offs: it can do more of one thing that it wants only by doing less of another. The key to good decision making is to see those trade-offs explicitly.

In many cases it would help to quantify the trade-offs facing a museum. What will an extra, say, $50,000 a year buy? How many extra hours would it allow the museum to be kept open? Or, alternatively, how many students could be brought to the museum for a single visit or a series of visits using that money? Or how many teachers could be brought to the museum for a series of classes that would permit them to teach about art more effectively in the city's schools? Or how many members of a minority group that does not normally come to the museum could be brought in by a variety of outreach programs? Only by quantifying the choices and assessing what the explicit trade-offs are within the given budget can the museum officials feel that they have made a well-reasoned choice.

In some cases, of course, quantification is easier than others. It may not be clear what a $50,000 program of advertising, transportation, and free admissions would do to minority attendance. But a quantitative guess refined as experience accumulates is better than just a feeling about what should be done.

It is even more difficult to quantify the effects of increased spending on preservation and conservation. And yet, without at least some crude quantification, how can the responsible museum officials know whether funds are being well spent?

Because museum budgets are severely constrained, it is desirable to revisit two issues about the sources of funds for museums in this spirit of facing difficult trade-offs: the deaccessioning of items from the collection and the charging of admission.

Museum officials have a natural reluctance to sell (deaccession) works of art from their collections. In addition to the loss of the work from the museum's own collection, there is the concern that the painting or other object might no longer be available to the public in any museum or might even leave the country. Moreover, a work of art that goes from the expert hands of a museum curator to a private individual might not be cared for as well. These are legitimate concerns of anyone who feels responsible for the care and public display of the works in the museum's collection.

Although museum storerooms have many works of art that cannot currently be displayed because of inadequate space, and that may not have been displayed for decades, curators argue that works that are currently unfashionable may be of greater interest in the future. There is a concern, moreover, that selling objects from the collection may deter future gifts of works of art or may even deter cash contributions by prospective donors who come to regard the sale of the museum's art as an alternative source of cash for operating purposes.

In an ideal world in which museums were adequately funded, these arguments might well be fully persuasive. But in the actual second-best world in which museums are woefully underfunded, museum professionals have generally come to accept the sale of works of art from their collections, as long as the receipts from those sales are restricted to purchasing new works of art for the collection.

Perhaps surprisingly, when works are sold, they are not sold subject to restrictions that they may not be exported or that they must remain in the collection of a public museum. Imposing such legal restrictions would reduce the sale price for any object sold but would allay some of the concerns that museum officials have about their stewardship responsibilities.

Such restrictions that protected the care and public availability of deaccessioned works of art might also make museum officials willing to use the funds from such sales for certain types of operating expenses. Expenditures on the restoration or preservation of works of art in the collection may be seen as close substitutes for the acquisition of new works of art. Indeed, the restoration or preservation of a work that is already in the museum's collection may be a socially more productive way of adding to the museum's usable collection because it represents a virtual net addition to the world's stock of art rather than just a shift of ownership.

Funds spent on improving the security of the museum's collection (guards, electronic surveillance, etc.) or the internal climate of the museum (air conditioning, humidification, etc.) are similar in their effect to more technical museum work to restore and preserve works of art. Museum officials who see themselves as the stewards of the world's art might even find expenditures on restoration, preservation, and protection more worthwhile than expenditures on acquisitions.

I come finally to the problem of admission charges. I have already explained why economists would say that in an ideal world it would be appropriate to have no admission charge at all. Even when a charge is justified by the detrimental effect of additional visitors on the enjoyment of the museum by others, the level of the charge would ideally be set to reflect only this "congestion" effect and not with a view to raising revenue.

Museums must, however, live in a second-best world in which the lack of funding means that all of the museum's missions are served less well than would be ideal. There is too little restoration and preservation, open hours are too restricted, too little is done to attract members of the public who normally do not come to the museum, too little is done to educate those who do come, and too few specialized exhibitions are presented for relatively well-informed museum visitors.

Although an increase in admission charges would discourage some attendance, it would, at a minimum, permit the museum to serve its other missions more adequately. Museum charges are now quite low relative to what an individual would expect to pay for a similar amount of time spent at a concert or theater or sporting event. Although museums have been reluctant to increase general admission charges, they do impose extra fees for major travelling exhibitions with wide popular appeal, and the resulting revenue is seen as a significant contributor to annual budgets. Nevertheless, receipts from admission charges still finance only some 5 percent of museum operating budgets.

The decision of whether or not to raise admission charges should be based on a quantitative assessment of the likely results. How much would an extra dollar of admission charge reduce total attendance? How much additional revenue would be produced, taking into account the higher revenue from those who continue to come and the revenue lost from those who stop coming? What could the museum do with the extra revenue? What types of individuals would choose not to come if the admission charge were increased? Could special discounts for particular groups (e.g., students, senior citizens) or particular times during the week eliminate most of the adverse effect on attendance while still producing extra revenue from those visitors who are less sensitive to the price of admission (e.g., higher income groups and visitors from out of town)? Could some of the extra revenue be used to encourage attendance through public information programs designed to attract visitors or through activities at the museum that bring in additional visitors? In this way it might even be possible to increase total attendance while raising charges and net revenue. But even if that is not possible, the museum should face explicitly the trade-offs made possible by considering higher admission fees.

A Concluding Thought

Although museums are a small part of our economy, they are a vital part of our national life. Those who are responsible for museums rightly see themselves as the protectors of the treasures that our generation has inherited from the past, as the collectors of the creative activity of the current time, and as teachers who help the broad public to know and appreciate these works of art.

Ordinary market forces cannot support an appropriate level of museum activities. This is recognized by the public's willingness to support museums through contributions of money and art and by the government's support through grants and through the special tax treatment of charitable gifts.

But unless there is a dramatic change in our nation's priorities, museums will continue to have budgets that are too small to pursue their many missions at socially appropriate levels. Museum administrators and trustees will therefore be forced to confront difficult trade-offs among competing objectives. I hope that this volume can contribute to improving the quality of those choices.

I Panel Discussions

1   The Museum's Collection

Theodore E. Stebbins, Jr., Julia Brown Turrell,
Jay E. Cantor, and John Walsh

Theodore E. Stebbins, Jr.

It would seem a truism, and unnecessary to repeat, that the very heart of the older, established museum such as the Museum of Fine Arts can be found in its permanent collection. This is clear, at least, to most of us who devote our lives to these institutions. When we think of a museum, we think of its collection, and particularly of its great strengths. If you say "the Museum of Modern Art" to me, I imagine the gallery full of Matisses, or the one with their great Pollocks. When I think of the Philadelphia Museum of Art, I see the superlative group of Eakins paintings; for Chicago, I conjure up the great Seurat, *Sunday Afternoon on the Island of La Grande Jatte*. The collection is what gives the museum its identity, establishes its mission, and suggests its future. The collection also is often the most important factor in attracting the attention and allegiance of both its professional staff and its major supporters. Moreover, most museums, including the Museum of Fine Arts, place the care and preservation of the collections at the top of their mission statements.

Yet despite all this, I believe that while we pay lip service to the idea that the collection is central to what museums are about, we are in danger in our real lives of making the care, conservation, exhibition, storage, publication, research, and building of the collection into a secondary aim. As Philippe de Montebello has pointed out on several occasions, these are difficult and strange times for museums, and undermanned staffs turn increasingly to the production of temporary exhibits—with their hoped-for financial benefits to the museum, and the occasional moments of glory they can bring to the director and curator—while turning away to a considerable extent from their traditional job of caring for the permanent collection. My own view is that collections are akin to living organisms. Collections that are not cared for, that are not actively researched, conserved, published, and exhibited become

13

weak, and they may even die. Collections become especially vulnerable if they are left without specialist curators who study and champion them. Thus a distinguished modernist director, Andrew Ritchie, sold Yale's great collection of Tiffany glass in the late fifties because the material seemed tasteless and therefore irrelevant to the study of art history. More recently, during the past year, the Walker Arts Center sold the last of its T. B. Walker collection of nineteenth-century American paintings, including the now famous painting by Frederic Church, *Home by the Lake,* 1852, which set an all-time price record for an American picture at Sotheby's in May 1989. This deaccessioning was done with great deliberation and care, a number of distinguished experts were consulted, and in many ways, the deaccessioning makes sense in view of the Walker's self-definition as a museum of contemporary art. But at the same time, no one can doubt that it was a tragic loss for Minneapolis and for the people of that area. It was the region's core collection of nineteenth-century American art, and it exists no longer. Surely the sale never would have happened if *either* the Walker or its neighbor, the Minneapolis Art Institute, had had at the time a curator specializing in the nineteenth-century American field. This is not to say that I believe deaccessioning to be de facto wrong. We do it regularly at the Museum of Fine Arts, and we try to do it carefully and wisely; but our rule is *never* to sell things that we dislike, because we know that taste changes. Rather, we do it only in narrowly defined areas when trying to upgrade the work of an artist or school. One of the great joys of working with a collection as good as ours in Boston is the opportunity to improve holdings that are already strong. To give just one example, no one would doubt that our collection of works by John Singleton Copley, numbering some sixty-two paintings and thirty drawings, is one of the great treasures of the museum, one of the reasons people come to the MFA. During the past decade, we have worked hard to make this great collection even more outstanding, in the process acquiring three more Copley paintings—the famous *Boy with a Squirrel,* the rare full-length portrait of *Colonel Nathaniel Sparhawk,* and a beautiful grisaille, *The Copley Family,* which includes a Copley self-portrait in it. One of these acquisitions came as a gift, one was a partial purchase and partial gift, and one was wholly bought. Purchase funds in these cases came from the sale of three of the weakest of our Copleys. I think deaccessioning works best where you have a strong expertise, and it is best when you upgrade within a given school, as the Museum of Modern Art did successfully recently with the purchase of their Van Gogh, or where you upgrade within the work of the same artist. We have slowly learned in our field that people, both scholars and the public, come to a museum for its strengths—that people go to Philadelphia to see Eakins, to New Haven to see Trumbull, to Sarasota to see Rubens, and so on—and that we need not all aim to have a broad survey of all of art history. In the fifties it was very popular for all museums to have a broad survey of everything; that now seems unnecessary and naive.

Working with a collection is extremely rewarding for the specialist, but sadly, in most of our museums, we have not yet learned how to convey this high priority of the collection to others. Both our public and our own trustees are likely to see our full storerooms either as representing liquid inventory, or as demonstrating that we already have more art than we need, both of which are quite wrong. The rise in the art market makes our collections worth more and concomitantly makes our lives more difficult in almost every respect. Most dangerously, current prices raise the specter of selling art to pay operating expenses, which would, I believe, have a devastating effect on the future of museums. Alan Shestack, I know, feels strongly about this. We have not been effective in making clear the museum's multifaceted role as a center of research, as a bureau of aesthetic standards, as a library of materials, styles, and signatures, and as the source for future rediscoveries, exhibitions, and inevitable changes of taste. A collection must be properly curated; if it is not constantly being improved, it may well decline. Ongoing research and publication is particularly important if the museum is going to be more than a storage facility and the curator more than a caretaker, as has already happened in some small museums and historical societies.

In my own field of American art, during the 1980s, the Henry Luce Foundation has made an enormously important contribution toward solving this problem. During the past seven years they have made grants to some 20 museums for research and publication of both scholarly and popular catalogues of the permanent collections. These catalogues set a standard for the American and modern fields. The Luce Foundation also funded the superb Luce Study Center at the Metropolitan Museum of Art, a computerized, open collection storage, which was completed this year. During the nineties, it looks as though museums may be forced to turn back to their collections, as the cost of special exhibitions rises and outside funding from business and government dwindles. It seems to me that this is not an unwelcome development, for our permanent collections are the essential reasons for the existence and survival of the museum, and they deserve our attention.

Julia Brown Turrell

There is a range of issues facing museums as they form collections. How to do so with great quality, with major works; and how to do it accurately, so the evolution and force of art is conveyed in a way that is responsible to cultural history and to art itself. How to develop a collection of strength and distinction so each museum is not a carbon copy of the next. How to do so both with limited resources and with a limited number of works of great quality, in a world that is intensely competitive.

Museums are in a difficult period with the myriad of pressures placed upon them to play many different roles in a community and to serve many different constituencies. At the heart of the museum's responsibility is to form and present its collection and to serve well its most important constituency—art itself.

I speak from the viewpoint of a director of a relatively medium-sized institution outside of a major urban center, a museum with distinctive architecture and an outstanding twentieth-century collection. This presents different issues and challenges from those of a large museum collecting many fields and periods. I also speak as a museum director with a particular concern about how best to collect and present the important art of our times for now and for future generations.

The current art market has complicated the task of museums tremendously, as has been well and frequently discussed. The rapid escalation of prices both at auction and in the galleries has taken many museums out of the market. Donors, because of this factor, and because of the current tax laws, are less willing to give. Another result of this money frenzy has been an uncomfortable shift in values whereby one is talking more about money than about art, and real value becomes harder and harder to ascertain. In the contemporary art world, the interplay of museums, galleries, artists, collectors, auction houses, critics and other writers, and the ever-present media results in a complex of powerful factors that influence reputations and prices.

Within this tangle of forces there remains the steady and compelling power of the art itself, and it is the job of the museum to fully respond to it. It is essential that museums work both with the market and independently of the market in their building of collections. Because the forces that drive the market are not the same as those that drive art, and because the goals of the two are not the same, the museum must keep its sights clear on what is important in art and not be overly influenced or driven by what may be important in the market.

I feel that in our turbulent times, and particularly in the area of contemporary art, it is more important than ever for the museum to be bold, to be steady, to be wise, and to be responsible—to art and to artists and to its public.

It is imperative for museums to plan for the future in response to the development and needs of art itself and to realize that continual institutional growth, change, and reassessment are required because the history of art continues to evolve.

By carefully assessing what has been an important force in the recent evolution of art, and taking on that work which may challenge some of the traditional spatial and structural constraints of many museums, I believe one can form an important collection of art of our time, even with limited resources. In marshaling one's resources and working with artists, collectors, dealers, and the auction houses to identify and purchase primary works, I believe one can still make a collection of substantial and lasting meaning even with limited resources. To have the courage of one's conviction, as an institution, and not to be swayed by the prevailing forces of fashion will bear real fruit.

One of the directions we are pursuing in Des Moines is to take advantage of our unique setting (which includes buildings by architects Eliel Saarinen, I. M. Pei, and Richard Meier) and our location in a beautiful park, by commissioning and purchasing environmental outdoor and indoor works for the collection. A major sited sculpture in stone by Richard Serra has just been installed, and works by Bruce Nauman, Robert Irwin, Siah Armajani, Bill Viola, Richard Fleischner, Ann Hamilton, and Mary Miss are in various stages of development. These are artists who are making a major contribution to the evolution of art but whose nonobject works and installations are less involved in the art market. We are also continuing to build the collection through seeking important individual works from 1940 to the present using the same combination of resources used by most museums: collection endowment funds, fund-raising to support individual works, careful deaccessioning to focus and strengthen the collection, and the seeking of donations. In the intensely competitive arena of contemporary art, with more and more museums and collectors around the world focusing on contemporary art, it is a challenge to identify and purchase important works while the price is still within the realm of possibility, and before the prize is snapped up by others.

Jay E. Cantor

My remarks will be partially economic and partially philosophical. I hope to suggest through a few digestible statistics what we all know from the banner headlines of the press reports on each season's rounds of major auctions. The market is hot, and prices are escalating at an incredible rate. The real impact of price increases on collectors, both private and institutional, has to be understood in light of broad patterns of collecting behavior.

The auction market represents only a segment of the art market, the other part being the trade—in itself a diverse group ranging from art consultants to private dealers to the traditional gallery, with a fair number of people dealing out of an attaché case sprinkled in. The auction market is, however, an increasingly large and visible component of the market. Moreover, the sales figures, by consistency, volume, and documentation, are the most reliable index we have of the art market. While we cannot quantify the entire market through auction records, we can discern patterns and examine changes that have occurred. We also have evidence that auction prices both mirror the market and influence it when we see dealers adjusting prices immediately after an auction.

The other half of my discussion will revolve around notions of collecting and the interplay among museums, private collectors, and the market. I want to glance back at market patterns of the last five years and to suggest some of the reasons for the changes that have occurred. Most price cycles in the art market last from three to five years. Significantly, the most recent five year period encompasses the 1986 tax law revision and demonstrates its impact on the art economy. You will forgive me if I take my figures from Christie's sales, but these are easiest for me to obtain. As we have enjoyed a fairly stable proportional balance with our major competitor over this period, I think our figures can be taken as a viable sampling rather than as a reflection of the redistribution of market share.

I will also concentrate on New York sales which, amazingly, have superseded London. This is an interesting footnote, as a decade ago, America was a provincial auction center.

Since 1984, Christie International's sales have increased annually at incredible rates: 1985–86, 8.2%; 1986–87, 50%; 1987–88, 10%; 1988–89, 63% (percentages are based on figures in pounds sterling). Our growth in New York has been similarly astonishing: 1985–86, 12.8%; 1986–87, 56.0%; 1987–88, 48.6%; 1988–89, 56.5% (percentages are based on figures in U.S. dollars).

In the 1960s, museums clearly held the center stage in making dramatic, high-priced art purchases. Beginning with the Metropolitan Museum's acquisition of Rembrandt's *Aristotle Contemplating the Bust of Homer* for $2.3 million, continuing through the 1970 sale of Velasquez's *Juan de Pareja* at over one million pounds sterling, to the Monet *Terasse at St. Adresse* in 1967, there was an optimistic broadening of the art market with museums in the lead. Such purchases may well have been a capstone—a fruition of 100 years of treasure hunting which had brought millions of works of art into the public domain. Museum professionals considered collections growth as a primary goal, and museum training focused on connoisseurship. Thoughtful acquisitions became the visible expression of the museum's professional activities.

Simultaneously, costly blockbuster exhibitions emerged as contenders for precious dollars of funding and began to erode the primacy of acquisitions as the focus of popular fascination with museums. Both of these activities are threatened by the current escalations in the market. Museums that cannot buy may also find it difficult to insure desired loans, and lenders in turn, because of the increased value and implied risk factor of a loss, have become increasingly unwilling to part with works. This is further complicated by the fact that we have a new breed of collector.

Scarcity and value in the market have combined with mobility in lifestyle to give art a different place in the domestic and emotional landscape of collectors. To put it bluntly, we have probably gone from the era of art collecting to the era of art consuming. In that scenario, art is acquired as an adjunct to other lifestyle decisions and can be changed as easily as one converts, say, from French provincial to Art Deco. Art has become, particularly through the good offices of art institutions, endowments, and the media, accessible and easy. A broader base of collectors now populates the marketplace, making, hopefully, studied but often highly personal decisions. These collectors are often disengaged from the traditional arena of museum affiliation and influence and from the familiar halls of plush, upscale galleries.

The new collector, who may never aspire to own more than a handful of works, pushes up prices and may well be invisible, aloof from the supplications of institutions. This collector is less likely to follow the lead of earlier generations who were the donors of important objects and collections. Older generations have absorbed the philanthropic instinct, at times outside of financial self-interest; it remains to be seen whether ready-made fortunes carry with them the same civic impulse. Furthermore, survival of this donor instinct, as we all know, was dealt a severe, additional blow by the 1986 tax law which eliminated the financial incentive to give appreciated property. In addition, museums are competing with each other to attract nationally recognized collectors in specific fields in hopes of luring them from their home institution with promises of greater national celebrity.

One of the few remaining opportunities for museums to lure gifts is in the form of bequests. Appreciated art becomes a liability in an estate and a drain on liquid assets. If the attraction of high prices and the ready accessibility of auctions, which perform especially well with estate material, do not distract heirs and executors, the bequest of art can be the most important potential source of acquisitions for all but the few institutions with generous purchase funds.

In the absence of a surviving class of philanthropic and nurturing trustees, and faced with other financial woes, the museum has turned increasingly to entrepreneurial or corporate leaders for managerial assistance on their boards. There is an expectation that these trustees will also provide much-needed funding, but they in turn assume they have been put on the board to provide the benefits of their business experience. These trustees often do not understand the difference between running the museum as a business and running it in a businesslike way. Hoping to convert practical managers into philanthropists, some museums, especially those in smaller communities, could find themselves with board members who have no interest in collections or collecting. Furthermore, in some institutions, curatorial departments lack a trustee collector to carry their banner and can find themselves at a singular disadvantage.

The curator is charged with encouraging fledgling or established collectors in the hopes they may also become donors. Curiously, at the very moment when this potential seems gloomiest, museums have awakened to the necessity of intimate familiarity with the marketplace. We see many more curators escorting collector groups to sales than ever before.

Many museums are also lumbered with a slow and cumbersome acquisitions process totally out of sync with the rhythm of the marketplace. Acquisition decisions reside with collectors, committees, and ultimately the board of trustees. The process was necessary in an era when the trustees, collectors themselves, were often paying for the art. With a new breed of trustee and greatly expanded professionalism of the museum staff, these procedures need to be streamlined.

Auctions will not wait, and after decades of having their property held captive for months pending a board meeting, dealers will not wait either. If they offer work to a museum, it is often the arcane, the difficult, the rare, or uncommercial object.

Collectors clearly have the advantage, especially the new entrants to the field. Those long engaged in the process can find it difficult to adapt to new price levels, even when their resources are adequate. New money enters the market and accepts it at its current level. Today's prices are the market. The secret desire for a return to the old days is not likely to be fulfilled because the old days are unknown to the new collector. I, of course, am not ruling out an across-the-board market adjustment.

Ironically, it may be high prices that pull people into the market, like moths attracted to a light bulb. The spotlight increases energy and activity, but it can be fatal. The heat of the art market simulates the fast-paced financial markets the new collector is familiar with. Art has become liquid—and the marketplace self-verifying.

As important private collections are drawn into the market by high prices, their freshness in the sales arena helps energize the bidding and escalate the selling price. Even the reappearance of a work of art after only a brief time off the market is not as catastrophic as it once was, since for new buyers, unfamiliar with a work's past history, the piece is a discovery, and price changes make it appear a bargain.

A recent and compelling example of this is a pastel by Mary Cassatt sold in June of 1984 in a Christie's American painting sale for $495,000. This large (25 × 32 inches) and dramatic work entitled *The Conversation* was reoffered in an American Paintings gallery four years later at $1,500,000 and found no takers. The owner then put it back at auction, this time in Christie's French Impressionist sale, where it commanded $4,510,000 only five years after its purchase at one-tenth of that price.

Liquidity, of course, can also encourage the pure speculator, and with that apparition in the market, we are all in trouble. While collecting may have become consuming, it should not be commodity trading.

Can museums participate in the market? Part of the answer, of course, lies in the collections policy. The institution that aspires to comprehensive overview, and one that hopes to build on selected strengths of the collection, can each find the market's scarcity defeating. On the other hand, specialized lacunas can be filled with objects that are not in the center of the market. While a Monet may be out of reach at $10 million, the truth is that the wealthier institutions probably do not need the kind of Monet that comes up, and the poorer ones would have been out of the market at one million.

Those who build collections on an existing strength appeal, in particular, to the specialist and scholar who finds it useful and convenient to see quality and quantity in concentration at a particular location. Such specialized focuses become visible attributes and promotable features of an institution—the museum as treasury and as monument demonstrating the power of plenty. The average visitor finds less utility in such aggregation. A broader chronicle probably provides greater functional utility for the community. And in days of decreasing assets and fewer traveling exhibitions, the permanent collectors will come into focus more clearly as the source of community interest in a museum. Museums are more likely to find collecting solutions in their basements—either by resurrecting previously neglected works or by finding material for deaccessioning.

The subject of deaccessioning is prickly and controversial, but it is an extremely important avenue for the museum which, while hurt by the rising market, might also benefit from it. As there is no right acquisitions or collections philosophy, there is no single acceptable rationale for deaccessioning. What I can suggest is that objects once in a museum are not sanctified in eternity, nor are they condemned to death if deaccessioned. The move from a basement rack or shelf to a Park Avenue apartment might be a step up, as the buyer who pays a good price is likely to care well for the purchase. It becomes part of the museum's new function not simply to be the custodian in perpetuity, but rather the educator and counselor to private preservers of art.

There is a lesson here from the countless historic preservation agencies who have deaccessioned houses with covenants to protect them. Furthermore, the sale of art is done to bring other art into the museum, so there is, in effect, no net loss and, in terms of the usefulness of the collections, a probable net gain.

Museums have participated more actively in the marketplace in recent years, as is evident from the figures reported in table 1.1. The responsibility to preserve, and the desire to build visible monuments is taking a special twist

Table 1.1   Museum Selling and Buying Activity at Christie's, 1984–89

Year	Institutions	Lots	Total Sales
Museum sales			
1988–89	88	844	$21,735,080
Violette de Mazia Collection sold for		440	7,865,720
the benefit of the Barnes Foundation			29,600,800
1987–88	86	1,277	14,237,912
1986–87	61	1,000	8,178,297
1985–86	37	997	6,425,306
1984–85	28	298	3,517,168
Museum purchases			
1988–89	93	142	37,543,678
No purchase figures available for previous years.			

Table 1.2

	American	Asian	Other	Total
Contemporary Art Sales Combined Totals: November 7 and 8, 1989:				
Dollars spent	39,410,580	9,136,600	34,279,300	83,014,680
% Dollars spent	47	11	42	100
Lots bought	236	41	153	420
% Lots bought	55	9	36	100
Impressionist and Modern Paintings, Drawings and Sculpture Collection by Mr. and Mrs. Paul Mellon; Impressionist and Modern Paintings and Drawings: The Mr. and Mrs. George N. Richard Collection; Important Impressionist and Modern Paintings, Drawings and Sculpture, Part 1—November 14, 1989:				
Dollars spent	49,027,000	88,715,000	94,616,000	232,358,000
% Dollars spent	21	38	41	100
Lots bought	17	25	26	68
% Lots bought	25	37	38	100
The Billy Wilder Collection: November 13, 1989:				
Dollars spent	15,763,000	3,822,500	13,055,900	32,641,400
% Dollars spent	48	12	40	100
Lots bought	42	12	31	85
% Lots bought	49	14	37	100

as museums confront the challenge to keep works of art in America in the face of the influx of foreign buyers. Again it is helpful to look at the statistics. In the most recent round of major Impressionist, modern, and contemporary sales, we see an interesting pattern of foreign buying (table 1.2). The American collectors demonstrated a strong preference in the contemporary field where the Japanese have only recently begun to make a showing. Asian buyers are still timid in the area of contemporary art and accounted for a small percentage of purchases. Even in the post-Impressionist and modern field, which was the core of the Billy Wilder collection, Asian buyers lagged behind American and other collectors. However, in the Impressionist arena, Asians bought a strong percentage of works, although not, as they had previously, all of the more expensive works.

Museums in America have undergone enormous physical expansion in the last few decades leading to an increase in memberships which, in turn, led to an increased need to keep members interested. Collecting activity has been a major component of that program. Collecting for a museum is incontrovertible evidence that it is, in fact, alive. Like an economy seeking continuous growth, museums have taken collection expansion as a sacred obligation. Collecting is often the reason a director or curator went into the field, a love of objects and the ameliorating influence of retail therapy. With this new market structure, and increasing competition from foreign buyers, the major lament is that the fun is gone. It is hard to collect; it is hard to convince the administration to pay attention to the collection.

The other side of museum work, the study and interpretation of the collection, has been suppressed in favor of the big and showy, audience-gathering, blockbuster. The staff spends an increasing proportion of their time filling out grant applications to the endowments or courting corporate sponsors. The small-scale, thoughtful, exploratory exhibition does not boost admissions.

American museums are rather frightened by the prospect of middle age, and little comfort is provided by the examples of great European institutions that are great without growing. American museums are too professionally oriented to sit still and too restless to retire. We may be at the end of a great era of collecting for institutions, but there are still significant opportunities.

The accumulated resources of American museums are a rich field for scholarship and an undiscovered territory for large segments of the population. Enlightened entertainment—the guiding principle of the creators of parks and museums a century ago—is still a positive potential for the museum public. The treasures of American institutions are a document of aspiration and a vehicle of inspiration.

In many ways, American museums have veered from their charter purposes. The frenzy of creation subsumed another, philosophical goal. Museum charters defined art as a means to an end—art in the service of education, moral uplift, and social betterment. And if original works of art were not available, these goals could be achieved through the use of casts and reproductions. Then suddenly new American wealth and a Europe impoverished by war made the unimaginable possible: great treasures could be purchased, and their acquisition became the major thrust of the museum.

New alignments in the market and a renewed understanding of what museums can and should accomplish will refocus attention on existing collections. Those collections will be revalued not only as a product of modern scholarship, but also in the light of revivals of older, forgotten, charter purposes. While we would all still like to be out there collecting, these new goals pose challenges in these complicated, not unimportant days.

John Walsh

Let me first say a few words as the 1989–90 president of the Association of Art Museum Directors, the AAMD, which represents about 140 of the larger art museums in this country.

When the trustees of AAMD learned about a year and a half ago that a group of world-famous economists, led by a former counselor to the president, planned to make a study of the economics of art museums, we had conflicting feelings. We were flattered, first of all, since we had been insisting to governments and policymakers for years that art museums had become a big force in the economics of our communities, and now we were going to be treated like one. We knew just how well timed your interest was, considering the financial bind that most of us are in, chronically or permanently. We hoped that economists would teach us something; at the same time, I am sure some of us feared that poking at our financial aches could lead you to mistaken diagnoses and maybe drastically wrongheaded treatment that you might prescribe and lend your prestige to.

The background papers, which I found fascinating—particularly on the subject of tax policy and marketing—showed that you don't have the answers either, and that we all still have much to learn about how museums function in the economy. I am grateful to each of you who wrote them. There is a lot there to argue about, but at the very least it is refreshing to read about our work and attitudes described from a sharply different perspective and in a professional jargon that is almost as arcane our own. I hope art museum directors will benefit a great deal from this meeting and the published proceedings.

Martin Feldstein asked me to speak on museum collections and especially my own personal experience. Given the peculiar situation of the Getty Museum, which is busy building a collection in a time of escalating prices and unfavorable tax laws, he suggested that I talk about collecting strategy, including the issue of specialization, and art sales by museums.

Our situation is nearly unique among art museums, for the Getty Trust is lucky enough to have the money to permit the Museum to compete for the best and rarest works of art in an increasingly dizzy market. (I am not sure that this actually gives me a better seat to observe the market. I sometimes feel I am down on the ground like Fabrizio, the young antihero of *The Charterhouse of Parma* by Stendahl, who rides into the middle of the battle of Waterloo but in the confusion cannot figure out what is going on, who is winning or losing, and for years afterward wonders whether that really was the famous battle he was in, or not.) In my six years at the Getty, we have been after an endangered species, the rare and important work of art. The competition is seldom from other museums, because their endowments for acquisitions have not risen with the astonishing inflation of the art market. Instead, it is almost exclusively from private collectors in America, South America, Europe, and Japan. These people, or the companies they control, have staggering amounts of cash to spend, often in currencies that have recently gotten stronger against the dollar. They often bid as though they have nothing to lose, confident that art will at least hold its value against other investments and may do better.

I would like to point out a few aspects of the mechanics of the market, not to my museum colleagues here, who know these things as well as I do, but to the economists.

The balance of forces has changed, so that now the auction houses dominate, whereas twenty years ago a much higher number of the most important works of art in the market were owned by private dealers or sold by them on consignment. In the good old days, not long ago, when dealers bought most of their stock directly from private owners, the dealers had great advantages: Nobody knew what they had paid, and therefore nobody could figure how high the markup was; it was not known that they had a particular work, so they could offer it quietly to various clients one by one; and, after a while, they could buy back works from their clients or take them in trade and resell them to other clients, sometimes making profits again and again on the same thing—in effect, managing in a spirit of quiet confidentiality a pool of art owned by successive generations of trusting clients. Now art dealers are forced more and more to buy at auctions. What they pay for something is public knowledge, so there is a limit to the markup. Higher and higher prices mean bigger investments for dealers when they buy, which has meant wider syndication to share the cost and risk, and this gives a bigger role for fretful backers and their accountants. Often dealers find themselves bidding against the same private collectors they would have hoped to sell to. Let me invent an example.

Let's take a collector, say Mrs. Haveamanet, who has a painting she bought from the dealer Sam Pfeffer for $200,000 in 1955. She has gotten old, the Manet is dirty, she wants the money to distribute to her children, so she goes back to Mr. Pfeffer. Pfeffer says they will gladly buy it back from her for $3.3 million, calculating that they can clean it, reframe it, and sell it for $4 million. Christibie's tells her that it will fetch $3.5 to $4 million at auction, maybe much more, and offers to pay her a guaranteed $3 million cash on the day of the sale. She might have preferred to dodge the publicity and make a quiet, private sale, but what the hell, all her friends are doing it, so the picture goes to auction. The Manet makes $3.8 million. The underbidder was the dealer Pfeffer, who stopped because he just did not think that the spread between what he would pay and what he would have to ask would be worth it. The successful bidder against Pfeffer is a client of theirs, a 36-year-old aspiring greenmailer who had been in to see Pfeffer a few times and bought a minor Renoir. This time he skips the middleman.

Auction houses have been shrewd in promoting auction sales as theater for large audiences of vicarious participants and admirers. They have gained the confidence of inexperienced collectors, who are apt to be afraid of being ripped-off by dealers and have come to believe that auctions are the best test of the fair market value of a work of art. So have an important class of sellers, the bankers and executors, who do not know much about art but who read the papers and have their worries as fiduciaries.

Thus the flourishing of the auction age, with highly publicized record prices that keep the log rolling. Thus the decline of private art dealing; dealers who have not fallen off the log are in an increasingly specialized trade.

The irony here is that museums have mostly been put out of the acquisitions game partly by what museums themselves have been doing to create art consumers. In the boom years since the mid-sixties, American museums have been hugely successful in making their programs popular, especially temporary exhibitions. They have played a big role, together with the media, in the broader consciousness of art that sharpens the appeal of collecting as a prestigious activity for those who can afford it. What is new is not status-seeking through art—we have had that for a hundred years. What is new is how widespread it has become and how much money it takes.

Museums have helped price themselves out of the art market, of course, by reducing supply—retiring works of art from circulation for ever. This might make you economists think that museums could manipulate the market in their favor by selling to relieve the scarcity. The trouble is that the things museums are willing to let go would not deflate the market—they are usually not very good and mostly consigned to storerooms.

Museums have been able to add amazingly little to their purchase endowments. Walter Annenberg's gift to the Metropolitan of an acquisitions fund of $15 million, and of $5 million to several other museums, was a complete surprise, the first thing of its kind that I can remember in many years. Passing the hat for individual purchases generally has not been a reliable method for most museums. But museums have been generating more purchase money by selling. Works of art that are minor or that have become redundant by virtue of subsequent acquisitions are culled and sold. This practice was not very widespread until the last decade, but recently it has been big business, indeed the key to shaping the collections by the staffs of many major big city museums with large collections, and others too. Jay Cantor provides some dramatic numbers. Even very well-endowed smaller museums like the Kimball and the Getty sell from time to time—always things that have been superseded in importance or are downright unexhibitable. To give credit where it is due, I should say that we usually sell at auction.

Let me add something about timing and specialization, from the perspective of our own collecting.

Paul Getty had very narrow interests—he collected antiquities, French furniture and decorative arts, and paintings, and that was all. But he left no restrictions on what we could collect after his death. In 1983, after his legacy had begun to generate income for the Trust and the Museum, we made a study of the collections and decided to expand their scope only very modestly. We were happy to remain relatively specialized. We thought it was simply too late to make excellent collections in many fields, no matter how much money you had, and that the world did not need another all-purpose art museum with a little from a lot of cultures and periods. We chose not to be a textbook but a well-edited anthology instead. We resolved to build the existing collections, first of all. Our choice of new fields was partly historical, staying within the arbitrary bounds of Europe from the Middle Ages until around 1900, and in part opportunistic, based on rough calculations of how we might do great things in the face of the actual realities of the art market. You might be interested in those decisions.

We decided to begin a collection of Old Master drawings because we had a chance to make an important collection that would make a distinctive contribution on the West Coast. We knew the supply in private hands was relatively abundant, and that for a time at least, prices would not go up unreasonably, since collecting drawings is not nearly as widespread as collecting paintings. Having bought mostly one by one, rather than in blocks, we now have about 300 drawings at a very high level of quality. It is still possible to buy superb examples by less-than-world-famous artists in the $20–50,000 range. The greatest and rarest, however, such as the work of Leonardo, Raphael, Dürer, and Rembrandt, make prices in the millions and are collected almost exclusively by private people.

Manuscripts came to the Getty in quite a different way. I do not think the trustees would have thought seriously about collecting illuminated manuscripts except for the historical accident in 1983 that brought Peter Ludwig, the German chocolate manufacturer, to decide to sell his private collection. He had bought the best medieval and Renaissance manuscripts that appeared in the market for twenty years or so. We could have his entire collection of 144 examples at a price much lower than the sum they would have made individually, because Ludwig wanted to see the collection survive more or less intact, and he was prepared to get less than top dollar to preserve his achievement. Again, we would have the only significant collection in the West. Since there were many important manuscripts still in private hands, we knew the collection could gradually be made even greater. But having retired dozens of the best privately held manuscripts, we could not help contributing to a jump in prices, and inflation has been fierce ever since. Our dollar now buys a fraction, perhaps a third to a quarter, of what it did when we started with manuscripts.

We began to collect European sculpture not only because it made artistic sense, but because we knew that there were many opportunities. Sculpture has always been undervalued relative to paintings and had fewer private buyers. In 1983 we imagined that there would be more for sale than there actually has been, and we did not reckon on the vastly higher prices that generally do not make the news but are very real. A bronze that cost $300,000 in 1983 can very easily cost $1.5 million today. Our rate of acquisition has fallen off, partly as a result of not having adjusted our expenditure much for inflation and partly because of the sheer scarcity of the things we want the most.

Our decision to begin a new collection of photographs was perhaps the most dramatic from both the artistic and economic point of view. There were good art-historical reasons for including photographs in a collection like ours, but we would never have dreamt of doing it without another of those never-before-or-since opportunities. We had a chance to bring together, more or less overnight, the three most important private collections in the world and a whole group of other smaller ones, altogether something close to 30,000 pictures. The timing was ideal. The bull market in photography in the late seventies and early eighties had leveled off. The major comprehensive collectors were willing to sell, but only to a buyer who would keep the collections together, like

Ludwig, so that their personal creations might be preserved. We removed a very large number of the most important photographs from the market forever, and we saw a corresponding rise in prices (though nothing like as steep as was predicted). The photography market rose gently, in fact, until a couple years ago when a raft of new buyers entered the picture, including the Japanese. Luckily we are now looking for a relatively small number of great pictures, "fishing with a fly rod," as the curator says, no longer with a dragnet.

The purchases you hear about, though, are paintings. And the Getty often buys in the most inflated sector of the market, the best and rarest. Mr. Getty left us only the beginnings of an important collection, and it needed practically everything. We knew it would be expensive to build, and God knows we wish we had been able to start ten years or even five years sooner, because it has been expensive beyond our dreams. But we felt a duty to do justice to European paintings—again, because of the particular needs of Los Angeles and the West, and because we believed, and still believe, that we can still *be* an important collection, albeit relatively small and not evenly distributed across European history.

So far I have been speaking as the director of the Getty. Let me close with a few more general remarks.

Two trends bound up with the economy of art museums have been very evident in the past twenty years. Collecting, which formerly dominated our imagination, has played a smaller and smaller role in the life of our museums. Exhibitions, on the other hand, and I mean large, well-publicized loan shows, have become the commanding aspect of museum life.

From the mid-1970s onward, we have been seeing the end of a hundred-year era of collection building. I think this is true for most museums across the country, except for the very important subcategory of contemporary art, and of course, a few late-blooming but well-watered plants like the Kimbell and the Getty. During the collecting era, museums promoted the glamorous stereotype of expensive purchases, especially toward the end, by directors who did not mind exaggerating their own wily brilliance and publicizing their triumphs. this is the "chase and capture" mentality that made for high-profile careers and poor novels. Museums were buying works of art, all right, but many fewer than the stereotype would suggest. Mostly they were getting gifts.

American museum collections were formed above all by gifts, not purchases. The value of works of art given and bequeathed to museums—that is, works of art chosen by collectors and donated—must be vastly, vastly greater than the amount of money given or bequeathed to museums for purchases, whether earmarked endowments or contributions for purchases—that is, money spent by the curators and directors for works *they* chose. Our museums are the creations of such private individuals as Morgan, Altman, Lillie Bliss, Mrs. Potter Palmer, Arensberg, the Cone sisters, the Spreckels family, Andrew and Paul Mellon, Kay Kimbell, and J. Paul Getty, and on down an extraordinary list. Their private passions, their civic pride, and their desire to compete with each other by a kind of potlatch—outdoing one another with how much they could give away—these are the motives that built our institutions. I do not see much of this generosity these days. I suspect that this era of philanthropy by collectors is finished. It was already suffering before 1986; the loss of tax incentives for donors (well documented in the background papers) and the steep rise in art prices have made gifts and bequests much more costly. The drop in donations since 1986 has been dramatic, even drastic.

Attitudes are different, too. Today's newer art buyers seem to look at works of art as another speculative commodity. Their comprehension of the works of art, the kinds of satisfaction they take in owning and looking at them, their attention span—these rarely bear comparison with the great founder collectors of the past.

And I see so little active, knowledgeable new collecting of older art, whether Western or Oriental, that it is hard to imagine that we will have a new generation of philanthropists to add to museums' basic collections, even if tax laws change. With contemporary art, I am more upbeat. Our hope has to be that collectors of contemporary art who have formed bonds with museums are going to find ways to give or bequeath their collections. There have been some good examples set recently by the Meyerhoffers in Baltimore and the Sydney Lewises in Richmond, for example; and here in Boston, the great collections of Graham Gund and Stephen Paine have the potential to put the Museum of Fine Arts on the map of twentieth-century art. There are plenty of people out there who might respond to the force of good example on the part of other collectors. A big problem for museums, however, given the size of much contemporary art, is how to make space for it. I do not think that the only answer is building more and more galleries. More creativity on the part of the bigger museums in sharing works of art with smaller museums rather than warehousing them, taking on the management of collections and seeing to their widespread exhibition in other institutions, would have great appeal to potential donors and would give them an incentive to endow this kind of scheme.

Large traveling exhibitions are what museum directors seem to talk about most nowadays. When we are not doing deals for shows, we are complaining about them. The exhibition program has come to dominate the lives of museum staffs and to claim much of the attention and money for museum programs. Of course shows have had many important functions—recruiting a wider audience, fostering publications, teaching history of art to millions, and giving people a museum habit. One trouble, though, is that museums get hooked on the heady rush of income from exhibitions and acquire a kind of economic dependency on them. Another is that exhibitions have changed the audience's expectations about the purpose of a museum visit. The audience more and more comes to think of art as an event—if there is no show, why go to the museum? It is like a theater when the marquee is dark. The nonsensical thing, of course, is that museums often have in their permanent collections works of art far more important than the works they are borrowing and promoting—the ones that are here today and gone tomorrow. Our visitors have also been conditioned by temporary exhibitions to expect a more linear, programmed experience—a story line embodied in the installation, reinforced by labels, and murmured into your ear by the director. This can open one avenue to understanding for the visitor, but it may close many others. We often see robot-like behavior by our visitors and disappointingly little learning of the really useful kind, the kind that gives you power to discover things for yourself.

I am convinced that our museums, in order to prosper, are going to have to find ways to refocus attention on permanent collections. We need to broaden the base of visitors, make our collections the prime attractions, and help visitors more generously to enjoy them. This ought to make a healthier museum economy that is freer from the fluctuations of attendance for temporary exhibitions. But *ideas* are needed for the use of our collections. There was never a time when we needed to refocus so sharply on the quality and usefulness of the visitor's experience and recognise that experience for what it is: our fundamental contribution to society. How to make that experience more inviting, more natural, more intelligible, more memorable—that subject is going to repay all the study we can put into it.

Summary of Discussion

Charles T. Clotfelter began by asking if there is an inevitable conflict between curators wanting specialized collections and the public wanting to view a variety of art.

Theodore E. Stebbins, Jr. responded that the public does not really care about "gaps" in collections. What seems most important is to make a visit to a museum a pleasurable and meaningful experience.

Martin Feldstein asked whether that is an uncontroversial position among museum directors and curators, that they should strengthen collections through specialization rather than diversification. He wondered whether a focus on specialization rather than broad education represented a shift in the role that museums have seen themselves playing in the community over a long period.

James N. Wood concurred with Stebbins's view for cases where the collection meets the demands of the community; in other cases, he said, museums need to acquire at least some basic examples. He emphasized that teaching art history should not be the most important goal of a museum, because there are many other ways for people to learn it. Rather, museums should teach people to become excited about art and artists, and that often can be achieved more effectively through in-depth presentation of a few great artists.

Jay E. Cantor went on to say that museums first developed in the United States when communities were isolated and a museum was one way to develop a civic identity. In today's more mobile society, art is accessible by highway and airplane, so it does not need to be concentrated in one place. He felt also that having some museums concentrate on certain artists or time periods was important, but such concentrations may not encourage return visits as much as broad-based collections do.

Peter Temin concurred that focusing on the fall in the cost of transportation was a more fruitful way to study the long-term evolution of museums than focusing on the recent sharp rise in the price of paintings.

Martin Shubik turned to the topic of museums' selling, or deaccessioning, art. He speculated that the great flow of art into museums since the end of the nineteenth century may have stopped because the supply of important art (by dead artists) in the hands of private collectors has been virtually exhausted. This would explain why market prices of art have risen so much.

John Hale said that he was "delightfully flabbergasted by the calm acceptance of the idea of deaccessioning at least up to a middling level" of quality. In England the government encouraged museums and galleries to support their operations by selling art, which led to a political backlash against the practice. Hale mentioned two other concerns about deaccessioning: first, that respecting the wishes of past donors is important to maintaining the confidence of new donors, and second, that it is hard to predict what art will be important in the future. He reported also on the activities of the Advisory Committee to the Government Art Collection in Britain, which he chairs. The committee comprises the directors of the leading British art museums, and it is responsible for purchasing art to be used in government buildings around the world. The committee had unanimously decided not to sell their excess art but to explore the possibility of permanent loans to other institutions in Britain.

Richard E. Oldenburg added that there is an important difference between museums controlled by private trustees, as in the United States, and those controlled by the government, as in Europe. Although private trustees might wrongly choose to sell art for their own institution's operating expenses, he was even more afraid that local governments could "find it extremely convenient to build a new hospital out of the collection and see nothing wrong with that," so he found it more important to defend barriers against deaccessioning in that context.

Roger G. Kennedy noted that this discussion had been about reallocating funds from the liquidation of assets to other purposes, but there is also the related issue of what institutions should hold what kinds of art. He stated that there will be more determinations by the broader community as to where assets will be allocated in the future than there have been in the past.

John Walsh agreed that the common pattern is museums' selling works of art "that no museum would or should buy." In other cases, museums sell art that is outside the scope (for example, the time period) of the museum. The city museum in The Hague in Holland, however, has decided to "sell from the top of their collection" (Picasso, Monet) in a conscious attempt to shift the emphasis of the collection to contemporary art; this is a step that has not been taken by American museums.

Neil Rudenstine noted, however, that museums had recently purchased some works of art that could only have been afforded by selling very good works already held by those museums.

Marilyn Perry discussed the example of the Walker Museum in Minneapolis, which deaccessioned its founding donation in order to maintain its charter as a contemporary museum. She felt that two issues were raised by this sale: first, a museum's right to determine its collection policy, and second, whether storing art rather than selling it serves the public.

Cantor indicated that the speed with which the decision was made is also an issue, as the community might have chosen to retain the pictures. *Walsh* said that the paintings were offered to the Minneapolis Institute of Arts at a favorable price, but the Institute was unable to raise the necessary money.

Stebbins said that although the Walker's decision was consistent with their mission, he felt that no one was speaking for the people of the city or the state. *Harold M. Williams* responded that he was troubled by the idea that museums have that kind of responsibility to local citizens. By that logic, he said, if the Walker did not have the paintings, it should have an obligation to acquire them; in other words, it is not clear how the museum incurred an obligation to the city by the chance that it had those paintings.

Stebbins felt that Mr. Walker intended something when he founded the institution and that history should matter. *Kennedy* argued that the Walker heirs are directly engaged in managing the museum, and they fully participated in the decision to focus on contemporary work. Thus, the question here is not the obligation of the institution to the donors but rather to the local or even national community.

Hale returned to the more general issue of deaccessioning by expressing his fear that museum collections will be seen not as being held for posterity, but rather for financial convenience and personal taste. A view of museums as showplaces for "this year's model" could hurt the special relationship between the public and museums, and reduce donations.

Oldenburg concluded that a critical issue in deaccessioning is whether the work of art remains in the public domain or returns to private hands. When art prices were lower, it was easier to agree to sell the art to another museum. Today, museums feel compelled to sell art to private buyers in order to raise enough money to be able to purchase high quality art from private sellers.

Feldstein returned to a topic raised by Walsh, that of "sharing" art among museums. Noting that it might be more attractive to donors to know that their art would be on exhibit rather than spending a fair amount of time in storerooms, Feldstein asked what the general attitude was toward either joint purchases of works of art between two or more museums, or long-term lending from a collection.

Ashton Hawkins answered that the Metropolitan Museum of Art had experimented with both options. Their joint purchases "seemed not to be the wave of the future," and loans are essentially a short-term solution to storage problems. He concluded that most museums want to retain control over their collection and ultimately do with it what they think is in the best interest of the museum. *William H. Luers* noted that the Metropolitan has at any one time between five and ten thousand works of art on loan.

On a separate topic, *Richard N. Rosett* said his impression was that many great collections of art were given to museums before the income tax was instituted in the early twentieth century, and thus before there was any tax advantage to charitable contributions. In light of this history, he felt it was unclear why the recent reduction in the tax advantage of donating art (see the background paper by Fullerton, chap. 8 in this volume) was viewed as a crushing blow to donations.

Hawkins responded that most of the great art collections came into museums after World War I, when the income-tax rate, and thus the tax advantage to donations, was low. *Luers* responded also that one motivation for people to give large collections in the early days at the Metropolitan Museum of Art was that the giver was shaping the entire nature of the collection. He mentioned the John D. Rockefeller, Sr. gift to The Cloisters and the Nelson A. Rockefeller gift of primitive art as examples. Part of the problem today is that even a major gift to the Metropolitan would not shape any of their collections very much, except in a few areas such as Asian Art.

Rosemary Clarke addressed Walsh's remarks about the shift in the focus of the art market from dealers to auction houses. She felt there could be a disadvantage in the concentration of sales in a few auction houses rather than through many dealers.

Wood wondered whether the amount of loans being granted by auction houses had distorted the statistics of the so-called market value of art. *Cantor* responded that loans represented a very limited aspect of the market so they do not distort the overall statistics very much. In general, auction prices are a more reliable measure of market value than rumors about dealers' prices.

Feldstein mentioned studies that have compared the sale prices of the same work of art as it has come up to auction over long periods of time. The returns on holding works of art can be compared to the returns on securities. *Clarke* reported on a recent study of paintings reappearing in auctions from about 1650 up to 1985. The average real return after inflation was about 1.5 percent per year, less than the return on alternative financial assets. The comparison was essentially the same for the period after 1950.

2 The Museum and the Public

Anne d'Harnoncourt, Paul J. DiMaggio,
Marilyn Perry, and James N. Wood

Anne d'Harnoncourt

I will endeavor to get a few thoughts across about the very large issue of museums and the public. One thing that has struck me in the last couple of years is the importance of getting a *qualitative* sense of who the public are, what they want, and what we could do not only to give them what they want, but also to give them more ideas about what they *could* want. This has been brought to the fore particularly by the study sponsored by the Center for Art and Education at the Getty that has been going on for the last year and a half.

Looking at the quantitative aspects of museum attendance, I was fascinated to learn that attendance at the British Museum was about 4 million people in 1978 and 4 million people in 1987, both of which are impressive figures and suggest a kind of grand constancy to that audience. One of the most over-whelmingly visited museums in the world is the Hermitage in Leningrad, which has in the range of 4 to 5 million visitors—and until very recently, that was without any significant role of special exhibitions. Maybe we have been infecting our Soviet counterparts somewhat with our concentration on exhi-bitions. What always interests me when we measure museum attendance is that even though it appears to be very high today, in fact, if you look back at the history of museums, it has been high for a long time. I looked at the figures for the Centennial Exposition in Philadelphia in 1876: hundreds of thousands of people came over the span of six months.

I think that we as museum directors always face the question: What do overall attendance numbers actually mean? It seems to me that in fact part of what we need to think about are the qualitative questions: who the visitors are, where they come from, how they are changing over time, what they want, and what their experiences are.

One of the things that is most interesting about museum publics is their diversity. The Getty-sponsored study of eleven art museums, which brought together directors, curators, and educators at a recent conference, explored what museum audiences want or what we might want them to want, in terms particularly of education and information. However, the study told us a lot more than that. In watching one of the focus groups from this study recently, seeing a probation officer in the city of Philadelphia experiencing three minutes of ecstasy in describing Turner's *Burning of the House of Parliament* was pretty amazing. It was an extraordinary experience for him: he was enraptured with the painting, he had not read the label, he did not know exactly what it was. Although he knew it was a picture of an historic fire, it took us a while to realize what he was actually describing. But one of the things that we learned from seeing people describe their fundamental experiences in art museums is that not only are museum publics very diverse in themselves—where they come from, who they are, their age, their economic background, and so forth—but you never know who is going to have what experience in front of what object at what time.

That unpredictability affects the whole issue of what exhibitions museums present. You can market exhibitions, you can advertise them, but you do not really know if they will catch people's imagination, and whose imagination they will catch in what way, until they happen. Further, a great deal of what affects the attendance is word of mouth, which is not something that the museum controls at all. So I ask the question about exhibitions in general, and about blockbusters in particular: Don't we think that museums' continuing to be inventive in presenting works of art that they think are important—from all kinds of fields, in a diverse and lively way—is a terribly important thing if the museum public is to develop a continued interest in the museum as a whole?

I think that museum directors at the Getty conference were asking themselves: What do we as museums want? Do we want *more* public, do we want a *wealthier* public (as is implied in some of the studies I have read), do we want a *more diverse* public, or do we want the public that comes to have the *best possible experience?* If you have an exhibition that is enormously successful, there is a point at which it becomes really more uncomfortable for people to see the exhibition, because of its popularity. On one hand, you can be coldblooded about it and say, great, the more people you can cram through the door the better off you are. On the other hand, a museum's ultimate mission is not to have as many people as possible see the exhibition, but to have as many people as possible see the exhibition under circumstances in which it is possible for people to have a good experience, and that is something rather different.

I was quite disturbed by the background paper for this conference that posited the possibility or the necessity of museums' addressing two very different kinds of audiences. The paper argued that there is the collector-donor, sophisticated audience, and there is the general public audience, and museums ought to divide what they do and divide their resources to serve those two audiences quite separately. It seems to me that that may possibly undermine the whole mission of a museum, which is to bring as many people as you can to a kind of experience that they can only get in an art museum: direct contact with a work of art. You do not know what that experience is going to be and who will have it. So you have got to provide it, in a sense, with equal potential intensity for as many people as possible. You might not have expected that the probation officer would be excited about the Turner instead of something else, but he definitely was, that was the picture he picked, and people pick very surprising things with which to have very strong relationships.

So I think the idea of dividing our resources to cultivate donors on the one hand, and to please a general public on the other, is dangerous. Obviously, of course, we all do that to *some* degree. Every curator, every director, every educator, everybody in the museum, makes a choice as to whether to spend the next half hour persuading somebody to give you a picture, or working on an audio tape for an exhibition which you hope will make it a lot clearer to a lot of people. However, somehow it seems to me that these choices are still perceived as part of one activity, and not as two profoundly different ones related to two different audiences. My perception, at least, is that the audience, insofar as you hope it will grow and enrich itself (and the museum) in many senses of the word, is the same.

I am fascinated by the issue of museums struggling in their vision of themselves between being purveyors of education and of entertainment. How does the public see us? Do they see us as educating or as entertaining? Another thing that emerged from the Getty focus group study was that those two aspects of museum visits are not mutually exclusive; they blend together in individuals' minds. When people who had never been to the museum before talked about what it might be like to go, they talked about the fact that it was probably full of history and they wanted to learn. And the same people in response to the next question said, oh, I just want to let my mind go, and sort of drift with pleasure. It seems to me that knowledge and enjoyment, which have always been goals that museums have talked about, are intimately related to each other and should not be divided. We should not do one thing because we think it is educational and another thing because we think it is entertaining. If people know more about the art you are showing, they often get more excited about it.

The issue of marketing is a fascinating one, and one that raises every museum hackle that I know. It is an issue that we keep coming back to because no curator and no museum director wants to hang a gallery full of objects or install an exhibition and have nobody there. However, marketing has to do with products, and if you say, let us change the product to fit what the audience wants, that makes everybody nervous. This is further complicated because the audience changes over time, partly *because* of what products (i.e., what exhibitions, what works of art, what programs) you make available. I would love to know more about the long-term impact museums have upon their audiences, in terms of their collections, in terms of their philosophies, and in terms of their programs.

I believe that the impact will depend to some extent on geography. The Cleveland Museum, for example, has very consistently over a long period of time emphasized its collection. Among the great museums of this country, it is the one that has probably done more of that than any other—only recently has it become really involved with special exhibitions, and in still a relatively restrained way. There is probably no question that the public, the audience let us say, of Cleveland has rather different expectations, attitudes, interests, and experiences of art and of museums than the public in another city in which the museum does not have such great collections or focus on them with such intensity. Another example would be the Walker Art Center in Minneapolis, which has created avant-garde exhibitions, film series, performances, and mixed media events with a very deliberate and energetic attitude toward contemporary art: not just showing it, but showing it in particular ways, and concentrating on design and architecture at the same time. My guess is that the audience in Minneapolis have become not only accustomed to that over time, but their expectations and their interests—in short, they themselves—have expanded and changed because of exposure to the Walker. When you come to issues of how museums should deal with their public, obviously you want attendance to be high for many reasons; ultimately, though, it seems to me that you want the public to have an increasingly large sense of what art and museums can contribute to their lives and to their enjoyment—not only their enjoyment of art and museums, but of other aspects of life—and that is a very hard thing to put a number on.

I am trying to think about what you could compare museums to, because they are even hard to compare to each other, let alone to other kinds of institutions. Would we all say that museums have more in common with libraries than with orchestras, for example? Museums and libraries both have vast resources, so it matters what you put on your front shelf and what you put on your back shelf. Also, libraries do fundamentally presume to offer knowledge and enjoyment in the same kind of proportion, so it is an interesting analogy to make. There has been a fair amount of discussion of deaccessioning, but I think it would not quite occur to people to sell books in the library in order to make the library more successful; on the other hand, books do not have yet anywhere near the value of the works of art we were talking about.

Finally, it seems to me that the relation of museums to their public is one of the most interesting questions that any group can discuss. One of the most interesting comments in one of the recent Getty-sponsored sessions was from an historian of museums who said that thirty years ago, the people sitting around the table—the museum directors, the educators, the curators—would have had no doubts as to what the public ought to want, what their mission was, or what their relationship with them was. Our discussion today reflects the kind of existential anxiety that we all have about our survival, about our mission, about all of those people who are coming through our doors, and about how we are dealing with them. I do not say that our predecessors would have had no doubts, but they would have had far fewer questions and doubts, say forty years ago, than we do today.

Paul J. DiMaggio

My topic, the relationship between the art museum and the public, seems innocent enough. But, it is more complicated than it sounds, for the museum has several relationships with several publics. How an art museum chooses to allocate attention and other resources among them follows from how it chooses to organize itself and to define its mission.

Let us begin with the most straightforward dimension of the relationship: who visits U.S. art museums, and who does not. We know a lot about this, thanks to the National Endowment for the Arts' Research Division, which sponsored two studies undertaken by the U.S. Bureau of the Census, the 1982 and 1985 Surveys of Public Participation in the Arts. These studies provided the first reliable information on many of the cultural activities of Americans, including their attendance at art museums and art galleries. The following account of their findings relies heavily on an excellent report by Mark Schuster of the Massachusetts Institute of Technology, and on additional analyses that Francie Ostrower and I conducted at Yale.[1]

The findings of the SPPAs, as the surveys are called, are not surprising, but they are worth keeping in mind, because they tell us whom art museums are reaching, at least in some fashion, and whom they are not. In 1985, just over one in five adult Americans visited an art museum at least once—more than attended a jazz concert, listened to live classical music, saw a play, and attended a musical, and almost as many as visited a history or science museum. The major difference between the people who visited art museums and the ones who did not is that the visitors had spent more years in school. Almost half of the college graduates, and more than half of Americans with at least some graduate education, visited museums, compared to just one in twenty-five people whose schooling stopped in elementary school, and one in ten high-school dropouts (see table 2.1 for exact figures).[2]

---

1. J. Mark Davidson Schuster, "Perspectives on the American audience for art museums," report prepared for Research Division, National Endowment for the Arts (Cambridge: Massachusetts Institute of Technology, 1987), available on microfiche through ERIC system, ED294780; Paul J. DiMaggio and Francie Ostrower, "Race, ethnicity and participation in the arts: Patterns of participation by black, Hispanic and white Americans in selected activities from the 1982 and 1985 surveys of public participation in the arts," report prepared for Research Division, National Endowment for the Arts (New Haven, Conn.: Yale University, 1987).
2. Schuster, "Perspectives," 12–13.

Table 2.1   Percentage of Selected Groups Reporting Attendance at Art Museums or Galleries in 1985

Family income	
less than $5,000	16%
$5,000–$9,999	11
$10,000–$14,999	15
$15,000–24,999	19
$25,000–49,999	28
more than $49,999	45
Highest level of schooling	
Grade school	4
Some high school	11
High-school graduate	14
Some college	29
Four-year college graduate	45
Graduate school	55
Age	
18–24	22
25–34	25
35–44	27
45–54	23
55–64	18
65–74	16
over 74	10
Gender	
Women	23
Men	21
Race	
African-American	11
Euro-American	23
Other	25
Place of residence	
Central city	25
Metropolitan area but not central city	26
Not in metropolitan area	14
Occupation	
Professional	49
Managerial	37
Sales/clerical	27
Craftsmen	14
Operatives	9
Laborers	10
Service workers	16

Source: J. Mark Davidson Schuster, "Perspectives on the American audience for art museums," table 1a, report prepared for Research Division, National Endowment for the Arts (Cambridge: Massachusetts Institute of Technology, 1987), ERIC document ED294780. The author is grateful for Professor Schuster's permission to draw on this material.

Occupation and income are also related to visits to museums and galleries. Nearly half of people with family incomes of $50,000 a year or more visited, compared to 15 percent of those with incomes of from $10,000 to $14,999. Almost one in two professionals and three in eight managers visited museums, compared to one in six service workers and just one in ten operatives and laborers. Euro-Americans were twice as likely to have visited as African-Americans: 23 percent compared to 11 percent.[3]

One can use statistical techniques to assess the relative importance, in an explanatory sense, of the various attributes associated with museum visiting. When one does that, schooling emerges as by far the most important, dwarfing the effects of income, occupation, urban residence, race, gender (women visit more than men), and marital status (single and divorced people are more likely to attend than people who are married or widowed). Nonetheless, all of these factors are statistically significant predictors of attendance.[4]

There are several points worth making about these statistics. First, the SPPA data tell us about visitors rather than visits. That is, they tell us who attended at least once, but not how often they attended. On the basis of other research, we know that frequent visitors tend to be more upscale than occasional visitors.[5]

On the other hand, people who visit art museums are a more diverse lot than differences in participation *rates* might lead one to expect, because, as Schuster points out, many of the groups with the highest rates of visitation are smaller than groups with lower rates. For example, although people with family incomes of more than $50,000 a year are more than twice as likely to visit than people who earn between $15,000 and $24,999 per year, the latter constitute a larger proportion of the museum-visiting population because there are so many more of them. For similar reasons, more museum visitors have only a high-school degree than have attended graduate school, even though the latter are four times as likely to visit museums.[6]

Third, the visitor profile seems not to have changed much over the past thirty years or so: the museum public has remained substantially better edu-

---

3. Ibid.

4. DiMaggio and Ostrower, "Race, ethnicity, and participation." See table 2.2. Because of the focus of the report from which table 2.2 was taken, respondents were disaggregated by race/ethnicity and results reported separately for (non-Hispanic) Euro-Americans, African-Americans, and Hispanic-Americans. Although significant levels vary, due to the smaller numbers of respondents in the latter two groups, only the effects of gender (a dummy variable where 1 = female, between African-Americans and Euro-Americans) and SMSA (a dummy where 1 = resides in a Standard Metropolitan Statistical Area or SMSA, between African-Americans and Hispanics) differed significantly, and these only in 1982. None of the differences in coefficients within groups for 1982 and 1985 is statistically significant, except for the greater effect of SMSA for whites in 1985.

5. Paul J. DiMaggio, Michael Useem, and Paula Brown, "Audience studies of the performing arts and museums: A critical review," Research Division Report no. 9. (Washington, D.C.: National Endowment for the Arts, 1978).

6. Schuster, "Perspectives," 12–13.

Table 2.2   Logistic Regression Analyses Predicting Visitation of Art Museums and
                   Galleries for (Non-Hispanic) Euro-Americans, African-Americans, and
                   Hispanic-Americans

Independent Variable	1982			1985		
	Euro-American	African-American	Hispanic-American	Euro-American	African-American	Hispanic-American
Women						
b	.436	− .157	.101	.383	.276	.141
se	.047	.177	.202	.052	.203	.203
sig	d	NS	NS	d	NS	NS
SMSA						
b	.245	1.364	− .071	.495	.362	− .083
se	.051	.297	.298	.060	.269	.286
sig	d	d	NS	d	NS	NS
Age						
b	.001	− .000	− .012	− .001	− .007	.007
se	.002	.007	.009	.002	.008	.008
sig	NS	NS	NS	NS	NS	NS
Education						
b	.320	.279	.279	.312	.272	.155
se	.011	.040	.042	.012	.044	.037
sig	d	d	d	d	d	d
Income						
b	.115	.152	.226	.097	.208	.114
se	.015	.068	.076	.015	.065	.072
sig	d	a	a	d	a	NS
Occupation						
b	.255	.710	.444	.257	.385	.688
se	.050	.197	.219	.058	.217	.224
sig	d	b	a	d	NS	a
Marital status						
b	.415	.194	.019	.297	.252	.125
se	.056	.193	.234	.063	.218	.228
sig	d	NS	NS	d	NS	NS
Constant	− 6.29	− 7.07	− 5.02	− 6.23	− 6.34	− 3.98
Number of observations	13,905	1,656	941	10,872	1,385	790

Source: Paul J. DiMaggio and Francie Ostrower, "Race, ethnicity, and participation in the arts,"
appendix tables 3-1 and 3-2, report prepared for Research Division, National Endowment of the Arts
(New Haven, Conn.: Yale University, 1987).

Note: b = logistic regression coefficient; *se* = standard error; *sig* refers to level of statistical significance, where a = probability less than .05, b = less than .01, c = less than .001, d = less than
.00005, and NS = not significant. Coefficients and standard errors of the income variable are multi-
plied by 10,000.

cated, better paid, more professional, and more likely to be white than the population at large. How can this be the case even though museum attendance has galloped upwards during this period? For one thing, more Americans fit the visitor profile now—for example, more have college educations, fewer are blue-collar workers—than in 1960. For another, a larger proportion of the core public may be attending than did in the past, and they may attend more often.[7]

Fourth, the people who do not visit are not necessarily uninterested in art; many of them report watching shows about art on television, for example. Yet they do not appear to harbor a great sense of deprivation. People who already visit museums are far more likely to tell researchers that they want to visit more frequently than are people who do not visit museums at all. Nonetheless, if all the nonvisitors who reported wanting to visit did so, the proportion of Americans attending exhibitions would double. In other words, art museums may have a large untapped audience, but tapping it will require much effort.[8]

Statistics such as these provide a useful baseline for talking about the museum's relationship to its public, if only because it is difficult for museums to *have* relationships with people who do not enter their doors. But there is much more to the topic than such statistics imply. Indeed, all three of the terms in our topic—"public," "museum," and "relationship"—possess a variety of meanings, each related to different conceptions of the art museum's mission.

The museum public is what Walter Lippman called a "phantom public," an abstraction more useful for its ambiguity than for its denotative capacity.[9] Is the art museum's public the one in five Americans who visit museums? Is it the two in five who either visited in 1985 or told the Census Bureau's interviewers that they wished they had? Is it the three in five who neither entered an art museum nor regretted their failure to do so, and who therefore, some would argue, especially need to be awakened to the value of art? Or does the museum public consist primarily of organized stakeholders, visitors and non-visitors alike, who make their voices heard in public controversies?

For most art museums, at least three publics are salient.[10] The first, and in some ways most important, consists of patrons: wealthy individuals with a strong commitment to the visual arts, often as collectors, who are, or give some promise of becoming, committed to the museum as an institution. Such patrons are the major source of the private share of museum revenues: it is

7. Schuster, "Perspectives," 12–13. DiMaggio, Useem, and Brown, "Audience."

8. DiMaggio and Ostrower, "Race, ethnicity, and participation," ch. 4.

9. Walter Lippman, *The phantom public* (New York, 1925).

10. The first two categories are similar to those discussed by Professors Robert C. Blattberg and Cynthia J. Broderick in their contribution to this volume (ch. 11). The third is not included in their typology. Of course, many museums have more publics than this: students and art history faculty for university museums, artists for many museums of contemporary art, and so on.

they upon whom the museum counts for donations to capital and endowment campaigns and for gifts of art.

The second public comprises the many visitors who do not collect art, will never have the wherewithal or commitment to make major gifts, but who nonetheless visit museums, pay their admissions, patronize museum shops, possibly take out a membership, and account for the lion's share of attendance figures. Increasingly, museums, like other nonprofit organizations, are coming to see this group as a "market" for their services.

The third public is less tangible and more difficult to define than the other two, but no less important. In a sense, it can be said to consist of the 60 percent of American adults who neither visit museums nor want to, and who, by virtue of this omission, are believed by some to constitute a silent reproach to the art museum in its current form. Yet this 60 percent is notable for its *dis*engagement and thus cannot be called a public in the usual sense. Rather it represents a point of symbolic reference for a proxy public of organizations, agencies, and associations who seek to influence the art museum to widen its scope. Such corporate actors could not be more different from one another: some are artists, eager to expand the social impact of art; some speak for ethnic and racial minority communities whose cultures have been excluded from the fine-arts canon; some are agencies of government, concerned about what public grants to art museums are buying and whom they are serving; some are reformers working from within the museum community.

If the museum public is a multifaceted abstraction, so, in a way, is the museum itself. To be sure, art museums have charters, hold property, and take corporate action. But most museums lack that coherent core of undivided purpose that economists call a "utility function"—that is, a consistently ranked set of objectives, and rules for making tradeoffs among them. The problem is not that the museum lacks a mission, but that it has too many of them: acquisition, conservation, exhibition, and education, to mention a few. Some of these goals (education, for example), actually comprise several different objectives. To make matters worse, there is little general agreement as to how such objectives can most effectively be achieved, and a museum's performance in pursuit of most of them can be judged only indirectly.[11]

Art museums, like most other kinds of nonprofit enterprise, have developed a distinctive set of solutions to the problem of living with multiple goals. First, they have developed organizational structures that allocate different goals to different departments and different kinds of personnel: acquisition to curators, conservation to conservators, education to educators, maintenance activities to development officers and marketing departments, and so on. Second, they have staffed these positions with professionals, men and women

11. See Paul J. DiMaggio, "Nonprofit organizations in the production and distribution of culture," in *The nonprofit sector: A research handbook,* ed. Walter W. Powell (New Haven: Yale University Press, 1986).

whose technical training enables them to function, presumptively at least, without close supervision, detailed rules, or rigorous performance evaluation. Third, many art museum directors favor a management style and way of speaking that deemphasizes tensions among multiple missions (for example, by focusing on abstract goals with few operational implications or by avoiding explicit discussion of trade-offs among functions), both within the museum and in communicating to the outside. (Indeed, two Swiss economists have suggested that the role of the director is to ensure "that the production function connected with the museum's services is actively hidden . . . and cannot easily be detected"—a polite use of economics jargon to say that the director's job is to make sure that no one can figure out what the museum is up to.[12])

The result of these devices is that the museum can be seen as a confederation of groups of departments, staff, and trustees organized around different publics and objectives, overseen, in most cases, by the director and the board of trustees. At the cost of being exceedingly schematic and neglecting considerable variation within the art museum community, I would suggest that three such coalitions or "submuseums" are to some degree present in most large art museums:

Coalition I: The Patron's Submuseum. Here the patrons are the public, the curators (supplemented perhaps by development staff) are the heart of the museum, and acquisition, conservation, and research are the key functions. Curators serve patrons in a variety of ways, and patrons, in turn, donate objects and funds. Art historians and conservators are often a part of this coalition. The museum's relationship to this public is concrete, personal, and often intimate.

Coalition II: The Marketing Submuseum. Here the public, ranging in commitment from occasional visitors to members, is the "market." The key staff are marketing or membership personnel and their allies in other departments. This coalition's objective is to lure the market to the museum. In some cases, getting people inside the doors is equated with public education; in others, marketing is viewed as a means to ends that membership and admission income (and grants contingent upon robust attendance figures) can support. Although the market consists of concrete persons, this coalition views them abstractly as consumers.

Coalition III: The Social Submuseum. The key departments in this submuseum are education and outreach. The coalition's objective is to provide educational or social services to groups that are viewed as disenfranchised. The public consists of people who do not visit museums, or who do so rarely, and are defined categorically as children, minorities, the elderly, or the poor; and

---

12. Bruno S. Frey and Werner W. Pommerehne, "Economic analysis of the museum," in *Economic policy for the arts*, eds. W. S. Hendon, J. L. Shanahan, and A. J. MacDonald, 248–59 (Cambridge: Abt Books, 1980). On the issue of multiple goals, see Vera L. Zolberg, "Tension of mission in American art museums," in *Nonprofit enterprise in the arts: Studies in mission and constraint*, ed. Paul J. DiMaggio (New York: Oxford University Press, 1986).

of the staff of government and private agencies that claim to represent such groups, who are often served through special programs supported by soft money. If the language of coalition II comes from economics and business, the discourse of coalition III more often derives from politics or the social services.

This characterization of the staff and departments that belong to each of the three coalitions, or submuseums does not describe all art museums and may not fit the particulars of any museum perfectly. Although I have placed educators in coalition III, they are really a kind of swing group: in some art museums, education staff belong to the patron's museum, focusing their attention on relatively sophisticated programs for collectors or members. Similarly, although I identify public agencies with coalition III, they are likewise a swing group, at times contributing to scholarly or aesthetic goals that are unattractive to other publics.

But if the particular alliances vary from museum to museum, the tensions among these three relationships, publics, and missions are endemic and long-standing. Two of them—the patron's museum and the social museum—have vied for supremacy at least since the 1920s. The third—the marketing museum—is a product of changes in art museums, and in the world around them, that followed the Second World War.

The modern American art museum has many predecessors. Some, like the art academies, were coalitions of artists and patrons, with little interest in the public at large. Others, like Barnum's museums, anticipated contemporary theme parks in their concern with enticing the masses. But the most important early museums—the Boston Museum, the Metropolitan, the Art Institute, and a few others—were distinctively American in their orientation to public education and the common good. In those early days, education often held a rather precise meaning. Art museums, in many cases allied to local arts-and-crafts societies, would address the practical needs of designers and retailers, providing access to the best art works and designs in order to set a standard to which American craftspersons and manufacturers might aspire.[13]

As these institutions matured, however, European fine art became available, and acquisition drove out education as the primary mission. In many cases, when the founders died or retired, and a second generation of trustees took control, coalitions of patrons and curators redefined the art museum as a temple of higher learning. In some cases, as in Boston, the animating philosophy was frankly aesthetic and antagonistic to broad public participation. In others, as in Chicago, where the founders' generation lingered longer and connections to the settlement houses focused attention on public service, the

13. See Neil Harris, "The gilded age revisited: Boston and the museum movement," *American Quarterly* 14 (1962).

art museum was somewhat less insular. Nonetheless, few art museums were unaffected by the shift in priorities.[14]

By the 1920s, a movement to replace the patron's museum with the social museum had gathered force within the museum community. In part, this was a rear-guard action mounted by an older generation, whose background was not, like many younger museum people, in art history or architecture, but in library work (like the Newark Museum's John Cotton Dana, the movement's leading figure) or in the arts-and-crafts societies (like Frederic Allen Whiting of Cleveland). In part, however, it represented a prescient drive to adapt the art museum's mission to the circumstances of a changing world.

The reformers, who came together in the American Association of Museums and who received considerable philanthropic encouragement, especially from the Carnegie Corporation of New York but also from the Rockefeller philanthropies, were united in their support of professionalization and their conception of the museum as "a social instrument," devoted to educating the public, broadly defined. Their program, to the extent they can be said to have had one, looked back to the charters of the 1870s: less attention to fine art, more to the decorative arts and design; more attention to local working-class publics and immigrant groups, less to the patrons and collectors; more accessibility, and less grandeur. At the same time, they recognized that the art museum had lost its chance to lead in the area of industrial design. Whereas the founders wanted the museum to set a standard for manufacturers and retailers, the reformers of the 1920s saw in the attractive exhibits of the modern department stores a model for the art museum to emulate.[15]

The reformers and their image of the social museum lost the battle of the 1920s and 1930s to a new alliance. The patrons accepted professionalism, but it was the congenial professionalism of the art historians, not the radical professionalism of the educators. Acquisition would remain the museum's primary function, even during the Great Depression.[16]

Yet the reformers set the terms of a debate that has persisted to the present; and the patron's museum would make room for the social museum, albeit in a subordinate role. If Dana was the exemplary reformer, a more viable model was the Pennsylvania Museum's Fiske Kimball, president of the American Association of Museums during the late 1920s. Kimball made Philadelphia a showplace of professionalism: it was he who, with Carnegie Corporation backing, gave Yale's Edward Robinson a place to do his research on visitors

14. See Paul J. DiMaggio, "Cultural entrepreneurship in nineteenth-century Boston" parts 1 and 2, *Media, Culture and Society* 4 (1982): 33–50, 303–22.

15. Paul J. DiMaggio, "Progressivism in the arts," *Society* 25 (1988): 5; and Paul J. DiMaggio, "Constructing an organizational field as a professional project: The case of U.S. art museums," in *The new institutionalism in organizational analysis*, ed. Walter W. Powell and Paul J. DiMaggio (Chicago: University of Chicago Press, 1991).

16. Lawrence Vail Coleman, *The Museum in America* (Washington: American Association of Museums, 1939).

and museum fatigue, and opened what was hailed as the first satellite museum in the growing commercial suburb of Upper Darby.[17] Yet Kimball's first priority was the collection: when the Depression hit, he closed down the branch and, eventually, the education department itself.[18]

If the educational museums of the 1870s were succeeded by the patron's museums of the 1910s, what Kimball and his contemporaries did was to internalize the opposing forces within the museum, divide them into different departments, and, as much as possible, deny the opposition. As long as the patrons could finance the art museum (or prevail upon local governments to subsidize the functions that they could not), this strategy was a success. But changes in the postwar era brought this accommodation under stress. As museums expanded, as state and federal subsidy came to supplement local subvention, as their needs surpassed their patrons' resources, a new public, defined first as a membership and, eventually, as a more diffuse market, took on increasing importance. Today few museum people would question the importance of the market that has flocked to their exhibitions and their stores. Yet the rise of this market has raised new questions about what business the art museum is in.[19]

The relative importance of the three museums and their publics has shifted with the museum's economic environment. When patrons could provide financing and art, they were the salient public. To the extent that government financing has been important, as it has been in many cities and was during the Great Depression and during the 1960s and 1970s, the social museum and the "disenfranchised" receive special attention. During the 1970s and 1980s, the market assumed new importance, both as a source of admissions and retail revenues and because attendance figures could bolster applications for government and corporate grants.[20]

Although many would argue that the museum's first responsibility is to art, the press of economic considerations is inescapable. In the short run, the inability of private patrons to meet escalating prices for art, and the political and fiscal agonies of the federal arts-policy enterprise, can only increase the salience of the public-as-market.

17. DiMaggio, "Constructing an organizational field."

18. This summary is based on research on the branch museum in the archives of the Carnegie Corporation of New York, the Philadelphia Museum of Art, and the Archives of American Art in New York City. The author is grateful to the staff of all of these institutions for permission to use the collections and help in doing so.

19. See Vera L. Zolberg, "Conflicting visions of American art museums," *Theory and Society* 10 (1981); and Vera L. Zolberg, "Tensions of mission in American art museums," in *Nonprofit enterprise in the arts: Studies in mission and constraint,* ed. by Paul J. DiMaggio (New York: Oxford University Press, 1986).

20. See Paul J. DiMaggio, "Can culture survive the marketplace?" *Journal of Arts Management and Law* 13 (1983); and Paul J. DiMaggio, "The nonprofit instrument and the influence of the marketplace on policies in the arts," in *The arts and public policy in the United States,* ed. W. McNeil Lowry (Englewood Cliffs, N.J.: Prentice-Hall).

Space does not permit a thorough discussion of strategic issues here. I would only suggest that, quite aside from the problems a market-centered strategy raises for the museum's mission, such a strategy is unlikely to be viable in the long run. For one thing, income earned through admissions and retail operations represents a limited, if indispensable, part of the art museum's operating budget—far smaller than is the case for theaters or symphony orchestras, for example. What this means is that large and hard-won percentage increases in admissions and retail income yield small increases in operating budgets. Altering this situation would require changing the museum's mission, structure, and mode of operations, and going into head-to-head competition with department stores, motion pictures, and theme parks. It is not obvious that museums would fare well in such competition (especially given their limited access to capital markets) or that they would willingly make the changes such a strategy would require.

For another thing, art museums, like other cultural institutions, benefited from a demographic windfall during the 1960s and 1970s that will not be repeated. Individuals with almost all of the characteristics associated with museum attendance—relative youth, college educations, white-collar occupations—became far more numerous than they had been before. During the past decade, real incomes and educational attainment have stopped growing, the baby-boom generation has reached middle age, and labor-force growth has shifted to low-income service occupations. In other words, the United States produced typical art museum visitors at an unprecedented rate for approximately twenty years, and now the growth has stopped. Art museums can no longer count on steadily increasing demand for their services.

The patron's museum is also unlikely to make a resurgence. As museums have expanded, they have priced themselves out of the market for Medicis. Moreover, stable, local, self-renewing upper classes—the most fertile soil for patrons of the arts—have been in decline, losing ground to a national corporate elite with different agendas. And uncertainty in the art market may jeopardize traditional relationships between curators and collectors.

I suspect that the potential of the social museum, of the museum as an educational force, has been underestimated during the past decade of federal retrenchment and social conservatism. Public art budgets, which have not really declined even though the federal share has fallen sharply, may rise significantly again; and, as always, public support will bring with it new opportunities for educational initiatives. On the other hand, government will not become so important a source of revenues as to displace the patron or the market.

In other words, in the short run, the art museum will remain a conglomerate: three museums serving three publics, the balance among them shifting with changes in the economy and public policy, and exhibiting considerable local variation. In the long run, there is substantial room for entrepreneurship; and, as other institutions have done in the past, the art museum may transform itself, for better or worse, into something quite different from what it is today.

The long run is beyond the scope of these comments, however. What it important for now is to recognize that the art museum has not one public, but several; that it is organized to carry on several kinds of relationship with these several publics; that the museum's allocation of attention among them is shaped by its fiscal and political environment; and that the museum's strategies towards these publics follow from and shape its conception of the purposes it seeks to serve.

Marilyn Perry

In the mid-1960s, as a young graduate student in London, I lived for several months in a damp and dingy eighteenth-century basement just off Baker Street that cost five pounds a week and stank of mildew. This in itself is hardly noteworthy, but the total lack of physical comfort compounded the stark realities of an extremely difficult period. I was penniless and as yet without friends. I had left my husband for a course of study for which I was inadequately prepared, and my mother was dying of cancer 5,000 miles away. What saved me—it is not too strong a word—was the proximity of the Wallace Collection, and, in particular, two paintings that I went to visit almost daily: Velasquez's *Portrait of a Lady with a Fan* and Poussin's *Dance to the Music of Time*. When I think of that period, its terrors and uncertainties are countered by the welcoming warmth of the Wallace Collection and the beauty of the pictures that had become my dearest companions. It was my first intimate experience of the consolation of art.

The Wallace Collection, of course, is a very select, even privileged, art museum, in that it exists solely to look after its holdings. It neither acquires nor lends; it is without novelty (except for the recent rehanging) or impending expansion. It is large enough to contain a great many treasures of very high quality, and small enough to feel at home in, to browse, to imagine that you know, or could know, every work. And, like our Frick Collection and the Isabella Stewart Gardner Museum, it preserves something very special that we have had to sacrifice in our larger institutions—the inescapable fact that these are works of art that have been lived with and loved. That they have served, in other lives before our own, as they will serve in others after ours, to comfort, or to challenge complacency, or simply to delight.

It is the capacity to move us, to inspire love, that distinguishes art from all other objects. At the inauguration of the National Gallery of Art in March 1941, Franklin Delano Roosevelt rose to accept, for the people of the United States, the new art museum built by Andrew Mellon and with the founding donations of old master paintings from Mellon, Samuel Kress, and Joseph

Widener. "Great works of art have a way of breaking out of private ownership into public use," he said. "They belong so obviously to all who love them—they are so clearly the property not of their single owners but of all men everywhere—that the private rooms and houses where they are hung become in time too narrow for their presence. The true collectors are the collectors who understand this—the collectors of great paintings who feel that they can never truly own but only gather and preserve for all who love them the treasures they have found."

The purpose of the art museum, in Roosevelt's felicitous phrasing, is to place works of art "into public use . . . for all who love them." It is a high and noble charge, for both museum and public, pronounced in an hour when the fundamental values of western civilization stood in jeopardy. Half a century later, it bears revisiting.

Consider the predominant current activities in our larger, more comprehensive museums. To judge from their own press releases (a selective but indicative source), two approaches characterize the ways that art is presented to the public: as trophies, and as entertainment. Both patterns have evolved from premises about the nature and function of the art museum that would have been foreign to Roosevelt's generation, but seem now to be largely taken for granted.

The first presupposes that the art museum must continually acquire more art. I do not here wish to debate the merits of the proposition, but rather to consider the consequences when—as increasingly seems to be the case—it is accepted without argument that regular acquisition of more art is one of the museum's key responsibilities. This is an activity that makes enormous demands upon the limited resources of available funds, staff time, trustee interest, and publicity. Repetition of the processes of acquisition tends to demote works of art from treasures of the human spirit to specimen types with price tags or glamorous prizes pursued through subtle campaigns involving owners, dealers, auction houses, and donors. Novelty, cost, and possession become the primary values. Ironically, and sadly, the more the collection—and, eventually, the building—are expanded, the more the public use of the art, in Roosevelt's sense in which art is treasured, familiar, and beloved, is diminished.

If possession of more works of art is the first issue, display of more works of art is the second. The constantly changing, mammoth special exhibitions of the last two decades have whetted the public appetite for borrowed art expensively packaged and marketed as sophisticated, revolving, popular entertainment. Nor is the public disappointed, since, so primed, it arrives in record numbers, diligently follows the "acoustiguide," and agrees that it has enjoyed a privileged and unrepeatable cultural experience—a perception reinforced by queues, crowds, publicity, and merchandise. No wonder that special exhibitions are widely perceived as the art museum's chief attraction.

Inevitably, these patterns affect the public's understanding and use of its art museums and its art. Presenting works of art as recently acquired trophies taking their places among earlier spoils emphasizes the least important elements of the preciousness of art—namely, current assessed valuation and the uniqueness of physical possession. Great works of art have always been collateral in games of power and social prestige, but today's spectacle of museums ceaselessly courting collectors and announcing donations, or *partial* donations, at market value in formal press releases, demeans an act of philanthropy to the level of a tax maneuver and compromises the dignity of the work of art. The public is invited to gape at a publicist's icon, and to marvel at the incomprehensible value of paint on canvas. Neither donor nor public enjoys the rewards of Roosevelt's "true collectors", who knew themselves as temporary stewards of great works of art "for all who love them."

Other dangers attend the special exhibition. Here, it is the massing of art under a guiding rationale that creates the event. Interpretation is central, even crucial, since objects have been assembled according to an interconnecting (and occasionally tenous) principle that usually requires explication. The necessity of justifying the purpose of the show tends to encourage hyperbole, just as its transience promotes a certain urgency. In effect, works of art are set performing, on limited engagement, in front of crowds that gather for an expensively produced event that is often both wonderful and unrepeatable. Perhaps even too wonderful. The public is quickly spoiled when art comes so beautifully prepackaged, ordered, and interpreted, with an entry, a middle, and a signposted exit near which the cash registers ring. You are told what is important. You do not get lost. It does not take all day.

Special exhibitions can be highly informative, stunningly beautiful, and unforgettable. But they are also, of necessity, a programmed experience, in which the viewer is essentially a passive spectator, enjoying the conglomeration of objects temporarily brought together for education and delight. The larger and more popular the show, the less opportunity for quiet contemplation. In consequence, as the special exhibition has come to dominate the public's expectation of its art museums, it has also tended to undermine the highest use of art.

An analogy may serve. Attending a performance of *Hamlet* without prior knowledge of the play may be a deeply moving experience, but one that is altogether different from knowing the great passages by heart. Only the solitude of personal reflection can move great art from the public to the private domain, to console our most intimate fears and longings, to comfort the loneliness of mortality.

Art's highest reward is personal discovery. Like falling in love, the experience is unique to the individual. It cannot be programmed. But it can be encouraged.

My hope, for the future of our art museums, is to find the permanent collection returned to center stage. This is not to abandon special exhibitions or even the quest for new acquisitions, but to refocus these activities in relation to the works of art at the heart of the institution—the masterpieces overlooked because they are always there. And this, of course, is precisely the point. We must return the great art in our public collections to what Roosevelt so aptly called public use.

There are heartening signs of change, of new or improved efforts to invite the essential discovery that works of art can enrich the pleasure or diffuse the pain of being alive. Very little is required: curiosity, imagination, longing, accessibility, and encouragement. New modes of presentation quickly kindle new ways of looking and response. Nor does it take long to realize that the more we explore, the more we discover. The greatest wonder of great art, always, is that it is at once timeless and timely. If we will but give it time.

Must we justify? Some years ago, a BBC commentator queried Kenneth Clark about the purpose of art. Lord Clark responded, "I can only ask you, what is the purpose of love?"

James N. Wood

In spite of the title of this conference, the museums here are represented by directors and presidents, not by chief financial officers. I take this as recognition of the fact that, while the public is an essential component of the economic life of the art museum, the complex and dynamic relationship between the two can only be grasped in the context of an institution's purpose and philosophy. And today, the pressure for change in the way we perceive the public, define our purpose, and solve the economic challenge is, I believe, greater than at any time since the creation of our original bylaws in the late nineteenth century.

When The Art Institute of Chicago's first major building was completed on Michigan Avenue in 1893, it was intended to express permanence: architectural permanence in a city conscious of its unsophisticated youth and a cultural permanence that presented the values of the founders as the goal towards which the public should strive. Its cornice was proudly adorned with names of the great figures of western art (Apelles, Giotto, Leonardo, Velasquez), most of whom are, one hundred years later, still not represented in the permanent collection. This facade advertised a product that did not then exist in Chicago. It was a litany of cultural heroes that the museum and the public were to venerate without the benefit of original works of art. Today, our priorities and goals for the public are the reverse. The originality and quality of the actual work of art are now paramount. Judging our founders by today's values, they appear authoritarian and often condescending to their public. But while that may have been the case, their sense of civic responsibility and their extraordinary generosity have become increasingly rare. Today when a name is carved on a facade it is far more likely to be that of the donor than of an artist.

One hundred years ago our collections were meager but there was a fundamental, and not entirely imposed, consensus of purpose among the museum, its supporting elite, and the public. Today, swollen as we are with rich and diverse collections, that consensus has broken down. This change presents us with both a major challenge in determining the future of our art museums and an indication of our success in including a new cultural diversity and developing a sense of personal taste in our public. The names on the Art Institute's facade now misrepresent the breadth of our aspirations as well as our collections. Clearly the role of the museum and the expectations of the public have changed in our society. However, the full implications of these changes are still unclear, and the longer we take to comprehend them, the greater the risk we run, both philosophically and economically, of losing our bearings and jeopardizing our future.

I do not presume to have any profound answers. What I would like to do is to look briefly at our public and then ask several questions that I feel may help us at least to focus the issues before us. Of the public visiting the Art Institute, over 65 percent have a college degree or higher, and over 60 percent have white-collar occupations. The average age appears to be slowly rising, and women outnumber men by a substantial margin. The annual attendance of between one and a half and two million fluctuates in response to the special exhibitions in any given year, but the total, as for most American art museums, appears to have plateaued. When the attendance of the Art Institute is combined with the attendance of the other institutions in the metropolitan area, culture in Chicago, as in most major American cities, consistently outdraws sports events. What is important for us however, is that it is not just on the size of these numbers that we, and many of our funding sources, judge our impact, but on their socioeconomic distribution. The result is that while our popularity is at an all-time high, we are criticized from within and without for not meeting our social obligations. This coincides with the final stage in a one hundred year evolution, from the authoritarian assumptions of the founding generation to the pluralistic goals and tolerance for ambiguity that characterize the profession today. In addition, the continuing erosion of the American public's leisure time, which had already shrunk 31 percent between 1973 and 1984, means those that do not receive exposure to the arts through family or school at an early age, have even less probability of discovering them later in life. Therefore, as we approach the financial problems that most of us forecast for the 1990s, we will be under the pressure, much of it self-imposed, to assure that time and resources go to increasing the breadth of our audience as well as its size. The audience growth targeted by fund-raisers and merchandisers has little in common with that demanded by our educational purpose, and it will take concerted effort to prevent our museums from developing serious cracks along this fault line.

Just as the question of who the museum's public should be changed dramatically in the 1960s, the self-image the museum presented to the public was transformed in the 1970s. Spectacular loan exhibitions and ambitious building programs attracted a new and larger audience and convinced the media that the visual arts and museums had a mass appeal and were even capable, on occasion, of creating celebrities. The simultaneous emergence to positions of authority of Tom Hoving and Andy Warhol saw the elimination of the last taboos separating art and museums from the media. With this transformation and the parallel explosion of the art market—with its succession of front-page, record-breaking sales—more and more of the public formed their opinions of museums and certain high-priced periods of art from the media, unencumbered by any firsthand experience of actual institutions or specific works of art. This has led to a dramatic increase in public awareness and fascination, but not necessarily understanding and support. While attendance has certainly been affected positively—and without that motivation for a first visit our collections have no chance to speak to a new audience—we have also become politically attractive, which is to say that we are seen as generating issues that can stir the emotions of a mass audience. As a result, long before the current debate on obscenity, museums were becoming increasingly subject to both liberal and conservative political pressure, the former advocating social and educational usefulness and the latter searching for deviation from moral, religious, and patriotic standards. The public that is aware of our existence has vastly increased, but so has the challenge and enormity of the task of transcending the impressions made by money and politics and providing educational opportunities that will convey our true purpose.

A final observation concerning our public is that it and the museum world we operate in are becoming increasingly international. Two recent quotes from *The New York Times* capture the dizzying pace of change. Demonstrators in Moscow besieging KGB headquarters "urged that the Lubyanka prison be turned into a museum of Stalinism," and Christopher Burge, president of Christie's, commenting on the projected total of possibly $1 billion from the November New York auction sales said, "It's a huge sum of money in art world terms, but in real world terms it really isn't that much." Clearly today anything, anywhere could and perhaps will become a museum, and claims for the monetary value of art can only be understood in terms of international investment strategies rather than the number of American dollars paid.

The erosion of the American museum's former position of international dominance has paralleled the decline of American political and economic power abroad over the past decade. Gone are the heady days of "American cultural Imperialism" to quote Jack Lang, when exhibition loans flowed basically one way from Europe, Asia, and Latin America, and little was sent back in return. While it was easy to dismiss Lang's complaint as inconsistent with French history and aspirations and to see it as motivated more by envy than by moral superiority, we now have no grounds for complaint as the rest of the industrialized world's major museums are rushing to adopt high visibility programming and pursuit of corporate sponsors coupled with the inevitable growing dependence on earned income. In several countries, and Margaret Thatcher's England is only the most apparent, the Americanization of a centuries-old support system is creating direct competition not only for loans, but for private and corporate support as well. Who among us has not been repeatedly besieged by the charming delegates of the "The Friends of" some French, Dutch, or British museum, requesting access to the choicer levels of our mailing lists?

It would appear that we have little choice but to compete gracefully by the free-market standards we have pioneered. Or, in the case of the Japanese, by a variation on these standards that is particularly seductive, but potentially more dangerous in the long run. Given their willingness to pay substantial outright fees for loans, fees that they invariably recoup through sale of tickets and catalogues (and obviously much more when the venue is a department store), the Japanese have set an example that, while we have not hesitated to profit from it, would if adopted here, be highly destructive to the whole not-for-profit structure that is central to the tradition and purpose of the American art museum. These changes in the international museum world are absolutely central to our subject, the museum and the public, and demonstrate clearly that this subject can only be fully understood within the context of the changing economics of art museums.

In my opinion, what is at stake as we enter the 1990s is the basic relationship between the public and the museum. The evolution over our 100-year history of the concept of who the museum's public should be; the growing role of the media in shaping the public's perception of the museum; and the advent of strong international competition for art, funding, and ultimately the public, all lead to a fundamental question: What is the authority we want our art museums to project and operate under today? To limit the question to a somewhat simplistic, but essential, choice: Should our authority be educational or economic? Are we to be justified by the merits of the experience we provide or by our ability to survive in a free-market economy? Are we to view our public first as citizens or as consumers?

The way we answer these questions, and clearly there are many options in addition to a straight either/or response, will determine both the economic choices we offer our museums and the way we define their purpose. The founding generation saw their public as potential converts, while we are under a growing pressure to treat them as potential customers. Economics are only the surface of the debate. The fundamental question is one of purpose. The authority of an institution which serves customers is derived from the belief that the customer is ultimately, if not always, right and that current sales and attendance figures provide the ultimate measure of success. The authority of an institution which provides an opportunity to experience art is derived from the recognition, over an extended period of time, by a critical mass within the society, that this experience is essential and enduring and deserves to be made a priority. If we treat our public as consumers we will target very different audiences (upscale women from 30 to 50 will undoubtedly head the list) than if we see our public as citizens equally deserving of an opportunity. In addition, I am very concerned that a narrow focus on economics at the expense of education will push museums to follow the disastrous tendency of our economy as a whole to pursue short-term goals and profit, rather than long-term investments.

To view the public as consumers is really a throwback to the museum's more authoritarian past. The customer is encouraged to accept the product that is offered, while a museum dedicated to an educational purpose will encourage a far more complex response. Its goal will be to develop critical appreciation where enjoyment and understanding are combined with the self-confidence to exercise an informed personal taste. The goal of such a museum is not a herd of customers but an individualized public which has learned what it *does not,* as well as what it *does* like.

I realize that I have strayed from a narrow focus on what our public is. However, we tend to define our public in accordance with the goals we derive from our purpose. Therefore, a frank look at our changing purpose is essential if we are to speak meaningfully of the public in relation to the economics of art museums today.

Summary of Discussion

Robert C. Blattberg began by saying he was disturbed to hear that the Metropolitan Museum of Art does not use the word "marketing" any more. He believed that museums should separate the two issues of defining their mission and obtaining the means to accomplish that mission. Museums also must decide whether their primary goal is to generate converts or to meet the needs of their current "customers." These goals are related, but they may also be in conflict in some ways. In any case, marketing can be a valuable tool for reaching whatever goals are chosen.

Harold M. Williams argued that the distinction between winning converts to art and satisfying the existing demands of the public is not as extreme as had been articulated. Museums need, first, to attract people into the museums. Then museums may decide that they want those people, or "customers," to "consume" something other than what they would choose to consume themselves. Traditional marketers try to serve a need or create a need, and they try to encourage repeat buyers. These goals apply to museums as well.

James N. Wood commented that he used the word "convert" to talk about the authoritarian past of the late nineteenth century. He contrasted that period with today's situation, when the question is whether to consider the audience "customers" or perhaps "citizens."

Richard N. Rosett related his experience as dean of the University of Chicago Business School, when he realized that a critical feature of a well-designed course is that at the last meeting students will understand a manner of discourse or language that at the first meeting they would not have comprehended at all. If museums want to educate people to comprehend the art that is exhibited, they need to do more than simply hang the pictures on the walls. They should direct the attention of young children, or of people who have not been to museums before and do not know about art, to works that are especially accessible to them, in the cause of getting them hooked on enjoying art. In other words, Rosett argued, there are people who can walk into a museum and find the paintings they are going to fall in love with, and there are other people for whom an art museum is new and mysterious. This segmentation of the market is not permanent—through education, museums can move people from the second group into the first one.

William H. Luers said he had learned that the words "customer," "asset," "product," and "market" accentuate the cultural differences between economists and museum curators and directors. For example, referring to a work of art as an asset emphasizes its monetary value or its place on a balance sheet, a perspective that is hostile to the way museum people view art and hostile to the way they want the public to view art. One example of this divergence of views is the recent effort by the Financial Accounting Standards Board to have museums declare their works of art as assets on their balance sheets and then depreciate them. Most people who go to museums refuse to accept the concept of art as a commodity. Luers also contended that museums are undertaking the kind of education and introduction to art proposed by Rosett. *Rosett* responded that even though museums do those things, many museum directors resist speaking about their audience as composed of disparate groups.

Neil Rudenstine said that one of the definitions of an educational institution is that it has a claim to know something that the students do not. This mission of transmitting knowledge makes a university different in many respects from other kinds of institutions that sell "products" in ways that are far more customer-driven. Museums, like universities, are educational institutions, broadly defined. They have some important responsibilities and functions that are not directly related to their larger public audiences. They must be market-sensitive, but that is very different from simply asking, "what does the customer want?" If we believe this, then we can try to clarify the answers to some questions that were raised earlier in the discussion—what do museums know, and how can they teach it? Because museums cannot offer courses per se, they have often defined their educational mission in a rather amorphous way, and the result is sometimes an amalgam of special exhibitions, lectures, catalogues, videos, school programs, and so on.

Peter Temin returned to the question of language in referring to "assets" and "customers." He felt that the choice of language mattered when people use language; they are formulating a way to think about a problem. The premise of the conference was that it would be useful for art museum directors to think about their museums from a different point of view from their accustomed one. He argued that a useful economic model of a museum with distinct audiences is the model of a multiproduct firm. This is the common situation in

U.S. firms. The function of central management in such a firm is to balance the resources devoted to the products, which requires understanding both the short-term and long-term relationships among them. One specific example for museums is that educating the less-informed public today will increase the number of museum members in the future.

Alberta Arthurs felt that museums should be encouraged to find places where the three markets identified by Paul J. DiMaggio can come together and reinforce each other. The Rockefeller Foundation funds special exhibitions which reach out to communities and try to extend the definition of art, instead of funding exhibitions that reinforce the image that the museum has already. The foundation also funds curatorial experiments within museums, that is, exhibits that reexamine and use permanent collections in various, innovative ways.

Martin Shubik said that it was very tricky to use loaded words such as market or customer because there is a fundamental psychological difference—a difference in "gestalt"—between viewing museum visitors as customers or as patrons. He felt also that the dichotomy that had been introduced between education and entertainment was totally false; anybody who is in education is in show business. The issue is to determine the right mix of show business. Finally, he said that museums must be clearer about whether they are educating the public for taste for yesterday's art, taste for today's art, or taste for tomorrow's art.

Blattberg emphasized the difference between museums catering to people's current taste in art and museums playing a missionary role with respect to people's tastes. He wondered if the current staff and organization of museums could play that missionary role, or if another form of organization could meet that goal more effectively.

Martin Feldstein asked what would happen to the number of visitors to museums if the admissions charge were raised by $1. Presumably the number of visitors would fall somewhat, but he wondered whether the directors had a quantitative sense of what the relative reduction would be.

Wood felt that attendance would fall very slightly at the Chicago Art Institute, but he was concerned that people would hear that "it costs $6 to get in," although that is just the recommended admission. *Anne d'Harnoncourt* thought that the effect would be relatively small at the Philadelphia Museum of Art as well. She noted that admissions increases are timed usually to go into effect when there are special exhibits occurring, in the hope that people will not notice as much. *John Walsh* said that Mr. Getty had specified free admission, but Walsh would like that extra dollar.

Harry S. Parker III noted that an increase in the daily admission fee would encourage people to become members of the museum, which would mean a partially offsetting rise in revenue.

Luers felt that a $1 change would not affect attendance significantly but would affect the willingness to pay the full suggested contribution.

Anne Hawley said that the Gardner Museum just started charging for the first time in many years, and although overall attendance is little changed, the charge has been a barrier to students with whom the museum is very popular. *Rudenstine* added that other museums have lower rates for students, with the long-term goal of building an educated audience.

Bruce H. Evans said that the Dayton Art Institute had just started charging admission, and most people whom they asked as they left the museum thought the visit was worth more than the fee. He suggested reserving the additional dollar for admission for something specifically to benefit museum visitors. *Feldstein* said that might be a useful way to market the increase but was probably a bad way to manage funds.

John Hale believed that the British public was much more price-sensitive than the American public, based on the comments of the other museum directors.

Theodore E. Stebbins, Jr. said that the Boston Museum of Fine Arts expected no decline in attendance from the recent increase in fee from $5 to $6.

J. Carter Brown said that when the Museum of Fine Arts first instituted an admissions fee, attendance fell sharply. *Feldstein* wondered if there could be a big effect of moving from free admittance to paid admittance but a small effect of marginal changes in the fee once it exists.

3   Museum Finances

Harry S. Parker, III, Thomas Krens, William H. Luers, and Neil Rudenstine

Harry S. Parker III

Since the late 1970s, the Fine Arts Museums of San Francisco have experienced financial gyrations of surpluses and deficits. Private expenses increased due to expansion on all fronts, while support from the city of San Francisco declined. The bills were paid by relying on blockbuster exhibitions, which were scheduled every two to three years. The result was recurring swings from surplus to deficit and back. By the mid-1980s, these swings masked an underlying structural deficit of about one million dollars (see fig. 3.1).

The risk of continued reliance on blockbuster economics—paying for operating costs with big show windfall profits—was becoming apparent. In addition, the decline of the blockbuster phenomenon in the United States made it clear that reliance upon this economic crutch was soon coming to an end.

In July 1987, the board of trustees charged the new director of the Fine Arts Museums with two, simultaneous tasks. The first task was to balance the budget of the private side of the museum without resorting to blockbuster shows. The second task was to undertake the organizational changes necessary to put the board of trustees clearly in charge of the private funds of the museum, so that they would have comprehensive and direct authority and responsibility for both the public (city) and private sides of the institution. Let me now discuss these two tasks in greater detail.

Budget balancing for the private side of the museum was achieved by three major strategies. First, we substantially increased annual contributions, primarily with the creation of the associates program. This program entailed both higher levels of trustee giving and trustee leadership in reaching out for new and increased support. For example, annual support has increased by 109 percent since fiscal year 1985–86, growing to $1,424,000 in the year ended 30 June 1989 from $680,000 in the year ended 30 June 1986.

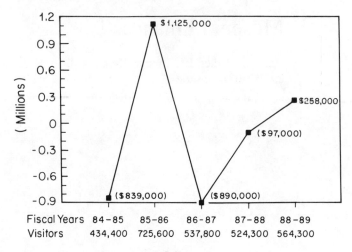

Fig. 3.1   **Operating surpluses and deficits**

Second, we cut costs by reducing privately paid positions by attrition (15 jobs in the last two fiscal years) and through other cost-containment strategies. With a current average job cost (salary and benefits) of $47,800, the attrition savings are now worth $717,000 annually.

Third, we adopted business plans to boost income from revenue-producing areas, especially general admissions, the stores, food and beverage services, and the sale of private viewings.

The outcome of these efforts was to shrink the operating deficit from $890,000 in fiscal year 1986–87 to $97,000 in fiscal year 1987–88, followed by a $258,000 surplus in fiscal year 1988–89.

The key organizational vehicle for accomplishing these financial changes was the creation of the Corporation of the Fine Arts Museums (COFAM) in the fall of 1987.

The basic organizational structure of The Fine Arts Museums is now as follows. The board of trustees is chartered by the city and county of San Francisco to govern two city-owned art museums: the M. H. deYoung Memorial Museum and the California Palace of the Legion of Honor. The board holds title to the art collection on behalf of the city, sets policies for the management of the museums, hires appropriate staff, expends city funds, and develops financial support from the private sector. COFAM is organized to manage the noncity fiscal affairs of the museums and to operate enterprise activities such as the museum stores.

The public and private sides of the museum were integrated in 1987 by making the COFAM board identical to the elected members of the museum's city board. Similarly, its top officers are the same. For example, the same person is president of both boards, and the city director of museums serves as COFAM's chief executive officer.

A related change in the governance structure was to tie the Fine Arts Museums Foundation more closely to the trustees. The foundation holds the museum's endowment and acquisition funds, and it serves as COFAM's investment committee. The foundation board was changed from being self-perpetuating to having its members elected by the trustees, and the president of the trustees has also become an ex officio member of the foundation board.

In sum, the new organizational structure has paved the way for comprehensive institutional policy making, planning, and management. From policy setting at the board level through implementation down the management line, there is now full accountability for all aspects of museum operations.

Thomas Krens

Discussions about the problems faced by museums today tend to focus on collecting. We are all keenly aware of the new power wielded by private collectors and the auction houses and the myriad problems this power poses for us. Museums have traditionally relied on the generosity of donors in order to strengthen their holdings, and, to a certain extent, have managed their collections through deaccessioning. The new economic climate in the art world is forcing many of us to pursue other strategies. A greater emphasis on operations may provide a way to address our problems.

The Guggenheim Museum is currently in the midst of a substantial capital-expansion program. Dramatic measures, including closing the museum to the public for eighteen months and thereby shutting off significant revenue streams, are forcing us to address long-term concerns about management, operations, and finances. Our starting point during this period is to apply traditional economic principles to the museum.

From an operational standpoint, revenue and expense streams are the key to understanding a museum's economic position. For most museums, operating revenues come largely from the audiences that we assiduously cultivate and develop. Admissions revenue is obviously related directly to the number of museum visitors, but so are membership income, unrestricted giving, annual appeals, and retail sales. The government has been another major revenue source, as have corporations and endowments. But how reliable are these revenue streams?

Unfortunately, audience growth is not going to continue at its former rate. Following World War II, there was a pent-up demand for culture. Museum facilities became larger, and more museums were opened to satisfy that demand. They became sophisticated and increasingly pleasant places for the public, partially through the development of special exhibitions and educational programs. These activities had the effect of stimulating and, conversely, satisfying demand. But we seem to be approaching a saturation level in terms of audience, and demand for our "product" is no longer increasing at rates greater than population growth. That will negatively affect all of the revenues associated with visitor rates.

From 1965 onward, the National Endowment for the Arts (NEA) has been very important for all of us, its matching-grants program a crucial catalyst for outside support. But by now everyone is familiar with many of the complications associated with government participation in cultural institutions. Beyond the issues of censorship and governmental control, the greatest complications have been economic. The NEA budget grew from $5 million in 1965 to $150 million in 1980. The beneficiaries of that support very quickly became dependent on it. In the 1980s, when the absolute levels of government support began to decline—and as museums became more competitive with each other for the same pool of funds—we have had to adjust to the inevitability that governmental support will continue to drop in years to come.

In the early eighties, funding from private corporations tended to replace declining government support. But that situation also became increasingly complicated as the decade progressed. Corporations once supported exhibitions through foundations that awarded grants based on some mysterious assessment of merit, or else there was an enlightened chief executive doling out money based on personal preference or connections. Now there are entire offices within corporations dealing with public image and nonprofit sponsorship. Corporations tell museums which exhibitions they want to see realized, depending on the tastes of their audience. Witness the preponderance of exhibitions devoted to Impressionist painters. In this way, museums have become part of the advertising program of corporations. As such, we are now competing with print media, sports events, television, and all the other ways corporations convey their messages. This diversification suggests that corporate support—like audience levels—is approaching maximum saturation, or may already be declining.

The other major funding source, endowments, seems to be no more promising. Since endowments have tended to be neglected, there has been a precipitous decline in the ability of the endowment to satisfy operating costs. For example, just twenty-five years ago, the income from endowments covered about 75 percent of operating expenses at the Guggenheim; now it covers about 20 percent.

This brief analysis of audience levels, government and corporate sponsorship, and endowment income points to a hostile environment in which museums will be operating during the coming years. As if the leveling off of revenue streams is not enough, we must also face grim realities on the expense side of the ledger.

The biggest single allotment in our budget goes for personnel, even though, in terms of salaries, our employees are still undercompensated. To survive in an increasingly hostile environment, we have to compete with the private sector. Not only do we need excellent curators, but we also need top-notch managers and administrators. We find ourselves in competition with banking and law firms for choice people; gone are the days when everyone at the museum could be paid less than $30,000 a year. This pressure on salaries will continue until we establish some sort of equilibrium with other sectors. The people who can be both good curators and good managers will be the ones who make a tremendous difference in the amount of revenue we are able to generate and will be crucial in solving our problems.

Other expense categories, such as technology and insurance, follow closely behind salaries and benefits. Because our industry has become technologically driven, the presentation of exhibitions and the ability to organize institutions professionally and manage them capably require an investment in computer technologies at an ever-increasing rate. The velocity of capital formation—not only in the United States but in Europe and Asia—has steadily increased the value of works of art in our collections, which has in turn increased insurance premiums.

Another major cost adding to financial pressures comes from maintaining capital-expansion projects. The past twenty years has seen the building of whole new museums and major additions, as well as sophisticated renovations. These expansions increase general carrying costs long after the projects are paid for.

All of these very general problems affect most museums today. Having recently taken over the directorship of an institution in New York City, I find myself facing a hostile economic environment head on. The balance between revenues and expenses at museums has always been marginal, but manageable. Breaking even is no longer a sure thing, however. And in the case of the Guggenheim, there is the somewhat anachronistic situation that only now are we aggressively going after a larger membership and trying to increase marketing and museum-shop sales. We are also emphasizing the development of collections and curatorial activities. All of these factors affect the ability of the institution to operate from a solid base.

Unforunately, although there are identifiable general problems affecting museums and cultural institutions, the solutions cannot be described so simply. Art museums do not fall into standardized categories. There are vast differences among them—differences in size, in location, and of course in collections. In spite of these differences, there is a semblance of similarity in that museums operate with similar guidelines and a common code of ethics.

Going back to the first source of revenue—the audience—we have to identify what differentiates one museum's product from another's. Vastly different strategies are required for operating them. The first step, though, is to focus on the nature of demand for the product from an operational standpoint. Is there such a thing as an incipient and expanding demand? Is demand leveling off? Is there an implied level of saturation of that demand? Once we understand the demand curve a bit better, we can begin to develop strategies for future operations management. Then we can begin a careful analysis of the stage of development of the particular institution. The Guggenheim is only fifty years old and is still in the process of developing its identity and operating structure. We are looking very closely at the curve of our own development, and how it interacts with the demand curve here and in the industry as a whole.

We believe that those institutions that are able to take a long, hard look at very difficult economic realities, then carefully and conscientiously develop and implement tailor-made strategies to address them, will be the ones that succeed in the face of the difficulties ahead.

William H. Luers

The finances of a museum are integrally related to the scholarly, educational, and aesthetic purposes of the institution. Philippe de Montebello, the director of The Metropolitan Museum of Art and unquestionably its decision maker on all issues dealing with art, education, and scholarship, and I, as the chief administrator, daily go about the task of integrating these sometimes competing, always essential aspects of museum life. It would be difficult to document just how we do this. Rather than enumerate the practical ways we have made this collaboration work over the past four years, I will formulate five propositions that describe some of the issues we have faced in keeping the museum artistically and financially vital.

Proposition I.   Over the past twenty years, the revenue sources of the Metropolitan Museum have expanded and become more diverse. As a result, the Museum has become involved in a larger universe of providers. It has become more difficult for the Museum to define its community. The staff-time needed to provide services to the larger, more diverse community has expanded, and administrative growth can appear to be disproportionate.

Proposition II.   As special exhibitions and other activities have resulted in increased attendance and revenues, it has become clear that strategies must be developed to assure that such activities preserve the Museum's scholarly and educational purpose and are not devised primarily as "profit centers" or "revenue raisers."

Proposition III. The larger the Museum becomes physically and programmatically, the more capable administrative and financial managers must be employed and adequately paid. This shift imposes on the Museum ever greater requirements to stimulate creativity and promote scholarship among the professional staff and to seek funds to enhance the salaries and research activities of curators.

Proposition IV. As prices continue to rise in the art market, museums have been less able to afford many desirable works of art. Simultaneously, changes in the tax law since 1986 have discouraged donors from contributing works of art to museums. Special efforts have become necessary to attract donations of art and to improve the tax environment through political lobbying.

Proposition V. As the economic environment of the city becomes more strained, the social environment becomes more impoverished. When caught in this dilemma, the Museum must direct its fund-raising efforts to a wider group—thereby confusing and, perhaps, even alienating its local community, unless special programs are designed to counter this trend.

The first proposition, to recapitulate, is that over the past two decades the revenue sources for the Met expanded and became more diverse, thus engaging the museum more actively in a larger universe of providers, but complicating our role in various ways. To illustrate this proposition: in 1967 the Met's annual operating budget was $6.98 million; 62 percent of the budget was from endowment income, 29 percent from the city, 5 percent from membership, 1 percent from gifts and grants, and 1 percent from other sources. There were no revenues in those years from admissions, from auxiliary activities, or from corporations in support of special exhibitions. The sources of income were largely derived from the New York area, and virtually no staff was dedicated to "development" and other fund-raising or revenue programs. In contrast, our budget in fiscal year 1989 was $68 million. We have increased our budget exactly tenfold in twenty years because of growth in the building, staff, and programs—and, of course, a general inflationary economy. When we look at our 1988–89 budget, we see a whole variety of new income sources, providing an important part of our income. In fiscal year 1989, Museum income was derived from the following sources: 20 percent from the city; 16 percent from gifts and grants; only about 14 percent from endowment; 14 percent from membership; about 13 percent from admissions; about 8 percent from auxiliaries (which include merchandising and restaurants); about 5 percent from special exhibitions; and about 9 percent from other sources. This broad revenue base is healthy in that we are no longer as dependent on one or two sources of income, but it also results in a larger staff serving a much wider body of supporters.

The increased diversity of income sources has brought with it a much greater need for the Museum's management to broaden and step up its activities with this larger universe of donors. Social events, correspondence programs, and the full range of development activities must be accompanied by modern computer systems, advertising, and new promotional techniques. Likewise, as relations with large corporations and tourist institutions grow, and as the merchandising and bookstore business increases, so has the staff—which has over 2000 employees and 600 volunteers. Museum management begins to take on the attributes and behavior patterns of a business. The Museum has an annual operating budget of over $70 million and 4.5 million visitors each year. This means that the Metropolitan offers its extraordinary resources to the public at a cost of about $15 per visitor per year. The key challenge is to manage such an enterprise without eroding its traditional scholarly and aesthetic role.

A concrete way to articulate the complex of issues arising out of this dilemma in the Metropolitan Museum is to examine some of the specific long-range and conceptual traps that can lead to conflict, confusion, and dysfunction within the Museum and its community. For example, the use of words such as marketing to describe the range of the Museum's promotional activities, or assets to describe works of art, or clients to describe visitors to the Museum can result in a breakdown of communications and functionality within the Museum. It sets administrators against curators and develops a "we-versus-they" mentality toward management. The language of marketing, with its lingo about "logos," in an art- and design-conscious institution can be offensive.

Moreover, the language of the advertiser and the market-trained professional can actually lead to flawed and failed efforts to promote a quality exhibition or activity. Note the disastrous campaign mounted in London to market the Victoria and Albert Museum. The language of marketing can and does provoke anger and fear of management's intention and sensibilities among curators. At the Metropolitan Museum, we therefore do *not* have a marketing office, a marketing individual, or a marketing committee. We go to great pains to discuss these issues in a way that encourages the professional staff to participate. We have found that intelligent publicity for scholarly activities to attract visitors works better than "marketing our assets to our clients."

Yet we carry out a wide range of activities that to others may look, sound, and be like the objectives of the dreaded "m-word." For example, we worked with AT&T to develop a series of highly publicized and popular recorded walking tours of the Museum, to try to give our permanent collection the same kind of excitement as our highly publicized special events. We also worked with *Business Week* to put out an advertising supplement on the Metropolitan Museum, which informed the corporate world of our Museum and earned us a substantial revenue in the deal. We also advertise in *The New York Times,* and other locations, and have been working with a creative group outside the Museum to improve our approach to regular promotional activities.

Within the Museum, however, we never refer to works of art as assets—because to do so would suggest that we intend to trade in them as assets—which we most certainly do not. Moreover, our visitors are not our clients. Should we begin to deal with our visitors for a commercial purpose, we would surely lose our mission as a great public museum. Show me a priest who refers to his parishioners as his clients, and I will show you a church in which bingo has become more important than baptism. Words, language, and concepts matter in seeking to preserve the mission of the large and financially stretched art museum.

The second proposition is about special exhibitions. As special exhibitions have been developed to expand museum admissions and attendance, it has become ever more clear that thinking of such exhibitions as revenue raisers, or profit centers must be avoided and that particular efforts must be made to preserve the scholarly and educational purposes of such activities. As we look back over the twenty years of experience with special exhibitions, we have seen our revenues rise and fall, year after year, depending to a large degree on whether or not a given year offered a major Impressionist or other blockbuster exhibition. An impression even arose that we began to become financially dependent on devising special revenue raising exhibitions, and that a bad year at the Metropolitan was a year when such an event had not been planned. Even though these so-called down years might be years with excellent and scholarly exhibitions, if they were not popular from the standpoint of finances, they were not seen as having contributed to the financial health of the Museum. This growing cycle of dependency of the Museum on the revenues from such exhibitions ran the danger of requiring the director and his curators to consistently devise at least one or two exhibitions a year that would enhance our revenues, thereby distorting the direction and approach to the mounting of Museum exhibitions.

Therefore, in 1989, under the guidance of Director Philippe de Montebello, working closely with Vice President of Operations Richard Morsches and Manager of Admissions Kathleen Arffmann, the Museum evolved a more balanced approach to special exhibitions and how they should fit into the pattern of the Museum's activities. For example, in 1989 we made the decision not to have advance ticket sales for our major Velazquez and Canaletto exhibitions for the fall of 1989. Looking back to the prior fiscal year (1988–89), when we had 4.5 million visitors—many of whom came to see the large, ticketed exhibitions of Degas and Georgia O'Keefe—one can see a significant addition to our admissions income from tickets sold through Ticketron. The decision not to ticket the two 1989 exhibitions was taken for a variety of reasons, and it clearly resulted in a drop of income for the Museum—even though attendance during that year did not drop significantly in comparison to the year before. The decision was designed to provide our public the opportunity to consider the special exhibitions as part of the general purpose and function of the Museum. Moreover, the director was concerned that if we used Ticketron, our visitors could too easily associate the special exhibitions with sports events or popular entertainment. He adopted the longer-term view that special exhibitions should make possible the building of a larger body of repeat visitors to the special exhibitions—thereby encouraging the growth of a loyal audience for the Museum. Over the long run this approach would expand our attendance to the Museum's collections, not make us dependent on special exhibitions, and enable us to demonstrate to ourselves and others that our exhibition schedule over the years was designed with a scholarly, educational, and public purpose rather than for its revenue raising potential. We are still examining this policy on ticketing to determine whether we are on the correct course or whether there might be some alternative way to supplement our income from particularly popular exhibitions.

We have surveyed our visitors frequently over the years to determine their likes and dislikes. One of our findings is that people who have good experiences in special exhibitions can be encouraged to become part of the larger Museum community that spends time in our permanent collections. Moreover, since we have a policy of asking for voluntary contributions and do not charge a fixed admission fee, the size of our admissions revenue is dependent upon the willingness of our visitors to pay suggested $5 admission. We want our visitors to feel good about their experience, to return, and even eventually to become members. Admissions has become, in recent years, a smaller percentage of our gross revenues. We have concluded that we will look on exhibitions as largely one of the multiple ways to develop a broader-based and more appreciative public. Admissions income will not and cannot be seen as a central factor in the mounting of special exhibitions.

In addition to this evolving attitude toward special exhibitions for our public, we have adopted in 1989–90 other programmatic ways to appeal to a broader and more diverse audience. In the fall of 1989, we began to keep the Museum open on Friday and Saturday evenings until 9:00 P.M., thus making the Museum accessible to the public longer during their traditional periods of leisure time. We have also provided special programing during these extended evening hours. The Museum has been greatly encouraged by the response to these weekend hours, and we have noticed that our visitors during these hours tend to be younger, ethnically more diverse, and in many cases new to the Museum.

The third proposition is that the larger the museum becomes physically, the greater the tendency toward enlarged management and financial staffs and the more these structures encroach on the work of the professionals. Therefore, ever greater efforts are required to find creative ways to stimulate the professional staff of the museum. In a trailblazing study written by Neil Rudenstine for the Mellon Foundation, a wide range of art museum directors in the United States were interviewed to find the most appropriate way in which private funds could assist museums today. One of the conclusions of this study was that the greatest benefit to an art museum would be to provide special sabbatical-like assistance to the key museum scholars to relieve them temporarily of the daily pressures of special exhibitions, the promotion of the collections, the management of departments, and the necessary negotiations with donors. The assistance would encourage them to conduct their scholarly work, revive their intellectual and creative talents, and free them of the stress of mundane museum activity.

When I first came to the Metropolitan Museum in 1986, I sensed that the Museum was undermanaged. The personnel office was given low priority, hidden in the back room of the Museum. The finance department was not adequately staffed, and our systems and computers were not sufficient to track our $70 million–plus budget, our $400 million endowment, our merchandising business, our $30 million capital budget, and the range of personnel issues that needed to be attended to. My focus was to work in those areas and try to improve them in order to cope with the large challenges of this expanding Museum. The cost of greatly improved management is increased by the fact that much of the staff required to work in the areas of finance, administration, and systems can only be hired from the competitive market. The competition, and therefore cost implication, for top curators and scholars is not as great as for senior financial managers and computer specialists. That is a fact of life. The growth of management and the high salaries of financial managers who are brought into the Museum have created structural tensions within the staff. As a result, the Museum, with the help of the Mellon Foundation and other supporters, has sought increasingly to provide special benefits to its creative professional people to enhance their role and their sense of vitality in the Museum. We must find ways to provide moments of peace and creative opportunity for the professional staff who function in an environment of "an active institution which works at a fevered pitch," to quote our director. We have also mounted a major fund-raising effort, strongly supported by our trustees, to enhance the salaries of our professional staff and make them somewhat comparable to the higher salaries we necessarily have to pay to attract the top-quality management.

The fourth proposition concerns the art market and the fact that museums are ill-equipped to deal with the radically different environment that has been created by the explosive prices of art. This environment has affected our ability to acquire new works and to exhibit collections, in part because of the cost of insurance, shipping, and travel. The Metropolitan, which was a regular and major participant in the acquisition of major works of art only seven or eight years ago, can now rarely compete or even think about the acquisition of major works of art that come on the market. Our endowment for acquisitions provides a cash flow of less than $3 million a year for the acquisition of art for our entire Museum, which has 19 curatorial departments. Therefore, our curators are too often frustrated because it seems futile even to think about major additions to our collections. In the past, 90 percent of our collection has come from gifts and bequests, but the tax law passed in 1986, which discourages donations of works of art to museums, has seriously restricted this vital source. There are only a few great donors who are prepared to provide funds for acquisitions. Fortunately, there are several in our Museum. Jayne Wrightsman, the head of our acquisitions committee, and Douglas Dillon, our former chairman, are two of several who recognize this major weakness in our financial structure in today's environment. They have dedicated large private resources to enhancing our capacity to make wise acquisitions. Moreover, Ambassador Walter Annenberg in his recent, generous gift to the Metropolitan Museum, provided us with $15 million for acquisitions, demonstrating once again his own wisdom and understanding of the plight of the large museum today.

Our hope in meeting this challenge is to encourage the Congress of the United States to amend the tax law so that donors will again be encouraged to give works of art to museums. But museums, like all cultural institutions, are not equipped psychologically or financially to mount major political lobbying efforts. The very scholarly and aesthetic environment we so hope to preserve in the Museum is the antithesis of the tough posture necessary to redress a tax and political environment now even more negative toward the arts.

Finally, the fifth and last proposition addresses the inner city. As the economic and social environment of the city becomes more strained and impoverished, the Museum must direct its efforts to raising financial support from outside the city by attracting foreign and American tourists, cultivating the European and Asian donors, and expanding the concept of the museum community. In trying to reach a broader community, the Museum could lose touch with, confuse, or even become alienated from its immediate surrounding community.

There are multiple responses to this particular challenge. The Metropolitan Museum, located in New York—one of the most generous cities in the world to its arts—has found it impossible to depend exclusively on the community of New York. Increasingly we find it necessary to look beyond this community for support. Other museums, such as the Guggenheim, are planning a response that creates a global museum, with museum networks around the world, serving communities on several continents with a range of curatorial staff and collections. Indeed, the Guggenheim represents probably the most radical museum response to the support limits of the local community. On the other side, a museum such as the National Museum of American History in the Smithsonian Institution in Washington, D.C., has undertaken an even more intense effort to relate that museum to its specific ethnic environment and to the ethnic environment of the United States—by shifting its exhibitions and displays to be responsive to the ethnic and national sensibilities of the diverse American community. While this latter museum's approach is to improve the capacity to relate more directly to the immediate community, the former is to expand enormously the community to a global scale.

The Metropolitan Museum does not intend to expand physically beyond its existing building and The Cloisters (its branch for medieval art at Fort Tryon Park) but indeed our horizons must expand to incorporate the world community, which is interested in our museum. We have increased our efforts with foreign visitors substantially by providing foreign-language services. We now offer brochures, maps, and recorded walking tours in six different languages at a tourist desk, where receptionists can welcome visitors at all times in at least six foreign languages. We are mounting efforts to increase our corporate support from Europe and Japan. Yet at the same time our relationship with immediate community in the city of New York—a city to which we make a financial contribution and from which we derive both a significant part of our identity and substantial support—requires special effort. The Museum is constantly seeking new ways to expand support from the city and our private donors, as well as ways to expand the participation of minorities in the work of the Museum. Our community outreach program is actively expanding. We are not satisfied that we are yet achieving our objectives and must do more through our educational program. These are dual responsibilities that must be met, both for the financial well-being and the public purpose of our museum.

The experiences of The Metropolitan Museum of Art, with regard to these various tensions that are at play between the financial needs and the scholarly purpose, are not unique. Simply put, the Metropolitan is such a large institution that we probably confront the problems on a scale that is more evident than with other museums. Our objective is to achieve appropriate balance in retaining the creativity and the financial soundness of the institution.

Neil Rudenstine

I will begin by assuming we are all reasonably familiar with the factors that are now creating difficult financial conditions for many American art museums. These include (among many things) an actual decline or at least "flattening" of important revenue streams; recent changes in federal tax laws; and a less robust national economy. In this talk, I want to focus on two rather different (but related) questions. First, is the current situation similar to those of several earlier eras, when museums were also financially hard pressed? Or, if the present moment is unusual in certain fundamental ways, can we define the most important differences and offer at least a tentative explanation of them? Second, if we assume that the current financial problems are not likely to disappear or change significantly in the near future, can we say anything useful about the realistic alternatives open to art museums as they try to deal with this more stringent set of economic circumstances?

I will concentrate primarily on those museums that are located in quite large cities; that are privately (rather than publicly) funded; that have existed for the better part of a century or more; and that are engaged in a wide range of activities, including major special exhibition programs. There are perhaps 8 to 10 institutions of this kind in the nation, and I will—especially when using statistics—normally refer to five representative examples. Clearly, by concentrating on this particular sector, one fails to address the considerable variety of situations faced by many small and mid-sized institutions throughout the century. At the same time, the major urban art museums do play a significant role in establishing a tone and defining a range of programs that inevitably have an effect upon large numbers of other museums.

Let me return to my first question: is the current economic situation similar to, or different in some fundamental ways, from earlier difficult periods? My own view is that the present predicament is in fact different. Let me suggest why.

Figure 3.2 consists of a bar chart which shows, for 1969, the *percentage of spendable income from endowment,* plus the *percentage of income for general operating expenses from city or municipal contributions,* for three major, urban art museums. As the chart indicates, the income provided in 1969 by only these two sources of revenue ranged from nearly half (46 percent) of one museum's entire budget to nearly four-fifths (79 percent) of another's.

Figure 3.3 shows the 1969 percentages for two similar urban museums— with one important difference. These institutions received no annual municipal contributions, and they made up for this lack by relying on admissions and memberships as an alternative. Endowment, plus admissions and memberships, accounted for 66 percent and 72 percent of all operating revenues at these two museums.

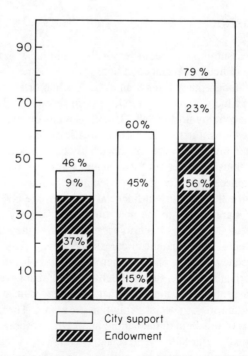

Fig. 3.2   Three major (private) urban museums, 1969: spending yield on endowment plus city/municipal operating support (as a percentage of total income)

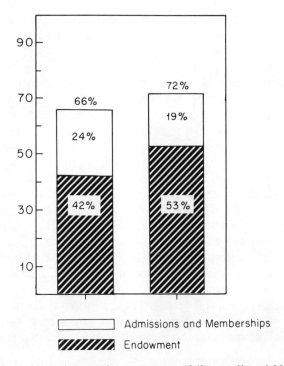

Fig. 3.3   Two major (private) urban museums, 1969: spending yield on endowment plus admissions/membership receipts (as a percentage of total income)

If we take the five institutions just examined, we can see that in 1969, the spendable yield on endowment, plus *either* municipal funds *or* admissions and memberships, supplied an average of 64.6 percent of all their operating revenues. This degree of quite steady support provided a considerable budgetary cushion, and left only a moderate revenue gap to be filled from other sources. Those other sources, moreover, were few in number and not very large: they consisted primarily of annual gifts (often from a limited number of highly committed patrons); exhibition revenues, which were then extremely small; and revenues from sales or auxiliaries, where the net income was also very small.

If we shift from 1969 to 1987, examining the same financial indicators at these same institutions, we can gauge the extent to which the economy of many of the most important American art museums has been transformed during the past two decades. The graph in figure 3.4 indicates what has happened to spendable endowment income as a percentage of total annual income—not including the figures for "auxiliary" or sales activities, since these numbers have varied considerably and can therefore distort the underlying budgetary picture. Altogether, the endowment share of total income dropped quite markedly, from an average of 40.4 percent in 1969 to 21.8 percent in 1987. At only one of the five institutions did the endowment percentage rise.

Figure 3.5 displays what has happened to municipal support at the three museums receiving such revenue. In two cases, the percentage dropped steadily; in the third instance, there was a modest rise, although the initial base of 9 percent was obviously very slim indeed.

Finally, in figure 3.6, we can see what changes occurred in the combination of endowment and municipal revenues from 1969 to 1987. Essentially, the three museums that in 1969 received about 62 percent of their total operating income from these two revenue streams alone, had by 1987 reached the point where they obtained only 37 percent of their income from the same sources. In short, during this relatively brief eighteen-year period, several factors combined to shift a number of major museums from only modest dependence upon earned income (from a very restricted number of sources) to a predominant dependence upon such earnings (from a considerably larger and more diversified number of sources). How this change occurred, and why, are extremely interesting questions which I would now like to explore, although there is not space to permit more than a brief discussion.

First, it seems clear that the change just described was almost certainly due to a number of causes. Some museums may not have attempted to raise significant new endowment funds between the late 1960s and 1987, they may not

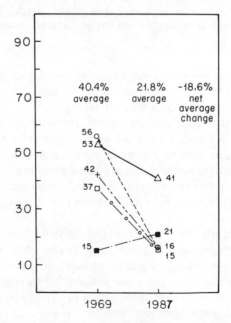

Fig. 3.4   Unrestricted endowment contribution (five museums)

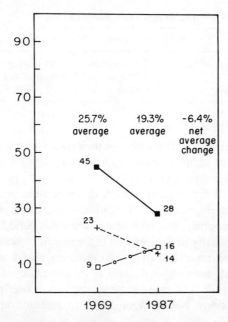

Fig. 3.5   Municipal contribution (three museums)

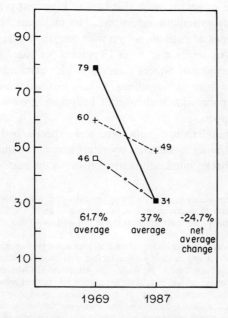

Fig. 3.6   Endowment plus municipal funds (three museums)

Table 3.1   **Operating Budget Expenditures (Averaged)**

	1980	1987	Percent Increase
5 Museums (excluding auxiliaries)	$ 13.6 million	$ 32.1 million	136%
4 Private universities	$132.6 million	$269.0 million	103%
4 Symphony orchestras	$ 11.6 million	$ 21.3 million	83%

have managed their endowments well, or their endowment spending rates may have been too high. Municipalities may have consistently cut their allocations to museums. While these and other factors undoubtedly played some role in certain situations, I am inclined to think that they were overshadowed by at least one other development: the extraordinary expansion of museum facilities, staffs, and programs that took place during this period. That expansion led in turn to an equally striking growth in the size of museum operating budgets. The rise was rapid and steep—so much so, that it would have been extremely difficult, even under the best of circumstances, for the growth of either endowment funds or municipal contributions to keep pace. As always, there were exceptions, but the figures are, on average, quite dramatic and revealing.

For instance, table 3.1 focuses on the time period from 1980 to 1987. It compares the average growth in operating expenditures—*excluding auxiliaries*—for our five museums, with that of four high-cost private universities and four large-city symphony orchestras. The museums obviously outdistanced the other types of institutions by a wide margin; in fact, the average rate of growth for the museums was about 13 percent per year.[1] Clearly, it would have required massive endowment campaigns, plus extraordinary rises in annual contributions from municipalities, to have enabled these two sources of income to keep pace with such overall budgetary growth-rates. And this simply did not happen.

Let us now examine more closely some of the specific budgetary items that played a role in driving up museum operating budgets so quickly. Figure 3.7 provides general background information. It shows the number of new Amer-

1. An analysis of expenditure-growth, for the same time period, of an additional 7 (only slightly smaller) museums indicates an average cumulative increase of about 130%, a figure that is only marginally less than that of the major museums, and still well above that of the universities and symphonies.

It would be misleading, however, to suggest that all museums experienced rates of growth such as those just cited. For example, a set of yet smaller (but well-known) institutions—including the Worcester Art Museum, the Carnegie, the Wadsworth Atheneum, the Albright-Knox, Columbus, and others—had an average growth-rate of almost exactly 100 percent between 1980 and 1987. These museum budgets, however, are very modest ($6 million average in 1987, compared with approximately $35–$65 million—excluding auxiliaries—for the largest urban museums), and these institutions are of course not generally located in major cities with large bases of potential support. Even a 100 percent growth-rate for museums of this scale, given their respective locations, is certainly non-trivial.

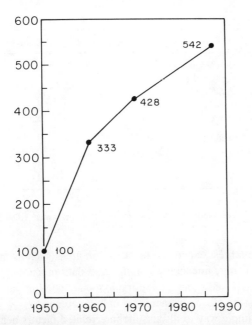

Fig. 3.7   Number of new art museums established in America, 1948–87
Source: Official museum directory.
Note: Figures include college and university art museums.

ican art museums created between 1950 and 1987: a leap from about 100
institutions just forty years ago, to nearly 550 at the present time. Even more
important, during the thirty-year period from 1950 to 1979, more than 100
existing museums in America added a total of over 10 million square feet of
new space to their physical plants. This amount of new construction is equal
to about 14 times the total space of the Louvre Museum.[2] Moreover, since
1980, the pace of building has not slowed appreciably: the number and size of
recently constructed or planned space additions to existing institutions is substantial by any standard.

The first part of table 3.2 indicates what happened to the number and type
of exhibitions at our sample of five museums from 1980 to 1987. The number
of exhibitions of any consequence grew by about 37 percent in just seven
years, and the number of major, large-scale exhibitions doubled. Such exhibitions are, of course, an important source of revenue for museums, but they
are also extremely expensive to mount. More exhibitions, by definition, require larger outlays of money, more space, and more staff time—all of which
drive up operating expenses.

Table 3.2 also illustrates developments with respect to museum staffs during this same time period: they increased about 25 percent at the five mu-

2. Karl E. Meyer, *The art museum* (New York: William Morrow, 1979), 271–84.

Table 3.2

	1980	1987	Percent Increase
Growth in Number of Museum Exhibitions at Five Large-Scale Urban Museums			
Total "advertised" exhibitions	105	144	37%
Large-scale national or international exhibitions with major catalogue	16	32	100%
Total Museum Staff Growth, 1980–87, at Five Major Museums			
Total staff	2,201	2,759	25%
Curators	150	159	6%

Source: Annual reports.

Note: Excludes small, short-term shows drawn entirely from permanent collections, without catalogues, etc.

seums, with the largest expansion occurring in areas such as merchandising, security, fund-raising, financial planning, and data processing. At the same time, the curatorial ranks (e.g., curators, associate curators, and assistant curators) at these same museums increased only 6 percent.[3]

There is no simple way to discuss the interrelated factors behind the statistics cited above. We can see, however, that many museums consistently took on greater and greater fixed costs during the time period under consideration, and these costs in turn created greater pressure for additional earned income. At the same time, in spite of these formidable pressures, it is also obvious that museums somehow managed to produce that new income at an enviable rate, and it is extremely important to try to determine how they were able to do this.

At one level, their success can be attributed to actions that the museums themselves undertook: these included the introduction of large-scale, special exhibition programs; a considerable increase in merchandizing activities; and a greater number of special events. But if such initiatives were to prosper, they required a large and responsive audience—much larger and more responsive than most, if not all, previous generations of American museum audiences.

3. An analysis of a larger sample (approximately 20 art museums) indicates a considerable variation in curatorial increases or decreases. Some smaller museums, for example, increased their curatorial numbers from 3 or 4 to 5, 6, or 7, and these changes produce quite large percentages. Since curators constitute, on average, only about 4 to 7 percent of most museum staffs, even quite modest shifts can lead to apparently significant changes when the absolute numbers are converted into percentage figures.

It is also true, of course, that the addition of custodians and security guards have accounted for a good proportion of the staff expansion at several museums, and one might well conclude that there is no reason why curators should keep pace with the growth-rates of those particular staffs. Nevertheless, many increases have also come in core administrative areas (often in financial or technology-related areas), and these additions do tend to diminish both the actual and the psychological strength or role of the curatorial ranks relative to others—especially when new administrative staff are not infrequently hired at greater salaries than senior curators are receiving.

The fact that this audience was actually, or potentially, in being, and that it could be drawn to museums with such consistency over a sustained period of time, was due, I believe, to several important tendencies that had been developing gradually in American society for a number of years and that finally converged to produce highly visible effects in the 1960s.

First, there was the deep and widespread transformation of American attitudes toward all of the arts during the postwar period—a transformation that began to take place around 1950 and that constituted a major watershed in the history of American culture. The visual arts seem to me to have emerged from this period of intense activity as the dominant set of aesthetic forms in our society. And insofar as art can be given an institutional structure, the museum has become the predominant American arts institution of our time. Let me stress that this development seems to me to be a peculiarly American phenomenon: one can find approximate analogues in a few other countries, but there are also many obvious exceptions.

A great many factors—several of them quite familiar to us—played a part in creating this new situation. These include, for example, the clear emergence of America (especially New York) as a major creative center for work in painting, sculpture, and other visual arts, beginning in the late 1940s; the increasing presence of photography, film, and video as pervasive presences in the everyday life of America; the postwar growth of art history as a fully mature academic field of study in this country, with the result that far more university graduates began to show a greater interest in and knowledge of the visual arts; the realization on the part of the publishing industry that handsome art books—with good illustrations—could command an unexpectedly large market; the proliferation of reproductions of works of art (whether as photographs, postcards, posters, or media images); the enormous postwar growth of tourism, made possible by air travel, permitting hundreds of thousands of Americans to visit the cities and museums of Europe in a totally unprecedented way; and finally, the spectacular and heavily publicized boom in the art market, beginning as early as the 1960s. Museums, sensing this powerful and widespread interest in the visual arts, began to respond actively and imaginatively to meet it. Yet these institutions could not possibly have capitalized on the new situation so successfully had it not been for one additional, rather subtle, but I believe extremely important factor. This concerns the very nature of visual arts experience, and the way in which that experience relates to the structure of the museum as a physical environment.

As we know, virtually all institutional presentations of art (such as concerts or plays) require a spectator to be present at a specific place for a well-defined period of time. Silence and immobility are imposed upon spectators, and high ticket prices usually restrict the number of events that most individuals are likely to attend.

But the process of looking at works of visual art is obviously different and varies greatly among individuals. The experience can be private, silent, and meditative; but it can also be much more social—involving such simple but important activities as walking through the galleries, talking with friends, taking time out for lunch, stopping by the museum book shop, or going to the auditorium to hear a lecture. Indeed, the very flexibility or malleability of visual arts experience—including the fact that museum environments are large and unrestrictive, and that museum visitors have essential autonomy to control and alter the nature, rhythm, and duration of their visit—has enabled the museum as an institution to accomplish in economic terms what no other high-culture arts institution has been able to manage. That accomplishment can be described as a striking increase in "productivity," based chiefly upon the fact that museums learned to take much fuller advantage of their attractive and highly fluid interior spaces, as well as their ability to create a quite wide range of revenue-producing activities capable of appealing to a larger and more diverse set of audiences.

From an economic point of view, this advantage sets museums decisively apart from other arts institutions, including not only theaters and symphony orchestras, but also opera, dance companies, and even the cinema. The number of museum "seats" or places is very flexible; the tickets are relatively inexpensive; the visitor controls the length and the itinerary of the "show," which can go on all day; indeed, several different kinds of shows can take place simultaneously.[4]

In other words, as museums created new programs and activities (and new kinds of physical spaces), they inevitably also changed the actual nature of the museum experience. Some individuals would continue to come in order to look intensively and quite privately at particular works of art. But many visitors would now come because they had begun (perhaps unconsciously) to think of the museum as a kind of large indoor culture park: an architecturally elegant, congenial, open, variegated, thoroughly animated, inviting, climate-controlled environment. The museum, meanwhile, found itself in the quite complicated but still fortunate position of not having to make clear-cut choices that were unduly limiting: up to a point, at least, the institution could remain magnetically elitist in its fundamental commitment to high culture and great art, while also becoming more accessible, more popular, and more democratic. This general development created, of course, a number of internal (and sometimes externally visible) stresses, and it led to some quite serious debates—as well as some confusion—concerning the fundamental identity and basic purposes of art museums. These matters are far from being resolved, and they require continued analysis and clarification. Nonetheless, in spite of all the attendant problems, it was this complex transmutation of the

4. Although other arts institutions (theaters, etc.) have the advantage of drawing audiences in the evening, after work hours, museums have, of course, also begun to take advantage of evening hours—either to keep their galleries open, or to hold openings, previews, and other special events. In addition, museums have the great advantage of being open all day on both Saturday and Sunday.

museum environment and the museum experience that permitted the "economic miracle" of the last two decades to take place.

If we step back for a moment in order to summarize, we can see that there was a profound change in the value that America accorded to the visual arts during the postwar period, and this change stimulated museums to alter their environment in such a way as to increase productivity dramatically. This unique combination of circumstances and capacities enabled museums to respond rapidly, ambitiously, and successfully to the changed cultural circumstances of the 1960s, 1970s, and 1980s. A recognition of this unique combination also helps account for the fact that museum budgets grew so significantly in so short a period of time; that the endowment and municipal proportion of total income declined steadily; and that so many museums shifted from being only modestly dependent upon earned income to being critically dependent upon it.

Let me return for a moment to the second question I posed at the beginning of this paper. Given the more difficult economic conditions that art museums are now facing, what realistic alternatives are available to them as they confront this new set of circumstances?

It does not seem to me, for example, that many museums could return to the far more "subsidized" economic situation they enjoyed in the 1960s. If we calculate the amount of additional unrestricted endowment necessary to enable our group of representative museums to recover their 1969 endowment position, we discover that it would require about $40 million and $60 million for the two institutions at the low end of the scale, and $150 million and $400 million for the two museums at the high end of the scale. Municipal contributions would also have to rise at a very steep rate (for several successive years) to recoup what has been lost. In short, any full-scale return to the "old economy" seems to me highly unlikely, although a more limited effort in this direction may well be plausible.

I also doubt that the extraordinarily successful earned-income formula of the past twenty years can be replicated in the next ten to twenty years, even if that were a desirable goal. If our earlier analysis is correct, the enormous and sustained surge in museum revenues was made possible because the visual arts were rather suddenly blessed with much larger potential audiences than before, and because museums had not significantly exploited their potential for earned income. But the effort to exploit sources of earned income has of course been vigorously pursued with great success for the past two decades, and it is far from clear that there is any comparable amount of elasticity remaining in the system. One cannot, for instance, continue to double the number of large special exhibitions every seven years—in fact, it is far from obvious that the number per year can grow very much at all, or that even the present pace (given recent rises in insurance costs, plus other factors) can be easily sustained. Nor can one expect admissions and membership figures, or merchandizing revenue, to continue to rise steeply for an indefinite period of time: the most recent figures have already begun to show some tapering off of these revenue-streams at several institutions, and long-term demographic trends—which are almost bound to affect the nature and size of future museum audiences—offer even less cause for optimism.

Given these limiting conditions, what strategies do seem to make sense for museums? Clearly, no one set of policies will work for every institution: the diversity of American museums is such that individual institutions will inevitably have to evolve their own, particular solutions in the light of quite specific circumstances. But I would hazard a few suggestions that may have at least some degree of general applicability. None of them is novel, but they are perhaps worth emphasizing, even if only to underscore the obvious. All of them also have much more to do with addressing long-term budgetary issues than with solving immediate problems. Essentially, they invite us to think about the kind of economy museums might create for themselves over the course of the next two decades, assuming that such structural shifts require a substantial amount of lead-time and conscious long-term planning.

First, a continuing effort to obtain gifts and grants (as well as reasonable returns from appropriate forms of earned income) will obviously be required. Concerted attempts to alter the tax laws—in order to increase incentives for giving—are also critical. What needs to be recognized as one undertakes these initiatives, however, is that the future annual yield (as suggested earlier) is simply not likely to equal that of the recent past.

Second, it does, therefore, seem important for museums to do everything reasonable to avoid taking on significant new fixed costs in the next decade or so. New construction and new staff increases obviously add substantially to expenses: such fixed costs are essentially impossible to "shed"—the new wing cannot easily be dismantled—and they consequently magnify the pressure for more earned income. When such income was easier to identify, the case for growth was often a credible one. But that case, except in very unusual situations, is now far weaker. Sustained long-term control over the expenditure budget (with annual rises in the 6 to 7 percent range rather than several points higher) is consequently another goal to which museums should give considerable weight.

Next, as part of the effort to control expenditures (and to help carry out other fundamental museum purposes that relate to the permanent collection), it does seem an opportune moment to review the number, pacing, and scale of special exhibitions. Too often this issue is framed in terms of whether one is in favor of such exhibitions (or, to use the more nebulous term, blockbusters) or whether one is not. That seems an unhelpful way of formulating the question. Exhibitions clearly constitute visual, intellectual, and scholarly events that cannot be replicated through other means, and the loss of the best shows would be profoundly felt. At the same time, the current pace of the exhibition schedule at many (certainly not all) museums is such that curators, conservators, registrars, and other staff are often left with little time to do much more than manage the flow of such events; in addition, the quality of some shows inevitably suffers as a result of this highly pressured regimen.

Equally important, the amount of risk-capital required for large international shows has certainly grown dramatically in the past few years, and this makes their economic returns (quite apart from other factors) increasingly difficult to calculate. Rising insurance costs (which are beginning to outstrip the level of guaranteed government indemnities), sophisticated packing and shipping methods (attuned to higher standards in the field of conservation), and greater expectations concerning the quality and even bulk of catalogues have all combined with other factors to drive up the expense of major shows. As the logistical complexities and the total costs of special exhibitions become more daunting, museums will inevitably be compelled to weigh yet more carefully both the economic and other investments required to undertake at least the most ambitious ventures. A conscious policy of reducing somewhat the number of shows, therefore, might well yield several benefits. The extent of total financial risk could be lessened, and additional staff time might then be redeployed to attend to important needs related to the permanent collection. A more measured but nonetheless stimulating series of carefully chosen exhibitions would still infuse museums with the particular kind of vitality and the significant intellectual as well as visual experiences that such events obviously create. Whether such a shift in policy is economically feasible—and what its precise consequences would be—are difficult matters to judge. But the time seems ripe for a thoughtful consideration and systematic analysis of this issue.

Finally, I believe that similar consideration should be given—on a *continuing* basis, not only during campaigns—to the rebuilding of museum endowments. As already suggested, I doubt that the proportionate endowment levels of the 1960s can be achieved again. But if one takes the long view, then I suspect a great deal could be accomplished over a twenty or twenty-five year period, especially if this matter were to become a high priority for trustees and administrative officers.

Assuming that endowment funds will continue to be a primary means of helping nonprofit institutions maintain their independence and financial stability, then there is much to be said for developing an aggressive long-range approach to endowment formation—just as there is much to be said for maintaining endowment spending rates in the 4 to 5 percent range, rather than the current prevailing 5 to 8 percent range, since these latter rates are almost certain to erode steadily (perhaps quite rapidly) the purchasing power of endowments.[5]

5. There is of course no way to determine with great confidence a prudent endowment spending rate, particularly since the rate will naturally change over time, as economic circumstances change. If one assumes, however, that the internal inflation rates of most nonprofit, labor-intensive organizations are on average (over the long run) likely to be 2 to 3 percent above the Consumer Price Index (i.e., currently in the range of 6 to 8 percent per year), then one must necessarily

Today's immediate financial problems may well have to be dealt with rather pragmatically. But the current moment seems an excellent time to plan and to lay the groundwork for a future museum economy that might strike an interesting balance between the regimen of the present and that of the past. The new model, if achievable, would have a somewhat greater endowment cushion (with a more prudent endowment spending rate) than is now the case, plus a reduced dependence on earned income, with all of its associated pressures and problems. Special exhibition programs might be somewhat leaner, but not necessarily less stimulating or profitable. More time might then be devoted to permanent collections—which could themselves become the focal point for interesting exhibitions, as well as for thoughtful education programs. In short, museums would seek to sustain the essential vitality that has characterized them during the past two decades, but they would simultaneously attempt to create a somewhat different equilibrium for themselves, adapting to a new set of economic and other compelling circumstances.

Summary of Discussion

William H. Luers opened the discussion by describing the Metropolitan Museum of Art's recent decision led by museum director Philippe de Montebello to stop selling tickets for special exhibitions. He noted the three main benefits to ticketing—the museum's visitors know when they will be able to see the exhibit, attendance tends to be higher, and the museum receives the extra money. For this year's shows, however, visitors will pay just the usual voluntary contribution, a change that will probably cost the museum over $1 million and probably result in a somewhat lower attendance. Luers explained three reasons for the costly change in policy. First, selling tickets through Ticketron puts the museum in the entertainment business suggesting Broadway theater and football games. Second, selling tickets suggests to some that the exhibition was created to make money, even when the real intention is artistic. Third, the museum felt that encouraging repeated visits to great ex-

---

reinvest a similar portion of one's total return simply to maintain the purchasing power of endowment funds against inflationary encroachment. Estimates of long-term average total return on endowment investments will obviously differ, but few analysts are currently predicting figures greater than something in the 10 to 12 percent range. Hence, if the internal inflation rates of nonprofits can be held to about 6 to 8 percent, and if total returns are 10 to 12 percent (both *averaged* over a presumably long period of time), then the minimum "remainder" left to spend is about 2 percent (10 percent minus 8 percent) and the maximum is about 6 percent (12 percent minus 6 percent), with the "mean" being 4 percent. A mildly optimistic course, therefore, might be a spending rate of 4.5 percent, or at most 5 percent.

These calculations are meant to be essentially illustrative—not prescriptive—and they pertain to endowments related to the range of goods and services reflected in annual operating budgets. *Acquisitions* endowments (for the purchase of works of art) are rather different, mainly because the task of defining "inflation" is much more complicated (given the nature of the art market).

hibitions is the best way to build both audiences and a commitment to the institution and the collection. For example, people who come repeatedly spend somewhere between three and four hours in the museum; they are going to the exhibition plus seeing something else.

Ross W. Farrar followed by discussing the Boston Museum of Fine Arts' decision to sell tickets to an upcoming show through Ticketron. He played no role in this decision but would have if he still worked at the museum. He argued that, first, the price charged followed a precedent set by other museums in the city, and second, museums that are doing blockbuster shows should admit it and maximize their return. He felt it was important to implement the ticketing procedure in a way that does not "penalize a museum's current constituency." At the Museum of Fine Arts, for example, each member received a certain number of free tickets and could purchase others at a discounted rate. He admitted that the museum received a few complaints about not being able to go back into an exhibition after going through once, a restriction that is contrary to the usual museum experience.

Harry S. Parker III stated that The Fine Arts Museums of San Francisco were moving away from blockbuster exhibits for a while because of the financial turmoil they create.

Marilyn Perry suggested that the Metropolitan create an advertising campaign to emphasize the museum's recognition of its real purpose as a museum of art, not as alternative entertainment. She felt that there would be a positive response from the public, which would recoup some of the lost funds. She noted a new advertising campaign for the museum which is "sedate and handsome," and which *Luers* then described as the result of extensive interaction between the advertising people and the museum staff which resulted in the toned down, "handsome" advertising.

Martin Feldstein said that one rationale for blockbusters, quite apart from fund-raising, was that they brought in a larger public which would come back to see the permanent collection on some other occasion. He asked if that would be lost if museums shifted not just to a different pricing structure for exhibits but toward exhibits which have less market appeal per se.

Luers responded that future exhibits might turn out to be very popular, but they will not be designed or driven by the market. He mentioned the recent, very popular Siena exhibition as an example of this idea. *Bruce H. Evans* added that the Metropolitan's staff had conducted exit interviews which found that 90 percent of the people coming to the Siena exhibition had been to Siena, a situation he did not think would hold in Dayton.

James N. Wood emphasized that museums should not rule out popular exhibitions. He was concerned, however, that if museums make too much money using art loaned by other museums, those museums will demand that top-quality art be loaned in return.

Geoffrey Carliner raised several questions about blockbusters "as a member of the public." First, why is it not a good thing for all museums to have art loaned between cities so that people in Chicago can see New York paintings even if they cannot afford a plane ticket, and vice versa for the New Yorkers who cannot afford to go to Chicago? Second, why does there seem to be disdain for blockbusters which bring in people who almost never go to museums? Third, why were there huge increases in curatorial expenses and administrative costs in the year after the big blockbuster in San Francisco? Fourth, does not ticketing exhibitions reduce the personal inconvenience of waiting? Museums' sacrificing money in order to impose an inconvenience on patrons seems quite strange to him.

Luers answered that one alternative to selling tickets or having long lines is being used by the National Gallery of Art: tickets are given away marked with particular time slots. He continued that the Metropolitan Museum of Art is not in the least against very popular exhibitions, but it is concerned that the blockbuster name and the idea of moneymaking connected with it has tended to degrade the purpose of the exhibition for many directors. Creating an exhibition to make money and creating one to enlarge the body of people who understand an exhibition and an artist are two different things. *Harold M. Williams* thought that the Metropolitan's blockbusters did not look like just moneymaking ideas, and that there is nothing wrong with museums being viewed as entertainment. *Perry* said that the Ticketron-Museum differs substantially from the Ticketron–Metropolitan Opera because there is a lot to do in a museum besides going to see Degas. She hopes that museums would try to interest the public in a different way from other forms of entertainment.

Luers said that the Metropolitan makes two-year and five-year projections of costs and revenues, and they adhere strictly to a rule of spending less than 5.3 percent of the endowment. He said that not ticketing the special exhibitions this year would contribute to their largest deficit ever, but that it was important enough to return to the perceived purpose of the museum that over the next two or three years they will find other ways to raise revenue or cut costs. Conservative budgeting and aggressive pursuit of revenue have been key to the museum's management style.

Thomas Krens argued that solutions to financial problems are often specific to institutions, and he discussed several that apply to the Guggenheim Museum. The Guggenheim has the advantages of being relatively small (so it can change policies fairly quickly) and of having a great collection, two excellent locations (Fifth Avenue in New York and the Grand Canal in Venice), and a recognized name and building. He felt that the development field is nearly saturated in the United States but not in Europe.

Alberta Arthurs said the crucial question facing museums was how to reconcile the financial realities described by Rudenstine with the ongoing and expensive mission of reaching the public and bringing new people into the world of art.

Peter Temin wondered whether, as an alternative way to increase revenue, museums had considered renting "middling quality" works of art to individuals instead of deaccessioning them? *John Walsh* said that the Boston Museum of Fine Arts used to rent works of art to law offices, banks, and other businesses, but the program was dropped owing to the wear and tear on the art and the resulting conservation costs. *Farrar* added that one purpose of this corporate loan program had been to cultivate corporations as donors. However, the rising costs of conservation and insurance reduced the quality of the paintings the museum was willing to lend at the same time that corporations wanted to borrow higher quality works.

Richard E. Oldenburg felt that it was inappropriate to view expensive advance ticketing as the only alternative to free exhibitions. The old principle was that the admission fee covered the costs of a museum's basic operations, but that if a museum was unable to cover the costs of an unusually important exhibition that involved works of art from all over the world, then a modest additional charge was appropriate. When this principle had been followed, people understood that they were paying a little extra for a very special thing.

Feldstein responded that an "every tub on its own bottom" philosophy is not necessarily a very good way of running an institution. A museum could charge another dollar for a particularly attractive exhibit and then be able to do other things, or it could make the exhibit a break-even proposition, that tub exactly taking care of itself, but then it would be unable to do the other things. Is the special exhibit not a legitimate revenue source for supporting other activities of the museum?

Richard N. Rosett argued that it was a mistake simply to rope into the notion of a museum's mission the question of whether it should ever charge for a very popular exhibition. Rather, museum directors must realize that whatever their mission is, it cannot be achieved unless the stream of revenues and the stream of expenditures have a set relationship to each other. When thinking about whether to charge for blockbusters, or to charge admission at all, or to have annual fund raising campaigns, or to search for endowment, these two streams should be viewed as the tail of a dog, where the dog is the mission. The tail should not wag the dog, but neither should museum directors needlessly deprive the dog of the wagging tail. For blockbuster exhibitions, for example, the mission of a museum should determine what the exhibition is going to be, but the need to make revenues and expenditures match should lead to a decision about what to charge based on how popular the exhibition is likely to be.

4   The Museum and the Government

Andrew Oliver, Anne Hawley, and Sir John Hale

Andrew Oliver

This is a large subject, and I have made an attempt to cut it down to size. A few days ago I tore up everything I wrote, given the debate in Washington about public funding for the arts, so I intend to speak pretty much off the cuff. I will, however, try to give you some statistics. I was very pleased to have had an opportunity to meet with Charles Clotfelter earlier and to go over his paper (chap. 9 in this volume). I benefited from my conversation with him, and I am grateful to him in the first instance for spending some time with us in Washington.

Let me first say that, in my remarks, I will not comment on the tax laws through which the federal government allows tax-deductible donations to nonprofits, and I will also ignore the effects of the recent tax reform act. Nor will I discuss the appropriation of government funds for the federal museums, though they constitute a major portion of the federal contribution to art museums. I will focus rather on the three federal agencies that are housed in the Old Post Office building on Pennsylvania Avenue and 12th Street, namely the National Endowments for the Arts, the National Endowment for the Humanities, and the Institute of Museum Services. I am sure I cannot tell you anything you do not already know. Let me begin, however, with some statistics. I have glanced at the statistics in the background papers, and I believe some of them but do not accept all of them. I hope that you will be as skeptical of the ones I am about to deliver as I was of some of the ones that I read.

Now, what is the monetary value of the support that these three federal agencies give to art museums in America? And how does that monetary contribution relate to the total operating income of American art museums supported by the three federal agencies? In fiscal year 1988, the combined support to art museums by the Arts Endowment, the Humanities Endowment, and the Institute of Museum Services, including challenge grants, was just over $25 million. Now the total income of the 320 art museums that I view as being supported on a fairly regular basis by these three agencies is somewhere in the neighborhood of $800 million. To arrive at this last figure, I started with the total fiscal 1988 income of the 199 museums reporting to the recent Association of Art Museum Director's survey. I subtracted 15 percent, which is the sum of the income of the Canadian and Smithsonian art museums listed in that survey, and then I added $100 million, which represents 200 art museum budgets averaging $500,000 a piece, which is not just a figure out of the air; it is based on a careful scrutiny of a great number of annual reports. And even if that budget of 200 art museums times $500,000 is off by a factor of two in either direction, it does not radically alter the percentage figure. I judge federal support to be about 3.1 percent of the total. It might be as little as 2.9 percent, or it might be 3.3 percent. But it is somewhere in that neighborhood. You can be as skeptical of such figures as I often am. One should be. But the figure is not 10 percent, and is not 1 percent; it is 3.1 percent plus or minus a little bit. Now for any given museum, this percentage will vary. And it will obviously vary from year to year, largely because most of the grants given by the federal agencies (though not most of those by the Institute of Museum Services) are for projects, not for general operating support. So any one museum may go without federal support in one year and have a great deal the next. Also the larger the budget of the museum, the smaller the federal share is likely to be, and conversely, the smaller the budget, the larger the federal share is likely to be, provided the museum is a fairly regular applicant to government, and a regular recipient of grants. For a $10 million budget museum, this would amount to about $300,000, which in reality is probably a little high, and for a $500,000 budget museum, this would amount to $15,000, which likewise is probably a little low. Now 3.1 percent may seem at first glance to be an insignificant amount. Nevertheless, I think that everyone would agree that $300,000 to one museum or $15,000 to another is money that does not have to be raised from alternative sources. It is very real money.

More difficult to quantify are the intangible aspects of this federal support. I do not mean the leveraging or multiplier effect of the matching grant. Not that I underestimate this. Some would argue, however, that in many instances a government grant can be the last piece of a financial package, as well as the first piece, and that the leveraging effect is minimal. I can well appreciate the need and inclination for any member of the museum community to say in public testimony that the leveraging effect of the endowment grant is extremely important, but I am not certain that this is always the case. Yet what does the money mean? At the most basic level, it is the government setting an example, an endorsement by a panel of peers of the merits of a project. As a federal agency, the Arts Endowment should both be responsive to the needs of the art museum field and be an advocate for improvement and constructive change. Such ventures must take place in the context of the mission of the agency, which is twofold: to promote excellence and diversity in the arts, and to bring the arts to the broadest possible audiences.

Now at this point, there is an item I must turn to to make this a current statement. I want to draw attention to the new character who has entered the stage, namely the language attached to the appropriations act for fiscal year 1990, which provides funding for the Arts Endowment. I will read it, because even though it may seem to have nothing to do with our money, it turns out to be important. It says that "none of the funds authorized to be appropriated for the National Endowment for the Arts . . . may be used to promote, dissemi-nate, or produce materials, which in the judgment of the National Endowment for the Arts . . . may be considered obscene, including but not limited to, depictions of sado-masochism, homoeroticism, the sexual exploitation of children, or individuals engaged in sex acts and which, when taken as a whole, do not have serious literary, artistic, political, or scientific value." That is an ambiguous statement, to say the least, and I would like to report that my colleague who is head of the literature program at the Arts Endowment ob-served that because of the punctuation, the phrase "when taken as a whole, do not have serious literary, artistic, political, or scientific value" applies only to "individuals engaged in sex acts." This language and all else that has befallen us during the last ten months has had a chilling effect on the arts community.

We are pleased that a twelve-person commission is currently being ap-pointed to examine the panel review process and to improve the public's per-ception of the process. John Frohnmayer has stated in a letter sent to the arts community that this commission will ask whether the standard for publicly funded art is different from that of private art. Who decides what is to be funded with public funds? In this country it is not Congress, nor is it a minis-try of culture. On the federal level, it is a panel of peers recommending proj-ects to the Arts Endowment staff and setting grant amounts. Peer review pan-els that look at all of the applications in all of the fields, both in the visual arts and in the performing arts. They decide what is art, which art projects merit government funding, and how much money should be allocated to each proj-ect. The presidentially appointed National Council on the Arts reviews the panel's recommendations and then, lastly, the chairman signs off on the grants. This is not as easy as it sounds, because just to say that the peer panels have the say as to what is art and what art merits federal funds leaves open the question as to who selects the peer panels. This is an issue that has been de-bated at some length and will continue to be discussed. In all of the programs, it is ultimately the program director who makes up a list of individuals who are considered the appropriate people to represent different interests, view-points, and tastes around the country on the peer panel. My own lists, in the museum program, have been reviewed by the chairman, who, I am happy to say, has generally regarded them favorably.

All kinds of problems can arise: What happens, for instance, if a panel is capricious? What happens if an institution, a museum, once it receives a grant, goes beyond the stated project, either in the normal course of business—because all projects evolve from the time they came to us and are finally completed—or through deliberate provocation on the part of institution staff? The latter is a likely possibility in the next six to ten months. Here is another question that arises: Is there an edge beyond which it is inappropriate to go? If there is a limit, who decides where it is? Should we even be talking about an edge? Another kind of question coming to me and to my colleagues at the Arts Endowment, which I think is indicative of this chilling effect, often goes like this: "Will the project I have in mind fit within the new congressional language?" My answer is, "I won't answer that question. You make a case that what you are proposing to the Arts Endowment is art, and let the peer panels be the judge of that. You don't have to ask, as far as I am concerned, whether what you are doing is within the bounds of propriety or not."

Why have I spent so much time dwelling on this issue? I think that it has a very real bearing on the direction our funding is to go in the next five years. Out of the $25 million, that I said is the combined grant-making power of the three agencies, about one-third of it, something in the neighborhood of $8 million, goes toward the presentation of art, that is, exhibitions and related projects. The balance goes toward the preservation of collections and buildings, toward documentation, research, and publication of art collections, and toward education. In this climate, and I think that the present climate will last for a while, I believe that Congress will more likely continue or increase funds to the three federal agencies not in the realm of presentation, but in the areas of preservation, documentation, and education. And I would say that this tends to fit in very closely with the scenario that we have seen developed by Neil Rudenstine (see chap. 3 in this volume). It is in these areas that Congress can ultimately take unqualified pride in supporting American art museums and helping to underwrite the preservation of American values.

Anne Hawley

I will discuss government relations to art museums from my vantage point as a former director of a state arts agency and as a recently appointed art museum director. I led the Massachusetts Council on the Arts and Humanities during a ten-year period of rapid expansion. A sudden political attack in 1989 threatened to cancel all its accomplishments and eliminate the agency and state support for cultural institutions. As a newly appointed museum director, I now face the decline of government support for the arts, and, like my colleagues, must plan for this loss.

When I was appointed to the Massachusetts Council on the Arts and Humanities in the late 1970s, my conversations with Governor Michael Dukakis, with the chairman of the arts council board, with its members, and with leaders of the Boston business and cultural community, all shared the assumption that there would be expanding direct public support for the arts. We agreed that the expansion of the National Endowment for the Arts during the 1970s was one that the Commonwealth of Massachusetts should emulate, and further, that European models, particularly the French system, were something this country was now mature enough to strive for. With this implied mandate, I began my work in pursuit of substantial budget and program expansion.

Those of us toiling in this flinty soil could see across the Atlantic how the leadership of François Mitterrand dramatically increased government support for arts in France. By the end of his first term, Mitterrand had increased the budget for culture to the equivalent of $1 billion for programs alone. His grand capital programs such as the Picasso Museum, the Musée d'Orsay, the Louvre pyramid, and new regional museums were in addition to this extraordinary support. Our budgets were increasing, but the French set the pace. We watched in envy, but we also began to realize that Mitterrand's government was being canny about how to ensure that this support would continue. In personal conversations with Jack Lang, the French Minister of Culture, I learned that 15 percent of his administrative budget went to communications and press relations in order to keep pressing the case for French cultural funding by keeping public discussion of issues in arts and culture alive. Mitterrand (and Pompidou before him, I should add) was acting in the grand tradition of French kings and emperors, but he was also being a wily, modern politician.

In the United States, by contrast, the 1980s brought federal support for the arts to a standstill. The action was at the state level, and state arts agencies nationwide showed the kind of dramatic budget increases that had characterized the expansion of the National Endowment for the Arts in the 1970s. State support rose from $96 million in 1980 to nearly $260 million in 1989. Adjusting for inflation, this was an increase of 79 percent over the decade. Arts museums benefited from this expansion; from 1986 to 1987 alone, total state funding for art museums rose by 49 percent.

In Massachusetts, this expansion was made possible by a healthy and growing economy, strong support from the governor and senate president, and a strong board of directors for the Massachusetts Arts Council consisting of prominent business leaders, artists, a Nobel Prize-winning economist, and a major newspaper publisher. By mobilizing this leadership, communicating needs in the press, and organizing a state-wide network of advocates, the arts council advanced its support for culture in dollars from $2.3 million in 1978 to a high-water mark of nearly $23 million in 1988.

The Massachusetts Council on the Arts and Humanities had a programmatic and legislative agenda to drive this increase in funding. State government responded to this agenda by passing six laws during this period aiding cultural organizations, particularly museums. Those laws affecting art museums were amendments to the state bonding authorities enabling museums to qualify for tax-exampt revenue bonds which meant that capital projects could be financed by borrowing at interest rates below the prime rate. The Museum of Fine Arts in Boston used this device to help finance the new west wing. The most striking and controversial of this cultural lawmaking was the authorization of a $35 million bond for the Massachusetts Museum of Contemporary Art (Mass MoCA), a new contemporary art museum in North Adams, Massachusetts. The leader of Mass MoCA convinced the state that the museum would create an economic revitalization of the commonwealth's most depressed area.

Yet state funding for the arts barely kept pace with public demand for cultural programs. In 1970, 11 million people attended cultural programs offered by organizations funded by the Massachusetts Arts Council. By 1988 this had grown to 20 million, an increase of 82 percent. This growth occurred within a state with a total population of 5.3 million that increased less than 1 percent during the same period.

This decade of rapid expansion came to a halt when the state House Ways and Means Committee, in its proposed 1990 budget, abolished the Massachusetts Council on the Arts and Humanities and completely removed all cultural funding from the state budget. The state had a much-publicized fiscal shortfall of 10 percent in revenue, but in a $12.3 billion budget, the arts were the only function of state government targeted for elimination, a savings of one-tenth of 1 percent of the state budget.

Obviously, the arts took a symbolic hit, but it is interesting to review how the ensuing public debate was framed. The museum and cultural community rose up to assist with the fight to save the state funding. There was an effective lobbying effort; thousands of supporters poured out in a public demonstration at the state house, and thousands of letters were written. With few exceptions, the press, both print and electronic, ran positive editorials and human interest stories for over two weeks. But few advocates of continued state funding argued the intrinsic, ideal value of the arts. The museums in particular failed to mention the value of exhibitions, collecting, or even the very function of the museum in society. Instead, in an attempt not to appear elitist, they chose to emphasize two very functional areas. First, they discussed their material contributions in terms of the dollars they brought to the state's economy as employers, tourist attractions, and purchasers of services. Second, they pointed to the hundreds of thousands of children they served in an array of impressive educational programs.

Meanwhile, the leaders of the anticulture faction effectively and stridently countered these arguments through the *Boston Herald* newspaper and radio talk shows. The point man for the whole effort was Richard Voke, chairman of the House Ways and Means Committee, who polarized the debate by characterizing state expenditure for the arts as a frivolous subsidy for the rich, while programs for welfare mothers and pregnant teenagers were being cut. He continually pressed the argument that funding for arts should be private, and in a presumably expansive gesture, sent a $1,000 check to the Charleston Working Theatre, a struggling organization in his own district.

Not to be left out, the *Boston Herald* trumpeted its hostility to culture. It listed the annual operating budgets of prominent museums and performing arts groups, and estimated their endowments and net worths to be in the billions. Decrying state money for these rich and elitist institutions, it proposed the sale of assets for self-financing, and personally attacked some leaders of those institutions.

After much sound and fury, the proposed elimination of the Massachusetts Arts Council came to a vote in the House of Representatives. During the debate, Voke took the floor and, in a theatrically affected English accent with crescendoing shouts, denounced the public expenditure for the arts and condemned the arts council as elitist. In a final volley of rage, he accused the museums of "hiding behind the children" to gain public support. Despite his later claims to the contrary, Voke's hatred, and perhaps envy, for the so-called cultural class was palpable. Once again the Massachusetts legislature scarified the scabs of old enmities. The house voted to restore only 50 percent of the funds, and by summer's end, hundreds of staff at museums and performing arts organizations had been laid off.

During the early nineteenth century, American artists struggled to find an acceptable role beyond painting portraits of successful merchants and their families. For the artist, the times were rugged and characterized by a contemporary as "the dilemma of a land with neither a legendary past nor a poetic present."[1] Yet that same dilemma rings as plangently true at the end of the twentieth century as it did then. Our cultural memory is thin, and it is still by no means homogeneous. Our institutions remain dependent on private, individual support, and our flirtation with French-style cultural largess was abortive and fleeting.

De Tocqueville observed during his tour of America during the early nineteenth century that in a democracy the visual arts tend toward the mediocre. Without an enlightened and discriminating patron class, the artist had to serve larger numbers of citizens, most of whom were not discriminating. It is an old debate whether excellence is possible in a democratic system, but the Massachusetts Council on the Arts and Humanities had sought excellence anyway by emphasizing that only programs and institutions of high quality should be funded. Peer review panels, not legislators, made funding decisions. Compromises were not part of the process. This created a totally different culture of decision making than that of legislative compromise. The Massachusetts Arts Council's insistence on quality looked to many legislators like elitism, or worse, rejection of the amateur participation in the arts that boosted community pride through marching bands, community theater, and Sunday painting.

1. From *The diary of George Templeton Strong,* as cited by Neil Harris in *The artist in American society* (Chicago: University of Chicago Press, 1982).

While the arts council consciously worked to address these community art issues through programs in folk arts, education, touring performances, and exhibitions, these programs were never acknowledged by the politicians as important contributions. The lightning rod was always funding to "professional" and "high quality."

In thinking about this extreme swing in public support, I have reflected upon how the policies were made for the various programs the Massachusetts Arts Council planned and administered to support museums and performing arts organizations. For example, one program providing operating support gave grants up to $300,000 for the basic programs of museums; an education program granted substantial amounts, with several museums receiving over $400,000 a year for these services; an historical conservation program conserved important objects of painting, sculpture, and decorative arts. These three programs were planned by the arts council with major guidance from the museum community. And although public hearings were held to invite public participation, those attending were always the professional constituency being served, with little if any representation from the general public.

This pattern was common in other fields of the arts and it is safe to say that the Massachusetts Arts Council's major programs were jointly conceived by the funded constituency and the council. Was this then part of the problem? Would it have been wiser to have public policy formulated much more broadly, done through the legislative process rather than through professionals in the field who were advising and structuring programs?

A real dilemma for public funding is the public's total lack of understanding regarding the financing of cultural organizations. During the funding crisis in Massachusetts, the public demonstrated ignorance regarding who financed what; some thought these institutions were self-financing, others thought the entry ticket underwrote the costs, still others believed the city was paying fully to operate the museums, when in fact the city of Boston gives no support to any cultural organization. In the case of the museum education programs which the Massachusetts Arts Council was so heavily funding (one-third of the council's budget went to education programs), parents had no knowledge that the arts council was funding these programs. Why? Because schools resisted sending parents notes saying their child's museum education program was supported by this council.

Thus the Massachusetts Council on the Arts and Humanities failed to create informed public understanding of the reasons for the public tax support and its uses. It was never able to grab the media attention necessary to do this. It was always backstage, invisible in the panoply of cultural offerings. In a poll done by the *Boston Globe* on 12 March 1989, asking the public where cuts could be made in state spending, 47 percent said the Massachusetts Arts Council could take "a" cut; 43 percent said it should not. The closing of a much-loved museum due to financial failure would elicit public response, but the eradication of a public funding body that is not widely comprehended is an easy political victory in a time of fiscal crisis.

François Mitterrand's government is worth examining in this respect. In his first presidential campaign, a major increase of funding to the arts was part of the campaign platform. Jack Lang, his minister of culture, has related how important the cultural program was to the presidential campaign and reported that much attention was given to it. We can contrast that with how little attention was recently paid in the American presidential campaign to the arts policy positions of each candidate. In fact, we know that the positions were developed only in response to active lobbying for them on the part of the arts constituency.

Given this, and given what we know about the human condition in general, I fall back to the position that we must develop leadership in the public sector that supports the cause of funding the arts. Without support from the top—the president, the governor, the mayor—public support for our work will not develop. It will stagnate at best, and at worst be eliminated. I know from experience how far you can sail when you have the serious committed support of the chief executive in government. It makes it possible to accomplish extraordinary programs.

But perhaps in a culture so dominated by commercial culture—movies, rock, television—it will never be possible to have a public consciousness or commitment to the role the arts can play in the citizens' life. Certainly to judge by the stagnation of federal support and the miniscule nature of its size, the public policy is one of neglect. Compared to the growth of the National Science Foundation (NSF) during the last decade, the National Endowment for the Arts withers in comparison. The NSF budget, which was nearly $1 billion in 1982, had doubled to almost $2 billion by 1989, with 95 percent going directly to grants.

Several questions linger from this attack on the public funding at the state level that the arts community needs to try to answer and take action to address:

- Why was the attack so violent, so extreme? The state fiscal crisis, to put it in context, was facing a budget 10 percent out of balance.
- How can the public become informed about the need for public funding?
- What does this mean to art museums in planning their public programs?
- Where are we headed with public support for art museums and culture in American society?
- Is privatization of our cultural heritage really what the majority wants?

Sir John Hale

I would like to start by raising an issue that lay outside the brief not only of Rosemary Clarke's admirably crisp and thorough survey (in this volume) but also of the other background papers: the subject of cultural politics.

In their papers, Charles Clotfelter, Andrew Oliver, and Anne Hawley have opened my eyes to the extent of direct and indirect public funding in this country. In Britain we think of America in terms of the still lively creation and dispersal of collections—the background from which our own public collections sprang; the tax advantages that still have a sizable edge over ours; the high profile of your museum directors among the wealthy and influential members of their communities. Even after the gloomy session on museum finances, it is still clear that our own museums cannot draw on so continuous a tradition of private support and are forced to depend, directly or indirectly, more on the public purse. Now in both our countries, allocations from that purse pass through the filter of the choices and preferences of legislators and the representatives of public bodies. These men and women are all part of a political nexus. They have culture as part of their care. This is where political culture comes in.

In the United Kingdom, museums are in competition with the arts as a whole. Just to look at the center, the Minister for the Arts has a budget which has to service not just the national museums and the well-nigh insatiable new British Library, but the rate support grant for local authority spending on leisure-cum-cultural activities, and the Arts Council, with its responsibility to subsidize noncommercial theatres, opera and ballet companies, and nonmuseum centers for exhibitions of works of art. And within the museum sector, arts museums represent only one character in a crowded and clamorous cast. Nationwide, the rapid overall increase in museum visits is due largely to the appeal of the sciences and a nostalgia to identify with how people lived and worked in the past. The success of museumized open sites like Ironbridge Gorge in Shropshire or Beamish in County Durham arises from environmental and human interest issues that have soared past the fairly static enticement towards painting, sculpture, and the decorative arts. They offer an interest for which no previous intellectual preparation is seen to be required, from which no age, no race, no class, no educational background need feel excluded. Of course, precisely the same is true of the fine arts. Nonetheless, there is a perceived, if not a real, frontier there. You can see it operating in mixed collections with a fine arts component alongside the more popular archaeological, natural sciences, and historical displays. And the arts museum is further challenged by the growing cult of the fine house, where works of art are seen in the context of a way of life.

This mood is, of course, picked up by the councillors who are primarily responsible for the majority of our museums, and who are, moreover, begged to contribute to the impressive growth of independent museums, nearly all of which have an industrial, archaeological, or social history raison d'être.

Those who work in local government are, without doubt, respectful of their inheritance of museums which may include notable works of art. But only a minority have acquired, from family background or education, an empathic familiarity with them: British education starts with an indulgent paroxysm of self-expression and then stops save for the few who later take up the history of art. And it has yet to be demonstrated how widely art history leads to a love of art.

So the local authority sector is tempted, by its mind-set and the signals received by its political antennae, to go slow in its support—though of course, a domineering and attractive museum director can persuade them to go fast.

In moving to members of both Houses of Parliament, to ministers and their civil servants, we ask the same question: What, across the broad spectrum of activities and experiences summed up as "the arts," do they actually *like?* What have they been brought up to like and have time to like (for museum opening hours are calculated to appeal chiefly to the old, the unemployed, students and tourists)? And here we find another set of dice loaded against us.

For the liking element within parliamentary cultural politics extends primarily toward the arts that move or emit sounds, that is, that perform in a physical way denied to the mute, still objects on our own walls and plinths. Legislators prefer theater, opera, and ballet to the voiceless and indeed, non-voting representatives of the arts. They prefer a socially shared artistic experience rather than a one-to-one communion. Mrs. Thatcher is quoted as saying, when she opened the commercially sponsored Design Museum, with its plans to move with the product volatility of the times, that it was misleadingly named because "a museum is something that is really rather dead." And this state of mind makes it particularly difficult for politicians to sympathize with the archival function of collections like the Victoria and Albert Museum (the V & A) or the British Museum and the Tate, and the accompanying costs of storage, documentation, conservation, and staff time.

A preference for the arts that perform, and do it in the evenings, does not, however, lead to preferential subsidies. Personal liking does not erode the puritanical custodianship of the public purse when cultural matters are concerned, whether it is a question of universities, theaters and opera companies, or museums. There is, nonetheless, an especially dour, joyless sense of responsibility toward museums, an emphasis on the status quo, on good housekeeping, on keeping the fabric intact—rather than on the restoration of curatorial staffing levels or the support of acquisitions—that is dispiriting. Great concern is expressed for the taxpayer's money through scrutiny by Select Committees of the Commons, by the Public Accounts Committee and the National Audit Office. But when praise is, rarely, expressed, it is for administrative competence rather than for the acquisition of a masterpiece, or a feat of scholarship, or an increase in visitors. It is symptomatic that the recently announced hike in the triennial grants to national museums and galleries is to help them keep up with pay awards and maintain fabric. Purchase grants remain frozen. And this hits arts museums the hardest. It is a familiar British story: duty before conviction. Receiving funds from government is akin to being asked to a party because, oh dear, you've got to be there, rather than because you are welcome.

To turn to one of the topics raised by Rosemary Clarke, I have had the good fortune to have become, from 1973, a semi-professional trustee, first at the National Gallery, then at the Victoria and Albert, now at the British Museum. That an academic historian with neither a stock nor a share to his name could have such luck says something about our system. The polite incredulity that has greeted this aspect of my career in this country says something about yours.

Now the greatest number of trustees is appointed by the prime minister: all save one at the National Gallery, for instance; all at the V & A; 14 out of 25 at the British Museum, which, because of its long history, is a special case; and all the Museums and Galleries Commissioners.

In the past, the filling of vacancies was worked out by a carefully researched comparison of a short-list presented by the chairman to No. 10 and the proposals worked out by the prime minister's patronage secretary. No. 10 had the advantage of knowing what the board wanted, the board that of access to a wider trawl. It then suggested three names in order of preference and usually got the first one.

It is widely suspected that this intricate and careful mating dance is being interrupted by peremptory orders as to the choice of partners, chiefly those whose expertise in accounting, marketing, or civil-service common-sensicalness can inject into our furred veins the revivifying adrenalin of cost-effectiveness. There is something in this suspicion. It started, for me, in 1980 when I had put in, as chairman of the National Gallery, our usual list of who we wanted and who we didn't, and shortly afterwards received a phone call from one of the rejects saying he'd had a letter of appointment and could he come to see me to find out what the Gallery was all about? From a reverse viewpoint, it recurred when I received my own invitation from No. 10 to join the Museums and Galleries Commission three years later. A number of directors of national institutions, all friends, sent me Dear John letters saying "nothing personal, but we are contesting government's infringement in our traditional right to nominate to that particular commissionership." More interesting, though, than whether it is happening, is what good or harm it does.

Tycoon trouble-shooters brought in on an individual basis quickly see that the lack of business acumen within a museum is largely a myth. Contact with their colleagues shows them that museums are not on all fours with industries or retail networks or government deparments. They then, having sensed a different ethos, pitch in to support it. With rare exceptions, however, the rich do not suddenly change the habits of a lifetime and pour money into a new interest, and the ex-ministers and former heads of civil service departments find their influence in the corridors of power suddenly zero-rated.

Where the changed attitude to trustee selection has turned out to be harmful, at least in the short term, is at the V & A. There, in the wake of its independence from the tutelage of the Department of the Environment, a whole board was created which was overloaded in terms of business know-how, bushy-tailed about imposing efficiency, and not very perceptive about how to do it. It was not a board on which I felt at home and I'm afraid I left as soon as I decently could.

To sum up, the trustee apparatus has become, rather more than it was, a supplementary honors system for rewarding enterprise, and a reflection of government's feeling that museums are not very good at running themselves. But I don't think, with the V & A as an exception, that this change of emphasis has become a malign one. Poachers turn game keepers with remarkable celerity. In British eyes, the real danger to museums from a politically supported enterprise culture lies less in the appointment of trustees than in the influences brought to bear on the choice of directors.

Outside the national institutions, government's reach into the museum system is most directly through another arm's length body, the Museums and Galleries Commission. The interest here lies in the recent delegation to it by government of activities previously its own preserve, notably the running of the indemnity scheme which has transformed exhibitions at home and abroad, and the operation of the system whereby public collections can acquire works of art accepted in lieu of tax liabilities on an estate. In these ways, as in the transferring of responsibility for the maintenance of their buildings to trustees, government is cutting its own staff, pushing across inadequate sums to pay for their substitutes, and relying more and more on unpaid services, while retaining the financial power that can make it all work.

As a result, coupled with delegation is pressure on museums to become more self-sufficient. As neither tradition nor fiscal policies encourage enough private-sector support, they are left to imitate that sector's values, to be productive, to charge, to cut into their scholarly base, to compete, and to lower their sights to compete with other attractions. We are being invited—as are our government-funded universities—to commit that most heinous of academic crimes: *la trahison des clercs.*

Yielding in 1980 to great pressure, government's sense of duty did lead it to the creation of the National Heritage Memorial Fund with a budget today of £3 million, and access to the Contingency Fund in cases of exceptional urgency. The Memorial Fund has helped to save works of art from dispersal including those—like the Cuyp recently acquired for the National Gallery—born abroad but domiciled in the United Kingdom from an early date. But it was set up to preserve the overall heritage men and women had died for in war. The fine arts compete with landscape, wildlife, and great buildings. And as its purchasing power wanes, "heritage" will have to be construed more narrowly as works of art actually produced in the United Kingdom, to the detriment of the more international representation aimed at by museums. This makes the role of the National Art Collections Fund, a private body run by people who do have a commitment to the fine arts, more urgent than ever. But its constituency is United Kingdom–wide, and it has only £2 million per annum to spend. What will happen when internal customs barriers wither within the European Economic Community from 1992 can only be guessed at. But if nations, as seems likely, are allowed, at least for a while, to retain their own export laws and are able to make them work, what is the use if what is stopped cannot be bought?

We have, then, two converging problems.

On the one hand: how do we educate our funding masters—whether politicians, or, indeed, those who control corporations, or foundations without a specific fine-arts remit—to take joy in our silent witnesses to mankind's creative genius?

And on the other hand: because funding bodies are capable of responding to public taste, how do we alter the growing bias of museum visitors toward nonart collections or installations? For we certainly cannot judge the health of the arts sector by measuring the lines round the block for blockbusters, or visits to institutions whose appeal is as much due to their status as monuments as to what they contain.

Or is history itself voting against adequate support for arts museums?

Summary of Discussion

Richard N. Rosett began the session by raising three questions. First, do state-funded museums in France have the freedom to present exhibits like the Mapplethorpe show that caused the recent controversy in the United States, and if so, have they ever taken advantage of that freedom? Second, do our federal museums have that kind of freedom, and have they exercised it? Third, will elected officials ever neglect opportunities to win votes?

James N. Wood reported on an exhibition being sent from the Chicago Art Institute to the Pompidou Center in France. The exhibit originally included a portrait of Adolf Hitler, but Wood had been told that the portrait could not be shown in France. *Anne Hawley* said that she had seen many shows in France that were provocative. She felt that it was striking that one individual such as Senator Helms can have such a large effect in our democratic system.

As regards the Mapplethorpe show, *Alberta Arthurs* pointed out that it had been very popular before the mass of publicity, and that the arrangements for the show included protection of the images that offended some people. She felt that the attack on the show ignored the care with which it had been put in place and greatly exaggerated the obscene content.

Rosett said that economists often believe that if they could teach politicians economics, the politicians would not do bad things to the economy. Rosett felt that was a false view; if we want politicians to be tolerant of controversial art, we must first teach the voters to be tolerant. Politicians do what the voters want them to do.

Roger G. Kennedy said he was disturbed by too much passivity in dealing with the government. He said that the National Museum of American History is supported because it works hard to persuade particular representatives and senators to like some of the things the museum wants do do.

J. Carter Brown explained that the National Gallery of Art receives 80 percent of its funding from the government but is controlled by a board of trustees of which a majority are not officers of the United States government. Andrew Mellon wanted to insulate the museum from politics, so the board consists of four government trustees and five others. However, the budget does go through the regular appropriation process including review by the Office of Management and Budget. Brown felt that the museum had been fortunate in budget hearings and had, in the main received the funds they had requested.

Martin Feldstein raised the more general topic of how the National Endowment for the Arts affects the kinds of exhibitions that museums choose to mount. He wondered whether museums seek to do shows on subjecs that the funding panels tend to support rather than other kinds of shows.

Wood felt that most federal money has gone to projects that are the hardest to fund in any other way, such as more scholarly shows. *Richard E. Oldenburg* added that the most important visible effect of the NEA, in addition to scholarly shows, had been supporting contemporary art shows, which is the area for which corporate support is the most difficult to get. *Bruce H. Evans* said that the NEA funds provide great leverage for smaller institutions, because they demonstrate to potential sponsors that the project has been approved by other museum directors.

Andrew Oliver agreed that the NEA is the biggest help to institutions that have less access to alternative sources of funding, in terms of both the cash provided and the "statement" made by winning a grant. He continued that the purchasing power of the NEA grants had fallen more slowly during the Reagan years than it had during the Carter years, but the real decline that occurred had affected art museums' ability to put on exhibitions over the last decade. He believed that the same proportion of applications for exhibiting historical art have been funded as applications for exhibiting contemporary art.

Neil Rudenstine asked whether the Massachusetts situation described by Anne Hawley was idiosyncratic, or whether arts councils throughout the country are being affected in similar ways.

Hawley answered that when states have financial crises, the arts are held up as a "lamb to be slaughtered," and she mentioned previous episodes in Alaska and Illinois. *William H. Luers* described the "political theater" devised to protect the New York State Arts Council from threatened cuts by the New York State Legislature in its budget several years ago. Council Chairperson Kitty Carlisle Hart was extremely effective in leading the legislative hearings to support the council, there was a behind-the-scenes compromise on some projects, but there was no legislation passed to limit or restrict the distribution of funds by the council to arts groups. This episode dramatized the need for a more aggressive political strategy, on the part of art museums and other arts groups, with states and in Washington. Luers felt that directors, presidents, and particularly trustees can have tremendous political influence and can do a lot of consciousness-raising with politicians about their true political interests.

Feldstein shifted the focus of the discussion to the financial impact of the tax laws, which the background papers noted are much more important in terms of total dollars than direct grants are, especially excluding federal funding for the museums in Washington. What is the effect of the unrelated business income tax (UBIT) on, say, the Metropolitan Museum? *Luers* said that some changes in the tax proposed in the House of Representatives could cost the Metropolitan Museum as much as $1 million per year.

Don Fullerton felt that the current tax law, which says that some items being sold in museum gift shops are subject to tax while other items are not, must be almost unmanageable. He asked whether sales from outlet stores that are not located on the museum premises are subject to the same tax rules.

Luers said that the Metropolitan Museum cooperates with the Internal Revenue Service concerning the UBIT law because they think the current law is a good one. He said that the tax paid should not depend on where the object is sold because the educational outreach of the museum stores is very important for the promotion of knowledge about the fine arts and about the Metropolitan Museum.

5 General Overview

J. Carter Brown, Richard E. Oldenburg,
Harold M. Williams, and Roger G. Kennedy

J. Carter Brown

In terms of general overview I thought that I would not try to summarize the conference. I shall try to be general and touch on some basic issues that have come up.

I might perhaps start with being very specific about the National Gallery. Oscar Wilde said that "America's youth is the oldest of her traditions," and the National Gallery's differentness has become the oldest of its. Everyone assumes that the Gallery is completely sui generis, but in fact it is just another art museum in most ways, and we face many of the same issues that everyone else does. It is always the balance of envy. (I know when I moved to Washington as a young bachelor I noticed that the singles thought that they would be better off being married, and my married friends tended to wonder nostalgically whether they would not be better off single.) If you are a government museum you sometimes spend a lot of your time and energy envying people in other situations, and perhaps vice versa.

The National Gallery is a hybrid and so we are hard to classify. Both buildings were given from the private sector, as was and is all the art. Whereas, the maintenance, and all the fundamental underlying budget, is provided by the federal government, as was the land that we were built on. The temporary exhibition program, for example, is a complete mixture. The Congress says that they will only fund part; we have to go out and find private-sector funding while getting help from the federal side as well.

By law, we may not charge admission. We do not have certain other economic options open to us. For example, there is no parking to charge for. Our ticketing systems do not include an entrance fee because our interpretation is that that would be a form of admissions. Our ticketing policy is to increase the quality of the visit, as we were talking of earlier, by limiting the number of people in an exhibition to a manageable number at any given time, and helping, on humanitarian grounds, to keep people from wasting time standing in line.

Apart from pleading with the administration and two houses of Congress for our budget, we have many of the same kinds of private-sector fund-raising problems as everyone, particularly in terms of acquisitions. We envy our sister national institutions in other countries where, even if the grant amount has been frozen for the last couple of years, they do get rather solid chunks of government money to buy art. And, in special cases, the Louvre can go to the French treasury for special grants when they find something really good, or get special deals out of *dation*, a tax break in lieu of inheritance tax, if the object is given to the nation. This is how the Louvre recently got a fabulous Vermeer.

We have certain quirky policies. We do not rent our facilities to any outside groups. We limit the reproductions that we sell only to two-dimensional materials, so we are out of the souvenir business. And we do not deaccession anything other than duplicate prints. I will talk a little more about that in a minute. Another thing we cannot do, by congressional mandate, is go to our friends over at the National Endowment for the Arts for help.

The fundamental issues, though, that I wanted to address in a more general way, are some of what the Harvard Business School called "hidden assumptions" that I think we've been hearing. All of these discussions about semantics go quite deep, because of the fundamental point that the kinds of structure with which an economist is trained to deal are only partially relevant to the art museum.

A basic concept of business is to have a quantifiable goal. Although businesses do tend to have other criteria occasionally, fundamentally there is a bottom line; and the bottom line is calculable and controls the decision-making process, whether in profit centers, or in multiple markets, or in multiple products. However it is put together, it all comes out to one figure which is either expressed in black or in red.

Naturally, these financial questions also obtain in the museum field, but largely as a secondary matter. The financial dimension is a question, yes, of survival. But it is not he point. It is not the be-all and end-all. It is not the purpose of museums or why we are in—if you want to use the word—business.

A recent review in the *New York Times* dealt with the book, *Pricing the Priceless: Art, Artist and Economics,* by William D. Grampp. He is retired, apparently. He seems well named, to judge by his views, which are reactionary. At any rate, he takes the extreme sort of position that the arts ought to be put out to fend for themselves in totally economic terms. The first thing you do is dismantle the Endowments. There is no point of having any government support for the arts and they should just fend for themselves like everything else. However, even Grampp recognizes that "for museums there is not such a single simple guide. As non-profit organizations they are directed by other purposes, goals, ends, motives, desires, aspirations and the like, which taken together or separately offer no clear guide as to how they should conduct themselves or how well they had done so." I think that sums up what we have been talking about at this conference.

Economics should come into our thinking in museum administration as a means to an end, but not as the end itself. As Sir John put it so well, it is a different ethos. Peter Temin also very sensitively said we operate on a different premise. In the background papers, the reference to this economic concept of the "merit good" keeps cropping up, and it is nice to know there is a bin to put us in because that is, I think, where we belong. Bill Luers has talked about the parish church and I would submit that the most important decisions they make are not what supplier they go to for communion wine or whether there is a price break on wafers that month. The point is that they are in a different business from business. I agree that it is hard sometimes to define exactly all of what business museums are in. What art museums should *not* be in is a market mentality; and I think Neil Rudenstine, characteristically, summed it up in making the differentiation between being market-sensitive and being market-driven (see chap. 3 in this volume).

Now when it comes to the question of collections, we have all kinds of pitfalls. I was delighted that Bill Luers brought it up, so I don't have to, the extraordinary attack we are now undergoing as a field from the Financial Accounting Standards Board (FASB), which would like museums to carry our art collections on our balance sheets. Luckily, support for this position does not come from the accounting profession as a whole, many of whom are persuaded that the museum point of view on this is absolutely correct. Museums, as a matter of fact, have a broad base of support on this issue even from bankers and audit firms.

First of all, how on earth would you ever find any meaningful number to attach to these works of art if you took them at cost? Some of them came into the collections so early on that is meaningless. If you took them at market, it would depend which day you are talking about—with tremendous swings, and very questionable comparability. Individual works of art are very individual. They are not like stocks and bonds which can be measured and quoted hourly on the Big Board.

The ultimate question is usefulness. What good would it serve? On the contrary, there is always the minus that it gives the essential, underlying idea that these are economic goods, these works of art, tangible assets, and that they somehow, therefore, could help us solve our other ills. There is where the most dangerous misapprehension of the underlying assumptions come in. Boards of trustees responsible for some of the museums of this country are in fact largely made up from the business community, and they are not used to the idea of certain objects that are under their control not being available fungibly to cross the line into dollars. I was fascinated by Peter Temin's suggestion that now that we have government controls on museums you do not need to keep this line firm anymore because the only reason there ever was one was to keep museum directors from lining their own pockets (see chap. 7 in this volume). I thought that was taking it a little far.

In terms of the question of deaccessioning, I am not going to go into that in detail here. I think that the arguments pro and con have been brought up. The collections are held for posterity as part of our mandate, particularly if you are a national museum. On the other hand, I can sympathize with those who wonder how you are ever going to get art any other way these days.

There were, however, some comments made on this issue that I think need to be rebutted. There was the idea that the responsibility of the museum to the object can continue even if it is sold, by virtue of someone else possibly taking better care of the object than the seller would have. That is great, if you can place the work of art into another museum or even into the right kind of private hands. But if you put it up for auction, as you almost have to do to protect yourself, then you have lost control over who buys it. If it is good enough, chances are it will leave the country. If it is not good enough (which should be the one reason you are selling it), there is not much money in it anyway. If you sell through the private market process, then there are all kinds of other problems; a dealer is going to have to tell its client that the museum was irresponsible in letting it go for such a low price, to justify the new price that has been added on to it. It is a kind of no-win situation.

At the Gallery we have a different approach. We have a National Lending Service, and we put these objects very much to work. I was delighted to hear how many objects the Metropolitan lends. I know that the embassies are always in need. There are responsible institutions around the country that came late into the collecting process. I think collections can be shared.

On the question of exhibitions, we do not have time to go through the long litany of pros and cons. John Walsh's summary I thought was very germane (see chap. 1 in this volume). I would certainly subscribe to the need to try to do everything possible to emphasize the permanent collections. It is not as easy as it sounds. They are there—there is only so much you can do about rubbing people's noses against them.

What exhibitions do provide, however, is another way station along a continuum. If you pull back enough, you can see that really both of these alternatives—permanent installations and special exhibitions—are compromises. At the far end of the spectrum is all the art that is out there everywhere in the world. One can control it to some degree photographically, and put it on some great list, and select from it at will, and write it into texts and lectures, and try to shape it in histories and give it some point. But that is all done in the world of ideas: it is done without originals.

At the other end of the spectrum are individual works of art that just happen to be some place; they happen to have been collected, or they happen to have gone into museums or to be in their original ecclesiastical or secular setting.

And there you have the opportunity to come to them first hand. Who has ever had a better opportunity to focus on a work of art, one that is not even in a museum, say, than in little Borgo Sansepolcro, where you come and they open the doors and there is the Piero della Francesca *Resurrection?* It is the only thing there, and they know why you have come, why you have made this pilgrimage. That is the kind of experience, directly, or a single great work of art in the original and in its original context that cannot be reproduced even in an art museum.

Somewhere in the middle are the opportunities to see original works of art grouped together. Permanent collections are often large enough to offer some modicum of context. Temporary exhibitions can go a step further, assembling originals that are not normally together, so that a visitor gets a visual rationale, made wholly of originals, as a once-in-a-lifetime opportunity. Such exhibitions can be, I submit, the best of both worlds, although still a compromise, and only temporary. Never as complete as the treatise, they still make coherent sense, while offering the inestimable advantage of primary, direct experience. If you ever wanted to penetrate the artistic personality and achievement of Gauguin, for example, the overwhelming experience of the recent Gauguin show in Washington and Paris provided, I believe, a better way of doing it than coming upon the few Gauguins that are available normally on the walls of the National Gallery of Art.

It is a question of trade-offs. It is, at the same time, a question of not being taken over by the marketing mentality and trying to make these shows into something they are not.

From the economic standpoint, it is erroneous to assume, as was said here, that these exhibitions take funds away from acquisitions. I certainly know of few corporations from whom we have ever been able to raise money for support of a temporary exhibition that would have been interested in putting the same amount of money instead into some kind of art purchase. One has to be realistic about where the funding sources are.

The fact that temporary exhibitions do occupy the dimension of time should not be considered a minus. People procrastinate. If a show is there only temporarily, it does help, as Harold M. Williams said, get people into the house. It gets people into the habit of seeing works of art, reacting to them, and learning that they can provide an extraordinary experience. If that makes the permanent collection seem a little less urgent, it does not necessarily mean that fewer people see the permanent collection than if there had been no shows. I believe it expands the whole pie. But the subject is endlessly controversial. It is largely made so by the media attention to shows rather than to collections, giving us a false impression of who sees what at a museum; and by the kind of moneymaking atmosphere that surrounds some temporary exhibitions. I am delighted to hear the Metropolitan is deemphasizing that, as I know other museums want to do.

That leaves me finally with the future, which is where everybody conveniently runs out of time. The concept of expansion is one that I believe we must challenge. It is not an inexorable conveyor belt, you do not have to go on adding wings and growing for the sake of growth, acting on that hidden assumption, the American expansionist mentality, which I think needs rethinking. We are paying for the expansions. Meanwhile, the curators are sometimes now an increasingly small percentage of the overall staff. This does not mean that there is necessarily less curatorial activity going on, on an absolute scale. It does mean that we have got to have more maintenance people and guards and so forth to take care of more space.

The encouraging thing is that people are going to art museums. I would call your attention to a survey that was made this year in our area, in which they found that museum-going was the most popular leisure activity in the region—with 55.3 percent of the area adults having visited a museum in the previous year; as against, for example, live theatre, 32.1 percent; Kennedy Center, 28 percent; any professional sport, 36 percent, and so forth.

The reasons that I am bullish about the long-range hold that art museums are going to have on people are fundamentally the reasons that Marilyn Perry has put forward (see chap. 2 in this volume). I think people do fall in love with works of art, and as Francis Henry Taylor once said, "it is like love; it takes." It has a lot to do with exposure. Temporary exhibitions are among the strategies that foster that exposure. They can offer an opportunity of providing one of those moments when people get hooked. Robert Frost talked about the "immortal wound." If you can just provide that one experience, then people are going to want to come back and back.

To do that, I think the future really depends on education and not necessarily education inside the museum. To me where the battle should be waged is on school boards and out in the communities of America in changing the value system, in getting citizens to appreciate the relevance of our cultural heritage in general and our visual heritage in particular. Then when people visit museums, they come with their own "furniture of the mind," and they will have something to which to attach these new experiences.

There are specific things we can do to try to help. Tax laws are very high on our agenda. We have not discussed them that much, but there is a brilliant background paper by Don Fullerton on their history. Unfortunately, you cannot do much about the cost of works of art.

But rather than curse the darkness, I would like to see us light some candles. I believe that education and political action are probably the flames to which our fuel might best be directed.

Richard E. Oldenburg

It is really very daunting to be asked to give an overview, when almost everything has been said and said very well. Nothing has been too cheerful as we look ahead to our future. But I think it is inevitable that a conference on the economics of art museums would be reasonably gloomy. It is said that when artists get together, they discuss the high price of paint, and I can assure you that museum directors do too.

There are, unfortunately, as many of us have pointed out, a lot of trends that are distressing. In hearing them discussed here or at other places, you often find them being described in tones of fin de siecle, ends of eras, and so on. While this may not have been too odd an idea in a year like 1989, it all sounds rather too dire. I like to think that there are also a few bright spots in terms of challenges, and opportunities, and above all in terms of what we continue miraculously to accomplish and offer. As we look around us, if indeed support is falling off, I think that it is certainly not because we have not been valiantly doing what we are supposed to do.

We have talked about so many of our problems. Forgive me for touching on some of them once again. We have talked about the rising cost of art, and I just thought that I might add in passing, that it is not simply the many-million-dollar paintings that have gone up; it is also lesser works and works in other media. For example, we did a study of acquisition costs at The Museum of Modern Art over the years. It was a lot easier to take chances with new paintings and sculptures in 1958, when we could acquire 66 at an average cost of $730. In 1988, we acquired 16 works at an average cost of $46,000. We can also turn to another medium for an outstanding example. In 1979, which is after all only 10 years ago, a print of Edward Weston's famous photograph, *Shell* (1927), sold at auction for $9500, which seemed very high at the time. In the spring of last year, a comparable print from the same negative sold at auction for $115,000 plus commission. In the field of modern and contemporary art particularly, costs have been rising across the board.

We discussed in this context the decline of private philanthropy and the new breed of consumer collectors. We also discussed many other problems, such as the evidence that museum attendance seems to have reached a plateau and that support from other areas was leveling off as well. At the risk of being repetitive, I would like to take a longer view of these problems. I have some claim to perspective, because I am surprised to realize that next week it will be 20 years since I first came to the Museum in the publications department. When I look back to see what I think are the major changes in that period, I view some of these problems in a larger context that I find useful for analysis.

I would say that the primary change, in the largest sense, is the change in the variety and the breadth of the sources of support on which museums rely. The major transformation, particularly in large museums, seems to be the transformation from institutions with an essentially private character, even when publicly supported to very public institutions, even though largely privately supported. By public, I mean in terms of responsibilities, expectations, accountability, their own self-image, and of course dealing with a much larger and diverse audience. There are many new masters, new people paying the pipers and calling the tunes. This makes life in the museum a lot more complex, and it makes museums more vulnerable. As Mr. DiMaggio pointed out, we have come a long way from the time when a few trustees and patrons made up modest deficits, when museums were not all that eager for large audiences, or at least were not prepared to make major efforts to lure them in (see chap. 2 in this volume). They certainly did not feel particularly accountable to the public in the running of museums.

Those changes were anticipated in the sixties and seventies, when a lot of the established institutions came under attack, and there were demands to be more responsive to community needs. Museums came out pretty well. I think we have a record of credibility and purpose, and we are generally recognized to have high standards. But the questions could not be ignored, and I think museums got the point.

So we started building larger publics for our programs and designing programs to attract them. And this was possible, as Neil Rudenstine pointed out, because of many factors—growth in sophistication, media attention to artists as celebrities and to new movements like Pop Art, and the right timing in many other areas (see chap. 3 in this volume). These programs needed more support than the old operations could provide without new sources of income. And so we turned first to the government. And as we know the National Endowment for the Arts (NEA) came into being in 1965, and was supplemented by the National Endowment for the Humanities and the Institute of Museum Services. Most of these grants were small amounts in relation to museum budgets. However, they were tremendously important, because so much of our budgets are allocated to the base expenses of keeping the doors open. It is that final small dollar share that allows you to realize the special project, the special exhibition—that means far more than its apparent impact on the budget. Now government support seems to have leveled off or to be eroding, and we even fear that it might disappear. Of course, the most significant government support is not grants from these agencies, but the support that has been given through tax incentives and exemptions. These have helped build our great collections and have made our museums what they are, the envy of museums all over the world. And it is, therefore, particularly ironic when we meet colleagues from abroad looking for advice on how to adapt the American system and apply it in other countries just as we seem to be dismantling it here, whether Congress is doing so consciously or unconsciously. Ahead of us we can see Congress exploring further steps in that dismantling in areas like the unrelated business income tax and in possible taxation of income from endowments. In the meantime, museums have had to assume new obligations to meet government regulations attached to the modest support we do receive.

When government support proved disappointing, we turned to corporate support, and to a remarkable degree this new savior came through. Until the late sixties and the seventies, the support from corporations for cultural activities was pretty modest. The large part was mostly in education or medicine. But when you look at the increase in arts support, the figures are amazing, particularly in terms of the kind of investment capital that we talked about yesterday that has made growth possible.

The Business Committee for the Arts was founded in 1967, and began to record the growth in corporate interest and contributions. In 1967, $22 million went from corporations to the arts in general. In 1985, $700 million went to the arts, of which about a quarter went to museums. And they calculate that over the past two decades, the decades I am talking about, about $1.35 billion has gone to museums in various forms. From a time when we did not even solicit corporations for annual support, corporations have now in many cases—like the Museum of Modern Art—become the largest single category giving support through the annual fund. They also give capital gifts and have helped to fund many of the new museums and museum additions in recent years. Above all, they sponsored the special exhibitions which have been the most prominent phenomena in building museum attendance. Now, unfortunately, here again we are in trouble. Corporations are pulling back. There are many reasons: mergers and acquisitions, retrenchments of major sponsors like oil companies, and, of course, tax changes here too. Most evident, and I guess most disturbing, is a change in attitude; the old rhetoric about community citizenship and quality of life is a lot less heard now. We get very frank bottom-line arguments, perhaps because of intense corporate competition and belt tightening. Corporations want to prove a direct impact of arts funding to justify its effects in terms of markets, demographics, and impressing government leaders. We hear phrases like "patronage that pays," "cause-related giving," and "affinity of purpose." This trend is underscored by the fact that we are getting more and more of our funds not from the philanthropic arm of the corporation but from the advertising, promotion, and other marketing budgets. And these agencies, in turn, are asking for major quid pro quos which, as we give in to some of them, threaten to debase our own currency.

During the past two decades, even more important to museums than the growth of corporate support is the extension that we have talked about to the much larger public, on which we are now increasingly dependent for earned income—from admissions, memberships, auxiliary activities, bookstores, and restaurants—and for fund-raising, as well. We have gotten a lot more sophisticated in wooing visitors, and one nice effect of that, I think, is reflected in the architecture of the museums we have built, which are certainly designed to be much more welcoming, less forbidding temples than they used to be.

We have discussed the phenomenon of special exhibitions, which has been one of our major tools. We all know we are too reliant on them. We want to build up new means of promoting our permanent collections; but we also know there is no substitute for the popular exhibition, whether we like it or not. They continue to affect the patterns we see in our finances and the work we do. We try to balance our programs to include exhibitions, of the highest quality hopefully, that will, at least for part of the year, draw in sizeable crowds. We know that attendance is not a good gauge, but it is a very seductive one because it can be easily quantified, unlike a lot of the other things we do.

All of these changes, and others, have made museums much more complex. We have had to create new departments to manage new services and respond to new obligations. Many people have observed that, as a result, museums have become much more like corporations—the corporations they are looking to for support. And others have observed that corporations have become more like museums, with collections, curators, and private museums, and no one knows where all that will end.

It's interesting to note that, except for Paul DiMaggio's comments, (see chap. 2 in this volume) the only issue I can think of that has not been very well covered at this meeting, although it is so central, is the whole issue of governance and what are the new demands made on people running museums. A director now is expected not simply to be a scholar and curator; he or she is to have business and marketing skills, to be an entrepreneur and negotiator, to handle union contracts, to lobby for legislation and government appropriations, to be a real estate developer—almost everything that you can think of, including social director. One of my museum colleagues recently said that the best training for a museum director now is to go to Cornell School of Hotel and Restaurant Management.

Needless to say, there are few of these omnicompetent paragons around. Since most of us are eventually liable to fail one or another of these tests, the turnover in directors is great. This is distressing to all of us, and I am quite convinced, very bad for our institutions.

Comparably, on the trustee side, museums have new trustees from the business world who can be very helpful but who have different expectations from trustees in the past. They may be very knowledgeable and committed to art, but their training is oriented to business concerns and the bottom line. As our nonart activities involving earned income and marketing increase, these trustees feel much more qualified to advise and direct museums because the business talents that they have can be applied very effectively. They can also exert their control more widely than before, since artistic and financial choices in museums today are not so clear. We ask ourselves every day what is an economic decision and what is an aesthetic, intellectual decision. A primary example is a special exhibition. An exhibition, of course, is a decision—a curatorial decision—of what you want to present and prove, and what you want to put together. But these days, it is often an immense financial gamble, and without the assurance of corporate support, or government support, how much can you ask of your trustees? If the support does not come in, or heaven help you, if the show is not a great success, you can have something that can skew 20 percent or more of your budget and result in a huge deficit.

These questions, I think, have become more difficult, and have made museums much more vulnerable. We expanded our programs, and if the support for them falls off, we have to worry about what will happen. In the good times we have enjoyed recently, we have been breaking even and feeling proud of it. What will happen in bad times? If we get lower endowment returns from lower market values? If there are declines in donations, memberships, attendance? All these things could perfectly well happen in even a modest down market. This is what worries us: we have to wonder what would be cut to reduce expenses. Probably not the empire of income-producing departments we have created, because those are the ones that will be needed or seem to be needed more than ever. Unless vigorously defended, what will go will be in curatorial areas, the backroom areas that are perhaps the more sensitive because least visible. I would say that if we are now going to stop building new museums and new wings, the primary goals for museums would be to shore up, to fund-raise for and endow those basic curatorial functions so that they will not be threatened in a storm. Then we can deal with the rest of our problems, whether they are exhibition costs or our auxiliary activities which may be churning large amounts of money more than making them.

So this overview offers many problems to be faced. Perhaps we are at an end of an era, although that sounds pretty cataclysmic. It is nicer to think we are at the end of a period of major growth, maybe approaching middle age, as Marilyn Perry suggested (see chap. 2 in this volume). Whatever it is, we find ourselves in a new phase. We have to adapt to new realities, and different institutions will respond differently. I think perhaps Neil Rudenstine is right that after prolonged growth we may have to batten down the hatches for a while (see chap. 3 in this volume). That needn't be bad. I think we all know that sometimes passion for growth and equating it with progress mask confusion, or at least allow you to not pay too much attention to analyzing your goals and missions. This can be a time to reconsider our future very carefully, to reassess the kinds of issues we have been discussing today.

I think one thing is obvious. Whether we are talking about the government or corporations or collectors or donors or the general public, we have got to learn to be more clear and eloquent about what we do and why, and what we uniquely offer. As Bill Luers has said, we have also got to become a lot more effective as lobbyists. I think we grew complacent. We assumed that everyone knew what we were talking about, since it was truth and beauty and quality of life. People like Mr. Voke and Mr. Helms are rude but not totally undeserved reminders that our arguments are not self-evident. I think we also have to recognize that some of these criticisms have touched nerves that may be more sensitive than we realized. There seems to be a large number of people who feel left out, hostile to being told what to like without much attempt at being persuaded. If we are better at presenting our case, we might do better at retaining and increasing the support we see falling away, and even find new support.

There are many other challenges that we have to meet. We have mentioned some of them here. We have to learn to serve our public better, which certainly will encourage them to come back more often. Any survey that we do at our

Museum, and I am sure at other museums represented here, indicates that the public that visits us knows less about art than we would like to think they do. And I know that is particularly true in a museum concerned with modern and contemporary art. We have to help our visitors more, if we want them to come back to us, to understand and enjoy what we are offering.

Despite the signs of attendance leveling off, there is a lot of room for further growth. We can greatly expand our public. We certainly have an obligation to try to do that not only with visitors from abroad but above all among the multicultural constituencies in our own cities. What are we doing wrong? If we really believe that love of art is not some elitist peculiarity and that we can offer pleasure and understanding to all, if they are properly introduced to it, then we are not bringing them in for that experience. There is much to be done, and I am still optimistic that museums can cope with these problems as they have with others in the past. Museums will not go away, because they serve art well and art is not going to go away. In the contemporary field, there is very exciting work appearing, even if it is not the new movement every minute that markets wish there were. Art reflects our times better than anything else I know, and museums are essential transmitters of its lessons and joys.

I am even guardedly optimistic about the new generation of collectors. After all, who knows who will be in the last chair when the music stops, holding the Jasper Johns?

Harold M. Williams

In introducing my presentation, Martin Feldstein has reminded me of Peter Drucker's comments on his 65th birthday when he said, "I still don't know what I want to be when I grow up." His introduction also illustrates a dilemma I sometimes face. Over the years, I have been very critical of the ineffectiveness of corporate boards of directors. I have also addressed the disastrous consequences of the takeover junk bond rage. When I do so, I am accused by the corporate community of being an academic or a bureaucrat or an unrealistic not-for-profit type. On the other hand, when I am critical of the museum world, some of my colleagues from the nonprofit world accuse me of having a corporate mentality. Another example. Some years ago we were in the process of acquiring a painting in England. The painting had been offered to a British museum for £4 million which they turned down. We negotiated the price down about a third, bought it, and applied for an export permit. At that point, the same British museum raised the funds and bought it. I happened to be in England shortly thereafter on a visit to observe the state of art conservation, visited conservators and training facilities, and saw the desperate condition of paintings from some of the country houses and the conservation needs of the museums. I was interviewed by the press and I made the observation that £2.7 million would have gone a long way toward urgently needed restoration of paintings. Of course, I was accused of self-interest. So, since I intend to try to be provocative today, you may find justification to discount what I am about to say.

I would like to begin, though, with a statement that is not provocative or controversial and thank Marty Feldstein and the Bureau for bringing this meeting into being. It has been an important one for all of us. It begins to appear that economics of art museums may not be oxymoron. But it is not clear to me to what extent our discussions reflect semantic differences, philosophical differences, or psychological phenomena. I suspect it is a combination of all three, but I would hope, at least semantically, that the discussion of the last day and one-half will bring us somewhat closer together. Many of the concepts and much of the terminology from economics or the business world apply, even if we call them by other names. For us to make like we don't market is totally unrealistic. We do market. And we do concern ourselves with marketing in many, many different ways. We may want to call it something different. If that makes us more comfortable, God bless. But on the other hand, if it makes communication among ourselves more difficult, then it is dysfunctional.

I do not know what there is about the psychology of the museum field. Are we threatened by the economic calipers of outsiders who do not reassure us by expressing an adequate level of love and affection for museums and art? Are we concerned that we are not understood and do not have a strong constituency that we can count on to protect us and to help us address our needs? As Dick Oldenburg has observed, we do feel vulnerable. We lack a large, committed, political constituency. We behave at times like a beleaguered, musunderstood minority.

Are we facing a midlife crisis? I think that is what we have been talking about. As we look at our future in the nineties, it is different—we cannot acquire art at these prices. Our operating costs are projected to outstrip our revenue streams limiting our ability to undertake essential new initiatives—a totally unacceptable condition. What do we do under these circumstances? How do we remake ourselves? To begin with, we need to reassess the need to acquire, and what drives it. The situation is not unlike that which seems to drive the corporate world—the bigger you are, the more prestigious, perhaps the better compensated. If you are not growing, you are dying. And therefore you have got to acquire because you have got to keep growing. Why? What are the alternatives?

We need to begin by defining our mission. The term "mission" has been used here five times in discussion, but not in the context of a prepared paper. The Getty sponsors the Museum Management Institute, a summer residential program for museum managers. Typically, participants have come up the curatorial route and now have managerial responsibilities. When they are asked to talk about the mission of their institutions, most of them cannot do it. Now either it has not been defined, or at least it has not been communicated. I suspect it is more the former. The definition of "collect, conserve, and exhibit" does not go far enough. As we look ahead, we must go further in defining what our individual missions are. They are not all the same for all museums. If we define the mission clearly enough, it will help us set direction and priorities and make operational decisions that follow from it in terms of audience, constituencies, collection, acquisition, activities to emphasize, and so on.

The process of defining mission will require us to address a fundamental question. And that is, how can a museum be great without growing? We have to learn from the Europeans and from the Wallace and the Frick and the Gardner about how to succeed without acquisitions and blockbusters. And we have to focus on other purposes that may be less obvious, less tangible, but increasingly important and desirable, in the next decade, whether it is scholarship, or more effective education, or long-term loans and exchanges of works of art with other institutions, or more imagination and creativity in the exhibition of the permanent collection (including bringing objects out of the basement). These are all issues that need to be addressed. I have seen very little truly creative use of permanent material in many of our collections. I share the concern raised earlier about trying to value art collections. I think it is an exercise in futility. And yet I am intrigued by one aspect. What if we privately were to value what is in the basement? Would we consider it differently if we realized the real value of what is in the basement? In a sense, if it is not on view, it does not exist. I know there are other values to what is in the basement, but are they equivalent to the real value of what many of us have squirreled away? In addition, if we looked at the cost of maintaining what is in largely dead storage—including space, utilities, insurance, staff, and so on, we might take a somewhat different view. Finally, consider the cost of new and expensive space we are building for storage.

I need to identify one important issue we have largely ignored. We have focused on the revenue side because it is easier to do and because it controls the level of expenditure. But we have not looked at how well we are spending money—or the unmet needs. What is the condition of maintenance in our museums? What is the adequacy of conservation? I can take some of the numbers in Dick Rosett's paper and work them differently to examine the relationship between the value of the collections and what we spend on conservation (see chap. 7 in this volume). When I do so I can at least express some concern about them. Perhaps they are adequate; perhaps they are not. But we have not looked at them systematically. What about the adequacy and effectiveness of resources dedicated to educational programs? And consider the lack of creativity in designing them compared to what goes on in history and science and technology museums. There are ways of gaining perspective on how well we are doing what we think we are doing. Focus group interviews, for example, can be very valuable. The focus group interviews that have been referred to have been very informative. There are all kinds of unexpected insights that fall out, such as that of the probation officer that has been referred to (see chap. 2 in this volume). For example, one of the things that we at the Getty found startling is that some people did not know the Getty Museum was a museum of art. There are some obvious things that can really help you.

One of the points that comes out of the focus group interviews of museum attendees and nonattendees that we have been sponsoring around the country is the comment, stated in various ways: "Nothing is happening at the museum. I have seen the permanent collection." Do we need "happenings" to get large numbers of people to attend? If blockbusters are too expensive and or dysfunctional, and it becomes increasingly difficult, if not impossible to finance the kinds of acquisitions that generate interest—what do you do? There have to be more interesting ways to make happenings, albeit not blockbusters, out of the permanent collection—including ways to use what is in storage. We also have to face the desirability of deaccessioning to be able to acquire and create happenings.

We have heard a number of very interesting comments about the subject of deaccessioning which reflect that some oppose it as an article of faith, while others are not certain how to decide what is appropriate. I appreciate the sensitivity relating to deaccessioning—much of it is very legitimate and appropriate—but much of it is clouded by emotion and dogma and consequently "straw men" or "straw people." Some of us might say there is no such thing as a justifiable deaccession. But once you assume there is, let us consider some of the comments we have heard here. The responsibility of the Walker to the populace of Minnesota is an example of a straw man. It is important, or is it even relevant, whether the Walker considered the interests of the citizens of the state of Minnesota when it decided to deaccession art of a period outside its range of collecting? I do not believe it is. Is it relevant that the art object would have been welcomed by another museum in the city? I do not believe it is. If you use the proceeds to acquire an object for the museum, why is it characterized as "wholesale" to deaccession at auction, but "retail" to acquire at auction? We are going to see more deaccessioning. If we want to acquire, we will need to deaccession. Directors need guidelines so they can have the comfort of knowing that they will not be scorned or criticized by their peers or trustees, and that their image and prestige in the field will not be tarnished. The Association of Art Museum Directors could certainly help clarify the issues and provide guidance on what will be an increasingly significant issue.

Now let us talk about marketing. We are doing it every day. We are going to continue doing it. We are going to do it better over time because we need to. One of the first things Martin Feldstein asked us was, "who are your markets?" Are we going to engage minorities? Are we going to try to attract new groups to our museums? How do you do it? It is marketing. Call it something else if you will, call it seduction. Call it whatever you want, but it is marketing. The differences are only a matter of semantics.

How about entertainment versus education? I had occasion just recently to talk about a television series on the arts to Joan Ganz Cooney who developed Sesame Street and other successful children's educational TV programs. She talked about how to get the kids to tune in the first time; then to listen to it, to stay with it, and not flip the dial; and finally to come back the next day. The objective is to learn, not to entertain. But you have got to entertain to attract and hold the children and for them to learn. You have got to get your audience. You have got to hold your audience. So if your objective is education, it is not indecent to entertain.

In the same vein, I agree fully with Marilyn Perry and her concept of love of paintings. But if you have not met her, you cannot fall in love with her. We have got to get people into the museum. And that is going to require marketing in all kinds of ways. Carter Brown addressed the need for more and better art education. That certainly would stimulate museum attendance. We at the Getty are devoting a fair amount of resources to supporting the development of more substantive art education programs in the public schools—not just in individual schools, but systematically through school districts. The program incorporates production, history, criticism, and aesthetics and is taught sequentially at least in kindergarten through sixth grade. And it is taking hold. Some people say our approach is wrong. Others say it is right. Frankly I do not care who is right. It has raised the level of appreciation for the importance of substantive art education in the curriculum. It is producing results within the schools. If others want to do it differently, let them do it their way.

I underscore Neil Rudenstine's assessment that the ability of museums to increase revenues year after year through the nineties will be increasingly difficult. We have pretty well exploited our previously untapped source, even without the threat of the unrelated business income tax. Given competing demands for public funds and the fragility of our own political clout, we cannot assume a favorable environment. The needs of health, welfare, and education are enormous. Museum attendance growth will probably slow. Perhaps we can raise the price of admission somewhat to offset it. Competition for private giving will increase.

The corporate sector is pretty well saturated, running into increasingly numerous, diverse, and conflicting demands and anticipating a decline in growth of corporate profits over the next period of time.

Finally, the outlook for endowment returns, given the quality of the markets today and the uncertain outlook, is not likely to be very robust. Certainly it will not replicate the bull market of the eighties.

At the same time, demographics are changing. And our museums are not responding adequately. What they are doing is, in many instances, uninteresting and irrelevant to an increasingly large percentage of the population of many of our urban communities, who do not identify with the culture of the Western Civilization—whether they are black, Hispanic, Asian, or Anglo who are not receiving the kind of education, either in history or art today, that would lead to identification or appreciation. How will public agencies respond to the funding needs of your museum if their constituents are not patrons and, at the same time, they have unmet medical, educational, welfare, and other needs? This is an increasingly urgent problem. And it is a problem not only for those who look to public-sector support. It is a problem for all of us who should be committed to attracting the public and interesting and educating them in the works of art that are part of our collection.

Reference has been made on several occasions to endowments and the portion that is drawn down for current purposes. Obviously, practice varies. Let me suggest one way of addressing it. If one begins with the assumption, which I accept, that the purchasing power of the endowment should not be eroded, then the endowment needs to earn enough to offset the impact of inflation and what is drawn down. On that basis, it may well be that what ought to be drawn down today is not more than 3 or 4 percent. Certainly any drawdown in excess of 5 to 5.5 percent is eroding the value of the endowment and invading principal.

Two last thoughts. Dick Oldenburg mentioned the trustees and governance. That is an area that we need to take a look at, defensively, if nothing else. Because if we go into the kind of economic crunch period that I expect, the behavior and response of our trustees can be pretty serious. How informed they are, and what their attitude is toward some of the issues we have been talking about are important. And I think we will find some of the same dichotomy there as that we have experienced here between economists and museum types. And so it is important that you appreciate that dichotomy and not reject it but try to understand it and be able to deal with it constructively— and now, before it becomes an issue or source of friction.

Finally, Carter Brown referred to William D. Grampp's *Pricing the Priceless: Art, Artists and Economics*. I have read it. It is polemic. But it poses some very interesting questions. I would recommend you read it. You will not like it. You will not agree with much of it. But do not dismiss it. Try to understand where Grampp is coming from. There are a lot of people who think that way. Perhaps even some on your boards. Certainly some of your supporters. The chapter on art museums particularly raises some very interesting questions, which we should all consider.

Roger G. Kennedy

I want to offer you some congratulations, then to offer you a two-part hypothesis, and finally to offer you a gift—in that order. It is always a pleasure to come to a gathering in which two distinct sets of people see two distinct sets of things as self-evident.

I want to begin with the congratulations because I think it is very important to underline what Neil Rudenstine has already talked about. Your achievement over the last couple of decades is absolutely extraordinary. What the art museum community has done for this country is unparalleled in its life and probably in the life of any western country—I don't know about the East! Let's observe the achievement of expanding the audiences and the depth of perception of those audiences; of widening those audiences and placing the visual arts at the center of American life—as it must be admitted—its performing arts are not. This is an achievement especially because it runs against the American grain. The disparagement of the past is inherent in our doctrine of progress.

Furthermore, while we are all looking for fresh audiences, I was struck by Neil Rudenstine's reference to Duke Ellington. We are the custodians of the Duke's legacy, including compositions that, of course, belong in the repertory of the Boston Symphony Orchestra—his late works for orchestra and chorus. Discovering materials you did not understand until you interpreted them, with the new audiences which many of you are reaching, means that you can learn, too. It is not just that we are instructing those audiences. As all of you know, they are instructing us. They are telling us things about ourselves we did not know before, about our ways of perception. So—congratulations, you have been doing a remarkable thing.

I want now to offer in hypothesis, an extension of a couple of economic themes that Harold Williams touched upon. The expansion of the last decade or two has produced a set of total returns that it seems to me are not likely to recur in the next decade or two. Sixteen or 17 percent annual average rates of total return in many endowments are not going to happen anymore, for, I think, the following reasons: those returns arrived in the presence of *decreasing* volatility, which is something to which trustees might pay a little attention, not *increasing,* despite a crash. I think they are unsustainable because price-to-asset values are still way out of whack, because price-to-dividend values are still out of whack, because the decline of liquidity in the collapse of the junk bond market seems to me to be almost as important as some of the sphincter motions of the Federal Reserve at the end of the twenties.

I also think that Mr. Gorbachev's removal of the IV-tube—defense production—that has sustained a deliberate Keynesian stimulus during the Reagan years is a very important factor. We are just not going to be having the Russians (as Mr. Nixon might have put it) to beat up on, and thereby stimulate our economies artificially. Under those circumstances, I think we can get used to the notion (as Harold Williams suggested) that it is not going to be easy for the endowments to bail out our improvidences any more.

Middle age is striking the arts community at the same time that perhaps something like those kinds of recurring middle ages that occur in economies is occurring more generally. Probably for some of the same reasons. We are at the end of a long cycle in modes of learning. The ways in which we have been learning and looking since the invention of print are now under assault. Their consequences, societal and economic, are under assault simultaneously. The epoch dominated by print carried with it very sharp emphases upon individuality on the part of the reader, upon individual exertion in capitalism, and upon religious self-determination. These print-dominated modes of learning are now under very significant assault—with an abyss of unknowable consequences lying out there before all of us. Television and the computer present to us a set of unknown and unknowable ways of relearning what we think we know. These are going to have profound effects on the way we "do business," you'll excuse the expression, all the time.

Let me suggest some things that may ensue: (1) the impoverishment of symbolic life; (2) an inhospitality to ambiguity; (3) a simulated reality that is out of scale but that replaces the reality of organic life (another child is perceived by some children as less alive than the box); and (4) the trivialization of all life into entertainment. Those phenomena are formed by one other, central to what we do in the museums, rooted in the real object, as distinguished from Disney: the major job of all of us is to set up a powerful opposition to (5) the decline of authenticity that arises from these new ways of learning.

Now, I want to get on to another tiny subject. At the same time these things are occurring in the United States, there are radical changes in the demographics. The obvious absence of any face of color here is illustrative of our problem. It is certainly interesting. Those demographics have certain characteristics that I think need underlining.

First, there will be, I believe, an increasing emphasis in this country upon *class,* and a declining emphasis upon *race.* One of the reasons for that is that the black community is not a homogeneous community. In the city of Washington, the majority of the blacks now do not live in the city. They live in the suburbs, and it is very likely (though the data are uncomfortable) that the average income of the black suburbanites is larger than the average income of the white suburbanites. Furthermore, second- and third-generation black suburbanites with substantial educations are now a fact of life. Not all blacks are poor (though they are the poorest of the poor—70 percent of the poorest of the poor are black). But blacks are not all identical, God help us. Nor, as a matter of fact, are people with Hispanic surnames. Young Hispanics now outnumber young blacks in this country, and of the 24 million people that came into our lives in the last decade, three or four million came into that life illegally from places to the south of us. Those people have two things in common. First of all, they have many reasons to regard the place from which they came as *accessible* to them, they continue to interact with that place, and regard it as *significant* in their cultural lives in a way that Europeans do not. Europeans do not keep going back and forth across the border and bringing relatives to reinforce their patterns of behavior. At least most of them do not. Hispanics are not all alike either. A rich Miamian from Cuba is not the same as a barrio resident in Los Angeles. We are going to have to get used, therefore, to the Hispanics as being the largest minority and the most rapidly growing one. Blacks are becoming divided between those who have made it, substantial in numbers, and those who are unlikely ever to make it, unless we alter fundamentally how we are coping with poverty. This is not a city/country discussion or distinction, nor is it a conservative/radical one. It seems to me the most significant single political event of 1989 to us in this country, aside from those in Eastern Europe, is the election of Douglas Wilder—a conservative black leader essentially representing suburban blacks. We are going to be seeing more of that interesting phenomenon.

Of course we are going to be in the lobbying business. But we had better know who we are lobbying and how they differ from each other. We had better be a little more respectful toward them. We are not very respectful. We are rather patronizing in the way we address ourselves to those audiencies. We do not know very much about them.

This leads me finally to the gift—after one final note. We are not likely to grow very much more in our place. It is a small museum, but there are those who love it. We are running at about a $30 million annual expenditure now, roughly speaking, and we are running about 7 million people through the place with about a third of the galleries being shut down for reconstruction. We do not want any more people. We want to do better by the ones we have got. God help us, we will do it by learning more about our visitors and learning from them about us. We have got, in our kind of place, as you may not, a very difficult job of re-staffing, so that we are in a position to continue to learn from them. So that they can help us give them what they deserve.

Now for the gift. Everybody is here because we would rather be doing the kind of work we do than other kinds of work we might do. Almost everybody in a room like this got here on purpose, one way or another. Even the economists here, who have got other kinds of work to do than the papers they did for this group. That is true because all of us have, one way or another, shared the experience that I want to share with you, thanks to a friend (John Julius Norwich). Here are the words of Pablo Casals, at the age of 93: "For the past 80 years, I've started each day in the same manner. It's not a mechanical routine, but something essential to my daily life. I go to the piano, and I play two preludes and fugues of Bach. I cannot think of doing otherwise. It is a sort of benediction on the house, but that is not its only meaning for me. It is a rediscovery of the world of which I have the joy of being a part. It fills me with an awareness of the wonder of life, with a feeling of the incredible marvel of being human."

I suspect that is why we are all sitting around here, because we believe in that experience.

II Papers

6   Art Museums in the United States: A Financial Portrait

Richard N. Rosett

6.1 Introduction

The Association of Art Museum Directors comprises approximately 140 museums in the United States and Canada that have in common the collection, preservation, and exhibition of works of art. They range from the great multicollection museums of New York, Chicago, Boston, and Washington, D.C. to museums highly specialized as to era, region, subject matter, and medium. Their collections include American, Asian, African, European, antique, medieval, modern, and contemporary art, art of the American West, and North Carolina folk art. There are museums that specialize in ceramics, glass, photography, portraiture, and sculpture. Their budgets range from a few hundred thousand dollars to well over one hundred million dollars. Half the members of the Association of Art Museum Directors (AAMD) are housed in buildings smaller than the store operated by the largest museum, New York's Metropolitan Museum of Art.

It is the nature of human institutions that their guiding spirits seldom are content. Opportunities for growth and improvement lie in every direction and could be seized if only there were more time, more money, fewer regulations of the sort that restrain progress and better enforcement of those that promote it. Art museums are no exception to this rule. There are vast populations to educate, mysteries to solve, decaying treasures to preserve, and new treasures to gather in. So it is that after almost half a century of unprecedented growth and prosperity, art museums in the United States, plagued by rising costs of acquiring, caring for, and exhibiting fine art, shrinking support from some

The data used in this paper were generously provided by the Association of Art Museum Directors. Millicent Hall Gaudieri, Executive Director of AAMD and Bruce H. Evans, Director of the Dayton Art Institute, were especially helpful. Without their support, this paper could not have been written.

traditional sources of revenue, and decreasingly supportive public policy, see themselves as faced with challenges they must struggle to meet and opportunities they may not be able to seize, frustrated by a growing disparity between what must be done and the means to do it.

Financial surveys of AAMD membership since 1985 confirm some elements of the museum dilemma and suggest directions in which solutions may lie, at least for some museums. Art museums taken as a group, are funded by individuals, foundations, and corporations; by national, state, and local government; by the income of their own invested endowments; and by what they charge for various services more or less related to or derived from their principal functions. While about one-third of the museums depend on all these sources, with none dominating, more than two-thirds depend on one or another of these sources for 40 percent or more of their revenue and are therefore especially vulnerable to the sorts of fluctuations suffered by any ordinary business that deals heavily in one market.

6.2   The Association of Art Museum Directors

Strictly speaking, the Association of Art Museum Directors, the principal art museum membership organization, is an organization of museum directors, not museums, but the requirements for membership include both the qualifications of the directors and of the museums. AAMD bylaws provide that, "active membership is open to persons who serve as directors of art museums which, by purpose, size and standards of operation meet the eligibility requirements established by the Trustees of the Association," and that, "Eligible individuals will be professionally qualified for their positions by a sufficient combination of art historical training, museum experience, demonstrated ability and adherence to the Code of Ethics of the Association."

The code itself, contained in a 30-page AAMD pamphlet entitled "Professional practices in Art Museums," briefly describes and enjoins the principal conflicts of interest to which museum directors are subject: self-dealing and profiting personally either from inside knowledge gained by virtue of the director's position or by trading on the reputation and prestige of the museum. "Professional Practices" also spells out the chief managerial responsibilities of the director and the function of the board, and provides guidance for hiring and firing directors, for acquiring and disposing of works of art, for cataloguing, preserving, exhibiting, and lending works of art, and for recognizing and dealing with conflicts of interest involving board members and directors. One sentence particularly significant in any discussion of museum finances deals with deaccession and disposal of works of art: "Deaccessioning should be related to [collection] policy rather than to exigencies of the moment, and funds obtained through disposal must be used to replenish the collection."

6.3   The AAMD Surveys

The AAMD's first membership survey, conducted in 1985, dealt with museum employees' 1984 salaries. It was augmented by a statistical survey of financial data and operating characteristics in 1985, and the survey has been conducted since then in the expanded format. A copy of the statistical survey questionnaire is reproduced as appendix A. The 1989 survey, which covered 1988 operations, produced 155 responses, approximately an 80 percent response rate. The financial data generally are not cast in a form that permits checks of internal consistency—and where checking is possible, it reveals inaccuracies, some of them considerable.

Problems arise from the design of the survey itself. In reporting revenues, museums were asked for total current operating income, and for all its components, with specific instructions to report the components of earnings from class tuition, stores, restaurants, and so on, net of direct costs. Interpretation of these instructions varied widely, with only half the respondents reporting total revenue as the sum of its components. As a result, about half the museums report total revenue well below total expenditure, many of them claiming at the same time that their budgets are not in deficit. In reporting expenditures, museums were asked for total operating expenditures, total salary and benefit expenditures, and expenditures on specific activities: curatorial service, conservation, administration, development, and so on. Because these specific components are not exhaustive, almost two-thirds of the responses show total expenditures that exceed the sum of the components by at least 10 percent. The bottom line is that the survey does not provide checks of internal consistency. Neither total revenue nor total expenditure can be tested against the sum of components, and these two numbers cannot be used to test one another, despite inclusion of the size of the museum's surplus or deficit in the survey.

The worst problems afflict the 1985 data. The survey was new, museum personnel were unaccustomed to the questionnaire, and questions went unanswered or were answered in ways that seem implausible, especially in view of disparities between that survey and the three that followed. The following three surveys were far better than the first. In most of what follows, I use the sums of expenditures and revenue data for the three years, 1986 to 1988, to describe the financial condition of these 112 museums. For physical characteristics, I have used 1988 data.

Some data problems arise from the organizational form of the museums themselves. Several of the Smithsonian museums share certain facilities, and university museums often are provided with services not reflected on their own books. The survey design makes it impossible to determine whether, in cases like these, there has been even an effort to allocate costs and revenues, much less whether the allocation is sensible. Despite these and other problems with the data, summary comparisons among the three years of data (1986–88) and among groups of museums classified in several different ways suggest that the data may be useful in forming a general picture of art museums' financial condition and addressing questions about changing patterns of museum funding. While the data cannot comfortably bear the burden of sophisticated statistical analysis aimed at discovering behavioral relationships, crude comparisons among aggregates and averages still can be illuminating. Even if it is not possible to estimate the demand for museum admissions or determine whether the industrial mix of a community shapes the revenue-producing activities of its museums, still it is possible to determine the financial condition of groups of museums and to explore the directions in which opportunities for improvement lie.

Of the 155 museums responding to the 1989 survey, 43 were excluded from the group examined here because key data items were missing or because they were Canadian museums. The excluded U.S. museums are about one-third smaller, on average, than those that are included, but beyond that, there is no obvious characteristic that distinguishes them except for the incompleteness of their survey responses. The 112 museums that remain after the exclusions include the half-dozen largest and are broadly representative of size, type, and region. In the discussion that follows, I frequently make comparisons of subgroups of museums to the 112 total, as though the group constitutes all art museums. The tedious repetition of this reminder seems worse than the modest misinterpretations that may result from its omission.

The AAMD surveys are like a series of snapshots, taken to give each member museum an idea of how it stacks up against the others. From these snapshots I have attempted to construct a portrait, not of the art museum, but of the getting and spending of art museums. What emerges is not one portrait, but several. Art museums, however varied their size and substance, are surprisingly similar in their spending on the main functions that are peculiar to them: collection management, conservation, education, and so on. They vary considerably, however, in the ways in which they fund these activities. It is upon the variation in the sources of funding and the related variations in spending that I have focused in an effort to gain an insight into how art museums might best exploit opportunities for growth or, under other circumstances, cope with adversity.

6.4   Geographic Distribution of Art Museums

Though a number of small cities boast art museums of excellent quality, and though there are museums in remote locations that attract visitors from throughout the nation, the great metropolitan areas of the United States enjoy an understandably disproportionate concentration of large, well-funded museums. Table 6.1 gives some of the statistics that illustrate this concentration. Of the 112 museums in the sample, 107 are located in 67 U.S. metropolitan

Table 6.1 Museum Characteristics by Metropolitan Area, 1988

Metropolitan Area	Number of Museums	1984 Population	Buildings (Sq. Feet)	Employees (Full-Time)	Attendance	Total Revenue	Total Spending
Largest 10	38	67,879	8,130	6,575	73,791	$1,449,113	$1,422,774
Percent	33.9%	28.7%	54.1%	65.8%	67.1%	69.9%	70.0%
Second 10	17	22,800	1,822	1,023	11,710	$ 208,426	$ 196,571
Percent	15.2%	9.7%	12.1%	10.2%	10.6%	10.0%	9.7%
Third 10	11	14,194	1,308	621	6,214	$ 98,919	$ 99,761
Percent	9.8%	6.0%	8.7%	6.2%	5.6%	4.8%	4.9%
Fourth 10	10	9,067	1,106	529	5,489	$ 93,883	$ 92,775
Percent	8.9%	3.8%	7.4%	5.3%	5.0%	6.5%	4.6%
Fifth 10	14	6,284	1,369	735	5,666	$ 132,243	$ 130,054
Percent	11.6%	2.7%	9.1%	7.4%	5.1%	6.4%	6.4%
Sixth 10	11	2,767	652	279	3,431	$ 44,321	$ 44,703
Percent	9.8%	1.2%	4.3%	2.8%	3.1%	2.1%	2.2%
Smallest 11	11	1,154	636	235	3,749	$ 47,035	$ 45,878
Percent	9.8%	0.5%	4.2%	2.4%	3.4%	2.3%	2.3%
Total	112	124,146	15,022	9,997	110,050	$2,073,940	$2,032,517
Total percent	100.0%	52.6%	100.0%	100.0%	100.0%	100.0%	100.0%

Note: Except for number of museums and employees, figures are in thousands. Attendance and dollar figures are three-year totals.

areas with a total population in 1984 of 124 million, or 53 percent of the total. The ten largest metropolitan areas, with 29 percent of the U.S. population have 38 of the 112 museums for which we have data. Though these are just one-third of the museums, they have more than half of the building space and exposition capacity, they employ two-thirds of museum employees, they entertain two-thirds of museum visitors, and their budgets account for 70 percent of all art museum spending. Museums, like other cultural institutions, as well as fine restaurants, financial markets, and wealth, are concentrated in large cities.

Museum funding flows to the metropolitan areas roughly in proportion to the attendance figures. Table 6.2 breaks revenue into the various reported sources. The sum of revenue from the various sources in table 6.2 falls short of the total reported in table 6.1 by about 17 percent, possibly because revenue is reported inaccurately or because the list of sources is not exhaustive. The overall picture is one of rough proportionality, as to total revenue, main components, and attendance, but there are striking exceptions which suggest a more useful way of classifying museums than according to the size of the metropolitan area.

Table 6.3 provides a clue to a more useful system of classification by showing that there are striking variations in the patterns of revenue source as we move from one group of metropolitan areas to another. Museums in the ten largest metropolitan areas, for example, derive a far greater share of revenue from federal funding than any other group. This is because Washington, D.C., the ninth-largest metropolitan area, is the home of the five Smithsonian museums, which receive 80 percent of federal funding for museums. Excluding Washington from the comparisons eliminates the disparity. Corporate funding, on the other hand, goes disproportionately to museums in the bottom eleven areas. Two of these museums have strong historical connections to particular corporations which account for their specializations—glass in one case and photography in the other—and for their exceptional success in obtaining corporate support.

From the largest to the smallest metropolitan areas, museums vary little in the proportions of their budgets dedicated to their various functions. Table 6.4 is more remarkable for the uniformity of its distributions than for striking departures. The greatest variations occur in the overhead spending on administration and development. For the purpose of understanding these and certain other budget variations, classification by size of metropolitan area is less illuminating than another scheme, classification according to the museum's principal source of revenue.

While revenue from the chief sources of art museum support flows to metropolitan areas roughly in proportion to attendance, this is not because all or even most museums are supported by the various sources in similar proportions. Rather it is because the several groupings of metropolitan areas tend to have a mix of museums, some heavily supported by one source, others by

Table 6.2 Sources of Museum Revenue by Metropolitan Area, Three-Year Totals, 1986–88

Metropolitan Area	Total	Federal Government	State Government	Local Government	Other Government	Corporate	Private	Endowment Income	Earnings
Largest 10	$1,151,662	$171,323	$70,089	$139,635	$5,294	$67,977	$327,487	$162,572	$207,285
Percent	66.8%	89.6%	65.4%	64.3%	17.7%	60.6%	70.5%	54.0%	68.9%
Second 10	187,852	6,791	5,912	47,432	1,753	11,579	48,666	41,170	24,549
Percent	10.9%	3.6%	5.5%	21.9%	5.9%	10.3%	10.5%	13.7%	8.2%
Third 10	88,609	3,012	3,653	14,339	762	6,567	28,996	17,274	14,007
Percent	5.1%	1.6%	3.4%	6.6%	2.5%	5.9%	6.2%	5.7%	4.7%
Fourth 10	91,599	4,062	1,615	7,970	19,674	10,873	19,102	16,040	12,262
Percent	5.3%	2.1%	1.5%	3.7%	65.7%	9.7%	4.1%	5.3%	4.1%
Fifth 10	118,856	3,073	12,523	5,476	143	5,204	20,787	47,900	23,750
Percent	6.9%	1.6%	11.7%	2.5%	0.5%	4.6%	4.5%	15.9%	7.9%
Sixth 10	40,740	1,131	8,026	257	2,101	790	7,468	11,410	9,557
Percent	2.4%	0.6%	7.5%	0.1%	7.0%	0.7%	1.6%	3.8%	3.2%
Smallest 11	44,603	1,716	5,367	1,911	215	9,130	12,209	4,450	9,604
Percent	2.6%	0.9%	5.0%	0.9%	0.7%	8.1%	2.6%	1.5%	3.2%
Total	$1,723,922	$191,109	$107,185	$217,020	$29,942	$112,121	$464,715	$300,816	$301,015
Total percent	100.0%	100.0%	100.0%	100.0%	100.0%	100.0%	100.0%	100.0%	100.0%

Note: Dollar figures in thousands.

Table 6.3   Percentage Distribution of Sources of Revenue by Metropolitan Area, Three-Year Totals, 1986–88

Metropolitan Area	Total (%)	Federal (%)	State (%)	Local (%)	Other Government (%)	Corporate (%)	Private (%)	Endowment Income (%)	Earnings (%)
Largest 10	100.0	14.9	6.1	12.1	0.5	5.9	28.4	14.1	18.0
Second 10	100.0	3.6	3.1	25.2	0.9	6.2	25.9	21.9	13.1
Third 10	100.0	3.4	4.1	16.2	0.9	7.4	32.7	19.5	15.8
Fourth 10	100.0	4.4	1.8	8.7	21.5	11.9	20.9	17.5	13.4
Fifth 10	100.0	2.6	10.5	4.6	0.1	4.4	17.5	40.3	20.0
Sixth 10	100.0	2.8	19.7	0.6	5.2	1.9	18.3	28.0	23.5
Smallest 11	100.0	3.8	12.0	4.3	0.5	20.5	27.4	10.0	21.5
All areas	100.0	11.1	6.2	12.6	1.7	6.5	27.0	17.4	17.5

Table 6.4   Percentage Distribution Among Uses of Funds by Metropolitan Area, Three-Year Totals, 1986–88

Metropolitan Area	Total (%)	Curatorial Service (%)	Conservation (%)	Education (%)	Library (%)	Operations (%)	Administration (%)	Development (%)
Largest 10	100.0	32.2	2.7	6.3	2.0	32.9	17.3	6.7
Second 10	100.0	28.9	2.6	8.1	2.9	24.5	22.6	10.4
Third 10	100.0	28.0	2.2	6.8	2.0	29.6	18.8	12.6
Fourth 10	100.0	26.4	1.9	7.6	3.0	31.2	26.7	3.2
Fifth 10	100.0	21.4	2.3	9.5	2.2	26.9	29.2	8.4
Sixth 10	100.0	25.5	2.5	6.7	1.9	32.3	21.1	10.0
Smallest 11	100.0	27.8	1.7	5.7	2.0	26.9	29.9	6.0
All areas	100.0	30.2	2.6	6.8	2.1	31.1	19.7	7.4

another. Art museums tend to specialize as to their sources of revenue even more than they specialize in the art they collect. The five Smithsonian art museums all receive at least 80 percent of their revenue from the federal government. The sixth museum, ranked according to support from this source, receives just over 50 percent, and no other museum receives more than 25 percent of its revenue from the federal government. State and local governments, too, concentrate their support on a group of museums with which they maintain special relationships, though not to the same degree as the federal government. There are groups of museums that rely most heavily on one or another of several private sources of revenue: contributions, endowment income, earnings from admissions, stores, restaurants, tuition, and a variety of service and rental charges. Under one-third of the 112 museums included in this study so spread their sources of revenue as to defy classification on this basis. Leaving aside the nature and quality of the collection itself, the readily observable characteristic that divides art museums most sharply is their principal source of revenue.

Policy decisions both by donors and museums tend to sort museums out according to principal revenue source. Governments condition their support for museums to suit public policy objectives which are not likely to be free of political considerations. Private foundations are guided by the policy objectives of their founders and their governing bodies. Corporations tend to favor museums close to world headquarters or which collect art linked somehow to the nature of the business. Museums seek support from these sources, weighing their own objectives against the potential donors' requirements. Museums vary in their admissions policies, the extent and effectiveness of their fundraising efforts, and their success in operating stores and restaurants. Revenue specialization is a product both of the environment in which a museum operates and of its own choices.

6.5 Sources of Museum Revenue

Table 6.5 shows the nine categories into which the 112 museums are divided, the number that fall into each category, and summary expenditure data for each category. Total revenue, the sum of revenue components, and total expenditure match reasonably well for the first six categories, but the last three show disparities, with the largest disparity in the category that contains almost one-third of the museums and accounts for almost one-half of museum budgets. The two categories with the largest disparities are those most affected by the ambiguity of the survey questionnaire. Both derive a substantial fraction of their revenue from tuition, store and restaurant profits, and other earnings.

Each museum was classified according to which of the eight broad revenue sources accounted for at least 40 percent of its revenue. Because of the ambiguity surrounding total revenue, I used the sum of the reported components of

Table 6.5   Museum Characteristics by Principal Source of Revenue, 1986–88

Principal Source	Number of Museums	Total Revenue	Sum of Revenue Components	Total Expenditure	Surplus	Full-Time Employees	Buildings (Sq. Feet)	Attendance	Endowment Market Value (1988)
Federal	6	$ 181,295	$ 185,289	$ 177,253	$ 498	1,315	1,754	27,866	$ 153,714
State	9	120,903	114,123	118,521	4,543	589	1,187	5,360	33,827
Local	11	167,563	161,923	153,356	11,621	888	1,630	7,835	73,882
Other government	4	36,281	35,079	35,391	1,407	273	468	3,040	6,108
Corporate	4	29,563	29,127	29,549	59	143	305	2,276	47,921
Private	23	277,840	275,903	268,659	3,096	1,461	2,094	14,045	201,223
Endowment	15	214,051	191,718	209,792	17,935	1,213	1,991	9,424	819,331
Earnings	6	87,798	91,946	124,307	2,558	601	690	4,387	158,437
Various	34	958,646	638,813	915,689	20,693	4,796	5,581	35,818	898,360
Total	112	$2,073,940	$1,723,922	$2,032,517	$62,408	11,279	15,701	110,050	$2,392,804

Note: Except for number of museums and employees, figures are in thousands. Attendance and, except for endowment, dollar figures are three-year totals.

revenue as the basis for calculating this percentage. Since this is the sum that best represents the amount of money available for spending on the museum's principal missions (as contrasted with operating stores and restaurants) it would have been the appropriate measure in any case. The categories are: Federal, State, Local (county and city governments), Other Government (a special category which seems to distinguish a particular way of funding a few state university museums), Corporate, Private (memberships, private foundation grants, and gifts), Endowment (endowment income earmarked for art purchases is excluded because it is not available for the ongoing operations of the museum), and Earnings (admissions, store and restaurant contribution net of direct costs, school tuition, and various fees). Thirty-four museums fell into none of these eight categories because their sources of support were diffuse rather than concentrated. These were classified as Various. The Various category includes five of the largest: the Metropolitan Museum of Art, the Chicago Art Institute, the Museum of Modern Art, the Philadelphia Museum of Art, and the Los Angeles County Museum of Art. For groups of museums classified in this way, I calculated the ratio of total revenue to the sum of revenue from the eight named revenue sources. The largest aggregate departure from a ratio of 1.0 is in the Various category, with a ratio of 1.2. Reported total revenue and expenditures tally reasonably in this and all other categories but one, Earnings, where expenditures are reported to be almost one-half larger than revenues for reasons discussed above. A minor anomaly of this classification scheme is that it places among the federally supported museums, one small university art gallery with a federal grant dominating its budget for just the three years of this study. It is small enough to be overwhelmed, statistically, regardless of how it is classified, so I left it where it fell, among the Feds.

Tables 6.6 and 6.7 together show the flow of financing to and from the several categories and illuminate the wide differences in the way museums are financed. The federal government provides (table 6.7) 11 percent of all museum funding, but the Smithsonian museums receive (table 6.6) 80 percent of federal support for museums, so that for the other groups, federal support ranges from less than 2 percent to just over 4 percent of total revenue. The Various category, with an aggregate budget five times larger than the Federal category, receives just 8 percent of federal support. Taking another example, private contributions (memberships, gifts, foundation grants, and so on) make up 27 percent of all museum funding, but less than 1 percent of it goes to Federal museums. The museums in the Various category, with aggregate budgets 5 times larger than the Federals, receive 50 times the private support.

To what extent is the pattern of museum funding due to choices the individual museums make, and to what extent is it due to factors beyond their control? Congress appropriated (over the three-year period, 1986–88) $191 million that went to the support of the 112 museums in our sample, but $153 million of it was earmarked for the Smithsonian art museums. Most of the rest

Table 6.6   Sources of Museum Revenue by Principal Source, Three-Year Totals, 1986–88

Principal Source	Sum of Sources	Federal	State	Local	Other Government	Corporate	Private	Endowment Income	Earnings
Federal	$ 185,289	$153,386	$ 10	$ 11	$ 0	$ 12,915	$3,849	$ 10,074	$ 5,044
Percent	10.7%	80.3%	0.0%	0.0%	0.0%	11.5%	0.8%	3.3%	1.7%
State	114,123	1,616	71,461	1,800	70	3,427	15,846	3,698	16,206
Percent	6.6%	0.8%	66.7%	0.8%	0.2%	3.1%	3.4%	1.2%	5.4%
Local	161,923	4,479	8,678	83,486	1,685	6,329	31,180	8,032	18,055
Percent	9.4%	2.3%	8.1%	38.5%	5.6%	5.6%	6.7%	2.7%	6.0%
Other government	35,079	1,466	795	9	25,363	527	3,996	716	2,208
Percent	2.0%	0.8%	0.7%	0.0%	84.7%	0.5%	0.9%	0.2%	0.7%
Corporate	29,127	1,239	566	262	3	15,333	5,384	2,154	4,186
Percent	1.7%	0.6%	0.5%	0.1%	0.0%	13.7%	1.2%	0.7%	1.4%
Private	275,903	6,101	3,907	7,966	497	20,733	162,256	35,778	38,666
Percent	16.0%	3.2%	3.6%	3.7%	1.7%	18.5%	34.9%	11.9%	12.8%
Endowment	191,718	5,532	4,423	673	97	5,501	31,453	114,483	29,556
Percent	11.1%	2.9%	4.1%	0.3%	0.3%	4.9%	6.8%	38.1%	9.8%
Earnings	91,946	2,073	1,814	639	12	4,103	16,260	21,576	45,469
Percent	5.3%	1.1%	1.7%	0.3%	0.0%	3.7%	3.5%	7.2%	15.1%
Various	638,813	15,218	15,531	122,175	2,215	43,253	194,491	104,305	141,625
Percent	37.1%	8.0%	14.5%	56.3%	7.4%	38.6%	41.9%	34.7%	47.0%
Total	$1,723,922	$191,109	$107,185	$217,020	$29,942	$112,121	$464,715	$300,816	$301,015
Total percent	100.0%	100.0%	100.0%	100.0%	100.0%	100.0%	100.0%	100.0%	100.0%

Note: Dollar figures in thousands.

Table 6.7   **Distribution of Revenue Sources by Principal Source, Three-Year Totals, 1986–88**

Principal Source	Sum of Sources (%)	Federal (%)	State (%)	Local (%)	Other Government (%)	Corporate (%)	Private (%)	Endowment Income (%)	Earnings (%)
Federal	100.0	82.8	0.0	0.0	0.0	7.0	2.1	5.4	2.7
State	100.0	1.4	62.6	1.6	0.1	3.0	13.9	3.2	14.2
Local	100.0	2.8	5.4	51.6	1.0	3.9	19.3	5.0	11.2
Other government	100.0	4.2	2.3	0.0	72.3	1.5	11.4	2.0	6.3
Corporate	100.0	4.3	1.9	0.9	0.0	52.6	18.5	7.4	14.4
Private	100.0	2.2	1.4	2.9	0.2	7.5	58.8	13.0	14.0
Endowment	100.0	2.9	2.3	0.4	0.1	2.9	16.4	59.7	15.4
Earnings	100.0	2.3	2.0	0.7	0.0	4.5	17.7	23.5	49.5
Various	100.0	2.4	2.4	19.1	0.3	6.8	30.4	16.3	22.2
All sources	100.0	11.1	6.2	12.6	1.7	6.5	27.0	17.4	17.5

went to support museums through the National Endowment for the Arts, The National Endowment for the Humanities, and the Institute for Museum Services. An individual museum might obtain federal funds by applying for a grant under one or another of the programs directed to their support or, occasionally by lobbying for funds to support an exceptional project. A successful applicant (such as the anomalous case mentioned earlier) might increase federal support for its own budget to an exceptional 40 or 50 percent for a year or two, but nothing the museums do individually or collectively is likely to change the aggregate picture presented in tables 6.6 and 6.7.

Other sources of revenue provide more promising directions in which to look for increased art museum funding. One-third of all museum support comes from private contributions, including contributions from corporations. But museums whose principal revenue source is endowment income receive only one-fifth of their funding from these sources. Is this like the case of federal museum financing in which redistribution of a limited pie is all that is possible, or could an able development officer help such a museum achieve a substantial increase in its revenue from private sources? Or to put the question differently, the museums in the Various category are, on average, larger than the museums in any other category except for the Federal. Are they large because they choose to exploit many revenue-producing opportunities, including some neglected by museums with dependable endowment or government revenue?

Though the federal government and the several state governments that support museums focus their support on a small number of institutions, other revenue sources are far more eclectic. Consider corporate support. While there are four museums whose revenue from corporations averages more than one-half their budgets, together they receive only 14 percent of all the money corporations give to museums. Corporate support for museums in every category except State and Endowment averaged above $0.5 million per museum for the three year period. The 34 museums in the Various category averaged $1.3 million in corporate gifts, and received 7 percent of their revenue from corporations. The 15 Endowment museums averaged under $0.4 million, 3 percent of their revenue. Other examples of the same sort could be drawn from these tables, but one suffices to illustrate the principle.

The classification scheme used here contributes to this disparity. Naturally, if we group museums together on grounds that a large fraction of their revenue comes from one source, the fraction coming from other sources will tend to be small. But choices made by the museums themselves also contribute to the great variations in revenue patterns. A well-endowed museum may pass up opportunities for corporate or foundation support, possibly to avoid constraints such support sometimes carries and possibly because a secure revenue source weakens the incentive to develop other sources. There is some evidence, in both the revenue and in the expenditure data, suggesting that museums do choose to specialize as to revenue source, and that the patterns we see are not merely reflective of the classification scheme.

6.5.1   Earnings

There are revenue sources that seem to be closed to certain categories of museum. State and local governments do not contribute to the support of federal museums, deferring to the U.S. Congress, both for the spending and the associated taxing. Foundations and corporations pursue a variety of support policies that limit eligibility for their generosity. Museums in home-office cities may have better access to corporate gifts than museums in branch-office cities. Foundations welcome those supplicants seen to be pursuing objectives or performing services that suit the foundations' own purposes, which may be narrowly defined. A museum may find that its specialization, its size, its audience, or its location place it beyond the pale for a particular source of revenue.

No revenue source is entirely exempt from externally imposed restrictions. Policies of donors themselves may limit or bar a museum's reliance on certain revenue sources. Conditions in the museum's charter, or attached to a gift or an endowment, may prohibit or limit admissions charges. Considerations of security may prohibit rental of space in the museum for receptions and banquets unrelated to the museum's own operations. Ordinary market considerations having to do with location, the size and nature of the local market, and the nature of the collection limit what can be earned through admissions and retail sales. What sets earnings apart from the rest of the revenue sources is the extent to which they can be enhanced by marketing techniques employed in ordinary retail trade: advertising, pricing, product management, and promotions. Table 6.8 highlights the retail components of earnings: admissions, store, and restaurant revenue.

6.5.2   Admissions Revenue

Whether or not to charge for admission is a policy question that may go to the very heart of a museum's mission. For many museums, offering the public free access to its exhibitions is a central purpose. Above the entrance to the St. Louis Art Museum the words chiseled in stone read, "Free to All." Even museums whose admissions charges make up a substantial portion of revenue often provide free or very inexpensive access to their collections on certain days of the week and to specific groups. Museums almost always admit members free and many extend the privilege of free admission to members' guests. The practice of privileged access for members may be thought of as a trade-off between the earnings component of revenue and private contributions. The 1988 AAMD data include the results of a special survey on admissions charges. There were 135 responses to the survey, with 69 reporting that they charge admission and 65 reporting free admission. Among our 112 museums, 68 report at least some admissions revenue.

Table 6.8   Earned Revenue by Principal Source of Revenue, Three-Year Totals, 1986–88

Principal Source	Total Earnings	Admission Revenue		Store Revenue		Restaurant Revenue		Other Earnings
		Total	Per Admittance	Total	Per Sq. Foot	Total	Per Sq. Foot	
Federal	$ 5,044	$ 0	$0.00	$ 179	$ 8	$ 635	$15	$ 4,230
State	16,206	4,128	0.77	4,467	446	479	24	7,131
Local	18,055	2,574	0.33	6,470	389	286	16	8,725
Other government	2,208	153	0.05	978	164	80	5	997
Corporate	4,186	979	0.43	996	585	143	*	2,067
Private	38,666	8,766	0.62	10,311	348	664	27	18,924
Endowment	29,556	5,985	0.64	13,010	266	(460)	(17)	11,021
Earnings	45,469	8,984	2.05	9,600	718	835	49	26,050
Various	141,625	50,420	1.41	38,198	389	1,797	15	51,211
All museums	$301,015	$81,991	$0.75	$84,210	$343	$4,458	$15	$130,365

Note: Total figures are in thousands of dollars. Revenue per admittance and per square is in dollars.

*Square feet not reported in this category.

According to the survey, more than two-thirds of the museums that charge admission provide free access for at least some portion of one day of the week, with more than half of these sponsored by a donor (in effect, a gift conditioned on the granting of some free access). About one-third grant free admission to school tour groups and to other youth groups. Students and senior citizens often are admitted free of charge or at a nominal fee; members almost always are admitted free. Still, admissions provide a source of earnings second only to the museum store's contribution except for museums in the Various category, where admissions are the largest source of earnings, and the Federal category, where admissions are zero. Unfortunately, no dependable inferences can be drawn from the AAMD data as to the effect of admissions charges on museum attendance.

6.5.3   Store and Restaurant Revenue

Almost every museum sells something to its visitors, if nothing more than postcards depicting reproductions of works it exhibits. The largest museum stores offer a wide variety of reproductions, books, greeting cards, craft products, gift merchandise, and jewelry both in their stores and through catalogue sales to national clientele. One hundred museums reported store revenue net of direct costs in 1988 ranging (net of wages and benefits) from a high of $4.22 million down to minus $56 thousand, with floor space ranging from the Met's 32,000 square feet to a small museum with 50 square feet devoted to what must be a single counter featuring postcard reproductions and a few books. The average museum store occupies 2,400 square feet.

Museum restaurants are less common than stores and far less profitable; only one-third of the museums report restaurant revenue. Aggregate restaurant revenue is less than 5 percent of aggregate store revenue. While only 2 of the 100 museum stores lost money in 1988, 7 of the 38 restaurants operated in the red. Taking account of the rental value of the space devoted to these activities makes the comparison even more lopsided. If a square foot of museum has a rental value of $10, 91 stores and 12 restaurants operated in the black. If the rental value is $20, these numbers fall to 82 and 6.

These results are manifest in table 6.8. Museum stores produce, per square foot, 20 times the restaurant revenue. While the period we are looking at is too brief to permit calculation of a reliable trend, museums seem to be responding sensibly to the disparity. Aggregate store space, which was 233,000 square feet in 1986, increased by 6 percent over the next two years while restaurant space fell by 8 percent from 311,000 square feet. A seemingly unprofitable restaurant may contribute to revenue production in other categories or provide benefits not easily measured. The restaurant may provide a tax-exempt fringe benefit for museum employees in the form of subsidized meals, or it may help attract paying visitors to the museum (about one-third of the museums with restaurants charge restaurant patrons for admission). The shift of space from money-losing restaurants to moneymaking stores is evidence that operating in the black is among the values that guide museum management.

6.5.4 Other Earnings

Museums' earnings include tuition charges, fees for the use of facilities, fees paid to the reporting museum for exhibitions it organizes and sends on the road, the net proceeds of benefit balls and banquets, and so on. The AAMD survey reports these earnings in five separate categories, the largest of which, other earned income, accounts for 16 percent of earnings and just 3 percent of all revenue. All five of these revenue sources are grouped together in the other earnings category shown in Table 6.8.

A few details concealed from view by grouping deserve special comment. There are six museums whose chief source of revenue over the three-year period covered by the survey was earnings. Each received a far larger than average share of its revenue from at least two of the subcategories of earnings, and all did somewhat better than average in most subcategories. Particularly striking is the fact that these museums earned 20 percent of their revenue (41 percent of their earnings) from class tuition, as compared with an average of 1 percent.

6.5.5 Endowment

The governing body and management of an art museum need to be especially farseeing to choose endowment-raising over other means of increasing revenue. Endowment's advantage is that its dependable revenue permits long-range planning, but raising it calls for direct participation by the director and members of his or her board. Success in obtaining substantial gifts is uncertain as compared with a professional marketing effort aimed at increasing memberships or improving admissions revenue. The immediate payoff may seem small relative to the effort. The aggregate market value of museum endowment in 1988 was $2.4 billion, with 91 museums reporting that at least some portion of their revenue came from endowment income.

Despite the 1987 crash, endowment income tied earnings for second place as a source of revenue and grew faster than any other source, increasing over the period by $29 million out of a total increase in museum revenue of $106 million. Table 6.9 shows how endowment was divided among the nine groups. In this respect as in others, the nongovernment museums differ sharply from the government-supported museums. Except for the Smithsonian museums, which are well-endowed, government supported museums have far less endowment than the nongovernments and a far larger share of their endowments are earmarked for art acquisition.

Endowments generally come from private individuals, most often in the form of bequests. The strong, systematic difference between the two broad

Table 6.9   Market Value and Income of Museum Endowment by Principal Source of Revenue, 1986–88

Principal Source	Number of Museums	Endowment Total (1988)	Payout Rate (1988)	Endowment Income (1986–88)	Endowment Income for	
					Operations (1986–88)	Acquisitions (1986–88)
Federal	6	$ 153,714	2.9%	$ 10,940	$ 10,074	$ 867
State	9	33,827	10.2%	8,339	3,698	4,641
Local	11	73,882	5.9%	14,698	8,032	6,666
Other government	4	6,108	21.4%	4,329	716	3,613
Corporate	4	47,921	3.0%	3,237	2,154	1,083
Private	23	201,223	7.6%	48,184	35,778	12,406
Endowment	15	819,331	7.2%	145,452	114,483	30,969
Earnings	6	158,437	5.9%	29,007	21,576	7,431
Various	34	898,360	5.9%	130,576	104,305	26,271
Total	112	$2,392,804	6.4%	$394,761	$300,816	$93,946

Note: Dollar figures in thousands. Income figures are three-year totals. Payout rates are for a 91-museum subset.

groups may result from museum decisions not to seek this form of support, or it may reflect donor reluctance to endow publicly supported institutions, except for well-defined purposes.

The endowment data reveal a sharp contrast between the Endowed and the Private groups. Similar in average spending, they are the extremes among the nongovernment museums in the average size of their endowments, and, excluding the Corporate group, the extremes in their spending on development. The Endowed group spends 7 percent compared with Private's 11 percent (or, in an even more striking comparison, 11 percent of the overhead budget compared with 19). The significance of this comparison lies in the mechanics of fund-raising. Annual membership drives, which rely on costly mass-marketing techniques, frequently are little better than break-even operations. They are nevertheless justified by the fact that they are the most effective means for discovering large individual donors, some of whom ultimately become the source of new endowments. Mass-marketing techniques are aimed at enrolling ordinary members at a modest annual fee, but opportunities are offered to enroll in special categories of membership at higher fees. Members in these special categories receive extra attention: invitations to special events, gifts which cannot be obtained by others and which identify them as exceptionally generous donors, and personal invitations from fund-raising volunteers (the Privates are served by more than ten volunteers per full-time employee, as compared with an overall average of four) and museum executives to enter even more rarified donor categories.

Over the three years, the average of all museum membership revenue grew by 27 percent. For the Privates it grew by 40 percent on a base that was already half again as large as the average for all museums; the Endowed managed just 9 percent growth on a base only one-half as large as the average. This suggests that in fund-raising, the Privates emphasize annual giving, possibly at the expense of endowed funds, while the Endowed do the opposite. As a result, the book value of the Private group's endowments (which is a better measure of success in raising new endowment than market value) grew by only 18 percent, while the Endowed grew by 21 percent. In annual giving, the Private group's 31-point excess over the Endowed's was achieved by spending half again as much on development and by giving up 3 percentage points on new endowment, possibly a worthwhile trade-off, but not necessarily. What makes this comparison interesting is that another group, the Various, surpassed both the Private and the Endowed groups in the growth of its endowment. The Various group's membership revenue grew by 14 percent and its endowment grew by 26 percent over the same three years, suggesting that in their vigorous pursuit of revenue on all fronts, they exploit the synergies available in the simultaneous search for expendable funds and endowment.

A rough calculation based on more detailed data than are presented here, comparing the Various group with the Private, suggests that its extra 8 points in book endowment growth produced more spendable endowment income in one year than an extra 26 points of membership revenue, and it cost less to produce. A similar comparison suggests that the Various group's strategy, although it calls for slightly more development spending, produces far better results than the Endowment group's strategy.

The 1987 and 1988 surveys reported the market value of investments, so it is possible to calculate approximate individual payout rates. Using the 1988 data, which are the most complete, I calculated the payout rates for the 91 museums that reported both the market value of their endowments and endowment income. These museums accounted for 99 percent of reported endowment. Table 6.10 shows the results, both in terms of the number of museums employing a given payout rate and the total value of the endowment possessed by the museums in each payout rate class.

An important question that cannot be fully answered by the AAMD data is the extent to which the growth in endowment income is the result of raising payout rates to levels that are not sustainable. In 1988, more than three-quarters of the reporting museums, possessing about one-half of the reported endowment, paid out 5 percent or more of their endowment's market value as investment income. Whether or not this is a sustainable payout level depends on the real rate of return on their investments. The real rate of return on intermediate term treasury notes and bonds over long periods has generally been under 2 percent. There have been sustained periods in which the average real return on common stocks has been above 6 percent, but there have also been long periods in which the return has been much less than 6 percent, and even negative. Without knowing how well art museums manage their investments, it is safe to say that payouts above 5 percent almost certainly represent invasions of capital, a policy that may be helpful as a temporary measure in deal-

Table 6.10   Museum Endowment Payout Rates, 1988

Payout Rate (%)	Number of Museums	Market Value of Endowment	Percent of Market Value
Less than 3	5	$ 349,072	14.7
3–5	12	753,277	31.6
5–7	24	581,984	24.4
7–9	18	476,817	20.0
9–11	15	44,947	1.9
11–13	2	8,390	0.4
13–15	2	10,386	0.4
15–17	2	131,673	5.5
17–19	2	24,601	1.0
19–21	1	1,353	0.1
Greater than 21	8	9,406	0.4
Total	91	$2,382,500	100.0

Note: Dollar figures in thousands.

Table 6.11   **Revenue from Private Contributions by Principal Source of Revenue,
Three-Year Totals, 1986–88**

Principal Source	Sum of All Revenue Sources	Total Private Contributions	Foundation Grants	Member Revenue	Other Private
Federal	$ 185,289	$ 3,849	$ 1,472	$ 578	$ 1,799
Percent	100.0%	2.1%	0.8%	0.3%	1.0%
State	114,123	15,846	3,595	10,858	1,392
Percent	100.0%	13.9%	3.2%	9.5%	1.2%
Local	161,923	31,180	4,458	20,496	6,226
Percent	100.0%	19.3%	2.8%	12.7%	3.8%
Other government	35,079	3,996	987	1,757	1,252
Percent	100.0%	11.4%	2.8%	5.0%	3.6%
Corporate	29,127	5,384	1,171	1,476	2,737
Percent	100.0%	18.5%	4.0%	5.1%	9.4%
Private	275,903	162,256	75,674	59,789	26,793
Percent	100.0%	58.8%	27.4%	21.7%	9.7%
Endowment	191,718	31,453	9,649	14,257	7,547
Percent	100.0%	16.4%	5.0%	7.4%	3.9%
Earnings	91,946	16,260	2,368	11,417	2,475
Percent	100.0%	17.7%	2.6%	12.4%	2.7%
Various	638,813	194,491	43,561	115,264	35,666
Percent	100.0%	30.4%	6.8%	18.0%	5.6%
Total, all sources	$1,723,922	$464,715	$142,935	$235,893	$85,887
Percent	100.0%	27.0%	8.3%	13.7%	5.0%

Note: Dollar figures in thousands.

ing with unforseen adversity, but not one that can be a long-term solution to
rising costs and declining revenue from other sources.

6.5.6   Private Contributions

Private contributions, accounting for 27 percent of museum revenue, are
reported in the AAMD surveys in the three categories shown in Table 6.11.
More than 90 percent of all the museums receive membership contributions
and foundation gifts and grants. About two-thirds receive other private contributions, sums often directed to particular projects and in larger amounts than
memberships. One museum of the twenty-three whose chief revenue source is
private contributions receives all its revenue—more than half the foundation
support granted to all museums in the group—from one foundation dedicated
to its support. Eliminating that single museum changes the percentage distribution of private support for the group from 59, 27, 22, and 10 percent of the
revenue sum to 50, 13, 26, and 12, a pattern of support consistent with the
overall pattern, with about half of all private support coming in the form of
memberships. When we examine expenditure patterns, we will see that this
group devotes an almost 50 percent larger share of its budget to development

than the average of all museums, reflecting the decision of these museums to pursue private contributions. Note that the effect of the decision spills over; corporate contributions are the only other revenue source from which they derive more than their share of revenue, surpassing all groups except for the one whose chief source is corporate.

6.6 Expenditures

If revenue patterns are partly the result of choices museums make, some evidence of these choices will be found in the expenditure data. Heavy reliance on fund-raising calls for spending on development. A successful store or restaurant requires good management. Heavy visitor traffic raises the cost of security and maintenance. Museums that must compete for revenue in the marketplace may count their costs more carefully than museums that enjoy secure sources of funding. The AAMD survey data contain strong traces of these and similar relationships, suggesting that museums do not have their funding patterns thrust upon them by circumstances beyond their control, but rather choose among them, and so might diversify to reduce the risk involved in depending heavily on one source.

6.6.1   Compensation Expenditures

Museum payrolls over the three-year period amounted to more than $900 million, 46 percent of their budgets. The fraction varies from a high among the Federal museums of just under 60 percent to a low for the Various museums of just over 40 percent. These figures are shown in table 6.12. Taking the five nongovernment groups together, compensation averages 43 percent of budget compared with 53 percent for the four government-supported groups.

Table 6.12   **Museum Compensation Expenditures by Principal Source of Revenue, Three-Year Totals, 1986–88**

Principal Source	Total Expenditure	Salaries	Benefits	Total Compensation	Compensation Percentage
Federal	$ 177,253	$ 93,120	$ 12,116	$105,236	59.4
State	118,521	40,096	10,700	50,796	42.9
Local	153,356	66,329	12,864	79,193	51.6
Other government	35,391	16,234	3,937	20,171	57.0
Corporate	29,549	10,910	2,128	13,038	44.1
Private	268,659	106,158	17,381	123,540	46.0
Endowment	209,792	89,287	14,338	103,625	49.4
Earnings	124,307	47,412	6,715	54,127	43.5
Various	915,689	321,779	60,766	382,545	41.8
All sources	$2,032,517	$791,325	$140,946	$932,271	45.9

Note: Dollar figures in thousands.

This disparity may be due to differences in the composition of the museum staff, salary scale, and head count. The data used here do not permit analysis that would allocate the difference. The Smithsonian museums pay according to civil service salary-and-benefit scales, and other government-supported museums may be affected by similar provisions. Among the nongovernment groups, the Endowment museums, enjoying the most dependable source of revenue, spend the largest fraction on compensation. The Earnings and Various groups, most likely to be disciplined by the marketplace, spend the least.

6.6.2 Overhead Expenditures: Development, Administration, and Operations

Allocation of costs among the seven spending categories shown in tables 6.13 is somewhat arbitrary. Museum directors vary greatly in the time they devote to development work. It is unlikely that proper allocation is made in every case between administration and development. Large, multicollection museums tend to departmentalize and to delegate administrative and development responsibilities to curators and their subordinates, transferring to their curatorial budgets costs that smaller museums would record in the overhead categories. Still, comparisons of expenditure and revenue patterns reveal relationships consistent with the idea that they shape one another. Take, for example, the relationship between development and private gifts. From the low of the Federal museums, which spend 1 percent of their budgets on development and get 2 percent of their revenue from private gifts, to the high of the Privates, spending 11 percent and getting 59 percent, the relationship between development spending and success in fund-raising is strong. The Corporate group comprises museums that enjoy special relationships with particular corporations, so spend only half the average on development. The Privates, which depend most heavily on contributions—especially memberships— spend 11 percent on development, a larger fraction than any other group and 50 percent above the average fraction for all museums.

The Federal, State, and Other Government groups, comprising museums that are part of larger institutions, spend the least on administration, while the Earnings museums, with multiple enterprises to manage, spend the most. Locally supported museums, unlike the Smithsonian museums and state university museums, are free-standing institutions and their administrative spending mirrors that fact. The Endowment group's 27 percent spending on administration, like its compensation ratio, may be a consequence of its relative insulation from market forces.

Operations, which includes security, energy, and other costs of building operation, displays such patterns less clearly, but there are some. The Federal group, with the largest fraction going to operations, must cope with the heaviest visitor traffic of any of the groups, 16 visitors per square foot over the three-year period as compared with traffic in the range of 5 to 7 for all other groups.

Table 6.13 Museum Expenditures by Principal Source of Revenue, Three-Year Totals, 1986–88

Principal Source	Total	Curatorial Service	Conservation	Educational Programs	Library	Operations	Administration	Development
Federal	$ 165,969	$ 54,293	$ 5,800	$14,959	$ 7,038	$ 61,615	$ 20,515	$ 1,749
State	95,262	31,594	2,877	4,960	1,364	32,040	15,496	6,929
Local	119,605	32,810	2,991	9,743	2,632	38,525	25,212	7,691
Other government	31,775	9,795	527	3,966	298	10,808	5,492	890
Corporate	21,119	6,863	634	761	925	6,020	5,160	755
Private	218,756	66,948	6,514	17,446	2,730	54,885	46,239	23,994
Endowment	164,382	36,745	5,944	10,738	6,866	47,752	44,697	11,640
Earnings	63,811	16,530	2,346	5,140	858	16,275	17,684	4,977
Various	562,541	180,880	9,611	30,224	8,150	181,227	103,823	48,626
All sources	$1,443,219	$436,458	$37,245	$97,936	$30,861	$449,148	$284,319	$107,252

Note: Dollar figures in thousands.

6.6.3 Program Expenditures: Curatorial Service, Conservation, Education, and Library

Tables 6.14 and 6.15 show how much museums in the nine groups spend on programs and how they distribute their program spending among the four activities that make it up. Federal museums, depending for certain overhead services upon the larger institutions of which they are a part, spend the largest fractions, 49 percent, on programs. The Endowed group spends the least, 37 percent. Among the rest, there is little variation from the 42 percent average.

Normalizing program percentages by calculating them as fractions of total program expenditures instead of the larger total that includes overhead costs, greatly reduces the variation in allocations and rearranges the rankings. For all nine groups, the bulk of program spending goes to curatorial service. A museum's curators are responsible for management of its collections. They recommend acquisitions, prepare exhibitions, perform research, and publish. When the public visits a museum, it is the curator's work they go (and often pay) to see. The Various group spends the largest fraction, 79 percent, on curatorial service, consistent with the observation that curators in this group bear more than average responsibility for administration and development. The Endowed museums, which spend the least on programs also devote the smallest fraction of program spending to this component, consistent with the idea that they are relatively independent of nonendowment revenue.

Conservation expenditures make up a small portion of museum budgets, 3 percent overall, and whatever meaning lies buried in the variations is not visible to the naked eye. The large expenditures on education by the Other Government and Earnings groups are not surprising. Other Government comprises museums that are part of state universities, and 20 percent of the revenue of the Earnings group comes from class tuition. The large library expenditure by the Corporate group is explained by the fact that two of the four own exceptional specialized collections and maintain fine libraries bearing on their specialization.

6.6.4 Capital Expenditures and Expansion of the Physical Plant

The AAMD surveys include data on total capital expenditures, but provide no details as to various uses. It is possible, from the data in Table 6.16 to construct a crude estimate of the fraction of the capital budget that went to expansion of the physical plant. Taking an approximate cost of $100 per square foot, virtually all the Federal capital spending went to the 4.6 percent increase in total floor space, while for the Various group, just over one-tenth of the capital budget went to the building program.

There is a rough correspondence between the picture provided by table 6.16 and the overall financial fortunes of the several groups. Local museums (as I shall describe in Section 6.9, "Coping with Financial Problems") responded effectively to declining public support and were able to pursue aggressive

Table 6.14   Percentage Distribution of Museum Expenditures by Principal Source of Revenue, Three-Year Totals, 1986–88

Principal Source	Total (%)	Curatorial Service (%)	Conservation (%)	Education (%)	Library (%)	Operations (%)	Administration (%)	Development (%)
Federal	100.0	32.7	3.5	9.0	4.2	37.1	12.4	1.1
State	100.0	33.2	3.0	5.2	1.4	33.6	16.3	7.3
Local	100.0	27.4	2.5	8.1	2.2	32.2	21.1	6.4
Other government	100.0	30.8	1.7	12.5	0.9	34.0	17.3	2.8
Corporate	100.0	32.5	3.0	3.6	4.4	28.5	24.4	3.6
Private	100.0	30.6	3.0	8.0	1.2	25.1	21.1	11.0
Endowment	100.0	22.4	3.6	6.5	4.2	29.0	27.2	7.1
Earnings	100.0	25.9	3.7	8.1	1.3	25.5	27.7	7.8
Various	100.0	32.2	1.7	5.4	1.4	32.2	18.5	8.6
All sources	100.0	30.2	2.6	6.8	2.1	31.1	19.7	7.4

Table 6.15   **Distribution of Program Expenditures by Principal Source of Revenue, Three-Year Totals, 1986–88**

Principal Source	Total Expenditures	Program Expenditures	Program Percentage	Percentage of Total Program Expenditure Spent on				
				Curitorial	Conservation	Education	Library	Total
Federal	$ 165,969	$ 82,091	49.5	66.1	7.1	18.2	8.6	100.0
State	95,262	40,796	42.8	77.4	7.1	12.2	3.3	100.0
Local	119,605	48,176	40.3	68.1	6.2	20.2	5.5	100.0
Other government	31,775	14,585	45.9	67.2	3.6	27.2	2.0	100.0
Corporate	21,119	9,184	43.5	74.7	6.9	8.3	10.1	100.0
Private	218,756	93,638	42.8	71.5	7.0	18.6	2.9	100.0
Endowment	164,382	60,293	36.7	60.9	9.9	17.8	11.4	100.0
Earnings	63,811	24,874	39.0	66.5	9.4	20.7	3.4	100.0
Various	562,541	228,864	40.7	79.0	4.2	13.2	3.6	100.0
All sources	$1,443,219	$602,500	41.7	72.4	6.2	16.3	5.1	100.0

Note: Dollar figures in thousands.

Table 6.16   Museum Space and Capital Expenditures by Principal Source of Revenue, 1986–88

Principal Source	Building Size (1986, Sq. Ft)	Change (1986–88, Sq. Ft)	Percent Change (1986–88)	Change in Square Feet, 1986–88, for			Capital Spending, 1986–88	
				Exposition	Store	Restaurant	Amount	Percent of Total Spending
Federal	1,676.3	77.4	4.6	74.1	1.4	0.0	$ 8.171	4.6
State	1,151.6	35.6	3.1	27.1	−2.3	1.3	11.670	9.8
Local	1,408.4	222.0	15.8	159.3	1.3	−3.2	52.931	34.5
Other government	478.0	−10.0	−2.1	0.0	−0.2	0.1	6 196	17.5
Corporate	190.4	115.0	60.4	11.8	−0.9	0.0	12 683	42.9
Private	1,887.8	206.3	10.9	105.5	4.4	−1.1	11.297	4.2
Endowment	2,072.1	−81.4	−3.9	10.0	20.6	−3.7	13.474	6.4
Earnings	703.4	−13.3	−1.9	−23.2	1.3	0.6	24.377	19.6
Various	5,452.2	128.9	2.4	−63.9	−12.5	−17.8	103.562	11.3
Total	15,020.2	680.5	4.5	300.6	13.0	−23.8	$244,361	12.0

Note: All figures except for percentages are in thousands. Capital spending in a three-year total.

building programs, in contrast to the State museums, whose financial problems were less tractable. Both the Earnings and Endowment groups reported decreases in space, and both of them suffered either slow growth or decreases in their principal sources of revenue. The Various group, financially the healthiest, seems to pursue a slow and steady policy.

6.7 The Collection

The least satisfactory data produced by the surveys have to do with the value of the art owned by museums. The most recent two surveys asked both for the face value of the fine arts insurance carried by the museum and the fraction of total value of the collection this number represented. The 1988 data contain 94 answers to the first of these two questions and 73 answers to the second, making it possible to calculate a rough valuation of the collections for two-thirds of the museums. The missing third includes all the Smithsonian museums and many of the largest museums. Some self-insure, some are insured by a larger organization of which they are a part, and others answered the first question but not the second, probably on grounds that there is no reasonable way to calculate the value of a collection so large that placing it on the market would profoundly affect market prices. Because the collections owned by art museums constitute the bulk of their assets—something in the neighborhood of 90 percent—I have attempted to reach an estimate of their total value. The estimates obviously are crude, but plausible. Table 6.17 gives the results. The method for calculating the estimated values in table 6.17 is as follows:

1. For the 73 museums that answered both questions, calculate the implied values of the collections and sum. Although the table shows these sums for the individual groups, only the overall sum was used, not the individual sums. In some groups almost every museum answered both questions, but in others many responses were missing. None of the Smithsonian museums responded, so that the insurance value shown for that group is the insured value of the collection of one small university museum. Almost all the Privates answered both questions. Total insured value was $3.7 billion. Question two asked for the ratio of insured to total value. Answers to question 2 ranged all the way from 1 percent to 100 percent. Using this fraction, the insured face values were grossed up and summed, giving a total value for these 73 collections of just over $12 billion. But that left one-third of the museums unaccounted for.
2. The 73 museums that answered both questions in 1988 accounted for just over one-third of total expenditures for all 112 museums. The collection value for the missing one-third was calculated by assuming that as a group the value of their collections was proportional to their total spending, giving a total value for all collections of just over $32 billion, the number

Table 6.17   Insured and Estimated Value of Art Collections by Principal Source of Revenue, 1988

Principal Source	Number of Museums	Face Value of Insurance	Estimated Value of Art	Average Estimate
Federal	6	$ 20,000	$ 2,756,137	$459,356
State	9	168,425	1,793,851	199,317
Local	11	449,960	2,312,875	210,261
Other government	4	350,360	584,415	146,104
Corporate	4	138,500	427,144	106,786
Private	23	946,083	4,362,786	189,686
Endowment	15	421,500	3,433,696	228,913
Earnings	6	283,057	2,117,559	352,926
Various	34	999,167	14,516,936	426,969
All sources	112	$3,777,052	$32,305,400	$288,441

Note: Dollar figures in thousands.

that appears in table 6.17. This sum was portioned out to the nine groups in proportion to their total spending.

The value of the collections may be half the estimated amount or three times. Whatever it is, it dwarfs the value of the other two major museum assets, endowments—$2.4 billion—and buildings—$2.3 billion. If the financial statements of museums looked like ordinary financial statements, the value of the collection would overwhelm the rest of the assets side of the balance sheet. But art museums do not include the value of their collections in their balance sheets. The explanation lies in the sentence quoted earlier from the AAMD pamphlet, "Professional Practices in Art Museums:" "Deaccessioning should be related to [collection] policy rather than to exigencies of the moment, and funds obtained through disposal must be used to replenish the collection." The collection is not a fungible asset.

Imagine that an art museum owns a collection worth $100 million, but that the collection is housed so miserably as to severely limit public access to it and even to place its preservation at risk (through inadequate climate control, poor security, etc.). By selling off about $10 million worth of its collection, it could build a better than average building to house, exhibit, and protect the remainder. Will the museum do so? Possibly, but not with the blessing of the Association of Art Museum Directors. The prohibition may seem senseless, but there is sense to it, nevertheless. Table 6.18 shows that over the three-year period, art museums received $280 million in gifts of art and purchased another $267 million, of which $94 million came from endowed funds especially earmarked for that purpose. In addition, an unknown portion of the remaining $173 million worth of purchased art may have been paid for with expendable gifts expressly intended for that purpose. Were it possible for a museum to sell art from its collection to pay current bills or fund capital proj-

Table 6.18   **Value and Number of Purchased and Donated Works of Art by Principal Source of Revenue, Three-Year Totals, 1986–88**

Principal Source	Purchased Art		Endowed Purchases	Donated Art	
	Value	Number		Value	Number
Federal	$ 29,090	1,057	$ 867	$ 16,476	2,126
State	8,145	998	4,641	7,794	2,519
Local	22,511	2,605	6,666	23,687	8,688
Other government	3,623	271	3,613	4,706	2,125
Corporate	3,595	950	1,083	2,739	2,221
Private	50,436	2,992	12,406	43,094	29,987
Endowment	37,926	7,176	30,969	19,649	5,514
Earnings	9,052	658	7,431	20,771	2,571
Various	102,420	48,554	26,271	141,329	22,020
Total	$266,800	65,261	$93,946	$280,246	77,771

Note: Dollar figures in thousands.

ects, the intentions of donors who require that their gifts enhance the collection might easily be frustrated. The director of such a museum would have difficulty providing necessary assurances to potential donors of art or of funds for the purchase of art. The prohibition against the sale of art except to allow the purchase of more art solves this problem, but raises another in its place.

Preserving and exhibiting art costs money. The mere expansion of the collection imposes growing budgetary requirements for storage space, security, climate control, conservation, and insurance. Exhibiting a growing collection calls for expanded curatorial service and, possibly, new exhibition space. A museum that succeeds in attracting gifts of art without at the same time attracting the funds needed to care for it and exhibit it, finds itself under increasing budget pressure.

6.8 The Effects of Size

Of the nine largest art museums in the United States, five are in the Various group that draws its revenue broadly from a variety of sources. These five museums—the Metropolitan Museum of Art, the Chicago Art Institute, the Museum of Modern Art, the Los Angeles County Museum of Art, and the Philadelphia Museum of Art—account for about 75 percent of the aggregate expenditures of the group. Table 6.19 gives several measures that show how large the big five are relative to the smaller twenty-nine. Tables 6.20 and 6.21 compare the revenue and expenditure patterns of the two subgroups. Comparison of the big five with the twenty-nine smaller museums in the group supports the idea that classification on the basis of revenue source uncovers homogeneous patterns of finance and budgeting. Aside from various measures of sheer size, such as total spending, building size, and attendance, the two

Table 6.19 Characteristics of Museum in the Various Group, Classified by Spending Level, 1986–88

Total Spending	Number of Museums	Total Revenue	Total Expenditure	Full-Time Employees (1988)	Buildings (Sq. Feet) (1988)	Attendance	Endowment Market Value (1988)
$50 million or more	5	$734,111	$698,640	3,608	3,435,230	23,356	$662,665
Percent	14.7%	76.6%	76.3%	75.2%	61.6%	65.2%	75.2%
Less than $50 million	29	$224,536	$217,049	1,188	2,145,843	12,462	$218,179
Percent	85.3%	23.4%	23.7%	24.8%	38.4%	34.8%	24.8%
Total	34	$958,646	$915,689	4,796	5,581,073	35,818	$880,843
Percent	100.0%	100.0%	100.0%	100.0%	100.0%	100.0%	100.0%

Note: Attendance and all dollar figures are in thousands and, except for endowment, are three-year totals.

Table 6.20   Principal Revenue Sources of Museums in the Various Group, Classified by Spending Level, Three-Year Totals, 1986–88

Total Spending	Total	Federal	State	Local	Other Government	Corporate	Private	Endowment Income	Earnings
$50 million or more	$438,855	$6,096	$9,446	$89,801	$ 704	$26,583	$135,333	$70,218	$100,675
Percent	100.0%	1.4%	2.2%	20.5%	0.2%	6.1%	30.8%	16.0%	22.9%
Less than $50 million	199,958	9,122	6,085	32,374	1,512	16,671	59,159	34,087	40,950
Percent	100.0%	4.6%	3.0%	16.2%	0.8%	8.3%	29.6%	17.0%	20.5%

Note: Dollar figures in thousands.

Table 6.21   Spending Patterns of Museums in the Various Group, Classified by Spending Level, Three-Year Totals, 1986–88

Total Spending	Total Expenditures	Curatorial Service	Conservation	Educational Programs	Library	Operations	Administration	Development
$50 million or more	$381,709	$121,915	$5,283	$18,896	$5,622	$138,382	$65,063	$26,549
Percent	100.0%	31.9%	1.4%	5.0%	1.5%	36.3%	17.0%	7.0%
Less than $50 million	180,832	58,965	4,328	11,328	2,528	42,846	38,761	22,077
Percent	100.0%	32.6%	2.4%	6.3%	1.4%	23.7%	21.4%	12.2%

Note: Dollar figures in thousands.

groups are remarkably similar in their revenue and spending patterns. For example, both groups receive one-quarter of their revenue from government sources—with the small museums doing better at the federal level and slightly worse at the local level than the large museums, but conforming well to the group pattern in both cases. Both groups receive three-quarters of their revenue from private sources, with the small museums getting a larger share from contributions and a smaller share from earnings than the large museums, but again, conforming to the group pattern.

The division between overhead and program budgets is almost identical for the two groups, 60 percent to 40 percent. The small museums spend more of their overhead budget on administration and development and less on operations. The program budgets of the two groups are nearly identical.

Four other groups each include one of the large museums: Federal, the National Gallery of Art; State, the Detroit Institute of Arts; Endowed, the Winterthur Museum and Garden; and Earnings, the Boston Museum of Fine Arts. Each accounts for a large fraction of its group's spending (ranging from about three-quarters for Boston to about one-fifth for Winterthur), and each conforms almost as well to the revenue and spending patterns of its group as the five various museums do to theirs.

6.9 Coping with Financial Problems

The AAMD survey museums, during the 1986–88 period, were adding space at an annual rate of 2.3 percent, slightly less than the 4 percent average annual rate that has quadrupled U.S. art museum space since 1950; employment was growing at about 6 percent; payroll, 10 percent; and total spending, 9 percent. Over the same two-year span, the Consumer Price Index was rising at a 3.8 percent annual rate and wages were rising at 2.8 percent. Program budgets were growing slower than overhead budgets, with the curatorial budget—which claims the lion's share of program spending—growing at a rate of just under 7 percent. In all but one of these measures every group showed at least some growth.

Not all groups fared equally well. Of the 680,000 square feet of building space added between 1986 and 1988, one-third went to the Locals, another third went to the Privates, most of the remaining one-third was divided between the Corporate and Various groups, and the endowed museums reported shrinkage of about 4 percent. While spending was up for all groups, the rates of increase ranged from a low of under 2 percent for the Corporates to a high of 15 for the Locals. For the three-year period, the 112 museums reported total budget surpluses amounting to $62 million on total spending of more than $2 billion. But at least one group reported a budget deficit in each of the three years, five groups reported deficits in one or another of the three years, and more than half the individual museums reported at least one of its three annual budgets in the red.

A great deal of attention is focused on the role of the federal government in contributing to the distress many art museums suffer. Decreases in federal funding have adversely affected almost all museum groups. For most, the effect on the overall budget was small because, except for the Smithsonian museums, no group received more than about 4 percent of its revenue from this source. Overall, federal funding for art museums rose about 8 percent from 1986 to 1988; this figure reflects a 12-percent increase for the Smithsonian art museums, a 4-percent increase in art museum funding from the National Endowment for the Arts, a 42-percent decrease from the National Endowment for the Humanities, and a 20-percent decrease from the Institute of Museum Services.

We have, then, a picture of modest growth, unevenly distributed among the museum groups, and frequently recurring financial difficulties to be dealt with. What are the sources of the difficulties, and how do museums cope with them? Museums, concentrated as they are in the largest metropolitan areas, recruiting professional staff in a national market, and purchasing works of art in an international market, tend to face similar rising costs, but because they differ greatly from one another in their funding patterns, the effect of the slowing growth or decline of a particular source falls heavily on some and lightly on others. They do not all respond in the same way. A common financial problem facing them all is that, at all levels of government, support for art museums is growing too slowly to accommodate rising costs. The responses of the State and Local museums provide an interesting contrast. They are similar in size and in many of the characteristics we have examined, but in one crucial respect they differ. All but one of the nine State museums are located in metropolitan areas, with a population in 1984 of 600,000 or less, while all but one of the eleven Local museums are in metropolitan areas with population of 900,000 or more. Thus they differed greatly in their access to private alternatives to their chief funding sources.

Local government's support for the Local museums grew at about a 7 percent annual rate. Federal, other government, and endowment revenue all fell, but they were small to begin with. To sustain a far greater rate of budget growth (between 11 and 15 percent, depending on which of two conflicting aggregates is used for the calculation) than local support would allow, the Locals turned to private gifts for additional support and were successful on almost every front, more than doubling private gift revenue between 1986 and 1988, and raising it from 14 percent of their revenue to 24 percent, while their local government revenue fell from above 53 percent of their revenue to below 50 percent. In their membership drives, rather than increasing the number of members, they concentrated on increasing the size of membership gifts and raised it from an average of $36 to $68. Even more effective, they doubled their revenue from private foundation grants and tripled the amount of large private gifts.

At the same time, state government's support for State museums grew at about 3.5 percent, half the Local rate. Like the Locals, they lost some of their support from other sources—federal, local, other government, and corporate—but unlike the Locals, there was not much they could do to make up their revenue shortfalls. They, too, made an effort to cultivate private gifts, but were successful only in the membership portion, starting from a much smaller base, and actually lost support in the form of private foundation grants and large private gifts. They were helped slightly by the fact that the market value of their endowments and the spendable income it produced doubled, but publicly supported museums have relatively small endowments, and even doubled they do not amount to much. How then are the state museums coping with their slow revenue growth? Between 1986 and 1988, they limited their annual spending growth to about 4 percent and dipped into reserves. They shrank their curatorial spending by about 5 percent, while the Locals grew by about two-thirds. The States limited expenditure growth in most program and all overhead categories, added very little new space, and purchased about one-third as much art as the Locals ($8 million versus $23 million). It is impossible to tell from the AAMD data whether these are long-term trends or whether 1986 through 1988 just happened to be three years that were good for the Locals and bad for the States.

Shrinking public support for museums is not the only cause of financial distress. Though the 1986–1988 data do not provide evidence for it, museums are vulnerable to the vicissitudes of local and national economic performance. Also, aspects of public policy other than direct support—primarily tax policy—affect museums. Museum store revenue fell dramatically in the three groups in which the store dollar volume was largest: Endowment, Earnings, and various. Between 1986 and 1988, reported store earnings fell 37, 19, and 46 percent for these three groups. These decreases may have been fluctuations of the sort that all retailers experience from time to time, and they may have been due partly to accounting changes in response to, or in anticipation of, tougher enforcement of the unrelated business income tax. Taking them at face value, museum earnings, on average, did not grow at all between 1986 and 1988, and for two groups, Earnings and Endowment, they fell by 13 and 17 percent, a far more serious blow to the Earnings group because half its revenue came from that single source as compared with Endowment's 15 percent. The Earnings museums maintained a 13-percent annual growth rate in their spending by increasing private giving at a 13-percent annual rate and by reducing their annual surplus from about $2.5 million to almost zero. Adding to the misery of the Endowment group's loss of earnings, they suffered a far more serious 17-percent decrease in private giving. They dealt with the problem and maintained a 14-percent growth rate by increasing their endowment payout from just over 5 percent to just over 7 percent, probably not a long-run, sustainable, real rate of return. For the various group, the decrease in museum store earnings was offset by increases in earnings from other sources—admissions, tuition, and fees—so that total earnings actually rose by 2 percent. Diversification seems to pay.

Another aspect of tax policy seems to have hit museums especially hard during the period under examination. The 1986 Tax Reform Act, by lowering the highest marginal income tax rates, by tightening the procedures for determining the value of contributions in kind, and by limiting deductibility to original cost rather than appreciated fair market value, had a severely depressing effect on donations of works of art to museums. Coming at a time when the rising level of fine art prices was already a burden for acquisition budgets, the immediate effect was dramatic. Between 1986 and 1988, the value of donated art fell 54 percent.

The decreases were felt by all but three of the nine groups, and in the groups that escaped the decrease, large 1988 gifts to a single museum in each of the three groups made the difference between plus and minus. The result of the change in tax policy may have been both an acceleration of giving in 1986, in anticipation of the change, and a permanent decrease in giving, in response to the change. The waters are slightly muddied by the fact that one museum received a single gift in 1986 that accounted for almost one-third of the value of all donated art in that year. I do not know whether anticipation of the tax change affected the timing of that impressive gift or the decision to make it. Deletion of this one gift from the data changes the magnitude, but not the direction of change, even in the group to which the fortunate museum belongs. Excluding it, total donations of art fell by 25 percent instead of 54 percent, and for the particular group, 52 percent instead of 80 percent.

6.10 Conclusion

Of the many cultural institutions striving for stable growth, art museums are among the more fortunate because their opportunities to substitute new funding sources for old are more numerous. The daily traffic of a museum combined with the expert knowledge resident within its walls is what enables the museum store to make its 10 percent contribution to the revenue of museums that depend primarily on earnings. It is the staff's expert knowledge that makes it possible for the museum to conduct classes that bring another 20 percent.

Most orchestras and opera companies have little to sell beyond the sound of their music. The most valuable assets they employ, the skills of their musicians, belong to the musicians, not to the institutions. A museum, in hard times, may trim one or another of its programs and lay off personnel without immediate visible effect on its principal public function, an option not available to the performing arts. The contribution of memento sales to an orchestra's revenue is trivial, and musical tuition income goes to the musicians, not to the institution.

Important to the growth of a museum is the expansion of its collection. Rich connoisseurs of music may bestow an occasional fiddle—again, most often upon an individual performer, not the institution—but nothing in the musical world matches the benefaction of the rich collector of fine art whose greatest wish is to share his or her treasures with the public. In the three years from 1986 to 1988, U.S. museums were given $280 million in art, more than half their total acquisitions in those years.

Museums, in their efforts to achieve stable growth, might explore the advantages of diversifying their sources of revenue, as about one-third of them, the group I have called Various, now do. The AAMD data cover too brief a period and are too shaky to prove the superiority of the diversification strategy followed by museums in the Various group, but there are two shreds of evidence. First, except for the Federal group, the average Various museum is at least twice as large as the average member of any other group, a fact possibly, but not probably, due simply to greater age. Second, the Various group exhibits sustainable rates of growth in every program expenditure category, ranging from 3-percent annual growth for conservation to 10-percent annual growth in the library budget. In all the other groups but two, at least one program was shrinking while another was growing—at a rate too great to sustain and suggestive of a need to repair a growing deficiency.

Not every museum will have all avenues of diversification open to it, and some of them will choose, for perfectly sound reasons, not to diversify. A museum created by the action of state government in a metropolitan area too small to provide adequate private support may have little choice but to suffer the pains of declining levels of state support. A museum created exclusively for the purpose of displaying a particularly important private collection and adequately endowed for that purpose may have little reason to seek other sources of revenue. Still, the data suggest that many museums do have such choices to make and, when pressed, they do explore new possibilities. Particularly striking in this respect are the museums in the Local group which in many respects seem to be moving toward revenue source patterns that resemble the various patterns.

My examples of museum responses to adverse revenue shifts depend for their merit on the reliability that remains when one set of moderately unreliable numbers is subtracted from another and then taken as a percentage. The examples make sense, but it would be easy to find other examples that make less sense. They should be taken, therefore, not so much as representations of what happened, but as illustrations of the potentialities suggested by patterns discernable in the AAMD data.

Appendix A
Association of Art Museum Directors Statistical Survey Questionnaire

Association of Art Museum Directors
1988 Statistical Survey

In completing this part of the survey, please use data from your most recently completed fiscal year. The analysis of data supplied in this portion of the survey is designed to permit each museum to compare itself with other similar institutions. The results of the survey will be published question by question with responses sorted numerically in descending order.

It is important that an entry be made for each element of requested data. Do not leave blank lines. If, for example, you do not have any income from a particular source, enter "0". If data is not available, please enter "N.A. Enter financial data rounded to the nearest whole dollar.

1. Facilities, Memberships and Attendance (see note)
   A. Total Building Space _____ square feet
   B. Exhibition Space _____ square feet
   C. Museum Store Space _____ square feet
   D. Food Service Space _____ square feet
   E. Total Number of Individual/
      Family Memberships _____
   F. Total number of corporate
      Membership/Contributors _____
   G. Total Number of Volunteers _____
   H. Annual Attendance (FY 1987) _____

2. Financial Data - Income, (FY'87) (see note)
   A. Total Current Operating Income (see note) $_____
   B. Government Support (see note)
      Federal Total $_____
         1. NEA $_____
         2. NEH $_____
         3. IMS $_____
         4. Other $_____
      State or Province $_____
      County $_____
      City $_____
      Other government $_____
   C. Private Support, including membership income   (see note)
      Corporate contributions $_____
      Foundations $_____
      Individual/Family
         memberships & contributions $_____
      Other private support $_____
   D. Investment Income (see note)
      For General Operations $_____
      For acquisitions of art $_____
   E. Earned Income, Net (see note)
      Admissions $_____
      Concerts, Lectures, Films $_____
      Museum Store $_____
      Restaurant $_____
      Class Tuitions $_____
      Special Events $_____
      Participation Fees $_____
      Other Earned Income $_____

Note: Please refer to "Instructions and Definitions" before completing survey.

3. FINANCIAL DATA — EXPENDITURE (FY '87 (see note)

    A. Total Current Operating Expenditures (see note) $_____

    B. Personnel (see note)
        Total salaries $_____
        Total benefits $_____

    C. Cost of Program and Support
        Activities. (Include salaries but
        exclude space allocation.)
        (see note)
                Curatorial, Exhibitions $_____
                Conservation $_____
                Education $_____
                Library $_____
                Security $_____
                Energy (HVAC, lighting) $_____
                Administration $_____
                Development $_____
                Building Maintenance $_____
                Capital Improvements/Additions $_____

    D. Surplus / (Deficit) (see note)

                FY 1987 Surplus (Deficit) $_____
                Accumulated Reserve (Deficit) $_____

4. ACQUISITIONS (see note)

    A. Cost of Art Purchased in FY 1987 $_____
        Number of objects:_____

    B. Value of Art Donated in FY 1987 $_____
        Number of objects:_____

    C. Amount of insurance carried on
        collections $_____

    D. Percent of estimated total value
        of collection covered by insurance   _____%

5. ENDOWMENT

    A. Current Book Value $_____
    B. Current Market Value $_____

Note: Please refer to "Instructions and Definitions" before completing survey.

| |
| Please do not write in this space |
| |
| AAMD Code # |
| MSA Code |
| |

Please return questionnaire to:
Association of Art Museum Directors
P.O. Box 941
Dayton, Ohio 45401

INSTRUCTIONS AND DEFINITIONS
1988 AAMD STATISTICAL SURVEY

1. FACILITIES, MEMBERSHIPS AND ATTENDANCE

A. Use square footage for all enclosed building areas, regardless of function.

B. Use square footage for areas used for display of permanent collection and/or temporary exhibitions.

C. Use square footage for all space devoted to store (sales, storage, etc.)

D. Use square footage for all space devoted to restaurant (dining, serving, kitchen, etc.)

E, F. Use "membership units": a family membership = 1 unit; an individual membership = 1 unit, a corporate membership = 1 unit.

G. Use total number of all volunteers (Trustees, Education Volunteers, Fund Raising Volunteers, etc.)

H. Enter the total number of visitors for all programs, including those participating in extension/outreach programs.

2. FINANCIAL DATA - INCOME

A. Include all current operating income. Current income is defined as income received and reported during the current fiscal year. Do not include deferred income (pledges or prepaid commitments for future years). Do not include include income for Capital projects such as building or major renovation.

NOTE: The figure entered here may or may not equal the sum of the following income areas due to differences in internal reporting procedures for restricted funds.

B. Include only dollar grants or contributions. Do not include in-kind contributions such as utilities, maintenance services, etc.

C. Include all private, contributed income including membership fees, program sponsorships and other funds donated by individuals, foundations or corporations whether the donations are restricted or unrestricted, so long as these donations meet the definition of Current funds.

D. Include income from all investments (endowment funds as well as funds invested in short term certificates of deposit). Do not include gains or losses on sales of investments unless these are "realized" gains that were treated as current income.
"General Operation" includes all income, whether or not restricted, for all purposes other than the acquisition of works of art.
"For Acquisitions of Art" should include all income from investments designated or restricted as acquisitions funds, whether these are "operating" or "restricted" funds.

E. Report all earned income as net of direct expenses (eg. wages) but do not net out space allocation or utilities.

"Admissions" should include both fees charged to enter the museum and fees charged to enter special exhibitions.

"Class Tuitions" should include tuitions and other charges made in conjunction with classes, workshops and other organized ancillary activities such as collector's groups, unless these are included above as categories of membership.

"Special Events" should include revenue from fundraisers such as benefit balls.

"Participation Fees" should include revenue from exhibitions organized by the reporting institution.

"Other earned income" should include such miscellaneous revenue as building rentals.

3. FINANCIAL DATA - EXPENDITURES

A. Include all current operating expenditures. Do not include depreciation.
In cases where a parent, or other institution (eg. city or university) provides services such as security, utilities, etc. please estimate the expenditures if you cannot obtain specific amounts.
NOTE: The figure entered here will not equal the sum of the following expense areas due to differences in internal reporting procedures for restricted funds and because wage information is duplicated in the Program and Support entries.

B. "Total Salaries" should include wages paid to part time and hourly employees as well as full time, salaried employees. Cost of services provided on a contractual basis (eg. Security, Accounting) should also be included.

"Total Benefits" should include any amount paid by the employer on such benefits as insurance, pension or retirement programs. Do not include FICA (Social Security). Do not include vacation, holidays or sick leave.

C. "Cost of Program and Support Activities" should include all allocable <u>direct</u> expenditures for each department/function such as wages, supplies, travel, insurance, exhibition expense, etc. Do <u>not</u> pro-rate support services, utilities or space utilization among program areas.

"Curatorial, Exhibitions" should include the Registrar's office.

"Development" should include all fundraising expenses including those of the Membership office. Include Public Relations and Marketing expenses in this category.

"Administration" should not include building maintenance, energy or security since these amounts are requested separately.
Do not include expenditures already netted out of revenue areas such as store or restaurant.

"Capital Improvements" should include any building or renovation program.
<u>Note:</u> In most cases the income enabling these expenditures will not have been reported in part 2 (above) since such income is not generally treated as "operating" income.

D. "Surplus" and "Deficit" should be defined in terms of Current Operating Funds after any transfers to or from restricted funds but before any adjustments for capital additions. Changes in Property Funds (depreciation or capitalized expenses) or Endowment Funds (contributions and/or realized or unrealized investment gains or losses) should not be reflected in this item.
    "Accumulated Surplus / (Deficit)" should be reported as the sum of any unappropriated fund balance plus working capital or cash reserve funds.

4. ACQUISITIONS

A. "Cost of Art Purchased" should include the total dollars spent on acquisitions from all sources whether "operating" or "restricted" (endowment income, contributed funds or the proceeds of deaccessions or fundraisers for this purpose). This item may include costs related to acquisition such as shipping and insurance if your institution's accounting system normally allocates such expenses to acquisitions.

B. "Value of Art Donated" may include either the value of a gift established by the donor at the time of the gift or the value of a gift established by your museum for insurance purposes in lieu of any value stated by the donor.

C. "Amount of Insurance Carried on Collection" - state the total amount of insurance coverage carried. If self-insured, state the amount of reserve carried.

D. "Percent of Total Value of Collection Covered by Insurance" - Divide limits of coverage of permanent collection by the total <u>current market value</u> of the collection. Total current market value may be estimated.

5. ENDOWMENT

Include funds treated as endowments, whether they are permanent, term or quasi endowments.

Appendix B
U.S. Art Museums, Grouped According to Size of Metropolitan Area in Which They Are Located

Ten Largest Metropolitan Areas

Asia Society Galleries, New York, NY
Brooklyn Museum, Brooklyn, NY
Frick Collection, New York, NY
Metropolitan Museum of Art, New York, NY
Museum of Modern Art, New York, NY
New Museum of Contemporary Art, New York, NY
Newark Museum, Newark, NJ
Pierpont Morgan Library, New York, NY
Whitney Museum of American Art, New York, NY
California State University Art Museum, Long Beach, CA
J. Paul Getty Museum, Malibu, CA
Los Angeles County Museum of Art, Los Angeles, CA
Newport Harbor Art Museum, Newport Beach, CA
Art Institute of Chicago, Chicago, IL
Chicago Museum of Contemporary Art, Chicago, IL
Institute of Contemporary Art, Philadelphia, PA
Pennsylvania Academy of the Fine Arts, Philadelphia, PA
Philadelphia Museum of Art, Philadelphia, PA
Asian Art Museum of San Francisco, San Francisco, CA
Fine Arts Museums of San Francisco, San Francisco, CA
San Francisco Museum of Modern Art, San Francisco, CA
University Art Museum—Berkeley, Berkeley, CA
Detroit Institute of Arts, Detroit, MI
University of Michigan Museum of Art, Ann Arbor, MI
Cranbrook Academy of Art Museum, Bloomfield Hills, MI
DeCordova and Dana Museum, Lincoln, MA
Harvard University Art Museums, Cambridge, MA

Boston Museum of Fine Arts, Boston, MA
Houston Contemporary Arts Museum, Houston, TX
Houston Museum of Fine Arts, Houston, TX
National Museum of American Art, Washington, DC
National Gallery of Art, Washington, DC
National Museum of African Art, Washington, DC
Hirshhorn Museum and Sculpture Garden, Washington, DC
National Portrait Gallery, Washington, DC
Amon Carter Museum, Fort Worth, TX
Dallas Museum of Art, Dallas, TX
Modern Art Museum of Fort Worth, Fort Worth, TX

Second Ten Metropolitan Areas

Center for the Fine Arts, Miami, FL
Akron Art Museum, Akron, OH
Cleveland Museum of Art, Cleveland, OH
Saint Louis Art Museum, St. Louis, MO
Washington University Gallery of Art, St. Louis, MO
High Museum of Art, Atlanta, GA
Baltimore Museum of Art, Baltimore, MD
Walters Art Gallery, Baltimore, MD
Minneapolis Institute of Arts, Minneapolis, MN
University of Minnesota Art Museum, Minneapolis, MN
Walker Art Center, Minneapolis, MN
Tacoma Art Museum, Tacoma, WA
Seattle Art Museum, Seattle, WA
La Jolla Museum of Contemporary Art, La Jolla, CA
San Diego Museum of Art, San Diego, CA
Montclair Art Museum, Montclair, NJ
Tampa Museum, Tampa, FL

Third Ten Metropolitan Areas

Denver Art Museum, Denver, CO
Phoenix Art Museum, Phoenix, AZ
Cincinnati Art Museum, Cincinnati, OH
Columbus Museum of Art,
    Columbus, OH
Taft Museum, Cincinnati, OH
Milwaukee Art Museum,
    Milwaukee, WI
New Orleans Museum of Art, New
    Orleans, LA
Chrysler Museum, Norfolk, VA
Albright-Knox Art Gallery, Buffalo, NY
Indianapolis Museum of Art,
    Indianapolis, IN
San Antonio Museum of Art, San
    Antonio, TX

Fourth Ten Metropolitan Areas

Wadsworth Atheneum, Hartford, CT
International Museum of Photography,
    Rochester, NY
J. B. Speed Art Museum,
    Louisville, KY
Memphis Brooks Museum of Art,
    Memphis, TN
Dayton Art Institute, Dayton, OH
Birmingham Museum of Art,
    Birmingham, AL
Rhode Island School of Design
    Museum, Providence, RI
Clark Art Institute, Williamstown, MA
Virginia Museum of Fine Arts,
    Richmond, VA
Yale University Art Gallery, New
    Haven, CT

Fifth Ten Metropolitan Areas

Gilcrease Institute of American Art,
    Tulsa, OK
Philbrook Art Center, Tulsa, OK
Worcester Art Museum, Worcester, MA
Everson Museum of Art, Syracuse, NY
Allentown Art Museum, Allentown, PA
Huntington Art Gallery, Austin, TX
Laguna Gloria Art Museum, Austin, TX
Toledo Museum of Art, Toledo, OH
Ackland Art Museum, Chapel Hill, NC

North Carolina Museum of Art,
    Raleigh, NC
Joslyn Art Museum, Omaha, NE
Tucson Museum of Art, Tucson, AZ
Delaware Art Museum,
    Wilmington, DE
Winterthur Museum and Gardens,
    Winterthur, DE

Sixth Ten Metropolitan Areas

Flint Institute of Arts, Flint, MI
Elvehjem Museum of Art, Madison, WI
Madison Art Center, Madison, WI
University of Kentucky Art Museum,
    Lexington, KY
Santa Barbara Museum of Art, Santa
    Barbara, CA
Munson-Williams-Proctor Art Institute,
    Utica, NY
Princeton Art Museum, Princeton, NJ
Lyman Allyn Museum, New
    London, CT
Ringling Museum of Art, Sarasota, FL
Telfair Academy of Arts and Sciences,
    Savannah, GA
Portland (Maine) Museum of Art,
    Portland, ME

Six Smallest Metropolitan Areas

Huntsville Museum of Art,
    Huntsville, AL
Sheldon Memorial Art Gallery,
    Lincoln, NE
Cedar Rapids Museum of Art, Cedar
    Rapids, IA
Snite Museum, Notre Dame, IN
Georgia Museum of Art, Athens, GA
Spencer Museum of Art, Lawrence, KS

Nonmetropolitan Areas

Buffalo Bill Historical Center,
    Cody, WY
Corning Museum of Glass,
    Corning, NY
Herbert F. Johnson Museum of Art,
    Ithaca, NY
Hood Museum of Art, Hanover, NH
Southern Illinois University Museum,
    Carbondale, IL

Appendix C
U.S. Art Museums, Grouped According to Principal Source of Revenue

Federal Government

Hirshhorn Museum and Sculpture
  Garden, Washington, DC
National Gallery of Art,
  Washington, DC
National Museum of African Art,
  Washington, DC
National Museum of American Art,
  Washington, DC
National Portrait Gallery,
  Washington, DC
Washington University Gallery of Art,
  St. Louis, MO

State Government

Ackland Art Museum, Chapel Hill, NC
Detroit Institute of Arts, Detroit, MI
Georgia Museum of Art, Athens, GA
North Carolina Museum of Art,
  Raleigh, NC
Ringling Museum of Art, Sarasota, FL.
Southern Illinois University Museum,
  Carbondale, IL
Spencer Museum of Art, Lawrence, KS
University of Kentucky Art Museum,
  Lexington, KY
University of Michigan Museum of Art,
  Ann Arbor, MI

Local Government

Asian Art Museum of San Francisco,
  San Francisco, CA
Baltimore Museum of Art,
  Baltimore, MD
Birmingham Museum of Art,
  Birmingham, AL
Brooklyn Museum, Brooklyn, NY
Chrysler Museum, Norfolk, VA
Gilcrease Institute of American Art,
  Tulsa, OK
Huntsville Museum of Art,
  Huntsville, AL
Memphis Brooks Museum of Art,
  Memphis, TN
Minneapolis Institute of Arts,
  Minneapolis, MN

Newark Museum, Newark, NJ
Saint Louis Art Museum, St. Louis, MO

Other Government

California State University Art Museum,
  Long Beach, CA
Elvehjem Museum of Art, Madison, WI
University of Minnesota Art Museum,
  Minneapolis, MN
Virginia Museum of Fine Arts,
  Richmond, VA

Corporate Contributions

Cedar Rapids Museum of Art, Cedar
  Rapids, IA
Corning Museum of Glass,
  Corning, NY
International Museum of Photography,
  Rochester, NY
Yale University Art Gallery, New
  Haven, CT

Private Gifts and Contributions

Amon Carter Museum, Fort Worth, TX
Chicago Museum of Contemporary Art,
  Chicago, IL
Cincinnati Art Museum, Cincinnati, OH
Columbus Museum of Art,
  Columbus, OH
Dallas Museum of Art, Dallas, TX
Flint Institute of Arts, Flint, MI
High Museum of Art, Atlanta, GA
Hood Museum of Art, Hanover, NH
Houston Museum of Fine Arts,
  Houston, TX
J. Paul Getty Museum, Malibu, CA
Milwaukee Art Museum,
  Milwaukee, WI
Modern Art Museum of Fort Worth,
  Fort Worth, TX
Pennsylvania Academy of the Fine Arts,
  Philadelphia, PA
Phoenix Art Museum, Phoenix, AZ
Portland (Maine) Museum of Art,
  Portland, ME
Princeton Art Museum, Princeton, NJ

Rhode Island School of Design
   Museum, Providence, RI
San Francisco Museum of Modern Art,
   San Francisco, CA
Snite Museum, Notre Dame, IN
Tacoma Art Museum, Tacoma, WA
Tucson Museum of Art, Tucson, AZ
University Art Museum—Berkeley,
   Berkeley, CA
Whitney Museum of American Art,
   New York, NY

Endowment Income

Clark Art Institute, Williamston, MA
Cleveland Museum of Art,
   Cleveland, OH
Frick Collection, New York, NY
Harvard University Art Museums,
   Cambridge, MA
Huntington Art Gallery, Austin, TX
Indianapolis Museum of Art,
   Indianapolis, IN
J. B. Speed Art Museum,
   Louisville, KY
Montclair Art Museum, Montclair, NJ
Munson-Williams-Proctor Art Institute,
   Utica, NY
Pierpont Morgan Library, New
   York, NY
Santa Barbara Museum of Art, Santa
   Barbara, CA
Taft Museum, Cincinnati, OH
Toledo Museum of Art, Toledo, OH
Wadsworth Atheneum, Hartford, CT
Winterthur Museum and Gardens,
   Winterthur, DE

Earnings

Boston Museum of Fine Arts,
   Boston, MA
Buffalo Bill Historical Center,
   Cody, WY
Cranbrook Academy of Art Museum,
   Bloomfield Hills, MI
DeCordova and Dana Museum,
   Lincoln, MA
Laguna Gloria Art Museum, Austin, TX
Telfair Academy of Arts and Sciences,
   Savannah, GA

Various Sources

Akron Art Museum, Akron, OH
Albright-Knox Art Gallery, Buffalo, NY
Allentown Art Museum, Allentown, PA
Art Institute of Chicago, Chicago, IL
Asia Society Galleries, New York, NY
Center for the Fine Arts, Miami, FL
Dayton Art Institute, Dayton, OH
Delaware Art Museum, Wilmington, DE
Denver Art Museum, Denver, CO
Everson Museum of Art, Syracuse, NY
Fine Arts Museums of San Francisco,
   San Francisco, CA
Herbert F. Johnson Museum of Art,
   Ithaca, NY
Houston Contemporary Arts Museum,
   Houston, TX
Institute of Contemporary Art,
   Philadelphia, Pa
Joslyn Art Museum, Omaha, NE
La Jolla Museum of Contemporary Art,
   La Jolla, CA
Los Angeles County Museum of Art,
   Los Angeles, CA
Lyman Allyn Museum,
   New London, CT
Madison Art Center, Madison, WI
Metropolitan Museum of Art, New
   York, NY
Museum of Modern Art, New York, NY
New Museum of Contemporary Art,
   New York, NY
New Orleans Museum of Art, New
   Orleans, LA
Newport Harbor Art Museum, Newport
   Beach, CA
Philadelphia Museum of Art,
   Philadelphia, PA
Philbrook Art Center, Tulsa, OK
San Antonio Museum of Art,
   San Antonio, TX
San Diego Museum of Art, San
   Diego, CA
Seattle Art Museum, Seattle, WA
Sheldon Memorial Art Gallery,
   Lincoln, NE
Tampa Museum, Tampa, FL
Walker Art Center, Minneapolis, MN
Walters Art Gallery, Baltimore, MD
Worcester Art Museum, Worcester, MA

7 An Economic History of American Art Museums

Peter Temin

American art museums present a somewhat contradictory face to the world. Considered as private enterprises, which most of them are in this country, they own a remarkable and remarkably valuable stock of physical assets: their art. Yet they are in a continual state of financial crisis. The primary task of this historical essay is to understand this paradox.

Even a perfunctory look at the history of art museums, however, reveals a further problem. The operations so in need of funds today seem to have had financing problems since the start of American art museums. In fact, museum histories claim that museums ran perpetually in deficit. This, as most of us know, is not possible, although the United States as a whole is trying to prove the contrary. The second paradox, therefore, is how art museums could appear to be in a state of perpetual deficit.

A more detailed look at the history reveals yet a third conundrum. Old museums do not seem to possess advantages from their age in attracting viewers. They are indistinguishable from new museums in attendance. Even though art typically cannot be sold, older museums do not seem to have cornered all the good art. This is the paradox. If art is so valuable, why didn't the older museums' head start have a greater effect on museum activities?

This economic history of American art museums will attempt to resolve these three paradoxes. I will show how they are the product of the particular way in which museums have grown in the United States. And I will suggest that some of the burdens of this history would be better abandoned.

The first paradox of American art museums is that they are both rich and poor. In any comparison of assets, art museums show themselves to be, not only the richest of museums, but substantial collections of assets by any stan-

The views expressed are those of the author and do not necessarily reflect those of any organizations.

dard. "It is something of a paradox, then, that the anguished cries of financial distress issue for the most part from art museums—and from the largest among them at that" (Meyer 1979, 59). Or, in the phrasing of the deputy director of the Hirschhorn Museum, "In terms of operating funds," American museums "are—for the most part—broke" (quoted in Thompson 1986).

This has always been true, as far as I can tell. The secretary of the Boston Museum of Fine Arts, Benjamin Gilman, stated in 1920 that the annual expenses of the museum were $200,000, while the income was only $160,000. The $40,000 deficit, he said, had "to be made up annually from principal" (Gilman 1921, 31). Were that true, the Museum of Fine Arts could not possibly be the thriving institution it is today. The "principal" would have long since vanished. This picture of museum finances must be seriously incomplete.

The key to this paradox is the distinction between the two budgets used by all museums. The art budget is used exclusively to purchase or maintain works of art. The operating budget is used for all the other expenses of the museum. An annual report typically reports the condition of the operating budget, with quite separate—and often casual—treatment of the art budget (Museum of Fine Arts 1988).

The most outstanding feature of these two budgets is their separation. It is impossible to transfer funds out of the art budget into the operating budget, even though the former typically has a surplus and the latter a deficit. This can be thought of as a wall around the art budget. We need to ask both about the cause and the effect of such a strict division.

This wall has its origin in what economists call "market failure." Art is bought and sold like any other good, and there is no reason to think that the art market works very badly. But art museums are not in the business of selling art. They are in the business of preserving it and using it for entertainment and education (Gilman 1921; Howe 1913–1946; Whitehill 1970). It is these markets that cannot work in textbook fashion.

The preservation of art is a process performed on behalf of future generations. They obviously cannot pay for or affect what we collect for them today. In addition, the exhibition of art has the some of the aspect of a "public good." Once established, the cost of showing an art collection to an additional person is exceedingly low. Even though it is possible to exclude people from museums—distinguishing museums from suppliers of pure public goods—the resource cost of admitting additional people to the museum is virtually zero. It follows that a competitive market price for museum attendance would be low also, too low to support the museum (Hansmann 1980).

Education is an activity with "externalities," that is, education has effects both on those being educated and on other members of society. Education in the arts not only uplifts the spirit, so we are told, but sets a tone for and affects the standards of taste of the community. It is to this externality that American art museums owe their special character.

America had no royalty, no ancient aristocracy to collect art. American art museums could not be started by opening up these existing collections. If art museums were to exist, they had to be started anew. And there had to be reasons for individuals to band together to form them. Prosperous private citizens began to do this in the flush of Victorian prosperity after the Civil War.

Industrialization began well before the Civil War, but the internal conflict was a watershed in the public awareness of it. Industry grew rapidly after the war, and the size of industrial plants and firms grew as well. Cities burgeoned, populated in part by immigrants drawn to work in the new factories and mills.

The bourgeoisie regarded these developments with mixed emotions. They were, of course, enriched by industrialization, and they were champions of it. They consumed their new income and they enjoyed their economic privileges. But there was a dark side of industrialization as well. The professional and managerial elite looked with suspicion on the growing industrial labor force. They were frightened by the new immigrants with new socialist ideologies. They feared—at least a little—for the stability of their social and economic position.

Public policies instituted to deal with this apprehension had their positive and negative faces. The less attractive part included the strike breaking and union busting that is such a prominent part of early American labor-union history. More hopeful was the effort put into public education and social reform to include the workers and immigrants within the American dream.

These two aspects of policy are shown graphically by two characteristic late nineteenth-century public buildings. Armories were built to house local militias and to provide indoor parade grounds for their drills. The enemy against which these militias defended can be inferred from the style and location of the armories. The buildings were imposing castellated fortresses. Although not fortified against artillery, they were defensible against handguns. And they were located in the midst of cities. The enemy was within, not without. The fear was of urban rioters, not foreign invasion. The militia was in theory—as it was often as well in practice in the late nineteenth century—a bulwark against civil unrest (Fogelson 1989).

The other building type, examples of which were less numerous before the First World War, presented a more benign face to the masses. Art museums were founded to educate the people's taste, to help them identify with the values of the successful industrialists. There was a powerful faith in education of all sorts at the time; knowledge alone was enough to cure many ills of society. Public education was supported. Information on social conditions and ailments was collected. Art was presented to the urban population by "cultural capitalists" (DiMaggio 1986).

Art and education were part of the same civilizing campaign. The Boston Museum of Fine Arts, for example, began its collection with plaster casts of classical sculpture (Whitehill 1970). The aim was not the preservation or stimulation of current art, but the encouragement of a classical education. The calm demeanor of classical statuary would communicate a multidimensional message to the urban public. It might also improve the design of American products.

But museums were not schools. The collection of pedagogic artifacts was quickly superseded by original works of art. The public benefactors who established museums were collectors of art as well as missionaries for artistic ideals. They began to donate parts of their collections and even to acquire works for the purpose of donating them to museums.

These newly rich individuals were responding to the Protestant ethic in general and to the Puritan creed in particular by amassing rather than consuming wealth. Calvinism had made a sharp distinction between earning money—which indicated that you were among the elect in the next life—and spending it—which tended to suggest the opposite. This contrast placed the potential elect on the horns of a dilemma, resolved for many by reinvesting profits in their firms. Providing a public monument was an alternative solution to this dilemma. It was an activity that both expressed wealth and preserved the ethical purity of the donor.

Providing for the public display of art did more than just express wealth. It also validated it. Patrons of art museums were creating a framework in which their possessions would be admired. They were shaping a popular culture in which art, particularly the art they had collected, had an integral place. They were shaping the design of American-made products to correspond more closely to their cosmopolitan tastes. DiMaggio (1986) has characterized this effort the "sacralization of art." The attempt to influence the taste of society clearly was not an activity in which the market worked well.

From the start, in contrast with European museums, American museums depended on private support. Since the market for exhibiting and preserving art could not work, an alternative form of support needed to be found. Philanthropy was the answer. Initial donors banded together to found a museum which then relied on continuing gifts for its continued well-being. The founders needed guarantees that their gifts would be used for the stated purposes. To attract additional gifts, they also needed to assure future donors that their funds would in fact be used for art and not for other activities.

The method of enforcement was the bequest. Resources were given to the museum subject to explicit constraints on their use. In practice, this meant that gifts of art had to be preserved as art, whether in the objects actually transferred or others bought from the revenues from their sale. And it meant also that funds donated had to be used exclusively for the acquisition and preservation of art.

The wall between the museum's two budgets served as this guarantee. It served the same function as a tax exemption in other philanthropic organizations. To qualify for tax exemption, an organization has to adopt strict accounting to show that donated funds have not been siphoned off for the benefit of the administrators. The rules for tax exemption enforce this condition

(Hansmann 1981). Art museums are tax exempt institutions, but the wall between the two budgets antedates their tax exempt status. It served as a guarantee, in the years before taxes were high enough to make tax exemption an issue.

Either individually or in small groups, these industrialists could dictate their terms to the museums they were creating. They typically insisted that their gifts be preserved. A 1920 bequest reveals the pattern. Katherine Bullard willed one-third of her estate to the Museum of Fine Arts (after two life interests expired) "for the purchase of prints valuable for their beauty, or for aiding the Curator of Prints in studying the subject of prints elsewhere than in the United States, or for both purposes, the same to be and remain a memorial to my late brother Francis." (Miss Bullard died in 1920, but the bequest only reached the museum in 1959 [Whitehill 1970, 726].) More generally, Laurence Coleman lamented in his 1939 survey of museums that, "although some of the leading benefactions are without restriction, there is on the whole too much tying down of permanent funds to the purchase of objects for collections" (Coleman 1939, I:191)

The Bullard bequest allowed for more than the purchase of art, but it precluded other expenditures at the museum itself. It therefore created the problem that lies behind the paradox at hand. As Mr. Dooley said in a famous parody of a Carnegie speech: "All I aks iv a city in rayturn f'r a fifty-thousan'-dollar libry is that it shall raise wan million dollars to maintain th' buildin' and keep me name shiny. . . . I stake ye to this libry, which ye will have as soon ye raise the money to keep it goin' " (quoted in Meyer 1979, 86).

It must be admitted that these restrictions were not totally inviolable. Museums, like many other economic institutions, fell on hard times during the Depression. They were dependent on private funds, and these funds were not forthcoming when profits were low. Under these conditions, uncommon flexibility appeared. Coleman reported in 1939 that, "the freedom of some institutions to fall back for running expenses during recent years upon the incomes of funds devoted normally to purchasing for collections was instrumental in saving both museums and the museum profession from something like wreckage" (Coleman 1939, I:191). Coleman talks only of spending the interest, not the principal, of dedicated funds. He talks also of the "normal" use of funds without specifying whether the restrictions were embodied in the terms of bequests or not. The flexibility therefore may have been limited.

The strength of fund restrictions in more prosperous times can be seen in the public firestorm that greeted the sale of paintings by the Metropolitan Museum of Art in the early 1970s. They were sold to finance the purchase of other paintings and sculpture by Velasquez, David Smith, and Diebenkorn. Even though the resources stayed within the art budget, the decision to sell was scrutinized closely by the *New York Times* and the attorney general of New York. New procedures were adopted in 1973 explicitly restricting the Metropolitan's freedom in transferring resources within the art budget (Rich

1975, in Lee 1975). One can only imagine the havoc that would have been wreaked by a decision to sell a Van Gogh to pay a curator or to pay for a roof repair.

Every museum deaccessions art. But it has been done secretly and only for the purpose of buying more art. Sold works of art are not recorded as sold, but rather expunged from museum records as if they never had been owned (Meyer 1979, 208–10). By this procedure, museum directors implicitly acknowledge the impropriety of their sales. The strength of these restrictions means that although museum directors can quietly evade the rules against selling art, they cannot in ordinary times violate the even stronger rule separating the art and operating budgets.

This raises, as directors noted in the 1970s, the question of who owns the museum. In their discussion of business firms, Hart and Moore (1988) identify ownership with discretionary power over the firm's physical assets. They test their definition on firms that are largely collections of human skills (like a software developer) and find that even there it best describes the limits of a firm. The art museum is at the opposite end of the spectrum. It is virtually a collection of physical assets *tout court*. The trustees exerted full control over these assets initially. But dead donors can only influence current actions through the medium of the state, and partial public ownership—whatever the source of funding—has been the result.

Meyer (1979, 211) argues that museums, that is, their trustees, do not own the art, but rather are its stewards. The trustees are in the position of corporate managers, not corporate shareholders. The owners are the public. Ownership rights are enforced, when need be, by state attorneys general. But, as Meyer acknowledges, the rights of ownership have only seldom—as in the case of the Metropolitan's deaccessioning—been employed. The directors normally exercise the rights of ownership with little interference from the public.

Museum directors use this freedom in part to attract gifts that will enlarge their collections. Perry Rathbone (in Lowry 1984) commented ruefully that many of these gifts were not dependent on the tax laws. The Museum of Fine Arts in Boston and the Metropolitan Museum of Art in New York were chartered in 1870. The Philadelphia and Chicago art museums followed in 1876 and 1879. They were started well before income or estate taxes had become a factor in the plans of their donors.

Economists thinking about a consumer's purchase of a good will think of two influences on his or her actions. The "income effect" describes the effect of the potential purchaser's income on the purchase of a good. For most goods, higher income promotes larger purchases. The "substitution effect" describes the effect of prices on purchases, that is, of the price of the good in question relative to other prices. A lower relative price also encourages purchases.

Think now of a gift to an art museum as the purchase of some service. As suggested above, the service may be a stake in the life hereafter. It does not matter. We do not have to specify the donor's underlying motivation any more than we have to explore the base motivations for buying a Mercedes rather than a Ford. As a result of the income effect, rich people will be inclined to contribute to art museums. And for a given income, the growth of tax deductions encourages gifts as well. Rathbone argued in many forums that the growth of taxes reduced gifts to museums by lowering disposable income. The negative income effect, however, has been offset by a positive substitution effect. There is no reason to think that the net effect of income taxes has been negative.

This is not to say that taxes have no effects, only that they often have offsetting effects. Even this does not seem to have been true of the 1986 tax changes. The reduction in marginal income tax rates has increased the cost of giving to museums. The resulting substitution effect seems to have reduced museum donations sharply. A first-page headline in *The New York Times* last May announced: "Donations of Art Fall Sharply after Changes in the Tax Code." The story reported that the American Association of Museums had found a one-third fall in objects donated to a sample of various types of museums between 1986 and 1987. The Association of Art Museum Directors found a two-thirds decrease in donations to art museums (*New York Times*, 7 May 1989, 1). While the income effect will offset at least part of these reductions in time, there is no doubt that the immediate impact of the tax change was deleterious.

Given the restriction on nonart expenditures, museums had to think of ways to raise money to finance the operation of the museum. They typically were able to attract donations for new buildings. A defined objective was a good substitute for art itself. Day-to-day activities were more of a problem.

Museums established in the nineteenth century began their lives with almost no professional staff. The trustees administered as well as supported the museum, assisted by a handful of paid assistants. The transfer of operating responsibility to a managerial staff was a gradual process, marked by trustee reluctance to sacrifice power or to admit the legitimacy of professional points of view. Only in the interwar period did trained art historians begin to dominate museum staffs (Rich 1975, in Lee 1975; Zolberg 1981).

Paying for these staffs was a continuing problem. Unable to solve it by themselves, many museums turned to the city government for help. The Metropolitan Museum of New York received land and a building from the city in Central Park and an annual operating grant for maintenance from the city (Meyer 1979, 26). To provide additional operating funds, the museum began soliciting memberships in 1873 at $10 a year. They had 600 members in their first year (Coleman 1939, I:183).

Boston's Museum of Fine Arts received only land from the city and found, in the 1880s, that the "annual deficits from operating expenses . . . were slowly but surely melting away the museum's modest unrestricted funds." The trustees therefore followed the example of the Metropolitan and initiated annual subscriptions of $10 to provide operating funds, giving free admission to the museum in return. "The subscriptions provided a helpful source of income, but deficits continued" (Whitehill 1970, 69, 83).

This, of course, is the second paradox. Museums continued to run deficits, but they continued to exist, even to prosper. As noted already, reports of deficits have been a constant of museum description for many years. How could museums exist if their activities were continually eating away at their capital?

The resolution is simple. The key is that the reports of deficits refer only to operating budgets. Museums had outflows: operating expenses. There must have been offsetting inflows, not every year, but on average, for museums to continue their activities. These inflows could not have come from the art budget, due to the restrictions on bequests. They must have been attracted by other means.

One such technique appears to have centered on museum construction. Museums solicited funds for new buildings or extensions of existing ones. They collected enough money and built sufficiently cheaply to provide unrestricted funds for the operation of the museums. Periodic moves or expansions were needed, therefore, not only to provide added space for new works of art, but also to provide new infusions of operating income. Many museums abandoned their central locations around the turn of the century for more elegant surroundings, providing a focus for fund-raising while turning somewhat away from the urban workers.

A better solution came in the years after World War II with the expansion of museum membership. As incomes grew in the postwar economic expansion, museums used this device to tap the market of consumers who were far less rich than the donors of art. In addition to appealing to the income effect, they relied on the substitution effect, soliciting tax-deductible memberships. Instead of a few large gifts, the museums pursued many smaller ones. These unrestricted funds then went into the operating budget that could be used for operating operations.

Museums also solicited unrestricted donations from patrons of the arts. Among such unrestricted gifts, the historian of Boston's Museum of Fine Arts singled out one from Martha Mercer in 1960 that provided the museum with over $200,000 in unrestricted funds throughout the 1960s (Whitehill 1970, 803).

These devices helped, but new needs for unrestricted funds have arisen in the past few decades. The government has increasingly overseen the operations of art museums. As tax-exempt institutions, art museums are subject to a variety of accounting and reporting requirements to assure the government of their compliance with the rules. As partly public institutions, art museums have had to justify their actions in other governmental forums as well.

The result has been a growing professional museum staff. Full-time, paid workers have replaced part-time volunteers. Trained people commanding professional salaries have replaced family members of donors and their peers.

The growth of personnel has led to the articulation of museums' internal structure, the formation of departments dealing with separate museum activities. The operating costs of museums have grown rapidly as a consequence. In the perpetual race between inflows and outflows, the outflow appears to be winning at the moment.

This problem contains the seeds of its solution. Professional staffs have grown because museums are subject to a great many more controls than a century ago, or even a generation ago. In fact, the pervasiveness of government support and supervision has given rise to a new kind of museum director. The amateur or donor was replaced in the interwar period by the art historian. In the last 20 years there has been another transformation. Many museum directors now have managerial training or an administrative background, rather than an education in art history. They are experts in dealing with the problems of large, modern institutions rather than old paintings or sculpture. As the problems faced by museums have changed, so have their staffs (Zolberg 1981).

The safeguards used a century ago therefore have become redundant. Museums are no longer run by amateurs who cannot be trusted to implement the wishes of donors. Instead, they are run by professionals who understand how museums must be structured to achieve their aims. No longer is it necessary to specify exactly how a bequest will be used to assure that it will be used to further the museum's ends. The law and the pervasive governmental supervision of museums will prevent the diversion of a bequest to the aid of a museum employee's lifestyle. Tax-exempt gifts are controlled and regulated precisely to avoid this.

It follows that the strict separation of the two museum budgets no longer is necessary. To the extent that it binds, it prevents the most efficient decision making; directors need to maximize subject to a constraint that could be removed. Government oversight will make sure that the director does not maximize his or her own income by selling off priceless works of art.

This leads naturally into the third paradox. Art museums have been given extraordinary paintings, sculptures, and art objects. These works of art have been protected against alienation, so that they have remained in the museum to which they were given. Those museums first in the queue to get works of art should have received the cream of the crop. Newer museums should have been playing catch-up, prevented from acquiring comparable treasures. Furthermore, art museums show their collection, particularly their prize elements. They use the collection to perform their missions of entertainment and education, in short, to attract visitors. It follows that older museums should have an advantage over newer ones in the competition for visitors.

I tested this proposition by looking at the correlation between various measures of art museum activity. The data were kindly supplied by Bruce Evans from the Association of Art Museum Directors. The association solicited answers to a questionnaire from about 200 art museums in the United States and

Canada. Roughly half of them (110) provided information on all the variables used here.

The museums are grouped by age in table 7.1. The data in the table suggest that there has been a gradually increasing rate of art museum formation. This accords with casual observation, even though the table may not contain enough information to confirm it. The problem is that the Association of Art Museums Directors's study does not include all museums. Table 7.1 contains data on 172 museums, but another survey listed 387 art museums existing in 1938. There were 224 public art museums, 115 college and university museums, and 59 others (Coleman 1939, III:663).

There may be several reasons why there are so few museums reported in table 7.1. One of them is that the data are retrospective, reporting the age only of museums that have stayed in existence through 1988. If some of the early museums had ceased to exist through merger, acquisition, or disbanding, then the number of museums formed in the early years would be undercounted. The appearance of an accelerating rate of art museum formation may be illusory.

Table 7.2 shows the data I have used, a small selection of the variables available from the Association of Art Museum Directors. Attendance shows the yearly attendance at the museums. It ranged from 10,000 to 7,099,600, with a mean of 315,000. Building size is the size of museum buildings in square feet. Full-time employees indicates the number of people employed full-time at the museum. The mean is less than 100 people. Considering the value of the physical plant, this is a small number of full-time employees, as

Table 7.1   AAMD Museums by Date of Founding

Date	Number of Museums
Before 1875	14
1876–1900	31
1901–1925	39
1926–1950	44
1951–1988	44

Source: Association of Art Museum Directors.

Table 7.2   Characteristics of the Data

Variable	Number of Observations	Mean	Standard Deviation	Minimum	Maximum
Attendance	128	314,595.7	722,545	10,000	7,099,600
Building size	128	138,784.3	201,312.2	6,000	1,515,120
Full-time employees	128	95.04688	182.4578	0	1,500
Total revenue	128	5,806,251	1.26×10^7	89,485	1.19×10^8

Source: Association of Art Museum Directors.

Table 7.3   **Correlations**

	Attendance	Building Size	Full-time Employees	Total Revenue	Last Year's Attendance	Age
Attendance	1.0000					
Building size	0.8060	1.0000				
Full-time employees	0.7739	0.9381	1.0000			
Total revenue	0.7102	0.8988	0.9668	1.0000		
Last year's attendance	0.9913	0.7636	0.7253	0.6516	1.0000	
Age	−0.0988	−0.2853	−0.2455	−0.2280	−0.0809	1.0000
Number of observations	110					

Source: Association of Art Museum Directors.

noted above. Total revenue is the total annual revenue of the museums, ranging from less than $100,000 to over $100 million.

Correlations between these variables are shown in the first four rows of table 7.3. It can be seen that they are all highly correlated. In other words, large museums are characterized by large budgets, staffs, buildings, and attendance. These variables interact with each other, and it is not possible or necessary here to disentangle them. Large attendance generates large budgets, and large budgets encourage large attendance. There is not need to decide which effect is larger, or whether both variables are large as a result of the effects of another index. It is enough to demonstrate that there is a statistical profile of large and small museums.

The fifth row of table 7.3 reveals that museums have a short-run history. Last year's attendance is virtually the same as this year's attendance and only slightly less highly correlated with the other variables than this year's attendance.

But museums have no long-run history that helps to explain why some museums have larger attendance than others. The bottom row of table 7.3 shows the correlation between the age of museums and the other variables. Age is an index derived from the categories of table 7.1 with an additional break introduced in 1960. Lower numbers indicate older museums. The correlation between age and attendance is far, far lower than between any other pair. In fact, the correlation is low enough to be indistinguishable from zero. More precisely, it is likely that a correlation of this size would be produced by chance alone from independent variables. There is no evidence that age and attendance are correlated at all.

This finding is all the more puzzling because the correlations between age and the other variables, while still relatively small, are significantly different from zero. In other words, newer museums are smaller in terms of their buildings, full-time employees, and revenues. But they are not thereby penalized in the contest for patrons.

The details are shown in table 7.4. The top row shows the lack of a trend in attendance by the age of museums. In particular, those museums started in the second quarter of the twentieth century (age category 3) have been very suc-

Table 7.4   Means of Variables by Age

	Age					
	0	1	2	3	4	5
Attendance	466	220	238	403	146	163
Building size	194	119	81	81	54	38
Full-time employees	223	188	130	114	92	92
Total revenue	13	7	5	5	3	2
Number of observations	145					

Source: Association of Art Museum Directors.
Note: Attendance and building size are in thousands. Total revenue is in millions.

cessful in attracting visitors. The other rows of the table exhibit declining trends over time. The older museums have used their age to accumulate floor space, staff, and revenues, even if not visitors.

Multivariate regressions (not reported here) show the same picture. It is hard to defend a functional form for regressions because the causal interaction of the variables is not clear. Museums with many employees use some of them to attract large attendance. But museums with large attendance can afford large staffs. When attendance is taken to be the dependent variable, whatever is taken to be the relevant independent variables, age is not a benefit. In other words, the results in table 7.4 appear also in more complex presentations of the data.

Tables 7.5 and 7.6 reproduce the earlier tables omitting the three largest museums: The Metropolitan Museum of Art, the Chicago Art Institute, and the National Gallery of Art. They are the only three museums with more than 500 full-time employees. Table 7.5 shows that omitting the upper tail reduces the means and the standard deviations of the variables. It can be seen in table 7.6, however, that the correlations between the variables are virtually unaffected. They were not a phenomenon of the largest museums.

How are we to understand this result? The histories of the older museums are replete with their conquests of donors and sources, their acquisitions of now priceless works (Burt 1977; Howe 1913–1946). And, as we have seen, museums cannot—with rare exceptions—sell their art. Why have these museums not been able to leverage their earlier start and their putatively superior collections into larger attendance?

I can suggest two possible hypotheses. The first possibility is that there is simply so much art in the world that it is impossible to corner the market. In the language of economics, the supply of art is very elastic. Museums then have a small percentage of the world's art, and new museums—suitably endowed—can acquire their share of it. It does not matter very much for new museums that old museums cannot sell their collections. Newcomers can simply add onto the stock of museum holdings.

The Getty Museum is surely an illustration of this point. Starting in 1982 with an endowment of $1.2 billion, it now has an acquisition budget estimated at 25 times the size of the Metropolitan's. More important for the point of view of this paper, it has an unrestricted budget large enough to provide all sorts of ancillary services to support its art collection and attract notice and visitors (Kimmelman 1988).

The projected Massachusetts Museum of Contemporary Art in North Adams suggests an alternative path. This new museum will be part of what will be a museum holding company centered on the Guggenheim. The plan is to collect art that is too large for other museums to exhibit, illustrating the variety of art that is available. It will also collect art that is being created today, underscoring the expanding size of the world's art collection (Weisgall 1989).

The second possibility is subtly different. Admitting that the supply of art is limited at any time, one could hypothesize that art is basically interchangeable. It does not matter which works of art a museum has, only that it has art. Although any particular work of art might be irreplaceable, its appeal to the public is easily replaced. Any museum, therefore, can find some work of art of which it can be proud and which it can use to attract visitors. People will visit the Louvre to see the Venus de Milo, and they will visit their local museum to see works by local artists.

Table 7.5   Data Characteristics without the Three Largest Museums

Variable	Number of Observations	Mean	Standard Deviation	Minimum	Maximum
Attendance	125	227,839.4	2362,298.2	10,000	1,594,070
Building size	125	116,094.1	126,671.2	6,000	750,000
Full-time employees	125	72.016	94.22417	0	474
Total revenue	125	4,299,609	5,864,698	89,485	3.6×10^7

Source: Association of Art Museum Directors.

Table 7.6   Correlations without the Three Largest Museums

	Attendance	Building Size	Full-time Employees	Total Revenue	Last Year's Attendance	Age
Attendance	1.000					
Building size	0.7659	1.0000				
Full-time employees	0.8254	0.8699	1.0000			
Total revenue	0.8690	0.8105	0.9293	1.0000		
Last year's attendance	0.9605	0.7584	0.8470	0.8434	1.0000	
Age	−0.1478	−0.3016	−0.2320	−0.1895	−0.1543	1.0000
Number of observations	107					

Source: Association of Art Museum Directors.

Whichever variant is correct, the implication is that history matters little for the success of museums. Either there is a lot of good art to acquire or it does not matter much which art you show. New museums suffer no handicap from their late arrival on the scene. They can establish themselves and attract visitors as well as their older peers. In fact, the downward trend in employment, building size, and revenue suggests that new museums may be more efficient than old in generating attendance from a given set of resources.

It is true that attendance is not the be-all and end-all of art museums. As noted at the start of this essay, museums were founded with multiple aims. Attendance does, however, provide an index of the museums's effectiveness. The building and the staff presumably are means to an end. The value of the collection is perhaps an end, but it is hard to observe. Attendance is as good a proxy for the success of museums in their multitudinous activities as we can get.

This conclusion reinforces the argument for the recommendation made earlier that constraints on museum directors should be loosened. There does not seem to be evidence of a great scarcity of good art. We consequently can relax a bit in our quest to preserve it. We should allow directors more latitude to run their museums in support of their objectives, only making sure that they are dedicating their resources to the museum's and not their own ends.

In today's buoyant art market, museum directors might decide to be on the selling rather than the buying side of art. They might even engage in what could be called an "art preservation project," selling art from their basements into private collections to raise revenue to care for the remaining objects. Some objects currently inadequately preserved and accessible would be placed in the care of private individuals and firms who would have fewer works of art and the resources to preserve and exhibit all of them. And such art works would be likely to reappear on the market again at some time in the future when museums would have the opportunity to reacquire them.

If possession of the classic artistic achievements that are the hallmark of our museums does not bestow on these museums a commanding lead in furnishing museum services, then the principle of inalienable art collections may not deserve the force it has acquired. The issue should be the museum staff's fidelity to the purposes of the tax-exempt, quasi-public institution, not to the wishes of benefactors who can see only the most visible aspect of museum operations.

References

Burt, N. 1977. *Palaces for the people*. New York: Little Brown.
Coleman, L. V. 1939. *The museum in America*. 3 vols. Washington: American Association of Museums.

DiMaggio, P. J., ed. 1986. *The nonprofit enterprise in the arts: Studies in mission and constraint.* New York: Oxford University Press.

Fogelson, R. M. 1989. *America's armories.* Cambridge: Harvard University Press.

Gilman, B. I. 1921. *Museum of Fine Arts, Boston, 1870–1920.* Boston: Museum of Fine Arts.

Hansmann, H. 1980. The role of nonprofit enterprise. *Yale Law Journal* 89 (April): 835–901.

———. 1981. The nonprofit enterprise in the performing arts. *Bell Journal of Economics* 12:341–361.

Hart, O. and J. Moore. 1988. Property rights and the nature of the firm. Massachusetts Institute of Technology, Department of Economics Working paper.

Howe, W. E. 1913–1946. *A history of the Metropolitan Museum of Art.* 2 vols. New York: Metropolitan Museum of Art.

Kimmelman, M. 1988. The world's richest museum. *New York Times Magazine,* October 23.

Lee, S., ed. 1975. *On understanding art museums.* Englewood Cliffs, N.J.: Prentice-Hall.

Lowry, W. McN., ed. 1984. *The arts and public policy.* Englewood Cliffs, N.J.: Prentice-Hall.

Meyer, K. E. 1979. *The art museum: Power, money, ethics.* New York: William Morrow.

Museum of Fine Arts. 1988. *Annual report.* Boston: Museum of Fine Arts.

Rich, D. C. 1975. Management, power, and integrity. In *On understanding art museums,* ed. S. E. Lee. Englewood Cliffs, N.J.: Prentice-Hall.

Thompson, N. L. 1986. Financially troubled museums and the law. In *The nonprofit enterprise in the arts,* ed. P. J. DiMaggio. New York: Oxford University Press.

Weisgall, D. 1989. A megamuseum in a mill town. *New York Times Magazine,* March 5.

Whitehill, W. M. 1970. *The Museum of Fine Arts, Boston.* Cambridge: Harvard University Press.

Zolberg, V. L. 1981. Conflicting visions of American art museums. *Theory and Society* 10 (January): 103–25.

8   Tax Policy Toward Art Museums

Don Fullerton

8.1 Introduction

As nonprofit organizations, art museums are exempt from federal income tax in the United States. This exemption does not mean that tax rules have no effect on museums, however. Far from it. The various tax instruments affect art museums indirectly but dramatically. They change the incentives of individuals and corporations to make donations of art, they change the relative cost of raising capital for museum projects, and they change the incentives of museums to make passive investments in securities rather than active investments in unrelated businesses.

Tax policy provides an extra incentive to make charitable donations through the deduction against income tax or estate tax for such gifts. At the current top marginal, personal income-tax rate of 28 percent, a dollar gift only costs the taxpayer 72 cents, because the government gives up 28 cents that might otherwise be collected.

For art museums, a particularly important form of donation is artwork that has appreciated in value since the time of acquisition by the donor. In this case, the taxpayer may get a "double incentive." Itemizers are allowed a deduction against ordinary income for the whole value of the gift, and, in addition, the regular tax system forgoes capital gains tax on the appreciation. Since the capital gains tax was raised by the 1986 Tax Reform Act to the ordinary personal rate, this additional tax forgiveness has become more important for some.

For example, suppose that a potential donor in the 28-percent rate bracket

Financial support was provided by a grant from the Olin Foundation to the National Bureau of Economic Research. The author is grateful for helpful suggestions from Charles T. Clotfelter, Marion Fremont-Smith, Saul Levmore, Jeffrey Owens, Joel Slemrod, Hilary Sigman, and especially Martin Feldstein. The research reported here is part of the NBER's research program in taxation. Any opinions expressed are those of the author and not those of the National Bureau of Economic Research.

has a painting now worth $10,000 that was purchased for $8,000. The $10,000 deduction saves $2,800 of tax on ordinary income, and giving the painting instead of cash saves another $560 of tax on the capital gain (the 28-percent rate on the $2,000 of appreciation). By saving $3360, under the regular tax, the donor only gives up $6640. If the alternative is to sell this property, we say that the price of a $1 dollar gift is only 66.4 cents. On the other hand, the appreciation on donated property might make the taxpayer subject to the "alternative minimum tax" (AMT), with more complicated rules as described below.

For those of us who have always lived with such a system, these rules may seem like the logical consequence of private giving to a public cause. The tax base is supposed to reflect one's ability to pay, and charitable gifts reduce this ability by reducing disposable income (Andrews 1972). In this view, the deduction is part of the definition of income, rather than a special incentive. An alternative view is that income before gifts is a proper measure of control over resources and therefore represents one's ability to pay tax. Donors can be said to feel just as much value from their gifts as from their other consumption expenditures, or else they would not give. They are buying privileges of membership, a plaque on the donation, a little prestige, or at least some personal satisfaction. There is no logical necessity to exempt gifts. This alternative view implicitly underlies the government's estimates of the "tax expenditure" budget, showing the amount of tax that would have been collected without each such deduction.[1]

Under either view, the tax system clearly provides more incentive for charitable gifts than if there were no deduction. If this incentive induces more donations of art, then tax policy affects art museums. This paper will look at measures of this incentive and its effect.

Similarly, the government does not tax the endowment income of charitable organizations like museums. There is no explicit effect, either tax or subsidy. However, taxes levied on the rest of the economy serve to raise the cost of other activities relative to the cost of museum activities. In this sense we say that there is an "implicit subsidy." With limited economic resources to go around, a tax system that discourages certain uses of resources necessarily encourages other untaxed uses of resources. The tax system thereby impacts museums. I discuss these implicit subsidies, while the paper by Charles T. Clotfelter (chap. 9 in this volume) discusses explicit government subsidies.

The next section provides an overview of the various forms of indirect federal aid to art museums. It measures the rate of the implicit subsidy, and it provides a rough calculation of the size of the tax expenditure. It briefly discusses the justifications for public support and provides empirical evidence on willingness to pay.

---

1. At the U.S. Treasury Department, Neubig and Joulfaian (1988) estimate that the total tax expenditure for the charitable deduction would have been $16.45 billion in 1988 under the old law, but it was reduced to $12.87 billion by the lower rates of the Tax Reform Act of 1986.

These preliminaries accomplished, following sections attempt to document the actual effects of tax policy on art museums. Section 8.3 discusses the tax rules for individuals' gifts in other countries, provides a brief history of rules in the United States, and considers the recent reduction of marginal tax rates and the inclusion of appreciated property in the alternative minimum tax. It finds that the reduction of rates in the 1986 Tax Reform Act may depress gifts to art museums by as much as 24 percent. Section 8.4 analyzes incentives provided by the income tax exemption and the unrelated business income tax. It finds that the combination of tax advantages does reduce the cost of capital, but the result is still not "unfair" to other businesses as long as the rules do not change unexpectedly. This section also discusses rules for gifts of art by firms under the corporate income tax, and bequests of art under the estate and gift tax. A final section offers conclusions.

8.2 Implicit Subsidy and Tax Expenditure

A precise estimate of the implicit subsidy going to art museums is not possible, but a rough calculation indicates that the implicit federal tax advantages may be larger than all other sources of federal aid. This section discusses the rate of subsidy, the fraction of museum funds from tax expenditure, the philosophical justification for subsidy, and survey evidence on desires to subsidize the arts.

8.2.1 The Rate of Implicit Subsidy

For some background information on those who give to the arts, consider table 8.1. For each income group listed in column 1, the weighted average of personal marginal tax rates is shown in column 2. Groups above $50,000 per year are all near the top marginal rate, and column 3 shows that almost all of these taxpayers itemize deductions and therefore receive an incentive for their gifts. Column 4 shows the percent of gifts in each bracket that is property rather than cash. The top income group gives up to 30 percent in property, but the relevant percentage for gifts to art museums may be even higher. Then, column 5 shows that gifts to culture are very highly concentrated in the uppermost income brackets—where taxpayers have high tax rates and itemize deductions. Therefore gifts to the arts tend to receive a larger implicit subsidy than most charitable gifts.

In the example above, at the 28-percent rate, the gift of property had a price of 66.4 cents per dollar given. This example was chosen to be representative, as can be seen in the last column of table 8.1. This column uses a general formula described later (appendix A, equation [3]) to account for gifts to culture in each rate bracket, with different percentages of the gift being appreciated property. Since the overall average price is 67 cents per dollar given, the tax expenditure is approximately one-third of total individual donations to culture.

Of the private support to art museums, most comes from individuals. As

Table 8.1   Marginal Tax Rates and the Price of Giving to the Arts

AGI Group (1)	Marginal Tax Rate (2)	Percent Itemizers (3)	Percent Property (4)	Gifts to Culture (5)	Price of Giving (6)
0–10K	2.0	5.1	8.4	.0	.98
10–20K	15.9	20.5	8.7	.0	.83
20–30K	17.9	43.1	8.5	.0	.81
30–50K	21.5	67.2	9.2	.0	.78
50–75K	27.8	85.3	12.9	16.6	.70
75–100K	29.1	85.3	14.8	10.9	.69
100–200K	32.2	92.6	17.2	17.5	.65
200K +	28.9	93.8	30.9	55.0	.67
Total				100.0	.67

Notes and sources (by column): (1) AGI = adjusted gross income, in K = thousands of dollars; (2) and (3) weighted average in each group, for the Tax Reform Act of 1986, from U.S. Treasury Dept.; (4) Statistics of Income (SOI 1988), Internal Revenue Service, for tax year 1985 (before appreciated property placed under the alternative minimum tax; (5) calculated from Clotfelter (1985b, 213) and SOI for 1985; and (6) calculated from appendix equation (3) using column 2 for t and g, column 4 for $(1 - C)$, $a = .5$ for the ratio of appreciation to value, and assuming that the alternative is immediate consumption. These prices apply to itemizers, but there are very few nonitemizers in the top few brackets with gifts to culture. See section 8.3.6, "Rate Reduction and Giving to Art Museums."

described later in this paper, some gifts are from corporations that can take deductions at their 34-percent rate. Some funds are received as bequests, deducted at various estate-tax rates. For the rough calculations here, suppose that the overall average of these implicit subsidy rates is about one-third. Another implicit subsidy to art museums is the nontaxation of investment income. In this case the tax expenditure is measured relative to the other extreme where that income also would have been taxed by one-third. A final possible component of tax expenditure is the nontaxation of operating revenues or earned income from admissions, sales, restaurants, parking, and other fees.

8.2.2 An Estimate of the Tax Expenditure

Consider the following sources of support in 1988 for the 155 art museums surveyed in 1989 by the Association of Art Museum Directors:

Operating revenue (earned income)	$122.4 million	14.0%
Private support (contributed income)	235.0	27.0%
Value of art donated	77.3	8.9
Total federal support	95.7	11.0
Total state and local support	168.7	19.3
Endowment income	173.0	19.8
Total	872.1	100.0

Annual budgets of museums usually leave aside the value of art that is donated, since budgets are supposed to account only for dollar flows. These donations represent additional assets to museums, however, and so they are part of "economic" income. This art also receives an implicit subsidy. These figures therefore show that 35.9 percent of total economic income is received in donations of cash and art.

With these figures, the tax expenditures can now be calculated. The deductions of gifts to art museums are worth about one-third of this 35.9 percent figure, or about 12 percent of economic income. The nontaxation of endowment income is worth another one-third of the 19.8 percent of income from this source, or 6.6 percent of economic income. A third form of tax expenditure is the nontaxation of net operating revenues. Estimates are not available here because the figures do not show all of the costs of the store, restaurant, parking, or special events. In combination, however, just the first two implicit federal subsidies provide 18.6 percent of museum income, an amount substantially larger than the 11 percent coming from all other direct federal aid. Since this direct federal spending includes the financing of five large government museums (see Clotfelter, this volume), the implicit subsidy for private museums must be much larger than direct spending.[2]

8.2.3 The Justification for Public Support

The purpose of this paper is to document the economic effects of tax rules on art museums, but a discussion of the philosophical case for implicit or explicit subsidies may help put these rules in perspective. Books have been written on this subject (e.g., Netzer 1978; Banfield 1984; and Weisbrod 1988), so the discussion here will be brief.

The primary economic argument for providing a government subsidy to art museums is that individuals should not be charged more for any service than the cost of providing that service to the individual. In the case of museums, the cost of an additional visitor may be very low most of the time, or essentially zero. In this case, an admission fee might discourage visitors who could benefit without imposing any costs. Economists say that the art museum is "nonrival," in the sense that many can benefit without using it up. Equivalently, we say that the cost of serving an incremental "customer" is less than the average cost. Note, by the way, that visits during busy times or for popular exhibitions might well cause crowding, so an appropriate admission fee could induce visitors to recognize the congestion costs they impose.

If visitors during uncongested hours are not charged, however, and others are charged only the incremental cost of their visits, then total revenue will be far less than the total cost of operating the museum. In order to stay in business, the museum would need some support.

---

2. Perhaps due to recent rate reductions, the tax expenditure estimated here is smaller than the estimate of Schuster (1986, 320) that "taxes forgone through various arts-related tax incentives provide three times the amount of direct aid to the arts from all levels of government."

Of course, not every service would deserve a subsidy just because the revenue that results from charging incremental costs falls short of the total cost of providing the service. To justify the subsidy, it must also be true that the total value to the users of the service at least equals the total cost of providing the service. Total costs and benefits must be measured empirically, and those who argue for a museum subsidy have implicitly judged that the condition has been met.

Another type of justification for public support of art museums is that benefits flow to many individuals in society and not just to those who visit the museum. The preservation and display of artistic treasures provide national prestige, educational benefits, cultural enrichment, and inherent aesthetic value. They provide the option of future visits, even to those who are not currently visiting. A self-supporting art museum would not take these other benefits into account, so we say these benefits are "external." Again the private market breaks down, because total benefits exceed the amount that can be collected. The size of the external benefit is subject to measurement, but a subsidy can correct the imbalance.[3]

Other arguments have been suggested as justifications for a subsidy of art museums. One of the most straightforward simply states that the public does not properly appreciate art museum services, and that a subsidy is justified to induce them to consume more than they otherwise would. The trouble with this so-called merit good argument is that it can be applied to anything that the advocate factors. It also is impossible to measure. Like most economists, I reject a case for government subsidy based on these paternalistic sentiments.

Finally, free admission to art museums can be more significant for the poor than for the middle- and upper-income groups. Statistical evidence on museum attendance shows that visits rise sharply with income, however. Feld, O'Hare, and Schuster (1983) find that the top income group, representing 8 percent of the population, accounts for 18 percent of the visits to art museums, while the bottom income group, representing 8 percent of the population, accounts for about 2 percent of visits to art museums.[4] Therefore, subsidizing museums cannot be justified as a favorable redistribution policy.

Feld, O'Hare, and Schuster (1983) also note that the benefits of visits to

---

3. See Baumol and Bowen (1966), Netzer (1978), Radich (1987), Scitovsky (1983), Simon (1987), and Weisbrod (1975) for discussions of external effects and the form of the subsidy.

4. Their data derive from the 1975 survey *Americans and the Arts* (Louis Harris and Associates). The 1988 survey does not show the number of visits on a comparable basis, and it has been criticized by Schuster (1988). It shows the following percent in each income group that visited art museums:

Income	Go	Do Not Go
$15,000 or less	39	61
$15,001–$25,000	57	43
$25,001–$35,000	59	41
$35,001–$50,000	61	39
$50,001 and over	73	27

museums are only part of their impact. They also calculate the distributional pattern of various sources of income to museums such as admission fees, donations, and government subsidies. Admission fees are paid by those in relatively high income brackets, donations are received from those in even higher income brackets, and the deduction for gifts is "paid for" by taxpayers who also lie predominantly in the upper brackets of the progressive personal income tax. On balance, the arts are mildly redistributive in the sense that those who finance them have income slightly higher than those who benefit.

8.2.4   Empirical Evidence on Willingness to Pay

Very little empirical evidence is available on the size of any external benefits. One exception is a study in Australia by Throsby and Withers (1983).[5] Their survey results "indicate an overall acceptance of public benefit accruing from the arts, with only a small minority expressing the attitude that they believe there are net cost and that arts education and general support are unjustified" (183). They find that "a mean willingness-to-pay over the whole sample lying between $97 and $155 is indicated. This range is far in excess of the current average level of expenditure out of taxes on the arts in Australia, which is in the region of $6 per head" (185). The authors provide no source for this $6 figure, but it appears to include only direct government expenditures. Additional, implicit subsidies are provided through the exemption of nonprofit institutions and the deductions for charitable gifts.

A less scientific survey has been conducted in the United States by Louis Harris and Associates (1988), and part of the results are summarized in Table 8.2. The question posed to respondents is misleading in the way it points out the huge cost of major federal programs such as national defense and education, compared to "no more than 75 cents per capita for the arts." It ignores the larger state and local expenditures on the arts (see Clotfelter, this volume), and the still larger indirect federal subsidies provided through the tax system. Nonetheless, the survey shows a majority of 56 percent willing to pay $25 more in taxes each year for the arts, and a larger majority of 70 percent willing to pay an extra $10. More reliable than the levels might be the trends over time, where each of these figures have been increasing steadily since 1975.

8.3   The Deduction for Charitable Giving

In our eminently democratic system, the right to vote is not the only voice we have in government decisions about the allocation of scarce public resources. When individuals or corporations decide to give to art museums in the United States, they effectively direct the allocation of tax expenditure dol-

---

5. They deal with the problem that survey respondents have incentive to overstate or understate their willingness to pay, depending on whether they believe that their taxes would actually depend on their answers. The questions are asked two different ways, and the truth is assumed to lie between the two alternatives.

Table 8.2   Willingness to Pay Extra Tax for Arts and Culture

Question: The federal government now pays out over $900 per capita for defense, $140 for education, and no more than 75 cents per capita for the arts. Would you be willing to pay $25 ($15, $10, $5) more in taxes per year for the arts, or would you not be willing to do that?

	1987	1984	1980	1975
$25 More				
Willing	56%	53%	51%	41%
Not willing	42	45	45	53
Not sure	3	2	4	6
$15 More				
Willing	62	61	59	46
Not willing	36	38	39	50
Not sure	2	1	2	4
$10 More				
Willing	70	66	65	51
Not willing	28	32	33	44
Not sure	2	2	2	5
$5 More				
Willing	75	72	70	58
Not willing	23	26	28	37
Not sure	2	2	2	5

Source: Louis Harris and Associates (1988, 105).

lars as well. The next section (8.3.1) reviews practices in several other countries and reveals that tax rules are characterized by considerable diversity. Many nations do not allow a deduction for charitable giving, and no other nation allows both a deduction for the market value of the gift and forgiveness of capital gains tax. The following subsection reviews past practices and reveals that even the United States did not always allow a deduction for charitable giving. In addition, with the deduction, changes in marginal tax rates have resulted in considerable changes over time in the net price of giving or amount of the subsidy. The section also looks at Internal Revenue Service efforts to ensure compliance, and recent changes in the alternative minimum tax. Finally, it simulates the effects of rate changes in the Tax Reform Act of 1986.

8.3.1   Rules in Other Countries

Tax systems vary widely, even among the 23 developed Western nations of the Organization for Economic Co-operation and Development (OECD). Table 8.3 summarizes some of the rules about deductibility from the individual income tax at the national level, but it ignores other special treatments of art museums that might exist under a subnational level income tax, a corporation income tax, a wealth tax, a capital transfer tax, or a value-added tax. Thus, this table should not be used to calculate the final tax price of giving in each country. It is only intended here to indicate the diversity of rules just among the national level individual income tax systems.

A large number of these countries allow no deduction at all for charitable donations. Several other countries allow deductions only under extremely restrictive conditions. Some allow deductions only for cash and not for the market value of any gifts of property, so that donors have no deduction for giving paintings to art museums. Denmark and New Zealand have very low upper limits that would not support large gifts of art. Luxembourg allows deductions for gifts only to state and municipal museums and not for gifts to any private museums. Ireland specifies a list of qualified beneficiaries that is extremely limited and apparently excludes any art institutions (Schuster 1986, 324).

Ireland and the United Kingdom provide a tax incentive or "covenant" that operates much like a tax deduction in some cases, as described further by Rosemary Clarke (chap. 10 in this volume). In Britain, the pay-as-you-earn (PAYE) system means that the taxpayer only receives net income, upon which tax has already been paid. In order for the charity to receive the tax that was

Table 8.3   **The Deductibility of Donations in OECD Countries**

Nation	Deduction
Australia	Gift of $A2 or more to specified charities
Austria	None
Belgium	Cash, BF1000 or more, to 5% of income or BF10 million
Canada	Up to 20% of net income
Denmark	Over DKr300, up to DKr1000
Finland	None
France	Up to 1% of net income (causes of general interest) or 3% (charitable foundations)
Germany	Up to 5% or 10% of net income
Greece	Up to 50% of net income
Ireland	None
Italy	None
Japan	Excess of ¥10000, up to 25% of income
Luxembourg	None
Netherlands	Excess of 1% of income or Gld120, whichever is more
New Zealand	None (credit up to NZ$200)
Norway	None
Portugal	Up to a ceiling
Spain	None
Sweden	None
Switzerland	None
Turkey	None
United Kingdom	Cash up to £240
United States	For itemizers, cash up to 50% of income or property up to 30% of income

Sources: Organization for Economic Cooperation and Development (1986); Price Waterhouse (1988); and Schuster (1986).

paid on a gift out of net income, the taxpayer must enter into a formal agreement or covenant to give certain amounts over a minimum number of years, recently reduced to four. Then the individual's gift is matched by a check from the government directly to the charity. Until 1980, the government would only match gifts at the low basic rate of tax, so that gifts from high-bracket taxpayers were "subsidized" at the same rate as those from low-bracket taxpayers. The subsidy under this system is less flexible than the straight deduction, and it does not accommodate gifts of property. Also, Schuster (1986) notes that the donor can put restrictions only on his or her portion of the gift, not on the government's share. In the United States, the donor can specify the use of the funds for the entire gift, including the government's implicit portion of support.

Also, in Britain, artwork may receive a conditional exemption from capital transfer taxes due upon gift or bequest if the recipient agrees to show it publicly. Upon sale, the government is able to use certain tax advantages in bidding for it. Some works of art may be accepted as payment in lieu of tax. In the French *dation* system, heirs may pay estate taxes with artwork or other objects and thus avoid finding buyers and paying commissions. For the eleven countries on this list that have a personal wealth tax, art is fully exempt in Denmark, France, and Sweden; fully taxable in Finland, Norway, and Switzerland; and given intermediate rules in Austria, Germany, Luxembourg, Netherlands, and Spain (OECD 1988, 55; Cummings and Katz 1987). These wealth and transfer taxes are not reviewed here, but U.S. estate and gift taxes are described in a later section (8.4.4).

8.3.2   A Brief History of Deductions in the United States

For most of the time since our nation was founded, there has been no income tax and therefore no indirect subsidy for charitable gifts. During the experience that lasted from 1861 to 1872, income-tax revenue reached 28 percent of total federal revenue (Ratner 1980, 142), but no deduction was allowed for charitable giving even though Congress thought enough about fairness to establish progressive rates, a deduction for other taxes paid, and an allowance for housing. That tax was repealed, and other attempts at income taxation were held unconstitutional, before the Sixteenth Amendment allowed the enactment of a new income tax in 1913. That tax allowed deductions for business expenses, interest paid, taxes paid, casualty losses, bad debts, depreciation, corporate dividends received, and income on which tax was paid at the source, but there was no deduction for charitable giving.

The deduction for charitable contributions was enacted in 1917, and it was limited to 15 percent of taxable income. At the same time, personal marginal rates began to reach significant percentages for a small fraction of taxpayers. Table 8.4 summarizes the historical development of the top personal marginal tax rate, the relevant rate for calculating the after-tax price of giving for the most wealthy art donor. This top rate jumped from 15 to 67 percent during the

Table 8.4   **The Top Federal Personal Income Tax Rate in the United States**

Years	Top Rate (%)
1913–15	7
1916	15
1917	67
1918	77
1919–21	73
1922–23	58
1925–31	25
1932–35	63
1936–39	79
1941	81
1942–43	88
1944–45	94
1946–51	91
1952–53	92
1954–63	91
1964	77
1965–80	70
1981–86	50
1987	38
1988–	33

Note: See the Tax Foundation, *Facts and Figures on Government Finance,* for footnotes describing some surcharges and other special rules.

First World War, but the 67-percent rate only applied to incomes over $1 million in 1917. The great majority of donors still received no incentive, or at most 15 percent, for charitable giving.[6] The top rate fell back to 25 percent for a period, and rose to around 90 percent for the Second World War. It is not clear how much revenue was actually collected at such high marginal rates, and recent rethinking in the United States has led to successive marginal rate reductions. The top rate fell to 70 percent in 1964, to 50 percent in 1981, and to 33 percent in 1988, even though the revenue from the personal income tax has been rising with the economy and has remained roughly constant as a fraction of total federal revenue.

As a simplification measure for those who would no longer have to record every itemized deduction, a standard deduction was introduced in 1944. It was originally 10 percent of adjusted gross income (AGI) up to some maximum, but it later became a flat amount and was incorporated into a zero-rate bracket. The incentive for charitable donations was thus removed for tax returns taking the standard deduction, initially 83 percent of the total (Clotfelter 1985a, 26). As inflation and real growth decreased the relative value of this

6. The 1917 law "levied no tax on net incomes below $37,700 in 1982 dollars and applied tax rates as high as 15 percent only for net incomes above $300,000, in 1982 dollars" (Clotfelter 1985a, 31).

standard deduction, until it was raised in 1971, the percentage of taxpayers taking the standard deduction fell from 83 to 52. Also, the limit on charitable deductions for itemizers was changed to 20 percent of AGI in 1952, to 30 percent of AGI in 1954, and to the current 50 percent of AGI in 1969 (20 percent for private foundations). Still, however, gifts of property cannot exceed 30 percent of AGI.[7]

These percentage-of-AGI limits are exceeded for only 0.2 percent of all itemized tax returns, but for 5.5 percent of returns in the topmost income group (Clotfelter 1985a, 27). Thus, even for those with hundreds of thousands of dollars of income, there is no immediate deduction for most of the gift of a $1 million painting. The percentage of contributions in property rises from less than 10 percent, at low incomes, to 60 percent for those above $1 million per year.

Over time, donors and their recipients learned how to take advantage of legal tax possibilities, whether those possibilities had been intended by Congress or not. Two examples of perceived abuse were corrected in the Tax Reform Act of 1969. First, in an arrangement that came to be known as a "bargain sale," the taxpayer could sell a piece of appreciated property to the museum at original basis, take a charitable deduction for the excess of market value over basis, and avoid tax on the entire capital gain. Consider a $10,000 painting sold for an original $5,000 cost. With a marginal tax rate of 70 percent, and an exclusion for half of capital gains, the $5,000 deduction would save $3,500 of regular tax plus $1,750 of capital gains tax. The $5,250 tax savings was greater than the $5,000 gift, so the after-tax price of giving was negative relative to an immediate sale. Thus, the individual could sell the art at market value for $10,000, or he or she could sell it to an art museum and receive a total of $10,250 (plus a plaque expressing gratitude for such generosity). It is not clear how much art arrived at museums in this way, and the perception of abuse may have derived from bargain sales to other charities of income-producing property such as rental real estate. In any case, the 1969 act requires the taxpayer to allocate the capital gain between the sale price and the gift (rather than assign all of the gain to the gift).

Second, prior to 1969, the gift of an artist's own work could be deducted at market value. Though perhaps not apparent at first, the artist then received twice the tax benefit of someone else giving the same piece of art. The reason is that the artist had not yet been taxed on the income from the unsold piece of work. Suppose, for example that an artist had two pieces of art, each worth $10,000, and that one was sold while the other was given to a museum. The deduction on the gift then offset the income from the sale, so the artist paid no tax on $20,000 worth of effort. In contrast, if a plumber donated an amount

---

7. For a deduction at full market value, property must be "related" to the purpose of the donee organization (such as art to an art museum). Contributions above either percentage limit may be carried forward for five years. Gifts may also be "partial" interests. See Commerce Clearing House (1988), Arthur Andersen (1987), and U.S. Congress (1969).

of effort worth $10,000, there would be no tax on any income from those plumbing services but no deduction against other income either.

The Tax Reform Act of 1969 changed these perceived loopholes and made other significant changes to the taxation of exempt organizations and charitable contributions. It eliminated the extreme form of the bargain sale, and it put artists on the same footing as other donors by reducing their deduction by the value of their effort, the excess of market value over the cost of materials. It increased the fraction of AGI that can be offset by charitable deductions, from 30 to 50 percent (except for private foundations and for appreciated property). It introduced a 4-percent "excise tax" on the interest and dividend income of private foundations, later changed to 2 percent and then 1 percent.[8] The act also changed some other specific rules for tax-exempt organizations. Finally, the 1969 act introduced the first minimum tax. This provision was intended to prevent high-income individuals from using various tax benefits to the point of paying almost no tax. The original minimum tax did not include any of the benefits to charitable giving, but the concept has expanded in ways to be discussed shortly.

Congress has always felt a certain tension between the desired simplicity of the standard deduction and the desired incentive of the charitable deduction. The Economic Recovery Tax Act of 1981 introduced the first charitable deductions for nonitemizers, but with initial low percentages, ceilings, and expiration after 1986.[9] With a full deduction, the nonitemizer's price of giving $1 falls from 1.0 to $(1-t)$, where t is the marginal tax rate. The years from 1982 to 1986 were intended as a trial period, and the provision was not subsequently renewed.

At the same time, the 1981 act significantly reduced the top marginal tax rate, from 70 to 50 percent. The after-tax price of giving $1 in cash thus rises from 30 to 50 cents for the highest income group. Data from surveys and the IRS indicate that low-income groups (with the greatest relative number of nonitemizers) give proportionately more to religious organizations, while high-income groups give proportionately more to cultural institutions. The act therefore contained a twist or combination of provisions that served to encourage giving to some charities, such as religious organizations, and discourage giving to other charities, such as art museums.

Finally, the Tax Reform Act of 1986 reduced personal marginal tax rates again (and it allowed the nonitemizers' deduction to expire). The personal exemption was increased significantly, so many low-income individuals fell from positive to zero marginal tax rates. Multiple rates were collapsed to just two brackets of 15 and 28 percent, but the benefits of the personal exemptions

8. This provision does not affect most art museums directly, but it may affect the income available for private foundations to give to art.

9. For 1982 and 1983, nonitemizers could deduct 25 percent of the first $100 of charitable donations, for a maximum deduction of $25. They could deduct 25 percent of the first $300 in 1984, 50 percent of all donations in 1985, and 100 percent of all donations in 1986.

are phased out by a 5 percent surcharge over a specified range of income. In other words, the marginal rate increases from 28 to 33 percent and then falls back to 28 percent at the highest income levels.[10] The 1986 act also broadened the tax base in several ways, including the full taxation of nominal realized capital gains.

8.3.3   The Individual Alternative Minimum Tax

Congress has always felt another inherent tension between the desire for incentives and the desire for actual and perceived fairness:

> Although these provisions may provide incentives for worthy goals, they become counterproductive when taxpayers are allowed to use them to avoid virtually all tax liability. The ability of high income taxpayers to pay little or no tax undermines respect for the entire tax system and, thus, for the incentive provisions themselves. (U.S. Congress, Joint Committee on Taxation 1986)

The Tax Reform Act of 1986 extended the list of preference items under the alternative minimum tax (AMT) to include the appreciated portion of donated property deducted under the regular tax. No individual could use this deduction to avoid all tax liability, in any case, because deductions for gifts of property are limited to 30 percent of AGI. Nonetheless, Congress effectively felt that some individuals were using the deduction to pay less than they should. The act retains the full deduction for cash and for the original basis of property given to charities, but it eliminates for some taxpayers the extra incentive provided by the forgiveness of capital gains tax. This single provision, perhaps because it is newly enacted, currently occupies the most prominent point of discussion about income tax policy toward art museums. As reported on the front page of the *New York Times,* 7 May 1989, a study by the American Association of Museums found that the value of objects donated in 1987 was 33 percent less than in 1986. Also, a study by the Association of Art Museum Directors that focused on art museums alone found that "the value of donations declined by $161 million, or 63 percent, from 1986 to 1988 for the 116 institutions reporting." The article includes statements about particular paintings that were not donated because of the 1986 act, and it goes on to discuss efforts in Congress to amend this provision.[11]

Several problems with these statistics are relevant to an overall evaluation of the minimum tax provision for appreciated property. First, these figures for donations are affected by other changes, such as the significant rate reduction embodied in the 1986 act. For our example of property worth $10,000 that

---

10. Other phase-outs, such as the $25,000 passive loss allowance, can make the marginal tax rate higher than 33 percent for certain taxpayers.

11. At the time of this writing, in October 1989, the Senate Finance Committee has just approved an amendment by Senator John Chafee (R, RI) to repeal the inclusion of appreciated property in the AMT.

cost \$8,000, tax savings under the regular tax were formerly \$5,400 (\$5,000 from the deduction at a 50-percent marginal tax rate, plus \$400 from the forgiveness of capital gains tax at a 20 percent rate) and fall to \$3,360 (\$2,800 from the deduction at the 28-percent rate and \$560 of capital gains tax at the 28 percent rate). The price of giving thus rises from .460 to .664, even without the minimum tax provision.

Second, appreciated property is only part of the picture. Figures in *Giving USA* (1989) show increases every year in total donations to "arts, culture, and the humanities," as follows:

1984	\$4.50 billion	6.9% increase
1985	5.08	12.9
1986	5.83	14.8
1987	6.13	8.2
1988	6.82	8.1

Third, these figures might represent changes in the timing of gifts of appreciated property and therefore might not represent a change in the amount of such gifts. Proposals to place donations of appreciated property under the minimum tax were included in the discussions of tax reform during 1985 and early 1986, so donors could easily anticipate the loss of certain tax benefits after 1986. Any future planned donations were therefore more certain to receive the double incentive if made before the effective date in the legislation. Indeed, the study by the American Association of Museums reports that donations increased dramatically from 1985 to 1986, and that both the number and the value of works contributed in 1987 still represent modest increases over 1985. In some respects this showing is surprisingly strong, since we might expect that donations moved up to 1986 would more greatly reduce those remaining in 1987 and 1988. Furthermore, donations might be low while current debate considers further changes. With uncertainty about future legislation, potential donors might be induced to wait for more favorable tax benefits. In any case, it is too early to tell whether long-run gifts of art are affected by the inclusion of appreciation in the minimum tax.

Finally, in light of the stated purpose of the provision, it would be useful to know how many high-income individuals would otherwise have had low effective tax rates. To some, the greater equity is worth the loss of incentive. Even with the broader tax base of the minimum tax, the AMT rate is only 21 percent.[12] Unused deductions can still be carried forward and used against future tax liability for up to five years. And even if the excess is never used, the remaining subsidy is still the same as in other countries that tax the capital gain before allowing a deduction for the value of the gift.

---

12. In this case, the cost of a \$1 gift is 79 cents. Also, depending upon the taxpayer's mix of "exclusion" preferences and "deferral" preferences, an AMT credit may be available that can reduce the net cost of the gift in later years by a reduction of regular tax.

8.3.4   Enforcement, Compliance, and the Art Advisory Panel

Recently, Congress also became concerned about abuses by taxpayers who overvalue donations of property or otherwise overstate deductions. Data from the Taxpayer Compliance Measurement Program (TCMP) for 1982 indicate that 20 percent of donors overstate their deductions of all kinds (and 7 percent understate deductions). Donors of all sorts of property make one-third fewer errors, but the size of errors is one-third larger (U.S. Congress, Hearings, 1986). No statistics indicate the proportion of noncash gifts comprising art. However, tax shelter promoters made arrangements for taxpayers to "acquire objects such as limited edition lithographs, books, gems, and the like, hold the property for at least the capital gains holding period, and then contribute the items to a museum, library, educational institution, or other qualified donee at their 'appreciated' fair market value" (U.S. Congress 1984, 503). Moderate penalties were imposed if the overvaluation were discovered, but enforcement was generally viewed as difficult. Accordingly, the Deficit Reduction Act of 1984 instituted a requirement that a qualified, unrelated appraisal be undertaken before any deduction is claimed for property worth $5,000 or more. The appraiser can be subject to civil tax penalties for aiding and abetting an understatement of tax liability. Also, any donee that disposes of the property within two years must report what was received for it. Finally, penalties for overvaluation were increased.

For works valued at more than $20,000, the IRS generally considers whether to seek review from an official Art Advisory Panel, made up of 25 members including art dealers, museum directors, curators, and art scholars. This panel was established in 1968, and members volunteer their services without pay. The total operating budget for travel and other expenses is about $15,000 per year, and yet from 1977 to 1985, the panel reviewed 1565 cases involving 6717 items. It recommended adjustments for half of these items, by $115 million or 22 percent of the total $525 million claimed (U.S. Congress, Hearings 1986). These adjustments seem to have increased since 1984, to 73.5 percent of items and 36 percent of the value claimed.

Moreover, the IRS seems willing to establish special-purpose panels that last only a finite period. In response to a flood of cases related to a particular shelter scheme, the IRS in 1982 established an Art Print Advisory Panel that, through 1985, reviewed 1650 items upon which $219 million of deductions were claimed. In these cases it recommended adjustments of $216 million, a full 98.6 percent reduction from the amounts claimed (Anthoine 1987).

This combination of provisions would seem virtually to eliminate any possibility for abuse, but several minor advantages remain. First, note that the donor is still able to claim a deduction for the fair market value of the property, even though a sale would probably only provide the fair market value less a significant commission. Second, nothing in these provisions would seem to prevent the donor of a particularly valuable piece from obtaining several different qualified, unrelated appraisals. Even valid professional estimates are bound to vary to some degree, and the donor could pick the highest value for use as the deduction. Finally, note that the issue of appraisal would not even arise if the deduction were limited, as in other countries, to cash or to the original basis of appreciated property. Alternatively, if full capital gains tax were collected on the appreciated portion of the property before the gift were deducted, then any overstatement of value would increase the taxable capital gain by as much as it increased the deduction. In other words, even with correct valuation, the taxpayer under the regular tax still gets the double incentive of the deduction against ordinary income plus the forgiveness of capital gains tax.

8.3.5   The Effect of Incentives on the Amount of Giving

Many studies have attempted to measure the various determinants of charitable contributions, including the donor's income level, tax incentives, and other demographic characteristics. An important parameter for policy purposes is the "price elasticity," defined as the percentage change in giving for a 1 percent change in the after-tax price of giving. Similarly, the "income elasticity" is the relative change in giving for a 1 percent addition to income. Some of the equations and assumptions used to estimate these parameters are described in appendix A.

Some studies use data on the total amount of charitable giving each year, aggregate income, and an overall price (1 minus a weighted average of personal marginal tax rates). This aggregate time-series analysis relies mostly on statutory changes in marginal tax rates to measure the response in giving. Alternatively, some studies use one year's survey or tax return data for different households. This cross-section approach relies on differences in marginal tax rates and differences in giving, while trying to control for differences in level of income and other characteristics.

Researchers have been concerned not just with the size of the estimated price elasticity, but whether it is greater than 1. This value represents a critical benchmark in the sense that it determines whether the extra giving generated by the tax incentive is greater than the government's revenue cost. If the elasticity is less than 1, when a new tax incentive reduces the after-tax price of giving, then the proportional increase in giving is less than the proportional decrease in price. In this case, the individual's out-of-pocket cost actually falls. Since the individual's outlay falls while the gift rises, government must be making up the difference. The tax incentive is "ineffective" in the sense that the donee would receive more if the government just delivered their contribution directly without causing the individual's outlay to fall.[13]

---

13. Feldstein (1980) points out that individuals may respond to direct government support by donating less themselves. In this case, the critical elasticity is zero, and a percentage subsidy always works better than direct grants.

Early research tended to find elasticities less than 1 (Vickery 1975, 157), but more recent work has found larger responses. Martin Feldstein (1975a) employed a time-series of IRS statistics on itemizers in 17 AGI groups. He used several sets of assumptions, but his basic specification resulted in a price elasticity of 1.24. To include nonitemizers and data on wealth, Feldstein and Clotfelter (1976) used a national survey of 1,406 households that was conducted by the Federal Reserve in 1963–64. The basic estimate for the price elasticity was 1.15 in this case. Also, Feldstein and Taylor (1976) used individual returns from the Treasury Department tax files. The estimated price elasticity was 1.09 using 1962 returns, and it was 1.20 using 1970 returns. The time-series and cross-section approaches were then combined when Clotfelter (1980) was able to employ the Treasury's panel study of low- and middle-income taxpayers that were followed for several years. These data allowed exact measurement of marginal tax rates that reflect income averaging and optional forms of deductions. It resulted in an estimate of 1.40 for the long-run price elasticity.

These price elasticity estimates are all close to each other, especially considering the substantial differences in the nature of the data and the level of aggregation. More recent research concludes that the price elasticity of charitable giving is greater than 1, though perhaps not much greater than 1. This implies that donees receive more than the government loses in tax revenue.

An important caveat, however, is that each of these estimates refers to an aggregate elasticity. They implicitly assume that all individuals follow the same behavioral rule for all kinds of giving. In fact, even if the elasticity is constant for a given individual or group, we would not necessarily expect it to be constant across individuals or groups. Also, the estimation lumps together different commodities. A given consumer's needs or wants may not be the same for gifts to different organizations. Such differences might be important for the study of art museums, because of special features of those gifts. Art museums receive donations predominantly from high-income taxpayers who itemize deductions and who might have a sensitivity to price that is different from the average. They also receive a high proportion of gifts in the form of property, gifts that might have a responsiveness different from other donations.

Several studies have attempted to measure variations in price elasticities for different income levels or donee organizations, as reviewed in Clotfelter (1985a, 63–71). The results allow no clear conclusions, largely because of limitations in the data. On the one hand, tax return data allow the calculation of an accurate after-tax price of giving for each household, but they do not include wealth variables, nonitemizers, or donee organizations. On the other hand, survey data (such as the National Study of Philanthropy or the Consumer Expenditure Survey) include more detail on gifts, but they have fewer high-income households and less information on taxes.

Nevertheless, it is useful to look in more detail at some of the disaggregate results. In the first effort to distinguish types of giving, Feldstein (1975b) estimated elasticities for five different types of charitable organizations. He used 1962 IRS data on each type of giving in each AGI class. He found that the price elasticity ranges from 0.49 for religious organizations to 2.63 for other donees.[14]

Type of Donee	Elasticity with respect to:	
	Price	Income
Religious organizations	0.49	0.63
Educational institutions	2.23	1.22
Hospitals	2.44	1.08
Health and welfare	1.19	0.85
All others	2.63	0.65

Unfortunately, the data do not identify art or even culture as a separate category. Instead, museums are aggregated with other diverse organizations in the "all other" category. Art museums are probably more similar to educational institutions than to other organizations with which they are aggregated, but the estimated price elasticity is more than 2.0 in either case.

In a different breakdown, Clotfelter and Steuerle (1981) estimate elasticities separately for five income groups using the Treasury's 1975 tax file and the seven-year panel study of individual taxpayers. They include only itemizers (for whom charitable giving is recorded in the tax return data). The basic set of estimated elasticities are as follows:[15]

Income (1975 dollar)	Elasticity with respect to:	
	Price	Income
$ 4,000–10,000	0.423	0.552
10,000–20,000	0.732	0.578
20,000–50,000	0.972	0.646
50,000–100,000	1.253	0.827
100,000 and over	1.506	0.908

These results are consistent with those above for donee organizations, in that the more responsive, high-income groups give proportionately more to educational institutions (and art museums), while the less responsive, low-income groups give proportionately more to religious organizations.

No study reports elasticities separately for gifts of cash and gifts of property. The best available information is from Slemrod (1988), a study that is

14. However, Dye (1978) and Reece (1979) find that the price elasticity for religious giving is *higher* than for other categories. These studies use individual survey data, with less good tax information, while Feldstein uses aggregate IRS data for 17 income classes, with few observations.

15. In contrast, Feldstein (1975a) and Feldstein and Taylor (1976) included specifications for which the estimated price elasticity *falls* with income. For low-income groups, less variation in the price of giving makes it difficult to estimate accurately the price elasticity.

intended to investigate whether the previous estimated price elasticities are biased by misreporting of taxpayers who respond to higher tax rates by overstating their deductions, rather than actually increasing their donations. Slemrod uses IRS data from intensive audits conducted by the Taxpayer Compliance Measurement Program (TCMP) that include the donations reported by the taxpayer as well as the amount deemed by the auditor to be the correct amount of deduction. He estimates elasticities using both the reported and the corrected deductions and finds that the estimated price elasticity only changes from 2.04 to 2.34, and income elasticity from 0.35 to 0.27.

The important aspect of these data for our purpose is that they separate cash gifts from property. The paper by Slemrod does not report specific results for the two types of gifts, but says:[16]

> The results for cash contributions, which accounted for 87% of the value of all contributions by itemizers in 1982, are quite similar to the aggregated results—price elasticities in excess of two, which rise slightly when reported contributions are replaced by auditor-adjusted contributions. For non-cash contributions, the estimated price elasticity is approximately . . . one and the estimated income elasticity is approximately 0.1. Neither of these estimated coefficients changes much when auditor-adjusted contributions are substituted for reported contributions. (1988, 16)

The lower price elasticity for gifts of property may seem surprising, especially in light of the higher price elasticity for high-income donors shown above. However, much of this property may be secondhand clothes for resale shops or charities, rather than art for museums.

Finally, note that income elasticities are less than 1.0 in most of the results reported above. An implication is that a simple reduction of taxes that puts more after-tax income into the hands of consumers is not an effective way to increase their charitable giving. If the objective is to increase charitable giving, the most effective tax policy would target the price of giving for the most responsive donors.

8.3.6 Rate Reduction and Giving to Art Museums

A major goal of the Tax Reform Act of 1986 was to reduce personal marginal tax rates that took up to 50 percent of any additional income from work effort, savings, or any form of economic activity in the market. Such rates encourage taxpayers to stay home, to work outside the regular market, and even to evade taxes on market income. They interfere with financial debt/equity choices, entrepreneurship, and the balance of investment portfolios.

---

16. This study is not exempt from data and other problems discussed above that lead to considerable uncertainty about the estimates and some disagreements about their size. Additional problems led Slemrod to omit the specific results. In particular, the same weighted average price from appendix equation (3) was used both for cash gifts and for property, instead of using $(1 - t)$ in the regressions for gifts of cash and $(1 - t - a \cdot g)$ in the regressions for gifts of appreciated property.

For many reasons, lower marginal tax rates are expected to increase productive economic activity as well as to have positive feedback effects on tax revenue.

Given these favorable effects, rate reduction is consistent with the benevolent objectives of charitable organizations. Yet given that the incentive for gifts to charities is in the form of a deduction, lower marginal tax rates are also expected to reduce charitable donations. Thus, rather than oppose rate reduction, charities might favor maintaining the subsidy at prior levels by switching to a credit with the same revenue cost as the prior deduction.[17]

In any case, previously estimated price elasticities can be used to "predict" the effects of the 1986 rate reduction.[18] The tax reform is not expected to have any major effects through income elasticities, since it was approximately revenue neutral and distributionally neutral.[19] Data from the Treasury Department on the average change in the marginal tax rate in each income group is shown in columns 2 and 3 of table 8.5. The tax reform dropped many poor families off the tax rolls and thus lowered the average of the marginal rates in the lowest income group from 2.7 to 2.0 percent. It raised the lowest bracket from 11 to 15 percent, however, so the next group actually experienced a slight increase in their average marginal rate. All other groups benefited from substantial rate reduction, especially the top income group where the marginal rate fell from an average of 45.5 to 28.9 percent. Notice that the penultimate group is left with a 32.2-percent rate, on average, because many of these taxpayers are in the 33-percent bracket that precedes the final 28 percent bracket.

Columns 4 and 5 then employ appendix equation (3) to calculate the price of giving, using IRS data on the fraction given in cash vs. property, and assuming that all groups give property with value that is half appreciation.[20] The price of giving changes very little in the lower brackets that tend to give little or nothing to arts and culture, but it rises from .52 to .67 in the top income group that gives most to this category. The top income group gives proportionately more in the form of property, and the Tax Reform Act raises the capital

17. If all taxpayers were allowed the same rate of credit, a remaining problem would be that the subsidy would rise for low-bracket donors and fall for high-bracket donors, those who give relatively more to art museums.

18. These calculations do not predict actual giving for some future year, because they do not include income and demographic variables that would also affect actual future gifts. Instead, they isolate the effects of the price change, as if there were no other changes. They ignore the AMT. Tax rate changes in the 1986 act will be shown to reduce gifts, but higher subsequent income levels will raise actual subsequent gifts.

19. The Tax Reform Act shifted $120 billion of tax over five years from individuals to corporations, but the corporate taxes are implicitly paid through higher prices, lower wages, or reduced dividends. I assume that individuals feel no richer by shifting tax to corporations. No change in real income implies no effect through income elasticities.

20. Clotfelter (1985b) discusses the possibility that taxpayers in higher brackets have assets with higher gain-to-value ratios, and choose those with the greatest gains to give to charity. On the other hand, these assets are less likely to be sold for consumption and more likely to be held until death to avoid capital gains tax. "The two factors thus tend to offset one another, to what degree it is impossible to say" (p. 207).

Table 8.5   Predicted Change for Individual Giving to Arts and Culture

AGI Group (1)	Marginal Tax Rate %		Price of Giving		Price Elasticity (6)	Gifts to Art and Culture ($ millions)		% Change Gifts (9)
	Old Law (2)	TRA (3)	Old Law (4)	TRA (5)		Old Law (7)	TRA (8)	
0–10K	2.7	2.0	.97	.98	−0.47	.0	.0	.0
10–20K	15.7	15.9	.84	.83	0.32	.0	.0	.0
20–30K	20.9	17.9	.79	.81	0.56	.0	.0	.0
30–50K	26.4	21.5	.73	.78	0.75	.0	.0	.0
50–75K	32.8	27.8	.66	.70	0.90	173.2	164.2	−5.2
75–100K	38.3	29.1	.61	.69	1.04	113.3	99.3	−12.4
100–200K	41.9	32.2	.57	.65	1.17	181.8	154.7	−14.9
200K +	45.5	28.9	.52	.67	1.71	573.0	370.8	−35.3
Total						1041.3	789.0	−24.2

Notes and Sources (by column): (1) AGI = adjusted gross income, in K = thousands of dollars; (2) and (3) weighted average in each group, from U.S. Treasury Dept. TRA = Tax Reform Act; (4) and (5) calculated from appendix equation (3) using column 4 of table 8.1 for (1 − C), a = .5 for the ratio of appreciation to value, and assuming that the alternative is immediate consumption. The old law uses column 2 for t, and g = .4t. TRA uses column 3 for t and g; (6) calculated from prices in column 4, the average income in each group, and coefficients in Clotfelter and Steuerle (1981). The appropriate income measure is AGI "minus the tax liability that would have been due if no contributions had been made" (Clotfelter and Steuerle, 424), calculated using Treasury data on average AGI and tax liability in each group, SOI data on gifts, and column 4 prices; (7) calculated from total gifts in SOI for 1985, and proportions given to culture in Clotfelter (1985b); and (8) calculated from appendix equation (4) using columns 4 through 7.

gains rate from a maximum of 20 to 33 percent. Column 6 then shows the price response derived from the variable elasticity formula of Clotfelter and Steuerle (1981) using IRS data on 1985 incomes and column 4 data on prices.[21] The price elasticity ranges from very low values in the lowest income group to 1.7 in the highest income group. Finally, column 7 uses data from the IRS on the 1985 level of gifts from each group, and from Clotfelter (1985b) on the allocation of gifts in each group.

With these figures, appendix equation (4) generates the new hypothetical amount of giving in each group shown in column 8, and the percentage change shown in column 9. The top income group has the largest elasticity, the largest increase in price of giving, *and* the largest amount of giving to the arts. As a consequence, their gifts fall by 35 percent, and the total for all groups falls by 24 percent.[22]

8.4 Other Taxes Affecting Art Museums

As nonprofit organizations, art museums do not pay corporate or personal income tax. No tax is paid on receipts from donations, membership dues, admission fees, or income to the endowment. Moreover, in some special cases, art museums can issue tax-exempt bonds to finance capital projects at an interest rate that is lower than the market rate for taxable debt. To serve their visitors on the premises, art museums can operate, and pay no tax on income from, a parking lot, a restaurant, and a gift shop.

Several tax provisions affect some art museums directly, however. If it is organized as a private operating foundation, for example, the art museum might pay a 1 or 2 percent excise tax on income of the endowment.[23] If it operates a business that is not related to its charitable purpose—such as a

21. Since the estimating equation is more complicated than appendix equation (2), Clotfelter (1985a, 69–70) shows that the price elasticity is calculated by $4.31 - 0.54[\ln(Y)] - 0.50[\ln(P)]$.

22. The nonitemizers' deduction was previously set to expire after 1986, so the Tax Reform Act had no effect on their price of giving. Calculations here pertain only to itemizers, but gifts of nonitemizers are highly concentrated in low-income brackets that give little or nothing to arts and culture. Including gifts to the arts of the few nonitemizers in high-income groups, the total change is 24.1 rather than 24.2 percent.

23. Loosely speaking, every nonprofit organization is a private foundation unless it qualifies as a public charity by being an educational, religious, cultural, scientific, or social-welfare organization with a high fraction of funding from gifts or from charging for related services. "This requirement is designed to insure that the organization is responsive to the general public" (U.S. Congress 1969). Thus an art museum can qualify as a charity by receiving enough gifts or by charging fees for admission. A museum that operates on the basis of a large endowment, rather than ongoing gifts or admission fees, might have to pay the excise tax. In general, private foundations are also subject to a lower (20 percent) limit on AGI that can be deducted by donors, and to other operating restrictions designed to prevent undue accumulations of wealth and private gain (self-dealing rules, payout requirements, excess business holding limitations, and restrictions on the nature of grants). However, a private "operating" foundation can qualify for the higher limits by using two-thirds of its assets to carry out its programs. Thus, even if the art museum is a private foundation and pays the excise tax, it can receive deductible donations of up to 50 percent of AGI by having most of its assets in art that is open to view. See Fremont-Smith (1965, 1972), and the *1989 U.S. Master Tax Guide* (Commerce Clearing House 1988).

restaurant off the premises or the sales of objects other than prints of its art—the museum must pay the unrelated business income tax (UBIT). In addition, the income tax on other corporations may affect their charitable donations and thereby affect art museums. Each of these tax provisions is discussed in turn.

8.4.1   Income Tax Exemption and the Cost of Capital

Many observers have pointed to various tax exemptions as forms of subsidy that allow "unfair competition" with other small businesses that must pay tax when providing some of the same goods and services. It is said, for example, that a private health fitness center must pay tax while the YMCA can provide the same services without tax and therefore at a lower cost. Wages and salaries are subject to the same payroll and personal income taxes, so the tax exemption must be said to lower the cost of capital rather than of labor. Is there really a cost advantage? The U.S. Treasury (1988) notes that:

> Because the nonprofit organization enjoys a . . . higher rate of return on other uses of its capital, including passive investments, the relative "opportunity cost" of entering a particular business . . . can be equivalent for taxable and exempt organizations. As a result, taxable and exempt businesses may be in the same relative position with respect to the decision whether or not to enter a particular business.

To help evaluate these views, appendix B provides a general framework that measures the cost of capital, defined as the gross-of-tax rate of return that a project must earn to cover taxes and the opportunity cost of the funds. The opportunity cost is the net return that the funds could have earned in some other investment. This cost of capital is shown to be identical for taxable firms and nonprofits, as suggested in the above quote, as long as the tax applies to economic income indexed for inflation. The cost of capital for the taxable firm could be *higher* if depreciation allowances at historical cost are insufficient to cover replacement cost, and it could be *lower* for taxable firms if they are allowed an investment tax credit or accelerated depreciation in excess of economic depreciation at replacement cost. Thus the taxable firm *could* have a cost advantage over nonprofits.

This equivalence result does not depend upon whether the funds for the project are obtained from taxable debt or equity. Whatever the actual source of finance, the project always must cover the return that could be earned by putting the money into taxable bonds. The private firm pays taxes on income from the project, but it has a lower opportunity cost of funds because it can only earn the net-of-tax interest rate on this alternative. The nonprofit pays no taxes, but its project has the higher opportunity cost of covering the full market interest rate that could have been earned instead.[24]

The U.S. Treasury (1988) goes on to say:

24. One potential problem is that the nonprofit does not earn the same rate of return on its holdings of debt and equity. The return on the project should be compared to the next best opportunity, that is, whichever rate of return is higher. For untaxed institutions, the interest rate on

Nonetheless, when tax exemption is combined with other governmental subsidies—such as the ability of some exempt organizations to issue tax-exempt bonds, access to lower postal rates, exemption from certain federal excise taxes, and exemption from certain state and local taxes—an exempt organization's cost of producing goods and services for sale is further reduced.

Lower postal rates and exemptions from state and local tax are considered by Clotfelter (in this volume), but the issue of tax-exempt bonds fits nicely into the framework developed here.

The cost of capital depends on the alternative rate of return that the investment must cover. If the exempt organization trades off more of the project against having more interest-bearing endowment, then the above analysis holds. If interest-bearing endowment is fixed, however, and the organization is allowed to use tax-exempt debt to finance the project, then the relevant cost is the tax-exempt interest rate. Since that rate is less than the market interest rate, the cost of capital is reduced. Thus a government-connected museum that can issue tax-exempt debt can provide services more cheaply.

The next section makes use of this analysis to consider specific issues of the unrelated business income tax. In particular, the issue is clouded by an inherent contradiction between the desire to subsidize one activity (that may have external benefits) and to treat similarly a competing activity (that may not have external benefits).

8.4.2 The Unrelated Business Income Tax and "Unfair" Competition

Despite the doubts just raised, this section will follow existing literature in assuming that the nonprofit's exempt status does confer a real or perceived cost advantage.[25] One question is whether this cost advantage is justified by external benefits, and another question is whether the cost advantage results in "unfair" competition.

In section 8.2, I discussed how tax advantages may be justified by spillover social benefits and/or the cost structure of museum services. If these benefits are sufficiently large, we might *want* certain nonprofits such as art museums to be subsidized not only through deductions for gifts and exemption of passive investment income, but through exemption of active business income as well. They could then provide more of the desired art.

The Revenue Act of 1950 effectively decided that the deduction for gifts and the exemption of passive investment income were sufficient subsidy. It introduced a separate tax at the corporate rate on the nonprofit's active business income that is not "substantially related" by having a causal relationship that "contributes importantly" to the accomplishment of the organization's exempt purposes, other than the mere need for funds (U.S. Treasury 1988).

---

taxable bonds is usually higher than the return after corporate tax on corporate stock. Thus, even if the funds come from donations, the cost of funds is the interest rate on taxable bonds.

25. See Copeland and Rudney (1986) or Schiff (1988) for examples.

Table 8.6   **Unrelated Business Income and Compliance with UBIT**

	Percent with Unrelated Business Income		UBIT Errors (Millions of Dollars)	
	1973–74	1979–83	1973–74	1979–83
Private foundations	1.2	1.5	0.4	3.7
Public charities	2.8	5.8	16.7	4.0
Civic associations	1.7	7.7	1.4	0.9

Source: Grabowski and Soffer (1988).

These rules have been modified in piecemeal fashion by Congress, Treasury regulations, and the courts. They have come to be viewed as complex and arbitrary, and their scope is still a subject of some debate.

Relatedness is now determined item by item, so separate accounts must be kept even within a single gift shop. The sale of an art print is exempt, but the sale of a T-shirt with the museum logo is not. What about the sale of a T-shirt with art printed on it? The museum is left to decide such details, subject to IRS and court objections, so it has every incentive to make aggressive interpretations.[26]

Moreover, these administrative difficulties lead to problems of enforcement and compliance. The IRS estimated that the voluntary compliance level (VCL) for unrelated business income was only 21.2 percent in 1973, and 46.3 percent in 1983 (U.S. Internal Revenue Service 1988, F-24), but they believe that the increase is due to broader examination coverage rather than to increased compliance. Grabowski and Soffer (1988) provide further results of IRS examinations, as summarized in table 8.6. They show that the UBIT errors of private foundations have increased ninefold between the 1973–74 period and the 1979–83 period. In the public charity category, UBIT errors have declined 76 percent over the same span, even though the percentage of public charities with such income has increased from 2.8 to 5.8.

Total UBIT revenues are less than 0.05 percent of the corporate income tax (Rose-Ackerman 1982), but this figure may not reflect its true revenue impact. Without this provision, much more business activity might be undertaken by exempt organizations instead of corporations, with a loss of corporate revenue. Also, the provision is intended to "regulate" the activities of nonprofit organizations, since, without it, substantial untaxed commercial activity could divert an organization from its primary purpose and make it accountable neither to donors nor to shareholders.

Yet the primary purpose of UBIT is not related to the size of the external benefit, the need for revenue, or the desire to regulate. The provision is intended primarily to address the perceived problem that the exempt organiza-

26. The Boston Museum of Fine Arts recently tried to help advertise their Egyptian exhibit by selling chocolate mummies in the gift shop, but this item was deemed to be subject to UBIT.

tion operating in an unrelated business would have an unfair advantage over other private business in the same activity.

Even with a cost differential, Rose-Ackerman (1982) points out that there may be no ill effect on other private business. First, if the nonprofit represents a small part of the total market for that particular good or service, it will have no effect on the equilibrium price and therefore no effect on other private business. Second, suppose that the nonprofit's activity does affect the price, but that other private firms face no significant fixed costs of entry or exit. In this case, any other firm can shift out of that activity and into a different activity where it can earn the same equilibrium market rate of return it earned before, with no adverse effects. Third, if there do exist costs of entry or exit, other private businesses could reasonably be expected to anticipate competition from nonprofits at the time of their initial commitment to the industry and thus to make only investments that cover the fixed cost and still earn their required rate of return. That is, the fully informed taxable firm would only undertake investments that improve its situation, so the differential rates of return do not inflict any injury. Fourth, even if the nonprofit's competition is unanticipated, the reduced return to the other private businesses might not be unwarranted if the industry is not initially competitive and thus affords an unusually high rate of return.

The only remaining case with a potential problem is where the industry initially is competitive, the nonprofit's entry is unanticipated, the nonprofit's activity is large enough to affect the market price, *and* the other private businesses would incur significant fixed costs of leaving this activity or entering another. For this reason, Rose-Ackerman concludes that UBIT is "exactly the wrong way to respond to the problem" (1982, 1037). It encourages nonprofits to concentrate in activities judged to be related, where they are more likely to affect the equilibrium market price. And since tax rules keep modifying the definition of unrelated activities, UBIT keeps imposing unanticipated windfall gains and losses. "It appears, then, that the tax on unrelated business activity creates more unfairness than it can possibly prevent. It should therefore be repealed" (p. 1038).

Rose-Ackerman provides a very useful analysis, but it does not support her own conclusion. The complete repeal of UBIT would represent the largest possible unanticipated change to existing tax rules in this area. Nonprofit organizations would probably expand in certain familiar activities, rather than enter many diffuse activities, where private firms have invested much fixed capital and are earning only normal competitive rates of return. The repeal of UBIT would thus reduce returns to existing businesses and impose large capital losses.

The analysis is correct that differential rates of return are not unfair so long as private businesses know about the differences before they enter the activity. Any tax change can impose windfall gains and losses, hence the adage "an old tax is a good tax." The implication for tax policy in this case is to minimize changes by nailing down a workable definition of related activities that does not require constant revision. Any unchanging definition avoids being unfair to private businesses, but administrative and compliance costs can be minimized by a definition that does not require multiple books and arbitrary classifications.

Similarly, a tax on museums' unrelated business is not unfair as long as they know the rules beforehand or can exit without cost. A tax on museums' *related* services might be unfair, since they cannot exit from their primary responsibility. Again, as discussed above, the tax exemption for related activities can be viewed simply as a way to encourage museum services that have important social benefits, and even a tax exemption on unrelated activities could be viewed as another way to enable them to expand those museum services.

8.4.3 The Corporate Income Tax Deduction

While the corporate income tax does not apply to the primary and related activities of art museums, it does affect the donations made to art museums by other corporations. Such donations were not deductible under the corporate income tax until 1935, but it was fairly easy for corporations to make charitable expenses look like business expenses. As a consequence, early data on corporate charitable contributions is not very reliable. From 1936 to 1980, while corporations were allowed to deduct contributions up to 5 percent of taxable income, data in Clotfelter (1985a) show that gifts increased 14 times in real terms, from $91 million to $2.32 billion (in 1972 dollars). As a fraction of net income, however, these gifts were 0.28 percent in 1936 and 0.79 percent in 1980.

The maximum fraction of taxable income was raised from 5 to 10 percent in 1981, with little effect on most firms.[27] Only 7.5 percent of corporations make contributions of more than $500 per year, and less than one-quarter make any contribution. These differences are related to size and profitability, as contributions were made by 35 percent of profitable firms and only 2 percent of loss firms (Useem 1987). Contributions were made by 80 percent of corporations with assets exceeding $0.5 billion (0.1 percent of all corporations), and these account for 50 percent of all corporate gifts. Still, most of these firms give less than 5 percent of income, and corporate giving averages less than 2 percent of corporate income.

Corporations and individuals donate similar percentages of income, on av-

---

27. The 1981 act also reduced the measure of taxable income, however, so the limit on deductions for some firms may actually fall. Also, firms may use a figure like 5 percent as a rule of thumb, or as a goal for enhancing their corporate image. For example, the Greater Minneapolis Chamber of Commerce honors area firms giving at least 5 percent of income. The lower measure of taxable income may have made it easier for some firms to attain that goal. Minneapolis reports that they honored 45 firms giving 5 percent in each year from 1979 to 1981, and from 71 to 76 firms in every year between 1983 and 1986.

erage, but corporate income is considerably smaller. Thus corporate gifts are about one-fifteenth the size of individual gifts (Clotfelter 1985a). In the non-religious, nonprofit sector, where private gifts constitute 22 percent of total resources, corporate gifts account for only 2 percent of the total (Useem 1987).

For sufficient detail to isolate contributions to art, table 8.7 uses data collected by The Conference Board in their survey of major corporations (Troy 1984; Platzer 1988). For the major categories of beneficiaries, the table shows that gifts to health and human service organizations have fallen steadily from 42 percent of corporate gifts in 1972 to 28 percent in 1986; gifts to education and to civic organizations have increased slightly over the same period as percentages of corporate giving; gifts to the "other" category have fallen somewhat; and gifts to culture and art have more than doubled as a percent of total giving, from 4.1 percent in 1972 to 11.9 percent in 1986. The penultimate row of the table shows that total corporate gifts have increased from $1.0 billion to $4.5 billion over the period, so the category of culture and art has clearly been a major beneficiary of this trend. The bottom row shows that these gifts have almost doubled as a percent of pretax income.

The table also shows components of the culture and art category, where gifts to museums have increased from 1.8 percent of the total in 1974 to 2.3 percent in 1986. Gifts to art funds and councils and gifts to other categories have remained fairly stable. The most dramatic increase within culture and art is the subcategory for employee matching gifts. In other words, corporations are starting to direct their own gifts to the organization favored by their workers.

These breakdowns also depend on size and other characteristics of firms. Large firms are less likely to give to health and human services and more likely to give to education and to civic organizations. Gifts to culture and art are somewhat related to size.[28] Differences are more dramatic by industry. Firms in printing and publishing have been giving about 20 percent of gifts each year to art and culture, and the seven firms in the survey from the stone, clay, and glass industry are giving 38 percent to art and culture. Even more startling, the subcategory for museums gets 32 percent of the total gifts from this industry.

Why might a corporation make a donation, and how might taxes affect the donation? A firm trying to maximize profits for shareholders would seem to have few charitable motives, but donations might still be part of a package the firm can use to increase profits or share values indirectly. When Galaskiewicz (1986) asked top managers to rank a set of firms, he found that those with the largest giving programs were ranked as the most successful, even controlling

28. Among firms giving less than $500,000, the median firm gives 8.9 percent to culture and art, and among firms giving $5 million or more, the median gives 11.6 percent to culture and art (Platzer 1988).

Table 8.7   Beneficiaries of Corporate Support as Percent of Total Giving

	1972	1974	1976	1978	1980	1982	1984	1986
Health and human services	42.0	38.5	39.3	36.9	34.0	31.0	27.7	28.0
Education	36.9	36.0	37.3	37.0	37.8	40.7	38.9	42.9
Culture and art	4.1	7.3	8.2	10.1	10.9	11.4	10.7	11.9
Music	—	1.1	1.1	1.5	1.5	1.5	1.4	1.4
Museums	—	1.8	1.9	2.5	2.4	2.5	2.1	2.3
Public TV and radio	—	1.7	1.2	1.6	1.6	1.4	1.3	1.3
Art Funds and councils	—	1.0	0.7	0.8	0.9	0.7	0.6	0.7
Theaters	—	0.4	0.4	0.6	0.7	0.8	0.6	0.8
Cultural centers	—	—	0.9	1.0	1.1	0.8	1.0	0.7
Dance	—	—	0.1	0.2	0.3	0.3	0.2	0.3
Libraries	—	—	0.2	0.3	0.3	0.2	0.2	0.2
Employee matching	—	—	*	*	0.2	0.4	0.6	0.9
Other	—	1.0	0.7	0.7	0.8	1.1	1.1	1.0
Not identifiable	—	0.3	0.7	0.9	1.1	1.6	1.6	2.3
Civic and community	9.1	10.4	11.0	11.4	11.7	11.7	18.8	13.2
Other	6.6	7.7	4.2	4.5	5.6	5.2	3.9	4.0
Total	100.0	100.0	100.0	100.0	100.0	100.0	100.0	100.0
In billions of dollars	1.0	1.2	1.5	2.1	2.4	2.9	4.1	4.5
Percent of pretax income	1.0	0.9	0.9	0.9	1.0	1.7	1.7	1.9

Sources: Troy (1984) and Platzer (1988).

Note: Category percentages do not add up to exactly 100 because of rounding. The percentage breakdowns by beneficiary category are based on survey responses from a different number of firms each year. The smallest number of companies was 370 (for 1986), and the largest number was 799 (for 1972). In the last two rows, however, the totals and percent of income figures reflect contributions of all U.S. corporations.

*Less than 0.1 percent.

for actual earnings and other measures of performance. Second, the publicity surrounding large gifts can act as a form of advertising. A certain kind of image can attract customers. Third, gifts to the community can make the community a more desirable place to live and work, possibly reducing labor costs. Fourth, the managers of the firm may be acting on their own motives rather than maximizing the profits of the firm. Several models of this type are reviewed in Clotfelter (1985a). Finally, a more tax-oriented reason for charity might lie in the double taxation of corporate source income. If the shareholders were going to be giving a certain amount to charity anyway, and if they can agree on the set and mix of beneficiaries, then they can save even more of the total tax on that income by making the donations at the corporate level instead of paying the corporate tax and then making donations out of personal income from dividends.

These alternative theories of corporate giving have implications for the effect of tax changes on donations. Both charitable expenses and advertising are deductible, so a change in the statutory corporate tax rate has no effect on the price of giving *relative* to the price of advertising. Thus, if gifts are a form of advertising, changes in the corporate rate may have no effect on gifts. But if shareholders want the corporation to donate for them, then the corporate rate does affect the overall price of giving. The actual effect of the corporate rate on gifts is subject to empirical investigation.

Large corporations with most charitable donations are all in the top corporate rate bracket, so cross-section data does not include enough variation in after-tax prices to allow estimation of a price elasticity. They generally find an income elasticity that is less than 1, as reviewed in Clotfelter (1985a). The corporate rate has changed over the years, however, so Schwartz (1968) and Nelson (1970) use time-series analysis to find price elasticities from 1.36 to 2.00, and from 1.03 to 1.18, respectively. Income elasticities may be less than 1 or greater than 1. The most recent and most thorough estimates are provided by Clotfelter (1985a), who uses two different samples (an aggregate time-series, and pooled observations of asset classes over time), two different after-tax price variables (one based on a constructed marginal tax rate and one based on an average effective tax rate), and several different measures of income (pretax income, post-tax income, or net cash flow). He obtains price elasticities between 0.20 and 1.75, and income elasticities between 0.40 and 1.14.

As pointed out by Clotfelter, differences among these estimates are attributable directly to differences in the variables used to measure prices and incomes. For the after-tax price of a gift at the margin, the conceptually correct variable is 1 minus the statutory marginal rate. The aggregate or pooled data do not supply a single marginal rate, however. When early work by Schwartz and later work by Clotfelter use the ratio of corporate taxes to corporate income (the average effective tax rate) as an approximation of the correct marginal rate, they get *high* estimates of the price elasticity. Nelson attempts to construct an estimate of the weighted-average marginal tax rate, and he gets *low* price elasticities. When Clotfelter conducts complicated calculations of the statutory rate bracket faced by each firm in each asset class in each year—again to approximate the correct marginal rate—he gets price elasticities only from 0.20 to 0.57, depending on other specifications.

For income elasticities, early work by Schwartz and later work by Clotfelter again find similar distinctions based on the measure of income. The use of after-tax income implies elasticities less than 1 (as low as 0.53), and the use of after-tax cash flow implies elasticities greater than 1 (as great as 1.34).

These kinds of differences make it difficult to conclude anything definitive about the effect of taxes on corporate contributions to art museums. There is no consensus about the best estimated price or income elasticities, so there can be no certainty about predictions based on any one set of elasticities. For this reason, no attempt is made here to simulate the effects of the Tax Reform Act of 1986, as was done for changes to individual tax rates and giving. Clotfelter (1985a) seems to prefer price and income elasticities of 0.4 and 1.1, respectively, and he uses these values to find that the repeal of the corporate tax would reduce gifts by 7.2 percent. Although the price of gifts would rise by about 85 percent, the after-tax cash flow would increase by 17 percent, nearly offsetting the price increase (p. 221). In the case of the 1986 act, both effects work to reduce gifts: it reduced the statutory marginal tax rate (increased the price of giving) and simultaneously increased corporate tax burdens by $120 billion over 5 years. Still, the analysis is complicated by other changes such as the reduction of individual tax burdens and the possibility that corporations act on behalf of shareholders who can see through the corporate veil.

8.4.4   The Estate and Gift Tax

Aside from brief intervals, 1862 to 1870 and 1898 to 1902, the federal estate tax has been in operation continuously since 1916. It was initially levied at rates from 1 to 10 percent, and during World War I from 2 to 25 percent, with an exemption of $50,000. The current gift tax was enacted in 1932. The estate and gift tax rules were modified several times until 1942, when the exemption was set at $60,000 and the rates extended to 77 percent. This $60,000 exemption was fixed in nominal terms for the next 34 years, with the result that the number of taxable estates increased from 1.1 percent of all deaths in 1942, to 6.5 percent of all deaths in 1976 (Pechman 1987, 350).

In 1976, the exemption was converted to a tax credit that was equivalent to an exemption of more than $120,000. The top rate was reduced to 70 percent, and the estate and gift taxes were unified. In 1981, the unified credit was set to be increased in stages up to the current exemption equivalent of $600,000, the top rate was reduced in stages to the current top rate of 50 percent, and the deduction for marital bequests was increased from 50 percent to the current 100 percent of the estate. As a consequence of these changes, taxable estates have fallen back from 6.5 percent of deaths in 1976 to 1.5 percent of deaths in 1985. In relation to total federal budget receipts, the estate ad gift tax has fallen from a peak of 2.3 percent to a current 0.9 percent (Pechman 1987, 370).

The gift tax represents a very small portion of this revenue, but its purpose clearly is to prevent the erosion of the estate tax base that would be made possible through inter vivos transfers to the same individuals. Under current rules, each spouse can give up to $10,000 per year tax-free to each child or other beneficiary, and excess gifts apply to the $600,000 lifetime exemption of the unified estate and gift tax. Similarly, the "generation-skipping transfer tax" is designed to prevent erosion of the estate tax base through trusts that provide income for the lifetime of the next generation (the children), where the remainder is given to the following generation (the grandchildren). Under all of these taxes, charitable donations are fully deductible.[29]

In 1985, 30,500 estates were taxable. These estates were worth $32.7 billion, but exemptions and deductions reduced the taxable portion to $24.4 billion. The total charitable deduction was $4.5 billion, an amount somewhat larger than corporate charitable deductions but still one-tenth the size of individual income tax deductions. The estate tax revenue after credits was $5.0 billion, one-fifth of the estate tax base. The great bulk of the wealth is in the largest few estates, however. Estates over $5 million account for 2 percent of taxable returns but 36 percent of the tax (Pechman 1987, 239).

While the estate tax is not a significant source of revenue, it still takes 40 percent of the taxable base for gross estates over $10 million. Thus the major reason for the tax may be its redistributive effect, or perceived redistributive effect. Bernheim (1987) has even suggested that the estate tax leads to a *reduction* in total tax revenue, by encouraging more inter vivos transfers of assets to children whose income is then subject to lower personal marginal tax rates.

While charitable bequests are a small portion of total charitable giving, they are a crucial source of art for museums (see Richard N. Rosett, chap. 6 in this volume). This difference is related to evidence that the distribution of charitable deductions under the estate tax is even more skewed than charitable deductions under the income tax. Charitable bequests constitute less than 1 percent of small estates, but this fraction rises to 48 percent of the largest estates (Clotfelter 1985a, 230). These large estates are more likely to give to museums. Detailed data are not available, but Clotfelter (p. 232) indicates that bequests to religious organizations account for two-thirds of total charitable bequests of small estates and less than 1 percent of total charitable bequests

---

29. Depending on the desires of the donor, arrangements can be made to split up the control of the assets, the income from the assets, and the remaining interests in the assets, through charitable remainder trusts, pooled income funds, or charitable lead trusts. See Arthur Andersen (1987). Although art may be left in the control of an heir for his or her lifetime before donation to a museum, these trusts are most commonly associated with income-producing property.

for the largest estates; bequests to educational, scientific, and literary organizations show no clear relation to estate size; and bequests to other charitable organizations (including foundations) increase as a fraction of estate size.

The largest estates provide most of the charitable bequests *and* give more than proportionately to the arts, so the price of giving to art museums depends on the top marginal rate under the estate tax even more than under the income tax. As is not true under the income tax, however, appreciated property is never subject to capital gains tax at the time of death. Instead, the "basis" for the heir is increased to the fair market value of the property at the time of inheritance. Thus, the forgiveness of capital gains tax is not an additional benefit of donation to charity, as it is under the income tax. The after-tax price of giving to charity, rather than to an heir, is just 1 minus the estate tax rate. The situation is more complicated under different alternatives, however, as described by Boskin (1976). If the alternative to giving property to charity at death is to consume the proceeds during life, then the relative price does involve the capital gains tax that would have to be paid upon sale. Or, if the alternative to a charitable donation at death is a donation to the same charity during life, the *relative* price may involve the personal income tax rate, the capital gains rate, the estate tax rate, and the interest rate that can be earned on funds retained until death. Nonetheless, most empirical studies of the price elasticity simply use 1 minus the estate tax rate as the price of a charitable bequest.[30]

Empirical work in this area finds that charitable bequests are related to the after-tax price, the size of the estate, and the age and marital status at the time of death. Most studies find very large price elasticities for charitable bequests. Interestingly enough, they tend to find that the price elasticity falls as the estate size becomes larger. When Boskin (1976) uses 1969 estate tax returns, for example, he finds that the elasticity with respect to estate size is 0.40 and that the price elasticity falls from 2.53 for the smaller estates to 0.20 for the largest estates. Using 157–59 returns, the price elasticity ranges from 1.8 for the smallest to 0.94 for the largest. Feldstein (1977) finds that the price elasticity ranges from 4.0 for the smallest estates to 0.3 for the largest estates. In contrast, Barthold and Plotnick (1984) find that the after-tax price is not a significant determinant of charitable bequests.

Finally, Clotfelter (1985a) uses more recent 1976 data, varies the functional forms, and recalculates previous results. He finds high price elasticities, ranging from 3.70 for the smallest estates (those with price greater than 0.8) to 1.77 for the largest estates (those with price less than 0.6). He also simulates the effects of recent estate tax changes, using 1.6 for the price elasticity of estates less than $1 million (and 0.4 for the elasticity with respect to estate

30. Similarly, when empirical work discussed in section 8.3.5 uses 1 minus the personal tax rate, amended for the capital gains tax, it assumes that the alternative to the current gift is current consumption. If the alternative to lifetime giving is donation at death, then the price in those regressions would involve the estate tax.

size). Because of uncertainties about the estimated coefficients, he uses alternative values of 1.0 or 2.4 for the price elasticity of large estates. Results suggest that the 1981 changes could reduce total charitable bequests by 34 to 52 percent, but could reduce charitable bequests of the very largest estates by 50 to 84 percent. As a consequence, if donations of art are concentrated in the largest estates, and if the price elasticity is as high as 2.4, then the 1981 reduction in the top marginal estate tax rate from 70 to 50 percent could have a very major impact on bequests to art museums.

8.5 Conclusion

Although art museums do not pay any substantial taxes, they are greatly affected by various U.S. tax rules. The individual receives a deduction for donations of art to museums, the estate gets a deduction for bequests, and the corporation gets a deduction for charitable gifts. These deductions might be viewed as the logical consequence of taxing a measure of income defined as funds available for personal consumption, excluding funds given to a public cause. Alternatively, they might be an explicit policy to encourage gifts. Whatever the justification, when taxes raise the cost of undertaking activities that are not deductible, these provisions clearly lower the relative cost of making donations. In this sense, art museums receive an implicit subsidy.

Art museums also are not taxed on investment income or on some related business activities. Again these provisions might be justified in a number of ways, but the effect of taxes is to raise the cost of other private activities and thus lower the relative cost of museum activities.

The tax expenditure is defined as the amount that would have been collected from museums if they had been fully taxed. In combination, this set of tax provisions is found to have a tax expenditure that is larger than direct federal expenditures on art museums in the United States. However, the amount of this tax expenditure or implicit subsidy has been falling in recent years because of reductions in the marginal personal income tax rates at which individuals deduct gifts.

A review of the empirical literature reveals that individuals and corporations are indeed fairly responsive to the incentive inherent in this deductibility. High-income taxpayers are found to be the most responsive to marginal tax rate, and they also tend to give the largest amounts to the arts. Therefore, the level of the top personal marginal tax rate is particularly important to art museums. Simulations here suggest that the personal marginal rate reduction in the Tax Reform Act of 1986 could greatly reduce gifts to the arts.

Other countries tend to have smaller implicit tax subsidies but larger direct spending on the arts. What might be the advantages or disadvantages of each approach? If the primary justification for public aid is the educational benefits of art museums, for example, then a government using the direct approach might be able to specify that arts funds be used for educational functions. Or, if the goal is to make art opportunities more accessible to a wider audience, it might direct funds toward traveling exhibitions. A disadvantage is that art funding is subjected to the political process.

The United States provides relatively more implicit aid. Deductibility is available for gifts to art museums that may be used for purposes specified by the donor rather than by the government. In effect, we seem to have decided that the possible advantage of direct spending is outweighed by the need to avoid undue political influence.

Appendix A
Price Elasticities and Simulation

In order to estimate price and income elasticities, researchers often assume that charitable behavior is determined by:

$$(1) \qquad\qquad G = AP^bY^c,$$

where G is the amount of giving, P is the price, Y is income, and A is a function of other characteristics. In this case b is the price elasticity, as can be confirmed by taking the derivative of G with respect to P: $dG/dP = bAP^{b-1}Y^c = bG/P$, so $b = (dG/G)/(dP/P)$. The income elasticity is $c = (dG/G)/(dY/Y)$. In this particular functional form, these parameters are constant across different prices and income levels (though giving is not). The next step is to take the natural logarithm of (1) and run linear regressions on:

$$(2) \qquad\qquad \ln(G) = \ln(A) + b \cdot \ln(P) + c \cdot \ln(Y).$$

Since equation (2) relates the consumer's spending on gifts to the price of gifts, it is essentially a downward-sloping demand curve. Giving falls when the price rises, but it is common to refer to the absolute value of the elasticity as a measure of responsiveness.

If the data separate the amount of cash gifts from the amount of appreciated property, then the after-tax price for total giving of the household is a weighted average of the price for cash gifts and the price for property gifts:

$$(3) \qquad P = C(1 - t) + (1 - C) \cdot [1 - t - a \cdot g]$$

where C is the fraction given in cash, t is the marginal tax rate for the deduction, a is the discounted ratio of appreciation to value, and g is the capital gains tax rate. The two tax rates are equal under current law, so for our example with the rate of 28 percent, equation (3) provides $(1 - t - a \cdot g) = 1 - .28 - (.2)(.28) = .664$ for the price of giving appreciated property. Also, this price implies that the alternative to the gift is consumption. If the alternative is a bequest, the estate tax matters (Clotfelter 1985b).

Each household is typically assigned the average fraction given in cash for its income group. The amount of appreciation is not available, but Feldstein and Clotfelter (1976) find that $a = .5$ provides the best fit for the data. Subsequent researchers typically assume this ratio.

A major purpose of estimating the price and income elasticities for charitable giving is to measure the effect of changes in tax policy. Since the form of equation (1) assumes that the elasticity is constant over a range of prices, the estimates can be used to "predict" changes in gifts even for a large discrete change in the after-tax price. Suppose that G_0 is the observed amount of giving, as determined by $A(P_0)^b Y^c$, and that tax policy changes the price from P_0 to P_1. The predicted new level of giving is $G_1 = A(P_1)^b Y^c$, but division implies that $(G_1/G_0) = (P_1/P_0)^b$. Then multiplication by G_0 provides:

$$(4) \qquad\qquad G_1 = G_0 \cdot (P_1/P_0)^b.$$

This equation "predicts" new gifts using only observations on old gifts, the statutory change in tax rates, and existing estimates of b.

Appendix B
The Cost of Capital

For simplicity, suppose that a firm pays corporate tax at rate u on earnings after deductions for economic depreciation at replacement cost. It faces a certain interest rate i and inflation rate π. It considers a hypothetical marginal investment that must earn a nominal required after-tax rate of return r, the discount rate. Suppose that the return c falls due to depreciation at rate δ, and is discounted at rate r. The equilibrium condition is that the marginal one dollar outlay must be matched by the present value of after-tax earnings (see Hall and Jorgenson 1967):

$$(5) \qquad 1 = \int_0^\infty c(1 - u)e^{(\pi - \delta)t}e^{-rt}\, dt + uz = \frac{c(1 - u)}{r - \pi + \delta} + uz,$$

where z is the present value of depreciation allowances at rate δ, discounted at $r - \pi$. Thus, with economic depreciation at replacement cost, $z = \delta/(r - \pi + \delta)$. We solve for c, substitute for z, and define ρ as $c - \delta$, the pretax return:

$$(6) \qquad \rho = c - \delta = \frac{r - \pi + \delta}{(1 - u)}(1 - uz) - \delta = \frac{r - \pi}{1 - u}.$$

Regardless of the actual source of finance, the firm could always forgo the investment and retire debt (or increase interest-bearing assets) instead, so the discount rate is the interest cost of the funds. In other words, because of arbitrage between this real investment and the interest rate alternative, these cost-of-capital comparisons pertain even if the investment is actually financed by equity of the taxable corporation or of the exempt organization.

For a taxable firm, the alternative is to save $i(1 - u)$ on its debt (or to earn $i[1 - u]$ on interest-bearing assets), so $r = i(1 - u)$ and:

$$(7) \qquad \rho_{\text{taxable}} = i - \frac{\pi}{1 - u}.$$

For a nontaxable entity considering the same investment project, the required rate of return that it can earn on other assets is $r = i$, the market interest rate. However, u is zero, so:

$$(8) \qquad \rho_{\text{nontaxable}} = i - \pi.$$

Thus, with no inflation, the cost of capital for the two types of investors would be identical. In fact, in this simple example with economic depreciation at replacement cost, higher inflation causes the cost of capital for the taxable firm to fall *below* that of the exempt firm. The taxable firm's cost of capital and effective tax rate may be even lower if it receives an investment credit or depreciation that is more accelerated than economic allowances at replacement cost. In the more general case, with historical cost depreciation and taxation of nominal capital gains, inflation might raise the cost of capital for the taxable firm above that of the exempt firm.

References

Andrews, William D. 1972. Personal Deductions in an Ideal Income Tax. *Harvard Law Review* 86, no. 2 (December): 309–85.

Anthoine, Robert. 1987. Charitable Contributions after the 1986 Tax Act and Problems in Valuation of Appreciated Property. *Columbia–VLA Journal of Law and the Arts* 11, no. 2: 283–314.

Arthur Andersen & Co. 1987. *Tax Economics of Charitable Giving.* 10th ed.

Banfield, Edward C. 1984. *The Democratic Muse: Visual Arts and the Public Interest.* New York: Basic Books.

Barthold, Thomas, and Robert Plotnick. 1984. Estate Taxation and Other Determinants of Charitable Bequests. *National Tax Journal* 37:225–37.

Baumol, William J., and William G. Bowen. 1966. *Performing Arts: The Economic Dilemma.* New York: The Twentieth Century Fund.

Bernheim, B. Douglas. 1987. Does the Estate Tax Raise Revenue? In *Tax Policy and the Economy.* Vol. 1, ed. L. Summers. Cambridge: MIT Press.

Boskin, Michael J. 1976. Estate Taxation and Charitable Bequests. *Journal of Public Economics* 5:27–56.

Clotfelter, Charles T. 1980. Tax Incentives and Charitable Giving: Evidence from a Panel of Taxpayers. *Journal of Public Economics* 13:319–40.

———. 1985a. *Federal Tax Policy and Charitable Giving.* Chicago: University of Chicago Press.

———. 1985b. The Effect of Tax Simplification on educational and Charitable Organizations. In *Economic Consequences of Tax Simplification*. Boston: Federal Reserve Bank.

Clotfelter, Charles T., and C. Eugene Steuerle. 1981. Charitable Contributions. In *How Taxes Affect Economic Behavior*, ed. Henry J. Aaron and Joseph A. Pechman. Washington, DC: The Brookings Institution.

Commerce Clearing House. 1988. *1989 U.S. Master Tax Guide*. Chicago.

Copeland, John, and Gabriel Rudney. 1986. Business Income of Nonprofits and Competitive Advantage. Parts 1, 2. *Tax Notes* (24 November): 747–56; (29 December): 1227–36.

Cummings, Milton C., and Richard S. Katz, eds. 1987. *The Patron State: Government and the Arts in Europe, North America, and Japan*. New York: Oxford University Press.

Dye, Richard F. 1978. Personal Charitable Contributions: Tax Effects and Other Motives. In *Proceedings of the Seventieth Annual Conference on Taxation*. 311–21. Columbus: National Tax Association—Tax Institute of America.

Feld, Alan L., Michael O'Hare, and J. Mark Davidson Schuster. 1983. *Patrons Despite Themselves: Taxpayers and Arts Policy*. New York: New York University Press.

Feldstein, Martin. 1975a. The Income Tax and Charitable Contributions: Part 1—Aggregate and Distributional Effects. *National Tax Journal* 28:81–97.

———. 1975b. The Income Tax and Charitable Contributions: Part 2—The Impact of Religious, Educational, and Other Organizations. *National Tax Journal* 28:209–26.

———. 1977. Charitable Bequests, Estate Taxation, and Intergenerational Wealth Transfers. In *Research Papers*. Commission on Private Philanthropy and Public Needs, vol. 3. Washington DC: Treasury Department.

———. 1980. A Contribution to the Theory of Tax Expenditures: The Case of Charitable Giving. In *The Economics of Taxation*, ed. H. J. Aaron and M. J. Boskin. Washington, DC: Brookings Institution.

Feldstein, Martin, and Charles Clotfelter. 1976. Tax Incentives and Charitable Contributions in the United States: A Microeconomic Analysis. *Journal of Public Economics* 5:1–26.

Feldstein, Martin, and Amy Taylor. 1976. The Income Tax and Charitable Contributions. *Econometrica* 44:1201–21.

Fremont-Smith, Marion R. 1965. *Foundations and Government*. New York: Russell Sage Foundation.

———. 1972. *Philanthropy and the Business Corporation*. New York: Russell Sage Foundation.

Galaskiewicz, Joseph. 1986. *Gifts, Givers, and Getters: Business Philanthropy in an Urban Setting*. New York: Academic Press.

Giving USA. 1989. New York: American Association of Fundraising Counsel, Inc.

Grabowski, Joseph, and Evan Soffer. 1988. Trends in Tax Exempt organizations. In *Trend Analyses and Related Statistics*. 1988 Update. Washington, DC: U.S. Internal Revenue Service.

Hall, Robert, and Dale W. Jorgenson. 1967. Tax Policy and Investment behavior. *American Economic Review* 57 (June): 391–414.

Louis Harris and Associates, Inc. 1975, 1988. *Americans and the Arts*. New York: National Research Center of the Arts.

Nelson, Ralph L. 1970. Economic Factors in the Growth of Corporation Giving. National Bureau of Economic Research Occasional Paper 111. New York: NBER and Russell Sage Foundation.

Netzer, Dick. 1978. *The Subsidized Muse*. Cambridge: Cambridge University Press.

Neubig, Thomas S., and David Joulfaian. 1988. The Tax Expenditure Budget Before and After the Tax Reform Act of 1986. OTA Paper 60. Washington, DC: U.S. Treasury Department.

Organization for Economic Co-operation and Development. 1986. *Personal Income Tax Systems.* Paris: OECD.

————. 1988. *Taxation of Net Wealth, Capital Transfers and Capital Gains of Individuals.* Paris: OECD.

Pechman, Joseph A. 1987. *Federal Tax Policy.* Washington, DC: Brookings Institution.

Platzer, Linda Cardillo. 1988. *Survey of Corporate Contributions.* New York: The Conference Board.

Price Waterhouse. 1988. *Individual Taxes: A Worldwide Summary.* London.

Radich, Anthony J., ed. 1987. *Economic Impact of the Arts.* Washington, DC: National Conference of State Legislatures.

Ratner, Sidney. 1980. *Taxation and Democracy in America.* New York: Octagon Books.

Reece, William S. 1979. Charitable Contributions: New Evidence on Household Behavior. *American Economic Review* 69:142–51.

Rose-Ackerman, Susan. 1982. Unfair Competition and Corporate Income Taxation. *Stanford Law Review* 34:1017–39.

Schiff, Jerald. 1988. The Unrelated Business Income Tax: An Economic Analysis of "Unfair Competition." Tulane University. Manuscript.

Schuster, J. Mark Davidson. 1986. Tax Incentives as Arts Policy in western Europe. In *Nonprofit Enterprise in the Arts,* ed. Paul T. DiMaggio. New York: Oxford University Press.

————. 1988. Perspectives on the American Audience for Art Museums. Massachusetts Institute of Technology, Cambridge, Mass. Manuscript.

Schwartz, Robert A. 1968. Corporate Philanthropic Contributions. *Journal of Finance* 23:479–97.

Scitovsky, Tibor. 1983. Subsidies for the Arts: The Economic Argument. In *Economics of Cultural decisions,* ed. W. S. Hendon and J. L. Shanahan. Cambridge, Mass.: Abt Books.

Simon, John G. 1987. The Tax Treatment of Nonprofit Organizations: A Review of Federal and State Policies. *The Nonprofit Sector,* ed. W. W. Powell. New Haven: Yale University Press.

Slemrod, Joel. 1988. Are Estimated Tax Elasticities Really Just Tax Evasion Elasticities? The Case of Charitable Contributions. NBER Working Paper no. 2733. Cambridge, Mass.

Throsby, C. D., and G. A. Withers. 1983. Measuring the Demand for the Arts as a Public Good: Theory and Empirical Results. In *Economics of Cultural Decisions,* ed. W. S. Hendon and J. L. Shanahan. Cambridge, Mass.: Abt Books.

Troy, Kathryn. 1984. *Annual Survey of Corporate Contributions.* New York: The Conference Board.

U.S. Congress, Joint Committee on Internal Revenue Taxation. 1969. *General Explanation of the Tax Reform Act of 1969.* Washington, DC.

U.S. Congress, Joint Committee on Taxation. 1984. *General Explanation of the Revenue Provisions of the Deficit Reduction Act of 1984.* Washington, DC.

————. 1986. *General Explanation of the Tax Reform Act of 1986.* Washington, DC.

U.S. Congress, Hearings before the Oversight Subcommittee of the House Ways and Means Committee. 3 June 1986.

U.S. Internal Revenue Service. 1988. *Income Tax Compliance Research.* Publication 1415:7–88. Washington, DC.

U.S. Treasury. 1987, 1988. Testimony of O. Donaldson Chapoton before the Subcommittee on Oversight of the House Ways and Means Committee. 22 June 1987; 9 May 1988.

Useem, Michael. 1987. Corporate Philanthropy. In *The Nonprofit Sector,* ed. W. W. Powell. New Haven: Yale University Press.

Vickery, William. 1975. Private Philanthropy and Public Finance. In *Altruism, Morality, and Economic Theory,* ed. E. S. Phelps. New York: Russell Sage Foundation.

Weisbrod, Burton A. 1975. Toward a Theory of the Voluntary Nonprofit Sector in a Three-Sector Economy. In *Altruism, Morality, and Economic Theory,* ed. E. S. Phelps. New York: Russell Sage Foundation.

———. 1988. *The Nonprofit Economy.* Cambridge, Mass.: Harvard University Press.

9 Government Policy Toward Art Museums in the United States

Charles T. Clotfelter

Governments since antiquity have taken an interest in the arts and often have provided significant support for the creation and preservation of works of art. It is not surprising, therefore, that government policies have had an impact on art museums in the decades since their emergence as major arts institutions. In this country, the principal form of governmental support for art museums has been the various tax provisions exempting them from certain taxes and providing for contributions to them to be deductible. But in the last 25 years, other forms of government support in this country have become prominent as well. This paper focuses on government policy other than the federal tax provisions related to charitable contributions and the treatment of income of tax-exempt organizations; these tax provisions are treated separately in Don Fullerton's paper (chap. 8 in this volume).

The first section of the current paper presents some background on public policy toward the arts in general and art museums in particular, beginning with a brief history of government support of the arts in America. The background section continues with a discussion of the major issues in the perennial debate over arts policy—the debate over whether it is desirable for the government to support the arts and, if so, in what form. The last part of the section examines the specific political context of arts policy at the federal level since 1965, the year Congress established the National Endowments for the Humanities and the Arts. The second section of the paper presents some sum-

The author is grateful to Marshall Adesman and Robin Langdon for research assistance and to Duke University for financial support; to the Association of Art Museum directors and the National Endowment for the Arts for unpublished information; and to Edward Banfield, Bruce H. Evans, Don Fullerton, Millicent Hall Gaudieri, Sherman Lee, Michael Mezzatesta, Andrew Oliver, Richard Schneiderman, J. Mark Davidson Schuster, Steven Rathgeb Smith, Alice Whelihan, and Margaret Wyszomirski for helpful comments and discussions. Errors committed and opinions expressed in the paper are the author's responsibility, however.

mary measures useful in assessing the extent and composition of government support for art museums. The third section deals specifically with federal policies and programs toward art museums, including federally sponsored museums, the major granting agencies, and certain indirect subsidies other than the tax provisions noted above. The section also discusses the likely effects of these federal programs. The paper's fourth section examines the policies of state and local governments toward art museums, including direct support and indirect aid via exemption from taxes. A final section concludes the paper.

9.1 Arts Policy and Politics

It is impossible to separate the consideration of public policy toward art museums from that of arts policy in general, or from the theoretical and political debates that have surrounded arts policy. I begin with a short history of government support for the arts and then turn to the contemporary debate over arts policy, focusing where appropriate on art museums in particular.

9.1.1 The Antecedents of U.S. Arts Policy

Government support for the art museums and other forms of art in the United States is often compared unfavorably with that provided by European countries. Symbolized by such renowned institutions as the Louvre, the countries of Europe are said to have carried on a tradition of government support for the arts dating from ancient Egypt and Greece. First, through the court patronage of numerous kings and princes, support for the arts was carried on by the succeeding national governments.[1] In contrast, governments in the United States, before the 1960s, provided little direct support for the arts, relying instead on favorable treatment under the property and income taxes. So complete was the absence of direct government support that, as late as 1966, Boston's famed museum could proclaim in gold letters in its central rotunda:

> Museum of Fine Arts.
> Founded, Built and Maintained
> Entirely with the Gifts of
> Private Citizens.[2]

The reliance on tax subsidies to support art museums and other arts institutions is typical of the more general American pattern of allowing charitable

---

1. See Lee and Henning (1975, 5) and Schlesinger (1988, 1) for discussions of the history of government support of the arts in Europe.
2. Rathbone (1984, 46). The inscription was removed when the museum received a grant from the Commonwealth of Massachusetts of $100,000 to pay for school children to enter the museum free of charge.

donations to support many services that are largely provided by government in Western Europe.[3]

To be sure, there were isolated instances of government support of the arts before the 1960s. President James Buchanan appointed a National Art Commission in 1859, but it was disbanded two years later. In 1910, Congress established the National Commission of Fine Arts, as an advisory body to deal with such questions as the location of statues and monuments in Washington, D.C. (U.S. Commission of Fine Arts 1953, 7). Later, to oversee works of art in federal buildings, the government set up a Section of Fine Arts in the Treasury Department. The federal government provided its first direct support for the arts during the Depression, through the Arts Project of the Works Progress Administration. By 1938, this program had funded some 17,000 pieces of sculpture and over 100,000 easel paintings.[4] Then in 1941 came a significant turning point in the government's support of art museums, the dedication of the newly built National Gallery of Art, paid for by and filled with the collection of Andrew Mellon.[5] Whereas the Smithsonian had previously been the repository for some artwork, the National Gallery would become the flagship of a group of federal art museums in Washington, which by their existence constitute a not insubstantial component of the entire federal policy towards art museums in the United States today.

But the acknowledged turning point in federal policy toward the arts came in 1965, with the passage of the law setting up the National Foundation on the Arts and Humanities. Championed by Presidents Kennedy and Johnson, the idea of a national arts administration was the subject of several years of spirited debate in Washington. What emerged were two separate funding agencies, the National Endowment for the Arts (NEA) and the National Endowment for the Humanities (NEH), authorized to make grants to individuals and institutions. From its beginning, the NEA's mission has included making the arts more widely available to the public and strengthening arts organizations.[6] Both of the endowments were set up so that their scope and their power would be limited. Congress made it clear that it was not interested in sustaining the operating costs of arts institutions. Grants were to be made only for specific projects, not general institutional support, and all grants would have to be matched by private funds, with no more than half of the support for any project coming from the federal grants. Congress also went to lengths to limit the possibility that bureaucrats might exert undue control over the creative pro-

---

3. Several European countries allow a tax deduction for charitable contributions, but most of these are limited in scope. See Schuster (1986) and Don Fullerton's paper in this volume (chap. 8) for international comparisons of tax provisions affecting contributions.

4. See Netzer (1978, 53–54) and Banfield (1984, 42–47).

5. Taylor (1975, 44); Schlesinger (1988, 19).

6. See National Foundation of the Arts and the Humanities Act of 1965 (PL89-209: 29 Sept. 1965), *U.S. Statutes at Large* 79, 845.

cess. The bill stated: "No department, agency, officer, or employee of the United States shall exercise any direction, supervision, or control over the policy determination, personnel, or curriculum or the administration or operation of any school or other non-Federal agency, institution, organization, or association."[7] In addition, both of the endowments have operated from the beginning under another important institutional control: the use of peer review panels to evaluate grant proposals. This structure, like that used in the National Science Foundation, was looked to as an important safeguard against the possibility that politicians or bureaucrats might seek to impose their artistic preferences on the arts community.

9.1.2 Issues in the Arts Policy Debate

Basic to a consideration of government policy towards art museums and other arts institutions is an awareness of several perennial issues that arise in one form or another in most discussions of arts policy. A fundamental question, of course, is whether the arts merit any government support at all. Related to this basic question are two rather specific issues that deserve separate consideration. One is the alleged elitist character of the arts and support for the arts. The other is the fundamental question of what constitutes art and what that implies about the use of reproductions.

Should the government support the arts? That the arts are deserving of government support is, for some, an unarguable truism,[8] but in describing government policy it is important to consider the specific arguments pro and con. Among the arguments offered to justify the public support of the arts, perhaps the most familiar to economists is the notion that art and arts institutions produce beneficial externalities, or that they have the character of public goods. It is a widely accepted conclusion of welfare economics that, when the number of people an activity can serve can be increased at little or no additional cost, such goods tend to be undersupplied by the market, presenting one justification for government intervention.[9] A second but related argument for government support is based on the idea that art is an essential element of our cultural heritage and that government must act on behalf of future generations to protect it. Arthur Schlesinger makes the analogy to another realm in which the government is heavily involved: "Surely government has as strong [an] obligation to preserve the cultural environment against dissipation and destruction as it has to preserve the natural environment against pollution and decay."[10] A third justification for supporting the arts is the "merit good" argu-

---

7. Ibid., 846.
8. For example, former NEA chairman Livingston Biddle (1984, 90) wrote, "Of course our government should support the arts!"
9. For discussion of the public goods justification for government support for the arts, see Austen-Smith (1980) and Abbing (1980).
10. Schlesinger (1980, 19). Also see Netzer (1978, 23) for a discussion of this argument.

ment, the notion that art is among that special group of commodities that society deems of such importance that they ought to be provided by government.[11] All of these justifications find expression in the 1981 statement of a task force appointed by Ronald Reagan: "There is a clear public purpose in supporting the arts and the humanities: the preservation and advancement of America's pluralistic cultural and intellectual heritage, the encouragement of creativity, the stimulation of quality in American education, and the enhancement of our general well-being."

To these justifications, critics have raised several objections. Some argue that the public goods argument does not apply to arts institutions, especially not to art museums. Museums clearly have some characteristics of public goods, but it is doubtful that excludability is a serious problem in their case.[12] Regarding the notion of cultural heritage, van den Haag maintains that classical art and music have no more justification for subsidy than many elements of popular culture:

> We have marvelous things in our museums. But they did not get there through government activities and did not celebrate those activities or our national history, cultural or political. The contents of our museums have nothing to do with our national life. . . .
>
> Tin pan alley, jazz, rock, or baseball are more important in the celebration of American values, not only in the working classes and among adolescents, but also in the upper classes and even among educated groups. They need no subsidy. (1979, 66)

Similarly, Banfield (1984, 11–15) compares art to religion; although both affect the public interest, supporting either one, he argues, is simply not a proper role of government. Another argument against government support of the arts is that the support itself will harm the arts. The "deadening hand" (Netzer 1978, 59) of government will harm the creative enterprise, it is argued, by inserting bureaucratic meddling into artistic decisions. Van den Haag (1979, 68) argues that government support of the arts must inevitably become indiscriminate, ultimately reducing potential support for the best artists. Another argument that is often made against government support for the arts is that the distribution consequences of such support is undesirable. Because of its importance, this argument is worth considering in somewhat more detail.

Are the arts necessarily elitist? One of the central recurring issues that arises in debates over public support for the arts is the tension between the perceived elitist nature of the arts and the populism that is embedded in American politics. Sometimes this issue is stated quite baldly, as in the statement that "arts-

11. See Rosen (1988, 55–56) for a discussion of this concept and Netzer (1978, 16) for a discussion of the idea in the context of arts policy.
12. See Hendon, Shanahan, and MacDonald (1980, 21) for a discussion of this point.

Table 9.1   Attendance at Art Museums and Art Galleries by Income and
                   Education, 1985

	% of Adults Who Attended in Previous 12 Months
Income	
Less than $5,000	16
$5,000–9,999	11
$10,000–14,999	15
$15,000–24,999	19
$25,000–49,999	28
$50,000 or more	45
Education	
Grade school	4
Some high school	11
High school graduate	14
Some college	29
Four-year college graduate	45
Graduate school	55

Source: Survey of Public Participation in the Arts 1985, cited in Schuster (1988, 12).

funding is in practice an income-transfer program for the upper-middle class"
(Bethell 1978, 136). More often, the elitist-populist issue manifests itself in
ways less obviously class-oriented, such as the forms of art that should be
supported (e.g., the "fine arts" vs. folk art), the kinds of institutions that
should be supported (established vs. "emerging"), and the regions where support should go (the urbanized Northeast vs. the hinterlands). That arts patrons
tend to be educated and affluent are facts that are confirmed by most surveys
of arts attendance. For example, table 9.1 summarizes the findings of a 1985
household survey regarding visits to art museums and art galleries in the previous year. For income classes above $5,000, the percentage of respondents
attending museums rises with income, with those in the highest income class
three times as likely to attend as those with incomes between $10,000 and
$15,000. The pattern for education is even clearer, with attendance rising
steadily with years of school.[13]

The geographical distribution of museums is also decidedly nonuniform:
there are both more museums and more museum-goers in cities and in the
more urbanized regions of the country. As an illustration of attendance patterns, in 1982 the percentage of adults who visited an art museum during the

13. Other survey data confirm the positive correlation between art museum attendance and
income. See National Research Center of the Arts (1981), for example, and Schuster's (1988)
discussion of it.

A complete assessment of the distributional impact of government policy towards art museums
would require an examination of tax subsidies as well as direct government expenditures. For
relevant studies of tax expenditures, see Fullerton (chap. 8 in this volume) and Feld, O'Hare, and
Schuster (1983). See also Wyszomirski (1982, 18).

year was 25 percent in urban areas, compared to just 16 and 17 percent in rural farm and nonfarm places, respectively.[14] Not surprisingly, such differences translate into regional differences in museum use. The differences among regions are less striking, but noticeable nonetheless. A survey conducted in 1985 showed that 31 percent of adults in the West had visited an art museum or gallery in the previous year, while only 19 percent of those in the South had made such visits. These differences may reflect regional differences in demand as well as supply.[15]

Differences such as these appear to underlie, or at least correspond to, much of the debate over arts policy in this country. To begin with, regional and economic differences in any class of public funding are certain to catch the attention of some members of Congress, and arts funding is no exception. It is no accident that the NEA's original mission statement contained the explicit goal to make the arts more widely available. Indeed, this outreach objective can be seen in most public programs supporting the arts. But the populist spirit manifests itself not only in the audiences to whom the programs will be targeted, but also in what kinds of art will be supported. In 1976, Senator Claiborne Pell, although a supporter of federal arts programs, took up the populist mantle in attacking NEH chairman Ronald Berman for funding esoteric projects that smacked of "mandarin culture" and praising the NEA for funding projects "at the grassroots level."[16] When argued along these lines, however, debate over arts policy can become nasty, with appeals to populism being rebutted with charges of "philistinism."[17] Defending Berman, William F. Buckley (1976) asserted that there is "no affirmative action for mediocrity." Indeed, the NEA was accused of "subsidizing mass entertainment and criticized for draining funds from elite arts organizations. Put crudely (but not untypically), the NEA has been funding 'cultural clambakes' at the expense of 'national treasures' " (Mulcahy and Swaim 1982, 318). When considering public support of art museums, arts institutions that serve relatively affluent patrons, it is important to understand the powerful political tensions that pull in the opposite direction.

What is art? One other issue that, in contrast to the previous one, is rarely discussed is the basic question of what constitutes art. For the case of art museums, the specific application of this question centers on the virtually universal acceptance of the principle that only *original* works of art are worthy of display. Another, heretical view has been put forth by Banfield (1984),

14. U.S. National Endowment for the Arts, Public Participation in the Arts by Urban and Rural Residents, Research Division Note no. 16, 27 May 1986.
15. Schuster (1988, 13). Similar findings for 1975 are reported in National Research Center of the Arts (1975, 16).
16. Mulcahy (1987, 325) and Will (1976). See also U.S. Senate (1976, 11) and Wyszomirski (1982, 22).
17. See discussion by Will (1976).

who argues that high-quality reproductions carry much of the aesthetic value (but not the historical value) of the original. If art museums were to display such reproductions, one could argue that there would be a much wider distribution in certain benefits of museum attendance. It is also possible that such dissemination would act to drive down the price of original works of art, though this would depend on the degree to which this practice were accepted by museums. At present, the notion of showing reproductions inspires little more than contempt in the museum world, so a consideration of a change in policy is purely academic. As one museum director told me, this view is "a travesty of what art is about." But whatever the effect of so legitimizing the use of reproductions, one unmistakable characteristic of government policy toward art museums in this country is the tacit acceptance of the principle that only originals can constitute art.[18]

9.1.3   The Politics of Arts Support Since 1965

As a political issue, the government's support of the arts surely receives much more public airing than one would guess by looking only at the share of public budgets devoted to the arts. One reason, as illustrated in recent controversies, is that the populist-elitist conflict inherent in arts policy debate often pits artistic expression on the one side against revered symbols and deep-seated beliefs on the other. Such debates influence government policy toward the arts at all levels of government.

Federal. At the federal level the "modern era" of government policy towards the arts began in 1965 with the creation of the NEA and NEH. Despite the built-in structural features designed to insulate the NEA and NEH from political manipulation, the charge has often been made that the endowments have become "politicized"; whatever the precise definition of that term, there is little doubt that arts support at the federal level has become entwined with politics.[19] One sign of the growing political activity surrounding arts funding was the creation of an arts lobbying organization, the American Arts Alliance, which brought together several national arts organizations, including the Association of Art Museum Directors (Wyszomirski 1980, 31). The elitist-populist conflict arose in various forms, among which was an alleged anti–New York bias in funding.[20] Populist policies were also pointed to as a threat

18. For a sympathetic commentary on Banfield's proposals on originals and reproductions, see Walzer (1984, 35).

19. See, for example, John Friedman, "A Populist Shift in Federal Cultural Support," *New York Times,* 13 May 1979.

20. See, for example, Richard F. Shepard, "New York Called a Principal Victim of U.S., State Arts-Financing Policies," *New York Times,* 29 January 1980 or Banfield (1984, 52). In one congressional hearing, Senator Ted Stevens of Alaska questioned the NEA director, Nancy Hanks, about what he viewed as a large percentage of NEA grants going to New York, Massachusetts, the District of Columbia, and California. He noted: "I do hope you urge your council to keep in mind the national aspect of this" (Carter 1977, 46).

to established arts institutions.[21] If the NEH's Berman met resistance in Congress, one of those who headed the NEA during the same period, Nancy Hanks, is credited with outstanding success in the politics of arts funding. During her tenure at the NEA, Hanks deflected the charge of elitism and generated support in Congress by distributing grants widely—including to state arts agencies—and by emphasizing outreach programs such as the Art in Public Places program.[22] Some in the Reagan administration wanted to do away altogether with the NEA and NEH, but the task force appointed by Reagan came back with a ringing endorsement of federal support for the arts and humanities.[23] Since its establishment in 1965, the NEA has been a bellwether for judging the government's disposition toward funding the arts. Table 9.2 summarizes the agency's appropriations over its history. In real terms, its budget grew rapidly over the first decade and a half of its existence, growing at an annual compounded rate of 18 percent from 1967 to 1979. But this growth was reversed in the wake of increased inflation and the Reagan retrenchments. Between 1979 and 1988, the real value of the budget declined by more than one-fourth. Even at its peak, however, direct federal funding for the arts in the United States has remained significantly smaller on a per capita basis than government support in Western Europe.[24]

The debate over government support of the arts leaves the realm of everyday politics when publicly supported art becomes offensive to vocal groups or legislators. Reauthorization hearings in Congress have often provided the forum for conservatives to attack what they view as wasteful, pornographic, or otherwise objectionable artwork supported by federal grants. But an especially bitter debate erupted in 1989 over the NEA's support of the work of two photographers—one whose work featured homoerotic themes and one whose photographs included the image of a crucifix immersed in urine. Conservatives in Congress denounced the artwork, and the Corcoran Gallery of Art in Washington decided to cancel a scheduled show containing some of these photographs. The Senate then voted to prohibit the NEA from supporting "obscene or indecent materials" and placed a five-year ban on federal support for

21. Michael Straight, deputy chairman of the NEA under Nancy Hanks, said, "Jimmy Carter's concept of the endowments is political. In the past, the endowments were apolitical, like the National Science Foundation and the National Institute of Health. Under the populous ethic of this Administration, the needs of the large organizations won't be met" (Friedman, "A Populist Shift").

22. For descriptions of the politics of arts funding under Hanks, see Banfield (1984, 66–81), Mankin (1980, 25–26), Mulcahy (1987, 326–39), and Wyszomirski (1987). Carter (1977, 48) attributes Hanks's apparent success to her ability to obtain support from Republican members of boards of trustees of museums and symphonies to keep the pressure on the Nixon administration.

23. See "Obscenity or Censorship?" *Economist*, 5 August 1989, and Presidential Task Force on the Arts and Humanities (1981).

24. Figures on exchange rates and government cultural spending presented in various articles (Cummings and Katz 1987) suggest that per capita federal spending on cultural agencies in the United States was no more than one-third of the comparable amount in Italy in 1982 and no more than one-fifth of the total per capita government expenditure for the arts and culture in France and Sweden around 1980.

Table 9.2   National Endowment for the Arts Appropriations, 1966–87

Fiscal Year	Appropriation in Millions of	
	Current Dollars	1987 Dollars
1966	2.5	8.5
1967	8.0	26.1
1968	7.2	22.4
1969	7.8	22.9
1970	8.3	23.1
1971	15.1	40.0
1972	29.8	75.2
1973	38.2	90.8
1974	60.8	132.5
1975	74.8	148.4
1976	82.0	153.0
1977	94.0	164.4
1978	123.9	201.9
1979	149.6	224.0
1980	154.6	212.3
1981	158.8	198.8
1982	143.5	168.8
1983	143.9	163.0
1984	162.2	177.3
1985	163.7	173.7
1986	158.8	164.1
1987	165.3	165.3
1988	167.7	163.7

Source: National Endowment for the Arts, *1987 Annual Report* (Washington, D.C.: Government Printing Office, 1988).

two institutions that had established the offending artwork.[25] In the words of the bill's sponsor, Senator Jesse Helms: "If someone wants to write ugly nasty things on the men's room wall, the taxpayers do not provide the crayons."[26] For their part, spokespersons for the art museum community warned of "de facto censorship."[27] Needless to say, the success of these sorts of challenges would imply a significant shift in government policy toward the arts in general and art museums in particular.

25. The artists were Robert Mapplethorpe and Andres Serrano. See Michael Oreskes, "Senate Votes to Bar U.S. Support Of 'Obscene or Indecent' Artwork," *New York Times,* 27 July 1989, 1. Specifically, the bill bars federal funding "to promote, disseminate or produce obscene or indecent materials, including but not limited to depictions of sadomasochism, homoeroticism, the exploitation of children, or individuals engaged in sex acts; or material which denigrates the objects or beliefs of the adherents of a particular religion or nonreligion."

26. Maureen Dowd, "Helms in Midst of Clash Between Art, Politics," *News and Observer,* 28 July 1989, 1.

27. Allan Parachini, "Helms and Arts Endowment: An Escalation," *Los Angeles Times,* 23 June 1989, sec. 6, p. 1. See also Anne Lowery Bailey, "Museum Officials Fear Outcries in Congress Will Stifle Arts Grants," *Chronicle of Philanthropy,* 27 June 1989, 5.

State and local. To consider the politics of arts policy at the federal level is to consider only part of the total picture, an assertion that is not very surprising once it is realized that state and local governments give art museums more aid than the federal government (see below). In a few states, where funding for the arts at the state level is comparatively generous, there have been debates over the distribution of state government grants not unlike those at the federal level. For example, the state with the first functioning state arts agency was New York, and grant making by that state's State Council on the Arts was criticized for having a New York City bias.[28] In apparent response to this kind of sentiment, the state legislature in fiscal year 1974 mandated that half of state arts funding be distributed among counties in proportion to population (Wyszomirski 1982, 14). As a result, the portion of state funds going to organizations in the city declined significantly over the next few years.[29] In Massachusetts, cuts in arts funding were denounced in part by representatives of relatively new arts institutions as having a disproportionate effect on their institutions as compared to well-endowed established institutions.[30]

As in the flap over NEA's support of controversial art, arts politics at the local level also offers examples of political fireworks. Two such examples are provided by the city of Chicago. In 1988, a heated political controversy with racial overtones arose when the School of the Art Institute of Chicago displayed a student's irreverent portrait of the late Mayor Harold Washington.[31] The next year, a controversy arose about another piece of art shown there, this time about a display which many considered to be a desecration of the American flag. In this instance, a committee of the Chicago Park District threatened to cut off support for the Art Institute of Chicago and seven other museums under its jurisdiction in connection with the flag controversy.[32]

9.2 The Extent of Direct Government Support

A useful beginning point in describing government policy toward art museums is to ask who actually runs the organizations. As noted above, the American experience in government support of the arts has been characterized by its indirect nature, in contrast to the European tradition of government-run museums. Most art museums are private, nonprofit organizations. A survey of the governing authority of art museums in 1979 showed that 60.2 percent of them were private, nonprofit organizations, and another 13.5 percent were

28. See, for example, Shepard, "New York Called a Principal Victim."
29. Grants from the State Council on the Arts to organizations in New York City fell from $23.1 to $16.9 million between 1976 and 1978 (Shepard, "New York Called a Principal Victim").
30. See William H. Honan, "Fight Is on in Massachusetts over Plan to Cut Arts Money," *New York Times*, 6 March 1989, 8.
31. For an account of this controversy, see the *Chicago Tribune*, 12 May 1988, and the following days.
32. See, for example, William Recktenwald and Robert David, "Park Funds Cutoff Threatened in Flag Flap," *Chicago Tribune*, 10 March 1989.

run by private educational institutions. The remainder were run by government or public institutions: 13.5 percent by public educational institutions, 8.6 percent by local governments, 1.8 percent by states, and 1.5 percent by the federal government (National Center for Educational Statistics 1981, table D.1). An earlier survey showed some regional differences in governing authority: New England had a particularly small portion of museums under the control of governments or state educational institutions, while regions outside of the Northeast were well above average in this regard.[33] Although private control is the rule, therefore, a few art museums are operated under the direct or indirect authority of government. At the federal level, the most prominent of these are the major federal art museums in Washington.[34] A comparable example at the state level is the North Carolina Museum of Art. Other museums, such as the Detroit Institute of the Arts and the Fine Arts Museums of San Francisco, receive the bulk of their support from state and local governments but are run by nongovernmental boards.

To measure the importance of government to art museums, it is necessary to do more than categorize institutions by governing authority. One reason is that virtually all museums receive some direct government support. Another reason is that museums differ enormously in size. As an illustration of this variation, in 1972 the largest 5 percent of all museums in the United States accounted for 46 percent of total operating budgets (National Research Center of the Arts 1975, 11). Among the art museums for which there are recent data—124 of the largest ones—similar diversity in size is evident. In 1988, the largest six out of that group (approximately 5 percent) accounted for 40 percent of the total operating income. Thus, if characteristics of museums vary systematically with size, it is important to note that variation.

Tables 9.3 and 9.4 present data on the sources of operating income of art museums in two different years. Table 9.3 shows the distribution of income for all public and nonprofit art museums in 1979. The largest source of income was clearly earned income, which included income from investments and net income from museum shops and restaurants, accounting for almost one-half of total income. Governments contributed a significant amount, however— over a fourth of the total. Despite the preponderance of the private, nonprofit form for art museums, direct government support far surpassed contributions as a source of income. Table 9.4 presents similar data for 1988, based on a

33. Percentages are based on 177 art museums surveyed out of an estimated universe of 340 art museums in 1972. National Research Center of the Arts (1975, xi, 14).

34. These are the National Gallery of Art, the National Museum of American Art, the National Portrait Gallery, the Hirshhorn Museum and Sculpture Garden, and the National Museum of African Art. While none of these museums is actually a line agency of the federal government, they receive appropriations from Congress and have government officials on their boards of directors. Of the National Gallery's nine trustee seats, four are reserved for the Chief Justice of the Supreme Court, the Secretary of State, the Secretary of the Treasury, and the head of the Smithsonian Institution. The other four museums are part of the Smithsonian, which is governed by a board of regents that also includes 8 government officials out of its 17 members. Both their governance and their dependence on federal funding set these museums apart from other major art museums.

Table 9.3   Sources of Operating Income, Art Museums, Fiscal Year 1979, as
                 Percentage of Total

Federal government	8.4%
State government	4.8
Local government	14.3
Foundations	5.4
Corporations	4.6
Individual contributions	6.3
Earned income[a]	48.4
Other sources	7.7
Total	100.0

Source: National Center for Education Statistics (1981, 47).

Note: The sample was weighted to represent all nonprofit art museums in 1978. Total operating income for all art museums was estimated to be $294,443,204. Percentage figures do not add up to exactly 100 percent because of rounding.

[a]Includes net income from restaurants and museum stores.

smaller sample of museums and disaggregating in order to separate federal museums and the two largest private museums, the Metropolitan Museum of Art and the Art Institute of Chicago. Divided this way, art museums clearly differ markedly in the extent to which they rely on government funding. At one end of the spectrum are the large federal museums, most of whose funding comes from government. At the other extreme in this table are the two big museums, which together receive 17.5 percent of their operating income from government. The remaining 148 museums present perhaps the typical distribution, with 23 percent of their income derived from government, which is approximately the same share implied by the 1979 survey summarized in table 9.3.[35]

9.3   Federal Policies and Programs

Although it accounts for a smaller share of government support for art museums than the combined total for states and localities, the federal government appears to exert a much more pervasive influence on these institutions than any other level of government. Part of the reason is obvious: there is one federal government, with only a few agencies concerned with art museums, while there are many governmental units at lower levels, with disparate policies. Another reason for the importance of federal policies is that granting agencies at lower levels appear to have adopted criteria set by federal agencies in making their own grants and have in fact taken federal grants to be an indicator of quality in judging the worthiness of grant applications. This section deals with federal policies toward art museums. It begins with the most

35. Probably the most noticeable difference between the 1979 distribution and that for the 148 museums is the much lower share of income derived from earned income in 1979.

Table 9.4   Sources of Operating Income, Large Art Museums, 1988

	Big 2 Museums[a]	5 Large Government Museums[b]	148 Other Large Museums
Total operating income ($ millions)	$101.1	$65.1	$733.4
Sources of income as percentage of total			
Federal			
NEA	0.4%	0.0%	1.0%
NEH	0.0	0.0	0.3
IMS	0.1	0.0	0.3
Other federal	0.0	83.3	1.0
State	1.8	0.0	9.9
County	0.0	0.0	2.8
City	15.2	0.0	6.4
Other government	0.0	0.0	1.6
Contributed income			
Corporate	3.9	7.3	5.1
Foundation	3.6	0.8	7.0
Individual	13.8	0.2	11.4
Other private	6.4	0.3	4.0
Endowment	20.8	6.3	20.2
Earned income			
Admissions	9.3	0.0	3.8
Auxiliaries and other earned income	24.7	1.7	25.1
Total	100.0	100.0	100.0

Source: Association of Art Museum Directors (1990), Metropolitan Museum of Art, and Art Institute of Chicago.

[a]Metropolitan Museum of Art and Art Institute of Chicago. Budget data obtained directly from these two museums only.

[b]National Gallery of Art, National Museum of American Art, National Portrait Gallery, Hirshhorn Museum, and National Museum of African Art

direct form of support, museums run by the federal government. Then it turns to the three major federal programs that provide grants to art museums, and to indirect federal subsidies other than tax concessions. Finally, it concludes with a discussion of the effects of these policies.

9.3.1   The National Museums

There is no more tangible manifestation of federal policy toward art museums than the National Gallery of Art and the other federal museums in Washington, D.C. These museums are very much in the tradition of the European support of art; and, although this is not the primary model of support followed in the United States, these museums constitute the bulk of the direct expenditures of the federal government in this area. An illustration of this importance can be seen by looking at the budgets for 124 large art museums in 1987. The total income this group of institutions received from the federal government was $65.8 million. Of that total, over three-fourths, or $50.4 million, was in the form of operating support provided to the five largest federal museums.[36] Although this share would be smaller if a larger group of museums were examined, it is clear that direct operating support to federal museums is a very large share of total direct federal support to art museums.

Two aspects of the national art museums deserve particular attention. The first is the obvious geographical concentration of these museums. They are all in the national capital. As will be emphasized in subsequent discussion, the geographical distribution of arts funding is every bit as much a political question as the distribution of military bases. Even though Washington is an exception to the general tendency to spread government programs into as many congressional districts as possible, the extreme concentration of this federal program may have an impact on the overall support for art museums. A second aspect of the federal museums is less a product of history as an explicit policy: these museums are open to the public free of charge. While this zero price policy may be efficient in an economic sense, when combined with the relative affluence of those who attend art museums the policy results in something of an upside-down subsidy.

9.3.2 Three Major Federal Programs

There are three federal programs that are responsible for the bulk of grants to museums: the NEA, the NEH, and the Institute of Museum Services (IMS). The National Endowments make most of their grants for specific projects through the process of submitted proposals and peer review. The grants are not intended for basic institutional support. As compared with the NEA, the NEH tends to support exhibits that emphasize the historical, as opposed to the aesthetic, aspect of art.[37] The IMS does make grants to museums for operating expenses and also devotes considerable attention to conservation efforts. Counting grants to all types of museums, the IMS spends slightly more than the NEA—$20 versus $19 million in fiscal year 1986—with the NEH third at $11 million.[38] For arts museums alone, however, the NEA is by far the most important source of federal funding, as indicated in table 9.5. Its size and its prominence make the NEA the most important federal agency affecting art museums and thus an agency worth looking at in more detail.

The NEA's explicit aim is to support the arts without dictating artistic standards. In its published mission statement, the agency states that its goals are "to foster the excellence, diversity, and vitality of the arts" and to "help

36. Association of Art Museum Directors, *1988 Statistical Survey*, 166. For a list of these five federal museums, see note 34.

37. According to one quip, the distinction is this: If the object is bigger than the label, it's sponsored by the NEA; if the label is bigger than the object, it's sponsored by the NEH.

38. U.S. Institute of Museum Services (1988, table D).

Table 9.5   National Endowment for the Arts and Institute of Museum Services
Allocation of Funds for Art Museums, Fiscal Year 1987
(in $ millions)

NEA museum program	
Special exhibitions	5.3
Presentation and education	1.4
Conservation	1.3
Catalogue	1.2
Collection maintenance	0.9
Other[a]	1.6
Total	11.7
NEA challenge grants[b]	4.1
IMS programs[c]	
General operating support	4.2
Conservation	0.8
Total	20.8

Source: National Endowment for the Arts, *1987 Annual Report* (Washington, D.C.: Government Printing Office, 1988), 96–115, 206–7; Institute of Museum Services, unpublished data.

[a]Includes museum training, special artistic initiatives, fellowship for museum professionals, special projects, and visiting specialists.

[b]Round Nine Challenge Grants, obligated in fiscal year 1987.

[c]Includes Museum Assessment Program I appropriation of $25,000.

broaden the availability and appreciation" of the arts. But the statement also stipulates that the agency "must not, under any circumstance, impose a single aesthetic standard or attempt to direct artistic content." [39] For museums, these aims translate into support for four basic activities: presentation of art (which includes education programs and special exhibitions), documentation, conservation, and training of museum professionals. One way of gaining an idea of the NEA's priorities is to examine the agency's spending for art museums in a recent year. Most of the agency's expenditures for art museums are included in two of its programs, the museum program and the challenge grant program, and table 9.5 summarizes fiscal year 1987 allocation of funds for these areas along with grants by the IMS to art museums. By far the biggest category of NEA spending for art museums is special exhibitions—short-term displays of related works of art, often obtained on loan from other institutions. For example, in 1987 the NEA made a grant to the Metropolitan Museum of Art to support the exhibition, "The Age of Correggio and the Carracci," and the accompanying catalogue. Another went to the Virginia Museum of Fine Arts to support a touring exhibition and catalogue of late Neolithic and early Bronze Age sculpture from the Cyclades Islands in the Aegean Sea. The second biggest grant category was the challenge grant program, matching grants that are conditional upon the institution's raising at least three times the amount from private sources. Among the other major categories of grants is

39. National Endowment for the Arts, *1987 Annual Report,* March 1988, 227.

conservation. The NEA, like the IMS, has emphasized conservation activities from the beginning. For example, the NEA has encouraged the development of regional conservation centers to serve the needs of several museums which might not otherwise be able to afford their own conservation staffs (Taylor 1975, 55). The agency's grants also emphasize storage, maintenance, and the cataloguing of collections. Among these functions, programs that increase the public's access to museum collections tend to be politically more popular than about anything else museums can do.[40] Special exhibitions have much the same appeal, but for the sponsoring museums they can have the added appeal (though never the guarantee) of profitability. Like the NEA, the IMS devotes a significant share of its budget for conservation, but the IMS's largest expenditure for art museums is for general operating support, a purpose to which no NEA funds are directed.

In implementing policy, the NEA operates under three important constraints. One is the prohibition against ongoing institutional support noted above; support may be given only for specific projects. A second is that all grants must be made on a matching basis only, with the NEA providing no more than one-half of the total cost.[41] The third constraint, which is really almost a defining characteristic of the NEA, is the reliance on peer review for awarding grants. Most observers would agree that peer review has acted as an effective antidote against the possible centralization of power over artistic funding and has quieted fears that the NEA bureaucrats would become "cultural commissars."[42] Still, it is the NEA staff that puts the panel together, and some maintain that the review panels can be easily swayed by the views of the agency's permanent staff (Carter 1977, 38).

9.3.3 Indirect Subsidies

Counting the income and estate tax deductions for charitable contributions and the nontaxation of endowment income, the federal government's indirect subsidies for art museums are probably at least as large as its direct expenditures.[43] Besides the tax subsidies, however, there are only two that are worth mentioning. One is the postal subsidy given to all nonprofit organizations, the value of which is unknown, probably small in relation to the tax subsidies, but not inconsequential in light of the active mail-order trade engaged in by the largest museums. The other form of indirect subsidy is one designed primarily

40. The interest in outreach has extended to the support of subsidiary galleries and mobile galleries set up in some states (Taylor, 1975, 64).
41. For a discussion of NEA policies, see Netzer (1978, 63).
42. See *New Republic*, 1 February 1985, and Schlesinger (1988, 20).
43. Taking all contributions to 155 art museums in 1988, including works of art ($235 plus $77 million), and assuming an average federal marginal tax rate of 33 percent (see Don Fullerton's paper, chap. 8 in this volume), the indirect subsidy would be $104 million. At the same rate, the tax exemption of endowment income accounts for an additional $58 million in indirect subsidy. This compares to total direct federal support for those museums of $96 million (Association of Art Museum Directors 1990).

for art museums—the federal indemnification program. Under this program, the federal government agrees to act as an insurer for works of art that are loaned, often by other governments, as part of special exhibitions. Although there is virtually no budgetary cost of the program, it has substantial value to art museums in terms of reduced insurance costs. A museum sponsoring an exhibition applies for indemnification for a portion of this value, specifying in detail how the works of art will be packaged, transported, and displayed. If the application is successful, the museum will typically be relieved of the need to purchase insurance on most of the exhibition's total value. There is presently a $125 million limit on each award, and museums must insure an initial portion of each exhibition as a deductible. The National Gallery's Gauguin exhibition in 1988 provides an illustration of how the program works. For this exhibition, the National Gallery borrowed paintings valued at more than $500 million from museums both here and abroad. The indemnification program provided insurance for any losses on the foreign loans over $10 million, up to $125 million. The museum had to buy insurance privately for the amounts not covered.[44] Table 9.6 summarizes the activity of the indemnification program from 1976 to 1987. In 1987 dollars, the face value of the art covered by the program increased from $189 million to $585 million over the period. In 1987, the program saved museums an estimated $5.6 million in insurance premiums. By comparison, federal grants from the NEA, NEH, and IMS to 124 of the largest art museums in 1987 totalled $11.8 million. In terms of economic value to art museums, therefore, the indemnification program is quite important.

9.3.4   Effects of Federal Policies

What has been the effect of these various federal programs on art museums? Some critics of government support of the arts have charged that such support, by its very nature, has harmful effects on art and artists. Banfield (1984, 67), for example, argues that public funding inevitably encourages arts institutions to engage in activities that have little to do with art. Van den Haag (1979) believes that public support must necessarily become arbitrary, with decisions being made on inappropriate grounds. Indeed, a Heritage Foundation report (Joyce 1981, 1051) found the NEA to be lacking in just such a manner, charging that its leaders had a "flawed conception of art." Among schools of art, some observers would argue that NEA grants have favored avant-guarde work at the expense of traditional schools of art. Yet the NEA's funding policies have also been criticized for seeking political support by pandering to the unsophisticated tastes of the public. The Heritage Foundation said of the projects receiving NEA support: "The best of these projects do no more than fos-

---

44. The amounts not covered included the $10 million deductible, losses on foreign loans over $125 million, and the U.S. loans. Estimates provided by Alice Whelihan of the NEA, 14 March 1989.

Table 9.6   **Art Objects Insured through Federal Indemnification Program, 1976–1987**

Fiscal Year	Number of Objects Insured	Face Value of Indemnities Outstanding (Millions of 1987 Dollars)	Amount They Would Have Paid in Insurance (Millions of 1987 Dollars)
1976	3,935	189.3	1.35
1977	6,708	230.2	2.65
1978	9,029	299.4	1.89
1979	7,442	242.0	5.11
1980	4,307	315.7	1.22
1981	4,605	240.4	1.26
1982	6,290	343.4	2.89
1983	4,094	362.4	1.75
1984	3,191	389.8	3.20
1985	4,494	405.7	2.03
1986	7,074	420.1	5.66
1987	8,484	585.3	5.64

Source: Annual reports on the Arts and Artifacts Indemnity Act, National Foundation on the Arts and the Humanities, Washington, D.C.

silize the popular culture of the past, and the worst are little more than high-flown welfare and employment schemes." It is difficult for anyone, let alone an economist, to make supportable judgments regarding the effect of federal policies on the quality of art being produced or exhibited, but it is possible to make some observations about the patterns of support and the apparent effects of federal policies. In response to the claims that a populist instinct has dominated grants made by the NEA, one can examine the geographical distribution of grants and the distribution by size of institution. It is also useful to consider the impact of federal grants on the types of functions performed by museums and on their modes of operation.

Geographical distribution. What has been the regional distribution of federal support for art museums? Has this support been distributed according to the location of the already established museums or according to population? Are review panels heavily weighted toward the regions with established institutions? In order to answer questions such as these in a rough way, table 9.7 shows the distribution, by region, of membership in advisory panels and of population; it also shows—for a sample of 116 large art museums—federal support of the museums and two measures of their geographical distribution. To highlight the possible concentration in the two states with a relatively large number of established art museums, separate figures are given for New York and California. The table shows, for example, that among the group of large art museums, the Northeast region has 32 percent of the total number of mu-

Table 9.7   Geographical Distribution of Government Support for Large Art Museums, Membership of Federal Advisory Panels, and Population

Percentage of U.S. Totals	Northeast	Washington, D.C.	South	Midwest	West	Total U.S.	Detail: New York and California as % of U.S. Total
116 Large museums							
Operating expenses, 1988	40	9	17	20	14	100	38
Support, 1988							
Federal							
NEA	28	1	17	36	18	100	32
NEH	37	0	16	29	18	100	42
Other federal	2	97	0	1	0	100	2
State	16	0	22	56	6	100	13
County	5	0	10	23	62	100	66
City	43	0	24	21	12	100	37
All government	22	16	15	27	19	100	32
Number of museums, as % of total	32	5	25	22	16	100	24
Total NEA grants, 1985	45	1	14	25	15	100	37
All Museums							
Challenge grants awarded, in constant dollars, 1978–87	38	2	15	24	21	100	34
Membership in NEA advisory panels							
1984	38	5	14	24	19	100	31
1988	32	4	19	21	25	100	25
Membership in indemnification panels							
1976	36	14	18	18	14	100	32
1984	28	21	13	18	21	100	44
1987	36	13	16	19	17	100	33
Population as % of total	21	0	34	24	20	100	19

Source: National Endowment for the Arts, unpublished printouts of panelists; annual reports on the Arts and Indemnity Act; Association of Art Museum Directors, unpublished tabulations of survey data for 116 art museums.

seums; the museums in that region are relatively large, accounting for 40 percent of total operating expenses. In contrast, the Northeast has only 21 percent of the nation's population. These three percentages offer three possible benchmarks for comparing the region's shares of federal support and membership in advisory panels. This same approach can be taken with the other regions as well.

Looking first at federal support, it is possible to see that NEA grants to art museums in both 1988 and 1985 were awarded more closely according to the distribution of art museums than to the distribution of population. The biggest deviations from that rule occurred in the Midwest and South. The Midwest, with 22 percent of the museums, received 36 percent of the NEA grants awarded to this group of museums in 1988, but only 25 percent in 1985. The South, containing one-fourth of the museums, received only 17 percent of NEA funds in 1988, which was its share of museum operating budgets. Comparing the distributions of NEA funds in the two years and the NEH grants in 1988, the most heavily concentrated toward the established areas (Northeast and New York/California) were the NEH and the 1985 NEA distributions. This would be consistent with both the elitist reputation of the NEH and a change in NEA between 1985 and 1988 favoring wider distribution of grants.

Another way to gauge the geographical bias, if any, in federal policy toward art museums is to examine directly the composition of the review panels selected to make awards. Information is available for two types of panels: the advisory panels used by the museum program of the NEA to judge grant applications and the panels used to make awards in the indemnification program. The geographical distributions of the membership of these two panels are shown in the table for selected years. These distributions closely parallel the distribution of expenditures for NEA and NEH grants, with the Northeast (and New York/California) being consistently overrepresented in comparison to their population but generally underrepresented in comparison to the region's museum expenditures. Over time, there appears to have been little trend in the pattern of representation. Even in the populist Carter administration, the Northeast continued to be represented on these panels in numbers far exceeding their share of the population, but less than the size of their art museums might justify.[45]

Size of institution. Do federal programs favor the large, established museums or do they favor smaller institutions? Table 9.8 addresses this question by examining NEA and NEH grants for a group of large art museums in 1988. As a percentage of the total income for these museums, both categories of federal aid are highest for museums having budgets between $1 and $2 million, with aid becoming relatively less important in the two higher budget categories. For the best-known museums, those in the highest budget cate-

---

45. See Netzer (1978, 73) for a discussion of the geographical distribution of NEA grants.

Table 9.8   Government Support by Budget Size, 144 Large Art Museums, 1988

	Operating Budget ($ millions)			
	$0.1 Million to <$1 Million	$1 Million to <$2 Million	$2 Million to <$5 Million	$5 Million or More
Number of museums	35	35	37	35
Government support, as % of total income				
Federal				
NEA	1.7	2.8	1.4	0.7
NEH	0.4	0.9	0.4	0.2
Other federal	0.5	0.0	1.1	0.2
State	19.6	10.5	8.3	8.5
City	9.0	7.0	5.7	7.7
County	0.5	3.1	2.8	2.5
Total government	31.8	24.4	19.7	19.7

Source: Association of Art Museum Directors, unpublished tabulation of survey data.
Note: Sample excludes museums in the District of Columbia.

gory, grants from the endowments are quite small indeed in relation to all sources of income. Indeed, this table makes clear that for art museums other than the major federal museums the NEA and NEH are not large sources of income in comparison with states and local governments.

Table 9.9 examines the question of size effects by focusing on two particular federal programs, the NEA challenge grants and the indemnification program. In this table, museums are divided by size and governance, with the five largest federal museums shown separately. For the group of 142 large museums responding to the 1988 Association of Art Museum Directors survey, it is possible to compare measures of these two federal programs with the distribution of operating expenses, although awards under both programs were also made to museums outside this group. For the challenge grants program, the big two museums received much less than their share of total museum budgets and the federal museums received none, leaving the remaining 135 museums with relatively more in challenge grants compared to their budgets. In contrast, the indemnification program shows quite a different pattern, with the number of items insured being almost exactly proportional to operating budgets. This program therefore represents a boon to the larger museums. In fact, if the average value of items insured increases with the size of the museum, the program would be even more skewed in favor of the largest institutions. In any case, it appears that most federal programs tend to help the largest museums less than proportionately to their size, the one exception being the indemnification program. Given the importance of this program in making possible the lavish and often profitable exhibitions of recent years, it is clear that federal policy does not favor the small museums in every respect.

Table 9.9   Distribution of National Endowment for the Arts Challenge Grants and Indemnification by Size and Governance of Museum

	Big 2 Museums	Next 30 Private Museums	5 Large Government Museums	Remaining 105 Museums	Other Museums and Organizations	Total
Total challenge grants awarded, 1978–87 (Millions of 1987 dollars)	4.7	31.5	0.0	20.6	11.6	68.3
As % of total for 142 museums	8	55	0	36	—	100
Idemnification program, number of items insured	9,215	22,429	4,983	11,724	21,615	69,966
As % of total for 142 museums	19	46	10	24	—	100
Total operating expenses (millions of dollars)	101.2[a]	366.5	57.8	189.3	—	613.6
As % of total for 142 museums	0	60	9	31	—	100

Sources: National Endowment for the Arts, unpublished budget documents; annual report on the Arts and Indemnity Act; Association of Art Museum Directors (1989).

[a]Corrected figures based on 1988 fiscal year.

Types of activities. Do federal programs affect how museums go about their work and indeed what work they do? From the point of view of art museums, there is probably no more important question concerning federal policy than this. Yet there is little hard evidence with which to draw conclusions. Based on the comments of observers of museums and arts policies, there are several kinds of activities of art museums that one might think would have been stimulated by federal programs. Since the NEA and IMS have programs explicitly designed to support such functions as conservation, the cataloguing of permanent collections, and exhibitions, it is certainly possible that these activities are more prevalent than they would otherwise be. Another function that has probably been stimulated by the federal programs toward art museums is simply administration. Several commentators have remarked that the documentation required for federal funds has increased the size of museum bureaucracies.[46]

One of the most controversial, and visible, of these activities is the special exhibition, a few of which come to be "blockbusters" by virtue of their size. Bringing together works of art from different museums, often from abroad, these exhibitions have assumed a prominent role in the public perception of art museums as well as their finances by drawing visitors who would otherwise not visit museums as often or at all. Although the most highly publicized of these exhibitions have been undertaken by the largest museums, they have had a significant impact on other museums as well. For example, the "Rameses the Great" exhibit hosted by the Mint Museum in Charlotte had a budget which exceeded all of the museum's previous 50 budgets put together.[47] The trend toward such large exhibits is not without its critics, though. Such exhibitions have been dismissed as "show business" and criticized for the potential damage that transporting works of art may cause.[48] For better or worse, in the view of most observers of art museums, federal programs have fostered the use of special exhibitions.[49] Not only does the NEA's museum group award its biggest share of grants for such exhibitions, but the indemnification program exists primarily to enable them to be undertaken.

Private donations. A fourth set of possible effects of federal policies concerns the ability of museums to attract private donations. There are possible effects in two different directions. On the one hand, federal funding of museums may have the effect of decreasing private contributions, as contributors see that the government is providing a new source of funding for items that would otherwise be bought with donated funds. There is evidence from studies of chari-

46. See, for example, Joyce (198, 1052).
47. "Mint Says Rameses was Great," *News and Observer,* 27 January 1989, p. 4C.
48. On "show business," see Taylor (1975, 62). On transporting art, see for example, Carter (1977, 45).
49. See for example, Carter (1977, 45) or Taylor (1975, 62). An opposing view is expressed, however, by the head of the NEA's museum program, Andrew Oliver, who argues that the NEA has merely responded to the desire of museums to put on exhibitions.

table giving that government spending may indeed "crowd out" donations, and this phenomenon may well apply to museums as well.[50] There is, however, no statistical evidence of this kind of behavior, only reports that private donors appear to viewing the federal government increasingly as a primary supporter of art museums.[51] Despite this possibility, museums appear to welcome the increased support they have received from federal sources over the past two decades, in that this decreases their dependence on private donors, some of whom have attempt to exert unwelcome influence on museums' artistic decisions.[52]

On the other hand, there is one federal program designed explicitly to stimulate private giving, the challenge grant program.[53] By requiring federal grant funds to be matched by private contributions, challenge grants can be seen as reducing a donor's net cost of giving a dollar to a museum. For example, consider a donor who is in a 30-percent tax bracket who makes a $1,000 gift to a museum. Normally, this taxpayer's net cost of making such a gift would be $700, reflecting the deductibility of charitable contributions for itemizers. However, if private donations are matched in a challenge grant program at a 1:3 ratio, the donor may realistically view his or her $1,000 gift as having a value of $1,333 to the museum. Counting this federal match, then, the donor bears a net cost of only 53 cents per dollar received by the institution. While there is no evidence on the effect of this kind of matching program on private giving, numbers such as these show the potential that the challenge grant program has for lowering the net cost of giving. Since there is quite a bit of evidence that donors are sensitive to the net cost of making contributions, it is likely that the challenge grant program does stimulate private giving to museums.[54]

9.4 State and Local Policies

Like the federal government, state and local governments have two sets of policies affecting art museums, those offering direct support and those working indirectly through tax exemptions.

9.4.1 Direct Support

All states and many localities give direct support to art museums. There are, as mentioned above, some state, municipal, and county art museums,

---

50. See Seaman (1980) and the discussion of these studies in Clotfelter (1985).

51. For discussions of individual and corporate donors, see Wyszomirski (1980, 29) and Carter (1977, 45).

52. Carter (1977, 47) reports that corporate contributors sometimes "try to throw their weight around." In this connection, see also Feld, O'Hare, and Schuster (1983, chap. 5) for a discussion of donor influence on arts institutions.

53. Nancy Hanks expressed the view that matching stimulates private giving. See Carter (1977, 46).

54. For a discussion of issues related to the effectiveness of matching grants, see Schuster (1989).

some of them comparatively large. More commonly, state and local governments make grants to museums. Unlike federal support of private museums, some of this direct support is for basic operating expenses, not just specially funded projects. As shown in tables 9.3 and 9.4, state and local support amounts to more than that received from the federal government. The largest art museums receive significantly more from state and local governments than they receive from all federal sources.[55] As table 9.8 shows, state support is especially important for museums with budgets under $1 million, while local support as a share of total budgets does not vary appreciably with size. Probably the most prominent form of state support of the arts is distributed through state arts agencies, of which there is one in every state. Table 9.10 presents information on appropriations to such agencies and other arts institutions, by state, in 1980 and 1989. In per capita terms, these appropriations ranged in 1989 from a low of $18 in Mississippi to a high of $623 in Hawaii. By far the largest state appropriation was in New York, with $51 million. And in most of the states, the real value of these appropriations is increasing. As is the case with federal arts funding, art museums receive only a small portion of these funds. In fiscal year 1986, they received 8.3 percent of the total.[56] As an indication of what kinds of functions the states support, table 9.11 shows state grants to art museums by activity. By far the biggest item is institutional support, which contrasts sharply with the NEA/NEH prohibition on such support. Next in importance is funding for exhibitions, an activity also supported heavily by the federal government.[57]

9.4.2 Tax Exemption

Most state and local governments exempt nonprofit institutions from income, property, and sales taxation, although practices vary.[58] Of these, surely the most important for art museums is the property tax exemption. Among arts institutions, art museums are exceptional for the value of their buildings and the contents of those buildings. The exemption of this property from taxation is the reason why Netzer (1978, 75) says that art museums get the most favored tax treatment among arts institutions. Indeed, from the perspective of

55. See table 9.2, based on a survey of all art museums in 1979. The 1988 survey of art museums conducted by the Association of Art Museum Directors (1989, 187) suggests that state and local support exceeds federal support by over 50 percent.

56. National Assembly of State Arts Agencies (58). The 8.3 percent figure would imply a total state appropriation for art museums of some $22 million in 1989. However, the AAMD survey shows that 142 museums received $67.1 million from states in 1987, so the NASAA data must not count all state support.

57. See Netzer (1978, 80–82, 247n) and Svenson (1980, 35–37) for discussions of state art agencies.

58. See L. Richard Gabler and John F. Shannon, "The Exemption of Religions, Educational, and Charitable Distributions from Property Taxation," in *Research Papers* of the Commission on Private Philanthropy and Public Needs (Washington, D.C., 1977), vol. IV, 2535–72. See also discussion of the property tax exemption for arts organizations in Feld, O'Hare, and Schuster (1983, 63–70).

Table 9.10   **State Legislative Appropriations for State Arts Agencies, Fiscal Years 1980 and 1989**

	Appropriations[a] ($ thousands)					
	Current $		Constant 1985 $		%	Per Capita
State	1980	1989	1980	1989	Change	1989
Alabama	525	2,476	720.83	2,250.68	212	60.7
Alaska	1,675	1,695	2,299.78	1,540.76	−33	322.9
Arizona	233	1,554	319.91	1,412.59	342	45.9
Arkansas	846	1,021	1,161.56	928.09	−20	42.8
California	7,891	14,604	10,834.34	13,275.04	23	52.8
Colorado	609	1,041	836.16	946.27	13	31.6
Connecticut	1,305	2,137	1,791.77	1,942.53	8	66.5
Delaware	123	785	168.88	713.57	323	121.9
District of Columbia	356	3,692	488.79	3,356.03	587	593.6
Florida	2,378	20,838	3,264.99	18,941.74	480	173.3
Georgia	1,102	3,248	1,513.05	2,952.43	95	52.2
Hawaii	1,545	6,747	2,121.29	6,133.02	189	623.0
Idaho	86	239	118.08	217.25	84	24.0
Illinois	2,246	7,509	3,083.76	6,825.68	121	64.8
Indiana	1,277	1,970	1,753.32	1,790.73	2	35.6
Iowa	313	825	429.75	749.93	75	29.1
Kansas	262	1,072	359.73	974.45	171	43.3
Kentucky	857	2,368	1,176.66	2,152.51	83	63.5
Louisiana	857	990	1,176.66	899.91	−24	22.2
Maine	180	622	247.14	565.40	129	52.4
Maryland	1,345	5,960	1,846.69	5,417.64	193	131.4
Massachusetts	2,300	19,539	3,157.90	17,760.95	462	333.7
Michigan	6,076	12,426	8,342.35	11,295.23	35	135.1
Minnesota	2,845	3,150	3,906.19	2,863.35	−27	74.2
Mississippi	307	496	421.51	450.86	7	18.9
Missouri	2,531	4,913	3,475.06	4,465.92	29	96.3
Montana	93	726	127.69	659.93	417	89.7
Nebraska	399	943	547.83	857.19	56	59.2
Nevada	87	269	119.45	244.52	105	26.7
New Hampshire	153	462	210.07	419.96	100	43.8
New Jersey	3,333	22,685	4,576.21	20,620.67	351	295.7
New Mexico	203	710	278.72	645.39	132	47.3
New York	33,285	55,987	45,700.31	50,892.18	11	314.1
North Carolina	1,379	5,005	1,893.37	4,549.55	140	78.1
North Dakota	101	214	138.67	194.53	40	31.8
Ohio	4,709	9,980	6,465.46	9,071.82	40	92.5
Oklahoma	552	2,670	757.90	2,427.03	220	81.6
Oregon	335	1,002	459.96	910.82	98	36.8
Pennsylvania	2,594	12,755	3,561.56	11,594.30	226	106.9
Rhode Island	359	1,440	492.91	1,308.96	166	146.1
South Carolina	941	3,119	1,291.99	2,835.17	119	91.1
South Dakota	155	338	212.82	307.24	44	72.2
Tennessee	517	3,506	709.84	3,186.95	349	19.7
Texas	1,215	3,310	1,668.20	3,008.79	80	95.4
Utah	1,088	1,603	1,493.82	1,457.13	−2	83.4

(*continued*)

Table 9.10 (continued)

State	Appropriations[a] ($ thousands)				% Change	Per Capita 1989
	Current $		Constant 1985 $			
	1980	1989	1980	1989		
Vermont	108	457	148.28	415.41	180	76.9
Virginia	1,230	3,771	1,688.79	3,427.84	103	63.9
Washington	579	1,756	794.97	1,596.20	101	38.7
West Virginia	1,563	1,845	2,146.00	1,677.11	−22	97.2
Wisconsin	719	1,881	987.19	1,709.83	73	39.1
Wyoming	63	206	86.50	187.25	116	42.1
Total	95,830	258,557	131,574.59	235,028.31	79	

Source: U.S. Bureau of the Census, *Statistical Abstract of the United States, 1988;* National Assembly of State Arts Agencies, unpublished data; *Economic Report of the President* 1989, 312.

Note: The GNP price deflator was used to adjust for inflation. That index was 85.7 in 1980 and 117.7 in 1987 and was assumed to be 129.5 in 1989.

[a]Includes line item appropriations for arts organizations passed through state arts agencies.

Table 9.11 State Support for Art Museums, by Activity, All States, Fiscal Year 1986

Activity	Number of Grants	Grant Amount ($ thousands)
Institutional support	137	$5,569
Exhibitions	146	1,428
Audience services	12	750
Repair, restoration, conservation	22	433
Marketing	4	69
Awards and fellowships	2	8
Other	216	1,453
Total	539	9,710

Source: National Assembly of State Arts Agencies (1989, 58, 80–81).

local communities, museums are often an object of civic pride and may well hold economic value sufficient to justify such favored status. One tangible bit of evidence of the importance attached to museums is the significant number of private, nonprofit art museums housed in publicly owned buildings; in 1972, 17 percent of such museums were housed in buildings owned by local governments.[59]

All together the property tax exemption for art museums is undoubtedly quite large, although it is difficult to estimate the size of the exemption with much precision. Two back-of-the-envelope estimates suggest the likely magnitude of this exemption. First, if one assumes that art museums constitute

59. National Research Center of the Arts (1975, 370). For discussions of the role of civic boosterism in explaining favorable treatment of museums, see Banfield (1984, 93) and Parkhurst (1975, 88).

one-fourth of the property of arts organizations, Netzer's (1978, 44) estimates for 1975 imply a 1988 value of taxes foregone on the order of $75 million for art museums.[60] A second approach is based on an estimate of the assessed value of charitable tax-exempt (noneducational) property of $54 billion in 1987. If 10 percent of the property of such charitable property is assumed to be held by art museums, then applying the same 2 percent property tax rate would yield an estimate of the foregone property tax on art museums of about $110 million.[61] Considering that art museums paid only about $1 million in property taxes in 1988, the value of this tax exemption appears to be very large indeed.[62] Counting the likely value of the income tax deductions, indirect support of art museums is probably greater than the total of all direct government support.[63]

The effects of the property tax exemption have been the subject of some speculation. Following a line of reasoning familiar in economics, Netzer (1978, 34) and Feld, O'Hare, and Schuster (1983, 141) have speculated that the property tax exemption makes arts institutions more capital-intensive than they would otherwise be, in that construction is subsidized relative to other expenditures. In the case of museums, which are among the most capital-intensive of nonprofit institutions, let alone arts organizations, it is not hard to believe that this bias toward bricks and mortar has had a significant effect. If one considers as well the exemption from personal property taxation of the assets contained inside art museums—the estimated value of collections considerably exceeds that of museums' land and buildings—the bias inherent in local tax exemptions is probably large. There is, however, no evidence on the degree to which these exemptions have affected the holdings or construction decisions of art museums.

9.5 Conclusion

Government policy toward art museums certainly exists, but it is decentralized, diffuse, and elusive. One reason for this is the federal nature of our government, where in state and local jurisdictions join the federal government

60. Netzer applied a 2 percent tax rate on an estimated aggregate property value of $7.5 billion around 1975. Considering the doubling of prices between 1975 and 1988 (203 percent increase in the GNP price deflator), and assuming 25 percent of arts property belongs to art museums, yields a figure of $76 million.

61. Twelve states with 33.1 percent of the nation's total assessed property value had an estimated $17.889 million in charitable (noneducational) property in 1986. Applying this ratio to the nation implies a total of $54.04 billion in charitable property. U.S. Bureau of the Census, *1987 Census of Government,* vol. 2; *Taxable Property Values* (Washington, D.C.: Government Printing Office, March 1989), xx, 4.

62. Unpublished data provided by the AAMD. These estimates of property value apply only to land and buildings and ignore the considerable holdings of property inside museums. In 1988, 155 art museums had collections valued at $22.5 billion. Needless to say, this property would yield a huge amount of revenue were it subject to taxation. Local governments also provide other indirect support in the form of auditing, accounting, payroll, building repair, and central purchasing (Parkhurst 1975, 88).

63. See Don Fullerton's paper, chap. 8 in this volume.

in exerting varied influences—through appropriations, tax exemptions, and other avenues of political influence. A second reason is the benign stand-offishness that has traditionally characterized the government's treatment of nonprofit organizations in this country. The United States has traditionally relied on the nonprofit sector to perform more public functions than is common in other developed countries, and it has provided tax incentives to encourage this to happen. Before 1965 government policy toward the arts was less clearly defined than that towards any part of the nonprofit sector other than religion because there was little legislation or administration at the federal level concerned with the arts. Certainly the United States had nothing in the way of a "cultural policy" to compare with the countries of Western Europe. The creation of the National Endowments for the Arts and Humanities in 1965 was undoubtedly a watershed event which, among other things, brought arts policy into prominence as an issue of public debate at the national level. But Congress has remained reluctant to establish a bureaucracy that would even appear to be able to impose artistic values. So there is great emphasis on peer review and matching grants in addition to the traditional reliance on tax exemptions. Stanley Katz has commented, "to have no policy is to have a policy. That we do not have a national cultural policy, in other words, means that we have made a decision . . . to leave to private and local institutions the determination of the decisions most overtly affecting the creation and conduct of cultural institutions" (1984, 36).

In general, then, the assumption that decentralization begets pluralism applies to our government's policy toward art museums. Art museums receive substantially more money in support from state and local governments than it does from the federal government. In addition, federal grants to museums are dwarfed by the implicit cost of the federal income tax deduction for contributions and by the value of the property tax exemption. Yet the federal programs are not without influence. Because of their visibility and their unity, they appear to have exerted an influence on how museums function. In part this may be due to the tendency of state agencies and private foundations to pay attention to the criteria and grants of the national endowments. Among the likely effects of federal policy has been to encourage special exhibitions. As has been pointed out, these exhibitions serve the financial aims of institutions while also serving the government's objective of wider accessibility. While the government's support for these exhibitions—through direct grants and the indemnification program—appears to have favored the large, established museums, the rest of the NEA's programs tend to favor smaller, less-established museums, at least as a percentage of their overall budgets. Taken together, the federal government's programs probably have increased the financial security of museums by giving them a new source of income, but it is also likely that the growth of this new source has probably reduced the growth in donative support for museums. Finally, it is possible to speculate on the effects of the forms in which the indirect subsidies have been given. Because of the favorable treatment, before 1987, of gifts of appreciated property, it seems highly probable that our museums have considerably more art in them—on display and in storage—than they would if all gifts had to be treated as cash gifts. As for the property tax exemption, it seems likely that this form of subsidy has probably encouraged museums to be more capital-intensive than they would otherwise have been. Needless to say, speculating about either of these effects is much easier than estimating their magnitudes.

References

Abbing, Hans. 1980. On the Rationale of Public Support to the arts: Externalities in the Arts Revised. In *Economic policy for the arts,* ed. William S. Hendon, James L. Shanahan, and Alice J. MacDonald. Cambridge, Mass.: Abt Books.

Association of Art Museum Directors. 1989. *1988 Statistical Survey.* New York: AAMD.

———. 1990. *1989 Statistical Survey.* New York: AAMD.

Austen-Smith, David. 1980. On Justifying Subsidies to the Performing Arts. In *Economic Policy for the Arts.* See Hendon, Shanahan, and MacDonald 1980.

Banfield, Edward C. 1984. *The Democratic Muse.* New York: Basic Books.

Bethell, Tom. 1978. Welfare Arts. *The Public Interest* 53 (Fall): 134–38.

Biddle, Livingston, Jr. 1984. Our Government's Support for the Arts: Nourishment or Drought. *Annals of the American Academy of Political and Social Science* 471 (January): 89–101.

Buckley, William F. 1976. Heading the NEH Pell-mell for Philistia. *Washington Star,* July 27.

Carter, Malcolm N. 1977. The NEA: Will Success Spoil Our Biggest Patron? *Art News* (May): 32–48.

Clotfelter, Charles T. 1985. *Federal Tax Policy and Charitable Giving.* Chicago: University of Chicago Press.

Cummings, Milton C., Jr., and Richard S. Katz, eds. 1987. *The Patron State: Government and the Arts in Europe, North America, and Japan.* New York: Oxford University Press.

Feld, Alan L., Michael O'Hare, and J. Mark Davidson Schuster. 1983. *Patrons Despite Themselves: Taxpayers and Arts Policy.* New York: New York University Press.

Hendon, William S. 1979. *Analyzing An Art Museum.* New York: Praeger.

Hendon, William S., James L. Shanahan, and Alice J. MacDonald, eds. 1980. *Economic Policy for the Arts.* Cambridge, Mass.: Abt Books.

Joyce, Michael S. 1981. The National Endowment for the Humanities and the Arts. In *Mandate for leadership.* ed. Charles L. Heatherly and Edwin J. Feulner, Jr. Washington, D.C.: The Heritage Foundation.

Katz, Stanley N. 1984. Influences on Public Policies in the United States. In *The Arts and Public Policy in the United States,* ed. Lowry, W. McNeil. Englewood Cliffs, NJ: Prentice-Hall.

Lee, Sherman E., ed. 1975. *On Understanding Art Museums.* Englewood Cliffs, NJ: Prentice-Hall.

Lee, Sherman E., and Edward B. Henning. 1975. Works of Art, Ideas, and Museums of Art. In *On understanding art museums.* See Lee 1975.

Lowry, W. McNeil ed. 1984. *The Arts and Public Policy in the United States*. Englewood Cliffs, NJ: Prentice-Hall.

Mankin, Lawrence D. 1980. The National Government and the Arts: A Policy Pastiche. *Aesthetic Education* 14 (October): 22–26.

Mulcahy, Kevin V. 1987. Government and the Arts in the United States. In *The patron state*. See Cummings and Katz.

Mulcahy, Kevin V., and C. Richard Swaim, eds. 1982. *Public Policy and the Arts*. Boulder, Colo.: Westview Press.

National Assembly of State Arts Agencies. 1989. *State Arts Agency Funded Activities: Analysis of Final Descriptive Reports, Fiscal Year 1986*. Draft report.

National Center for Education Statistics. 1981. *Museum Program Survey, 1979*. Washington, D.C.: NCES.

National Research Center of the Arts. 1975. *Museums USA: A Survey Report*. Washington, D.C.: Government Printing Office, January.

———. 1981. *Americans and the Arts*. New York: American Council for the Arts.

Netzer, Dick. 1978. *The Subsidized Muse*. Cambridge: Cambridge University Press.

Notebook. *New Republic*, 11 February 1985, 6.

Parkhurst, Charles. 1975. Art Museums: Kinds, Organization, Procedures, and Financing. In *On Understanding Art Museums*. See Lee 1975.

Presidential Task Force on the Arts and Humanities. 1981. *Report to the President*. Washington, D.C.: Government Printing Office, October.

Rathbone, Perry T. 1984. Influences of Private Patrons: The Art Museum as an Example. In *The Arts and Public Policy in the United States*. See Lowry 1984.

Rosen, Harvey S. 1988. *Public Finance*. Homewood, Ill.: Irwin Press.

Schlesinger, Arthur Jr. 1988. The New President and the Future of American Art. *Journal of Art* 1(December):1, 19, 20.

Schuster, J. Mark Davidson. 1986. Tax Incentives as Arts Policy in Western Europe. In *Nonprofit Enterprise in the Arts*, ed. Paul J. DiMaggio. New York: Oxford University Press.

———. 1988. Perspectives on the American Audience for Art Museums. Massachusetts Institute of Technology. Manuscript, February.

———. 1989. Government Leverage of Private Support: Matching Grants and the Problem of "New Money." Duke Center for the Study of Philanthropy and Voluntarism. Working paper, February.

Seaman, Bruce A. 1980. Economic Models and Support for the Arts. In *Economic Policy for the Arts*. See Hendon, Shanahan, and MacDonald 1980.

Svenson, Arthur G. 1980. The Administrator in the Administration of State Arts Agencies. *Aesthetic Education* 14 (October): 35–41.

Taylor, Joshua. 1975. The Art Museum in the United States. In *On Understanding Art Museums*. See Lee 1975.

U.S. Commission of Fine Arts. 1953. *Art and Government*. Washington, D.C.: Government Printing Office.

U.S. Institute of Museum Services. 1988. *The Nature and Level of Federal Support for Museums in Fiscal Years 1985 and 1986*. Washington, D.C.: IMS, February.

U.S. Senate. 1976. *Hearings before the Committee on Labor and Public Welfare*. 94th Congress, 2d sess., September 15 and 21. Washington, D.C.: Government Printing Office.

van den Haag, Ernest. 1979. Should the Government Subsidize the arts? *Policy Review* 10 (Fall): 63–73.

Walzer, Michael. 1984. The Popular Patron. *New Republic* (April 9): 33–35.

Will, George F. 1976. High Culture and Basic Politics. *Washington Post*, May 16.

Wyszomirski, Margaret J. 1980. Arts Policymaking and Interest-Group Politics. *Aesthetic Education* 14 (October): 28–34.

———. 1982. Controversies in Arts Policymaking. In *Public Policy and the Arts*. See Mulcahy and Swaim 1982.

———. 1987. The Politics of Art: Nancy Hanks and the National Endowment for the Arts. In *Leadership and innovation*, ed. Jameson W. Doig and Erwin C. Hargrove. Baltimore: The Johns Hopkins University Press.

10   Government Policy and Art Museums in the United Kingdom

Rosemary Clarke

Government support for museums and art galleries in the United Kingdom, while not generous by European standards, nevertheless provides the major funding source for the many national and local museums. Support is predominantly in the form of direct subsidies as, in contrast to the way it is in the United States, tax concessions in the United Kingdom are few so that museums receive little income from private donations. This pattern of subsidy has existed for many years but the Conservative government, since it came to power in 1979, has introduced a series of measures by which it hopes to reduce museum dependence on the state and to encourage greater contributions from individuals and companies through donations and sponsorship.

This paper aims to provide a picture of past and current government policy toward art museums and the art market. However, it should be noted that much of the published material and statistics cover all types of museums. Most museums are all-purpose, containing mixed scientific, technological, and art collections and it is only a small number that are devoted purely to fine and decorative art. Much of the following discussion, therefore, refers to museums of all types and does not always refer specifically to art museums.

The first section provides a brief history of government involvement up to 1945. The next describes the form and extent of direct subsidies at central and regional levels, while the third section reviews various tax concessions which provide indirect subsidies to museums. The fourth section covers the changes introduced by the Conservative government and examines the problems that face museums as they endeavour to come to grips with the "enterprise cul-

The author is grateful to Mr. D. Heaton of the Museums and Galleries Commission for help and advice, and to colleagues who have provided her with suggestions and comments at various stages of the work. She owes a large debt to people at the Policy Studies Institute, and especially Muriel Nissell and John Myerscough, whose publications, *Facts about the Arts* and *Cultural Trends,* have provided an invaluable reference. The responsibility for errors and omissions is her own.

271

ture." The fifth section looks at opportunities for raising income through admission charges, while the sixth section discusses the current system of regulating the export of works of art from the United Kingdom. The final section draws together some of the strands and concludes the paper.

10.1 Historical Background

The British government has only reluctantly taken on the task of financing museums and art galleries.[1] Royal patronage of the arts came to an abrupt end with the execution of Charles I in 1649, his art collection was auctioned by the Puritans, and for the next hundred years what patronage there was rested in private hands. A few private collections survived the Civil War, new collections started to be formed toward the end of the seventeenth century, and it was the bequest of one of these private collections to the state and offers of other collections at advantageous prices that eventually led to the founding of the British Museum in 1753. The £300,000 needed to fund and house the purchases, however, did not come from state funds but was raised by public lottery. State commitment did not stretch beyond an agreement to cover running costs, and the government's reluctance to finance additions to the collection meant that even the chance to acquire the Elgin marbles was not quickly seized on. When, in 1816, the government eventually bowed to pressure, it bought them for £35,000, a figure which left Lord Elgin considerably out-of-pocket.

The doctrine of laissez faire meant that the arts were not seen as an area for state intervention but, at the same time, the government was conscious of the growth of state collections across the Channel and elsewhere in Europe. Its ambivalent attitude is well summarized by Minihan who comments that while "reluctant to spend public money on ancient statues, it was somehow held to be a national disgrace if other countries managed to acquire them" (1977, 14). This reluctance was not restricted to statues: the state was equally unwilling to provide money for paintings. Private collections were growing and often opened to the public on request (the Stafford collection was open at regular hours) but the government resisted all pressure to establish a state gallery. It was not until nearly three-quarters of a century after the founding of the British Museum that the National Gallery was set up, in 1824, though it was not properly housed until 1838. Britain could now boast of a fine collection of art from various countries, but it still lacked a showplace for British artists. When, toward the end of the century, Henry Tate offered the country his collection, which included works by many British artists, the then government was, as ever, unwilling to provide state funds to build a gallery to house it and continued to prevaricate even when Tate offered to pay for this himself. A

1. In writing this section the author has relied heavily on Janet Minihan's book, *The Nationalization of Culture* (1977).

change of government resolved the matter, and the National Gallery of British Art (later to be renamed the Tate) opened in 1897, at Millbank, on the site of Jeremy Bentham's model penitentiary.

Several other national museums were also built largely from private funds, including the National Portrait Gallery (founded 1856), the Scottish National Gallery (1850) and the Scottish Museum of Antiquities (1780). Well might the Royal Commission on National Museums and Galleries comment in 1929 that "in general it is true to say that the State has not initiated. The Collections, whether artistic, literary or scientific, once formed by the zeal of individuals, and thereafter bestowed on or acquired by the State, have been maintained out of the public revenues at the lowest possible cost. The attitude of the State to the National Museums and Galleries has for the most part been a passive and mainly receptive attitude. Development has been spasmodic" (*Final Report*, 10).

An exception was the Victoria & Albert Museum: the commercial usefulness of art spurred the government to pay for the initial building, but, even here, it was the concern of the Prince Consort and others over the poor quality of design that had moved the government to create the Department of Practical Art which subsequently became the Department of Education and Science. The Victoria & Albert Museum, together with the Science Museum, formed part of this department, and it was only in 1983 that both museums gained trustee status.[2]

By the late 1920s, state funding of the national museums' operating expenses was well established, as can be seen in table 10.1. There was still a reluctance to fund additions to collections: the only two museums to receive substantial purchase grants were the British Museum and the Victoria & Albert. The National Gallery, which had received an annual purchase grant since 1855, had its allowance of £5000 increased by £2000 in 1927–28 to cover purchases for the Tate, which had no grant of its own. Even though a state role was not in dispute, there was concern over the level of funding, and a Royal Commission was set up to seek ways to reduce expenditure. It, however, reported that the "economy has already been pushed beyond the point of administration" (*Interim Report* 1928).

The national museums were concentrated in London and Edinburgh, but museums were also being established in the regions. This development was fostered by a growing belief in the educative importance of the arts and by the need to provide a wider range of recreational facilities as leisure time expanded for the working classes. The Museums Act of 1845 permitted town councils to found and maintain museums, and by the end of the century the

2. The government took a narrow view as to the commercial educative role of the Victoria & Albert. This is well illustrated by an anecdote reported by Minihan. It seems that Lord Palmerston, on viewing a collection of medieval Italian majolica recently purchased by the museum, asked, "what is the use of such rubbish to our manufacturers?" As a result, the collection had to be sold but was gradually bought back with the annual purchase grant (1977, 115–16).

Table 10.1   Government Grants to National Museums 1903–28 (£)

	Purchase Grants			Net Operating Expenditure		
	1903–4	1913–14	1927–28	1903–4	1913–14	1927–28
England						
British Museum	22,000	25,000	25,000	194,863	240,442	405,125
National Gallery	5,000	5,000	7,000	40,002	37,002	40,395
Tate	0	0	0	—	—	—
National Portrait Gallery	750	750	1,153	6,646	7,181	11,087
Victoria & Albert	11,000	10,400	16,000	n.a.	n.a.	n.a.
Wallace	0	0	0	10,657	18,291	19,042
Scotland						
Royal Museum	2,600	2,600	2,600	16,410	27,699	31,534
National Gallery	0	1,000	1,000	—	—	—
National Portrait Gallery	0	200	200	3,400	19,777	17,116
Museum of Antiquities	0	200	200	—	—	—
Total, museums	41,350	45,150	53,153	271,978	350,392	524,299
Total: all national museums & libraries	48,950	52,800	62,928	485,034	587,576	1,090,903

Source: Royal Commission on National Museums and Galleries, Interim Report 1928, Cmd. 3192, app. 3.

Notes: Net operating expenditure includes capital and current expenditure on buildings. British Museum operating expenditure includes expenditure on building repairs and utilities for National History Museum. Operating expenditure for the Victoria & Albert Museum cannot be separated from that of the Science Museum.

number of provincial museums was increasing rapidly. Museums set up under the Museums and Gymnasiums Act of 1891, covering England and Wales, had to be open to the public for not less than three days in every week free of charge, and in 1918 local education authorities were permitted to make grants to museums to encourage them to develop educational facilities for school parties. A limit was placed on the amount of money that might be raised on the rates (a form of local property tax) which was eventually removed in 1919. Nevertheless, private benefactors again played a major role: Miers (1928) noted that nearly half of the provincial public museums started between 1880 and 1920 originated from private collections, and Markham, writing in 1938, mentions that virtually all major building projects undertaken in the previous ten years had been privately funded. Town councils may have been given powers to establish museums, but it seems they were no keener than central government to provide funding. Of the 800 public and private museums surveyed by Markham, about 500 were inadequately financed and possibly 250 had "hopelessly inadequate finances" (p. 165). It is, therefore, hardly surprising he noted that approximately 50 museums had closed in the previous ten years.

Though state funding of the museums and galleries had ceased to be controversial, state subsidy of other forms of art was not provided. World War II provided a turning point. As part of an effort to maintain morale, the Council for Encouragement of Music and the Arts (CEMA) was launched, once again by private initiative though the government eventually provided funding. This was a great success, and, when the war ended, a natural sequel was the setting up of an arts organization to "encourage knowledge, understanding and practice of the arts in the broad sense of that term" (Chancellor of Exchequer, quoted in Minihan 1977); the Arts Council of Great Britain was established in 1945, so that from this time on, theatre, music and dance, as well as the visual arts, received state funding. In 1948, local authorities were permitted to spend a small proportion of revenue on arts and entertainment, over and above that spent on museums, and by 1972 final restrictions on the amount of spending were removed.

In 1965, a junior minister with special responsibility for cultural policy was appointed, and the arts gained a voice in government, albeit only as a division within the Department of Education and Science. From this has evolved the Office of Arts and Libraries with its own minister and budget.

The combination of private and state funding of museums had meant that today museums of every kind are to be found in all parts of the country. Because they are continuing to open—it has been estimated that on average a new museum has opened every two weeks since 1970 (Cossons 1987)—it is difficult to establish the exact number. There are the 19 government-funded, trustee museums treated as national by the Museums and Galleries Commission (1988), the most recent of which, on Merseyside, Liverpool, was formed from a complex of local authority museums in 1986. With this one exception, the national museums are all located in national capitals, though there are branches elsewhere in the country.[3] When Miers (1928) and Markham (1938) reported on regional museums before World War I, they both emphasized the haphazard distribution. Today, as can be seen in table 10.2, local authority museums are spread remarkably evenly when measured in terms of population—only London and Merseyside having fewer than 11.7 museums per million population. Nearly all these museums contain mixed collections, and the middle column gives some indication of the distribution of museums with art collections. This is somewhat less even, but only the Midlands appear to be noticeably less well provided for than other areas.

In addition to the public museums there are also many independent collections open to the public which are either nonprofit or run on a commercial basis. Other independent collections include those of universities, some of which are very fine indeed. The Museums and Galleries Commission estimated that in 1987 there were at least 150 university collections of which 76 were identified as of "undoubted national distinction." These, too, have generally been started with the bequest of private collections, one of the earliest

3. Branches of the National Portrait Gallery have been set up at Montacute (Somerset), Beningbrough (York), and Bedelwyddan (Clwyd), while the Tate runs the Barbara Hepworth Museum in St. Ives, Cornwall. The various branches of the Victoria & Albert Museum are all located in the London region.

Table 10.2   Museums and Galleries Open to the Public—by Region

Region	Local Authority Museums, 1983–84		Public and Private Art Museums, 1981		Art Collections in Country Houses, 1982	
	Number	Per Million in Population	Number	Per Million in Population	National Trust Houses	Other Country Houses
England						
Eastern	71	14.5	26	5.5	4	12
East Midlands	51	13.4	12	3.7	2	9
Greater London	28	4.2	51	7.2	2	3
Lincolnshire and Humberside	26	18.6	9	6.5	1	6
Merseyside	11	6.1	8	4.3	—	7
Northern	43	13.9	18	5.8	1	6
North West	55	11.7	30	6.4	2	12
Southern	58	13.2	32	7.5	2	13
South East	50	15.6	12	3.8	5	19
South West	49	13.6	22	6.3	7	9
West Midlands	70	13.5	21	4.1	3	7
Yorkshire	72	17.6	19	4.7	2	3
Total	584	12.4	264	5.7	34	109
Wales	35	12.5	16	5.7	1	4
Scotland	n.a.		40	7.7	—	14
Great Britain, Total	619.0	12.5	320	5.9	35	127

Source: For local authority museums—Myerscough (1986), table 7.4; for remainder—Nissel (1983), table 11.6.

being that of Ashmole to the University of Oxford in 1683. Some 35 National Trust houses contain fine art collections as do 127 other country houses (see table 10.2).

It is also worth mentioning that there are many major items of fine and applied art held by cathedrals and churches. Some government aid is provided to churches for building maintenance, thus enabling parishes to release funds for the conservation and, in some circumstances, display of their art property. Similar assistance is not available to cathedrals, many of which require extensive repair and maintenance. Hereford's recent proposal to sell the thirteenth-century Mappa Mundi to raise £7 million for building work (and to preserve its unique chained library) highlights the plight of cathedral chapters and anomalies in government aid which has been concentrated on art contained within museums and art galleries.

A century of private benefaction combined with increasing state funding has provided Great Britain with a large number of public museums and art galleries, many of which are free and, as we shall see, rely almost wholly on government aid for their running costs. These, together with the many independent collections, numerous historic houses and monuments, mean that most of the population lives within easy distance of a varied range of museums and historical buildings and sites.

10.2 Direct Subsidies

In the postwar period, the main changes in policy affected the performing arts following the establishment of the Arts Council of Great Britain. Government policy was limited to the acceptance of its role as main funder for the public museums and to providing a budget for the other arts, through the Arts Council, with policy decisions being directed at deciding how much to spend on the arts rather than how it should be spent.

There has never been a central "Ministry for the Arts", and currently funding for the visual arts continues through diverse bodies. The Office of Arts and Libraries, separated from the Department of Education and Science in 1979 (only to be merged again in 1981 and separated once more in 1983), handles most of the English national museums. Until 1983, the Department of Education and Science was responsible for the Victoria & Albert and the Science Museums and it was only in 1987 that the Natural History Museum passed from the department to the Office of Arts and Libraries. Scottish, Welsh, and Northern Irish museums are funded under separate votes for these countries. The Department of the Environment is responsible for historic buildings, including those owned by the state—such as Hampton Court, which contains a fine collection of pictures—and may make capital grants to museums through its funding of urban development councils set up in the 1980s to help revitalize specific urban areas. Occasional grants may also be received from tourist boards (funded by the Department of Trade) and from various government job creation schemes. Local taxes fund local authority museums. Finally, tax policy is determined by the Treasury.

10.2.1 Central Government Spending on Museums

With such a range of departments, there can be no definitive estimate of total government spending on the arts, but, for recent years, the government's annual paper on its expenditure plans provides a total figure, though it is only in the last ten years that spending on museums and other arts has been shown separately from that on libraries. Even now, these plans do not give a breakdown of Scottish, Welsh, and Northern Irish expenditure.

Until World War I, virtually the only art institutions to receive central government funding were the national museums but, after the establishment of the Arts Council in 1945, spending on the performing arts rose rapidly. The increase was particularly steep after 1965, and during the ten years from 1969 to 1979, spending on all the arts more than doubled in real terms. Funding of museums and galleries also rose during this period, but because of the increased expenditure on other arts, the proportion of the arts budget devoted to museums fell from 63 percent in 1949 to 39 percent in 1979, rising again to 47 percent in 1988–89.

Table 10.3 shows government direct subsidies to U.K. museums from 1949 to 1988. Up to 1979, the level of subsidy increased steadily, but the advent of the Conservative government in 1979, while not stopping the upward trend, introduced a more uneven pattern when measured in real prices, as can be seen in the bottom panel of the table. The large increase between 1985 and 1986 reflects the establishment of the new national museums on Merseyside and constitutes, in part, a transfer of funding from local to central government.

The Conservative government's declared objective to cut public spending and its emphasis on the merits of the market have changed both the social and economic climate. Museums will in future have to take greater responsibility for the management of their budgets and will be expected to earn a greater proportion of their income. To this end, the government has introduced changes in the method of funding national museums and is promoting measures to encourage donations and sponsorship.

In the past, government grants to national museums covered three main categories of expenditure: operating costs, buildings, and acquisitions. For most museums, a sum covering building maintenance and repairs was passed directly from the funding department to the government Property Services Agency which handled all building work. The remaining grant came as a vote: each museum's grant was calculated by estimating the running costs for the financial year and its expected receipts, and the resulting vote was the difference between these two amounts.[4] If a museum earned more than had been estimated, it could spend the excess, providing it did this before the end of the financial year. In the event that it failed to spend all the excess, the balance was surrendered to the Exchequer. Clearly, under this arrangement there was little incentive for museums to increase their income through trading activities or by seeking out donations and sponsorship. A similar arrangement operated for purchase grants, though, in this case, any surplus might be returned to the museum in the following financial year.

In 1986 the Minister for the Arts announced a change from vote to grant-in-aid funding. Under the new arrangement, the annual grant would be a given percentage of the assessed running costs, the museums having to raise the balance. Where receipts exceeded the target, these could be retained (without any offsetting grant reduction) providing they did not exceed 2 percent of the annual grant and 10 percent of the annual receipts. Under certain circumstances, however, transfer to endowment funds might be possible. Moreover, grants-in-aid are to be set on a three-year basis to enable museums to plan ahead. In order to avoid large transitional adjustments and consequent ineq-

---

4. A vote is a statement presented to the House of Commons of estimated expenditures during a financial year with a request for the necessary funds to be voted.

Table 10.3 **Government Direct Subsidies to Museums and Galleries**

	Central Government					Local Government			
	England	Wales	Scotland	Northern Ireland	Total	England	Wales	Scotland	Northern Ireland
	Spending at Current Prices (£ Million)								
1949–50	1.13	0.04	0.07	—	—	—	—	—	—
1959–60	2.44	0.13	0.21	—	—	—	—	—	—
1969–70	7.81	0.46	0.48	—	—	5.70	—	—	—
1974–75	15.28	1.38	2.09	—	—	18.80	—	—	—
1979–80	47.00	—	—	—	—	38.60	1.60	—	—
1980–81	58.00	—	—	—	—	52.30	1.50	—	—
1981–82	62.00	—	—	—	—	55.30	1.80	—	—
1982–83	82.00	—	—	—	—	62.70	2.30	—	—
1983–84	85.00	6.50	9.90	3.70	105.10	72.00	2.40	—	—
1984–85	92.00	6.90	10.10	3.90	112.90	82.90	2.00	—	—
1985–86	99.00	7.80	16.60	4.20	127.60	89.70	2.80	—	0.50
1986–87	114.00	8.00	12.20	4.60	138.80	81.40	2.90	13.40	0.50
1987–88	121.00	12.70	15.80	5.10	154.60	—	—	—	0.60

(continued)

Table 10.3 (continued)

	Central Government					Local Government			
	England	Wales	Scotland	Northern Ireland	Total	England	Wales	Scotland	Northern Ireland
Spending in 1985 Prices* (£ Million)									
1949–50	13.29	0.48	0.82	—	—	—	—	—	—
1959–60	19.06	0.99	1.64	—	—	—	—	—	—
1969–70	42.45	2.52	2.61	—	—	30.87	—	—	—
1974–75	50.93	4.61	6.97	—	—	63.67	—	—	—
1979–80	74.96	—	—	—	—	61.56	2.55	—	—
1980–81	78.06	—	—	—	—	70.39	2.02	—	—
1981–82	75.98	—	—	—	—	67.77	2.21	—	—
1982–83	93.93	—	—	—	—	71.82	2.63	—	—
1983–84	93.30	7.14	10.87	4.06	115.37	79.03	2.63	—	—
1984–85	95.83	7.19	10.52	4.06	117.60	86.35	1.98	—	—
1985–86	97.92	7.72	16.42	4.15	126.21	88.72	2.27	—	0.49
1986–87	109.20	7.66	11.69	4.41	132.95	77.97	2.87	12.84	0.48
1987–88	110.10	11.56	14.38	4.64	140.67	—	—	—	0.55

Sources: Central government: England, Wales, and Scotland—1949–75 *Appropriation Accounts;* England—1979–88 *Government Expenditure Plans;* and Wales, Scotland, and Northern Ireland—*Central Trends* (1989, 1). Local government: England—*Local Government Financial Statistics;* Wales—1979–84 as for England, 1984–87 *Welsh Local Government Statistics;* and Scotland and Northern Ireland—*Cultural Trends* (1989, 1).
*Deflated by GDP deflator.

uities, the amounts of the grants introduced for the 1986–87 year were based on the 1985–86 vote provision.

Table 10.3 shows government spending on museums; what is not immediately evident is that the national museums take the lion's share of the English museum budget, amounting to about 93 percent in 1988–89. Table 10.4 provides figures of the subsidies to the eleven "art" museums from which it can be seen that they have experienced a fairly constant level of funding (the rise from £54 million to £64.3 million in 1986–87 being mainly explained by the new Merseyside museum).[5]

The remainder of the central government budget for England provides grants for one or two smaller London museums and funds for museums in the regions which are channeled through the Museums and Galleries Commission. This is an "arm's length" body and can allocate its budget at its own discretion, as is the case with the Arts Council. It may also receive earmarked grants which it administers on behalf of the government. Similar funds are made available for Scotland and Wales through their respective offices.

The commission was originally established in 1930 as the Standing Commission on Museums and Galleries, but in 1981 it was set up as an independent body. Originally it had an advisory role as well as responsibility for liaising between national and provincial museums. With its change in status, various executive duties have been added. These currently include the monitoring of the nine Area Museums Councils (seven in England, one each in Scotland and in Wales), allocation of grants to the seven English Councils, funding of the Museum Documentation Association, administration of capital (generally for the housing of collections) and conservation grants for nonnational museums. It also takes responsibility for the Local Museums' Purchase Funds (administered for the Commission by the Science and Victoria & Albert Museums) and the acceptance of works of art in lieu of taxation, which will be discussed in more detail in a later section. The sums involved are shown in table 10.5.

The commission also has administrative responsibility for the Government Indemnity Scheme, whereby the government effectively acts as insurer for items lent to nonnational museums and galleries, including items from abroad, and in some circumstances from private owners. The advantages of this scheme are that museums avoid having to pay for insurance and, consequently, are more willing to make loans to other museums and exhibitions. Unlike the American scheme (see Clotfelter, chap. 9 in this volume), museums do not have to take out insurance for a proportion of the value, so that 1987–88 total annual value of upwards of £700 million covered by the scheme

5. These are the British Museum, National Gallery, NGM Merseyside, National Portrait Gallery, Tate Gallery, Victoria & Albert Museum, Wallace Collection, National Galleries Scotland, National Museums Scotland, National Museum of Wales, and Ulster Museum. The last three and NGM Merseyside are "all-purpose" museums with substantial art collections.

Table 10.4   **Government Direct Subsidies to National Art Museums (£ thousand)**

	Grants to Art Museums		Total Grants to National Art Museums		Art Expenditure as % of Government Expenditure on All National Museums	Grants to All National Museums	
	Operating	Purchase	Current Prices	1985 Prices*		Current Prices	1985 Prices*
1949–50	646.0	183.0	829.0	9,752.9	67.6	1,226.0	14,423.5
1959–60	1,401.0	451.0	1,852.0	14,468.8	66.7	2,776.0	21,687.5
1969–70	4,878.0	1,189.0	6,067.0	32,972.8	69.3	8,757.0	47,592.4
1974–75	10,285.0	1,190.0	11,475.0	38,250.0	61.2	18,756.0	62,520.0
1979–80	23,514.0	8,303.0	31,817.0	50,744.8	62.7	50,713.0	80,882.0
1980–81	30,338.0	9,875.0	40,213.0	54,122.5	61.5	65,428.0	88,059.2
1981–82	33,445.0	9,806.0	43,251.0	53,003.7	62.2	69,496.0	85,166.7
1982–83	36,020.0	10,558.0	46,578.0	53,354.0	62.2	74,920.0	85,819.0
1983–84	38,351.0	11,418.0	49,769.0	54,631.2	62.2	80,073.0	87,895.7
1984–85	41,494.0	11,295.0	52,789.0	54,988.5	61.5	85,839.0	89,415.6
1985–86	43,902.0	10,603.0	54,505.0	53,912.0	59.6	91,502.0	90,506.4
1986–87	55,764.0	11,466.0	67,230.0	64,396.6	63.9	105,256.0	100,819.9
1987–88	57,216.0	11,591.0	68,807.0	62,608.7	60.4	113,976.0	103,708.8

Source: Appropriation Accounts; Museums and Galleries Commission, The National Museums 1988.

Notes: In most cases the operating grant does not include any funds for buildings.
Purchase grant for National Museum of Wales is not shown separately from the operating grant.
*Deflated by GDP deflator.

Table 10.5   **Central Government Grants Administered by Museums and Galleries Commission (£ thousands)**

	Area Museum Councils*	Documentation	Capital	Transition	Local Purchases	Conservation	Research
1979–80	1,266						
1980–81	1,500						
1981–82	1,730		65				
1982–83	1,748	53	102				
1983–84	1,898	62	150				
1984–85	2,005	88	182		1,282	387	5
1985–86	2,194	72	300		1,282	150	8
1986–87	2,288	115	226	1,155	1,282	200	36
1987–88	2,622	113	220	1,019	1,280	238	18

Source: Museums and Galleries Commission, *Annual Reports*
*Seven English Councils.

represents a saving to museums of some £3.5 million in commercial premiums during that financial year (Museums and Galleries Commission *Annual Report,* 1988).

The Arts Council of Great Britain is the major source of funding for the performing arts but it also provides funds for the visual arts: in 1988–89 this amounted to £3 million, or 2 percent of its budget. The council is the main source of subsidy for exhibitions, and it also funds the Hayward and Serpentine Galleries in London. State patronage to individual artists is limited: the government has a small fund for the purchase of work by British artists, as does the Arts Council, while the British Council promotes and funds exhibitions of British artists abroad.

Compared with European Economic Community (EEC) countries, Britain spends relatively little on the arts as a whole but devotes a greater proportion to "cultural heritage." As can be seen from the top panel of table 10.6, whatever measure one adopts for assessing spending on arts and libraries—be it proportion of all government expenditure, spending per capita, or percentage of GDP—Britain is amongst the lowest spenders. The bottom panel of the table breaks down spending into different categories: cultural heritage (including museums), music and opera, theatre and dance. In all three categories, Britain spends less per capita than do Germany, France, and Italy. The study by the Commission of the European Communities only covers central spending, but it commented that local authority spending in the United Kingdom seemed unlikely greatly to affect the rankings (1989).

10.2.2   Local Authority Spending on Museums

As has already been explained, local authorities fund museums and galleries from the rates (a tax on nonagricultural land and buildings). However,

Table 10.6   European Communities—Spending on the Arts, 1985

	Spending on All Arts					
Country	Spending on Arts (ECU Millions) (1)	(1) As % National Budget (2)	Per Capita Spending Arts (ECU) (3)	(1) As % of GDP (4)	Spending on Arts (SPP) [a] (5)	Per Capita Arts Spending (SPP) [a] (6)
Germany	1,368.0	0.7	22.3	0.2	1,392.0	22.7
France	1,454.0	1.0	26.5	0.2	1,585.0	28.9
Italy	1,272.0	0.4	22.3	0.3	1,564.0	27.5
Netherlands	497.0	0.7	34.1	0.3	542.0	37.2
Belgium	224.0	0.5	22.8	0.2	270.0	27.4
Luxembourg	8.0	0.5	22.2	0.2	10.0	27.8
Great Britain	447.0	0.2	7.9	0.1	533.0	9.5
Ireland	22.0	0.2	6.3	0.1	28.0	8.0
Denmark	184.0	0.8	36.0	0.2	178.0	34.9
Greece	79.0	0.4	8.2	0.2	105.0	11.0
Spain	564.0	0.6	14.7	0.3	842.0	22.0
Portugal	56.0	0.4	5.4	0.2	78.0	7.6
EEC	—	0.5	19.1	0.2	7,127.0	22.0

	Spending on Visual and Performing Arts					
	Cultural Heritage[b]		Music and Opera		Theatre and Dance	
Country	% of Arts Budget	Spending per Capita (ECU)	% of Arts Budget	Spending per Capita (ECU)	% of Arts Budget	Spending per Capita (ECU)
Germany	20.10	4.48	5.50	1.23	28.70	6.41
France	28.90	7.65	14.20	3.78	7.50	1.99
Italy	32.80	7.33	24.30	5.44	7.00	1.57
Netherlands	29.10	9.95	11.90	4.07	4.50	1.52
Belgium	26.70	6.08	13.10	2.99	15.20	3.46
Luxembourg	24.00	16.94	2.10	0.56	2.30	0.56
Great Britain	36.70	2.92	13.70	1.09	12.80	1.02
Ireland	32.60	2.06	8.20	0.51	18.40	1.17
Denmark	24.20	8.75	4.30	1.57	28.40	10.25
Greece	—	—	—	—	—	—
Spain	32.60	2.91	10.00	0.89	3.50	0.31
Portugal	41.00	2.24	2.60	0.15	2.00	0.11
EEC	28.50	5.21	13.40	2.45	13.20	2.41
Average	34.30		10.00		11.80	

Source: Commission of the European Communities, The Public Administration and the Funding of Culture in the European Community (1989, 179, 180).

[a]SPP = standard purchasing power.

[b]Cultural Heritage includes architectural and archaeological assets, museums, and archives.

Table 10.7   Local Government Direct Subsidies to Local Authority Museums

	London	Metropolitan	Nonmetropolitan	Total England	Wales	Total England and Wales
		Net Revenue Expenditure at 1985 Prices[a] (£ Million)				
1979–80	4.3	20.3	28.5	53.1	1.8	54.9
1980–81	4.7	22.1	30.7	57.5	1.6	59.1
1981–82	5.4	21.4	30.8	57.7	1.8	59.6
1982–83	6.0	22.7	31.8	60.4	1.8	·62.2
1983–84	6.5	23.2	33.2	62.9	1.9	64.8
1984–85	7.8	23.8	33.5	65.2	1.5	66.7
1985–86	7.4	26.3	34.1	67.9	2.2	70.0
1986–87	7.0	20.1	27.9	64.7	2.3	67.0
		Spending per Capita (£ at 1985 Prices[a])				
1979–80	0.6	1.8	1.0	1.1	0.6	1.1
1980–81	0.7	1.9	1.1	1.2	0.6	1.2
1981–82	0.8	1.9	1.1	1.2	0.7	1.2
1982–83	0.9	2.0	1.1	1.3	0.7	1.3
1983–84	1.0	2.0	1.2	1.3	0.7	1.3
1984–85	1.2	2.2	1.2	1.4	0.5	1.4
1985–86	1.1	2.6	1.2	1.5	0.8	1.4
1986–87	1.0	1.9	1.0	1.4	0.8	1.4

Source: Local Government Financial Statistics.
[a]Deflated by GDP deflator.

some central subsidy may be included in the block grants which most local authorities receive, in order to adjust for regional differences in resources and needs. The allocation for museums is not earmarked and has moreover been estimated through a somewhat arbitrary choice of measure: square footage of relevant shopping and restaurant space. This central subsidy thus takes no account of the size, importance, or nature of the collections, which vary considerably due to historical circumstances and differences in the types of bequests, interests, and finances in the various regions.

Government figures for local authority spending on museums and galleries are given in table 10.3 and cover expenditure by all local authorities in the United Kingdom. Table 10.7 (top panel), using a different source, gives net revenue expenditure, at 1985 prices, by main category of local authority for England and Wales for the period 1979–87.[6] Over this period, subsidies have risen, until 1986–87 when English figures show a decrease.

In 1986, there was a reorganization of local government: before that time, London and the six major metropolitan areas had two-tier authorities but, in March 1986, the Greater London Council (GLC) and the six metropolitan

6. Figures for counties and districts have been merged to provide one figure for each type of authority.

county councils (the upper-tier authorities) were abolished. The removal of these authorities with relatively few functions but responsible for some of the major provincial museums (and other art bodies) generated considerable anxiety about future funding, and the implications were examined by the Education, Science and Arts Committee of the House of Commons (1984). It became apparent that the government had not thought through some of its proposals, and various compromises had to be made. In one case, various Liverpool museums were merged to form the National Galleries and Museums, Merseyside, thus transferring funding from the local authority to the central budget when it became the latest national museum in 1986. The government expected the smaller districts to fund other affected museums, promising adjustments in their block grants. However, problems in reaching agreement about the level of funding and appropriate shares left some of the arrangements predictably uncertain, such collaboration between districts not having been necessary in the preceding years. In order to aid transition, grants were made by central government to various bodies. In the first year following reorganization, grants paid, through the Museums and Galleries Commission, amounted to 75 percent of the GLC or metropolitan county council funding in the previous financial year. Grants have been reduced to 50 percent and 25 percent in succeeding years and ceased in 1989–90. The total sums involved are shown under the heading "Transition" in table 10.5.

It seems unlikely that reorganization accounts for the reduction in spending in 1986–87. The transition grants should have provided a cushion and, more pertinently, the reorganization did not affect the nonmetropolitan areas in England which also show a fall in spending. Moreover, although the Conservative government has conducted a fierce campaign to contain local authority expenditure, through rate-capping and other means, the local government financial climate after reorganization was not noticeably tighter than before. However, in recent years education costs have escalated, and since these represent a large share of local authority budgets, it could be that economies have had to be made elsewhere, including spending on museums.[7]

Future analysis of local government spending on museums will be further complicated by the forthcoming major revision of local government finance. This reform means that from 1990, local rates will be abolished and replaced by a community charge, or poll tax as it is commonly known. As this name indicates, it is a flat-rate tax on virtually all adults aged eighteen and over. Individuals with low incomes will receive rebates up to a maximum of 80 percent. The level of charge will be set by each local authority, which will raise about 25 percent of its total revenue from this source. The remainder will come from a revised block grant and a share of the business rates, the amount of revenue from these two sources being linked to the adult population in each area. The government's objective is to make authorities more accountable to

7. The author is indebted to John Gibson for suggesting this possibility.

their voters: local authority decisions to increase spending will mean a larger community charge. The reform is controversial. Local authorities will now only be able to determine the tax rate funding 25 percent of expenditure, instead of the previous 50 percent; redistributive effects are likely to be considerable since the previous tax was on property and payable by households, regardless of the number in the family. At this time, the government has not yet announced the size of the block grants to local authorities, so the level of community charge is not yet known and the implications for museum funding cannot be assessed.

Local authority museums benefit from the grants administered by the Museums and Galleries Commission, the most important of which are those made to the Area Museum Councils (AMCs). These grants, to aid conservation, display, traveling exhibitions, and information and training services, have to be matched by subscriptions and contributions from member museums. Scotland and Wales each have their own AMC, but so far none has been set up in Northern Ireland. In real terms, the size of the grant has hardly increased since 1979–80, and the total amount of money is small, individual councils receiving shares in 1987–88 that varied from £155,250 (East Midlands—recently separated from the West Midlands, which received £255,500) to £605,750 (South Eastern England). In line with government policy to national museums, the grant settlement will be made in future on a three-year basis in order to encourage planning; councils are being urged to supplement their income by sponsorship, in which area they have met with some success.

10.2.3   Independent Museums

A survey by the Museums Association found that about 42 percent of the income of independent museums came from public grants in 1985 (1987, 153). This seems a surprisingly large proportion, and unfortunately the survey does not provide detailed definitions of the type of museums it included in this classification, nor was the response rate very high. Some independent museums do receive public funds: a very few private museums receive grants from central government (e.g., Soane Museum) and local authorities make occasional grants. These local authority grants totaled an estimated £3.35 million in 1984–85, the last year for which figures are given by the Chartered Institute of Public Finance and Accountancy (CIPFA) in its Leisure and Recreation Statistics.

University museums receive a small amount of central government funding as universities receive a general grant from the government via the University Funding Council (formerly the University Grants Committee). This can include a nonearmarked contribution where the museum is recognized by the funding body. In 1986–87, the University Grants Committee only recognized 16 collections in 11 universities. Their selection contained fewer than one in four of the 75 collections the Museums and Galleries Commission identified as of national distinction. Local authorities may also contribute, but patterns vary from area to area.

10.3 Indirect Subsidies

10.3.1 Tax Concessions on Donations

The Charities Aid Foundation has estimated that, on average, British households donate only about 0.7 percent of their income to charity. This is a small proportion when compared with American households, but the British tax system provides few concessions to encourage charitable giving. In 1986 the government introduced a payroll scheme whereby individuals may offset charitable donations against tax up to a ceiling which is currently £480 per annum. Other donations by individuals and companies can be made by deed of covenant, by which the recipient can recover the tax at the basic rate, but a minimum time period of four years is imposed, which tends to discourage donors, especially companies. The tax advantages of this form of giving accrue to mainly to the recipient rather than to the donor, but giving has risen over recent years, particularly since the removal of the ceiling of £10,000 in 1986.

Another change introduced in 1986 allowed companies to offset single charitable donations against Corporation Tax up to a limit of 3 percent of the annual dividend. The company making the donation deducts income tax at the basic rate from the donation and pays this to the Inland Revenue; the net amount is paid to the charity, which can reclaim the tax from the Inland Revenue. Up to October 1987, total tax relief obtained in this way amounted to £20 million, out of a potential total of £500 million (Museums and Galleries Commission, *The National Museums* 1988, 16). How much the arts have benefitted is not known. The concession benefits larger, rather than smaller, companies because close companies are excluded and because donations are linked to dividends rather than turnover: as small companies are more likely to make donations to local museums, it would seem unfortunate that the concession has been set up in this way.[8]

In recent years there have been some very generous donations to art museums, including the donation from the Clore Foundation to the Tate; the Bernard Sunley funding of a much needed exhibition room for the National Gallery; the Getty endowment for the National Gallery purchase fund; the Sainsbury Centre endowment for Visual Arts at the University of East Anglia; and the Adeane Gallery donation for the Fitzwilliam at Cambridge.

---

8. A close company is one under the control of five or fewer participants, or of participants who are directors. If 35 percent or more of its shares are held by the public, the company does not fall into this category.

10.3.2   Sponsorship

The Association for Business Sponsorship of the Arts (ABSA) was formed in 1976 to encourage business support, and in 1984–85 total sponsorship money amounted to £15 million (Myerscough 1986). For firms, the advantage of sponsorship over donations is that payments can be deducted from profits providing such payments are (1) of a revenue nature (precluding the use of sponsorship funds to finance building work or art purchases) and (2) incurred wholly and exclusively for the purpose of trade. The sponsor relationship is thus one of a commercial nature, whereby the company expects tangible returns, and sponsorship money generally comes from the marketing budget. It is not surprising, therefore, that sponsorship for the visual arts has mostly been funneled into temporary exhibitions both in London and the provinces.

In order to encourage sponsorship by small and medium-sized firms, the government set up the Business Sponsorship Incentive Scheme (BSIS) in 1984. Awards, administered by ABSA, match company sponsorship funds: first-time sponsors are matched pound for pound, while additional money from existing sponsors is matched in the ratio of one to three. In the period from its inception until the end of 1988, the scheme has raised a total of £21 million of which £15 million came from business and £6.5 million from the government (Touche Ross 1988). In 1987–88, out of a total of nearly £3 million sponsorship money, £369,337 went to the visual arts, the government grant amounting to £177,200 (H. M. Treasury, *The Government's Expenditure Plans* 1989, Cmnd. 613). There are signs, however, that companies may be less willing to continue to provide sponsorship money as they believe that government is beginning to regard sponsorship money as a substitute for, rather than supplement to, public funding.[9]

A survey of art organizations' attitudes to fund-raising found that most put more effort into obtaining sponsorship than into obtaining corporate and individual donations (Touche Ross 1988). Certainly, as tax concessions on donations now stand, incentives to donors are not sufficient to encourage widespread giving from all households at all levels of income. Even sponsorship money has to be competed for—art museums and galleries perhaps offer less obvious benefits to marketing managers than the performing arts, not to mention sports events—and the amount of money raised through sponsorship and donation is likely to remain a small proportion of museum income in the immediate future. The average taxpayer in Britain, who has probably never completed a tax return (since income tax is deducted by employers under the pay-as-you-earn tax scheme), is probably unaware of the limited incentive

9. A spokesman for BP, which spent £1 million on the arts in 1988, is quoted as saying "If the government goes on reneging on its responsibility, we shall begin to pull in our horns a bit. We believe in a partnership with the government. There is no sign of us pulling the plug, but in the future we may say enough is enough" (*The Sunday Times*, 25 September 1989).

provided by the payroll scheme, so it not surprising that, by October 1988, only 100,000 individuals had enrolled (Touche Ross 1988).

10.3.3   Capital Gains Tax and Death Duties

The tax system has also been used to provide incentives for owners of heritage objects to make them available to a wider public, either through sales or through loans to museums. Neither capital gains tax nor inheritance tax (an estate tax) is payable on art objects bequeathed to national, local authority, and university museums.

Conditional Exemption from Tax

When an individual is given, or inherits, an object assessed by experts as "worthy of display in a public museum," provided certain conditions are fulfilled, exemption may be obtained from inheritance and capital gains taxes. The conditions are that the object is kept in the United Kingdom, maintained in a proper state of preservation, and accessible to the public (either through loan to a museum or by opening the house to the public). Should the owner decide to sell the object (or violate any of the conditions), tax is payable if it is sold at a public sale.

Private Treaty Sales and the Douceur

A further tax concession may make it worthwhile to sell the object by private treaty to a public museum rather than at an auction. Anyone selling a national heritage object, whether subject to conditional exemption or not, may gain by an arrangement designed to help retain art objects in this country. A simple numerical example is the easiest way to illustrate how both seller and purchasing museum can benefit.

Assume that the object is valued at £100,000 and has not been subject to conditional exemption from tax. On sale, capital gains tax would have to be paid by the seller. Let us assume that this amounts to £30,000. If the object is sold at auction for £100,000, the seller would therefore receive £70,000. If, however, the seller were to negotiate a private treaty sale with a museum, then he or she would receive £70,000 plus the douceur. This is usually 25 percent of the tax that would have been paid, and in this case is equal to 25 percent of £30,000, or £7,500. The seller thus receives £70,000 plus £7,500, a total of £77,500, which is paid by the museum. Both seller and museum benefit: the seller by the amount of the douceur and the museum because it has not had to pay the auction price of £100,000. No capital gains tax is paid to the government, so the indirect subsidy amounts to £30,000. In the case of objects subject to conditional exemption, the net price at auction would be the sale price less both the capital gains tax and the amount of inheritance tax that had been exempted. The douceur is then calculated as a percentage of the total tax and is added to the net of tax market price. The douceur may be 30 percent or even 50 percent, at the Inland Revenue's discretion, but 25 percent is usual.

Unfortunately, no records of such transactions are kept at the Capital Taxes Office, so it is impossible to estimate the extent to which such private treaty sales occur and the amount of this tax subsidy.

Acceptance in Lieu of Death Duties

Important works of art may also be accepted in lieu of death duties payable under the inheritance tax which replaced the capital transfer tax in 1986. Both these taxes are estate taxes—that is, they are donor based—and under the National Heritage Act of 1980, objects of special artistic or historical importance may be offered as payment in kind. As in the case of private treaty sales, a douceur is offered to induce individuals to take advantage of this arrangement, but unlike private treaty sales, it is fixed at 25 percent and there have been frequent calls for the amount to be increased to 50 percent or more. The administrative side is handled by the Museums and Galleries Commission which, following expert assessment of the object, advises the minister whether it should be accepted, advice which is usually taken. If an art object is accepted, the Inland Revenue is then reimbursed for the amount of tax from a fund set aside by the Office of Arts and Libraries for this purpose. Initially, a ceiling of £2 million was set on this fund, but it was subsequently agreed that in exceptional cases additional funds may be drawn from the Public Expenditure Reserve. As can be seen from table 10.8, it was necessary to call on the reserve fund when, in 1987, Constable's *Stratford Mill* was accepted to satisfy tax amounting to £5.5 million.

In its early years, the scheme was criticized for the extremely slow procedures. Before the Museums and Galleries Commission took over the administration, the Capital Transfer Tax Office might take a full year before deciding whether to accept an object. Another disincentive operated, in that interest charges were payable on any tax outstanding. This, combined with the slow administration in the initial years, meant that many owners and executors preferred to go to auction. Since 1987, such interest charges have been waived, and decisions are made more rapidly. One problem remained: on occasion, the tax offset negotiated may be less than the value of the item offered. This is

Table 10.8   **Works of Art Accepted in Lieu of Capital Transfer/Inheritance Tax**

	Tax Satisfied (£ thousand)
1981–82	1,463.5
1982–83	2,171.5
1983–84	815.3
1984–85	1,209.6
1985–86	2,132.3
1986–87	2,359.4
1987–88	8,627.5

Source: Myerscough (1986); Museums and Galleries Commission, *Annual Reports.*

especially likely to occur when collections are involved. The government has been repeatedly urged to allow tax credits which could be set against future liability for tax but has not agreed. However, in 1987, a precedent was set when Picasso's *Weeping Woman* was offered and valued at £1.2 million, a sum exceeding the amount of tax to be satisfied. A solution was found by allowing the Tate Gallery (assisted by a £0.9 million grant from the National Heritage Memorial Fund) to pay the balance of £1.015 million.

10.3.4 Other Taxes

All museums pay value-added tax (VAT) on trading activities, admission charges, and sponsorship monies. The tax is refunded on books. When objects are purchased at auction, VAT is payable on the dealer's margin: a strange anomaly is that this is refunded to local authority museums but not to nationals.

Museums also have to pay rates on their premises, though, if they are registered charities, they receive a rebate of 50 percent.

10.4   Current Situation

While the government has repeated on various occasions that state funding of the national collections will be maintained and that other sources of income, such as sponsorship and donations, will be viewed as additions, under the new funding arrangements government grants are no longer sufficient to cover the basic running costs nor are the purchase grants large enough to enable all museums to maintain an active purchase policy. The situation for local authority museums is less clear: they have always been run on less generous funding, and current uncertainty, generated by the forthcoming changes in local government finance, suggest that they too will be expected to augment their income by their own efforts.

In this section, we assess the impact of changes in government policy and examine the problems that museums face in responding to them. Due to the paucity of data on local authority museums, the main focus will be on the finances and problems of the national art museums.

10.4.1   Management of the National Museums

The trustees of the national museums take final responsibility for museum policy, while the director has the executive role. The trustees, who are unpaid and generally serve for a term of five to seven years, are usually appointed by a minister, often the Prime Minister.[10] The Scottish and Welsh Museums' trustees are appointed by their respective secretaries of state.

Relations between museums and the funding department (usually the Office

10. The P. M. appoints all trustees bar one for the National Gallery and the Tate, all of the trustees of the Victoria & Albert, but only about half of the British Museum's board of 25.

of Arts and Libraries) are by tradition conducted on the so-called arm's length principle whereby "prime responsibility for securing economy, efficiency and effectiveness in the use of the substantial public funds granted to the Museum, and the assets in its charge, rests inescapably on the Museum Council and officers" (Public Accounts Committee 1987, para. 24). Monitoring of financial administration and accountability, in respect of public funds, is exercized through periodic examination by the National Audit Office and the Public Accounts Committee.

The idea behind arm's length funding is that a museum can determine its own policy over a wide range of decisions. In the early 1970s, the government was disconcerted to find that it had no legal powers to force museums to introduce admissions charges, but, since museums depend so heavily on government finance, their technical independence may not enable them to persist in their objections for long. Independence, when the purse is held by someone else, can never be complete. Nevertheless there has been a general understanding that the government should leave management decisions to the museums: the state funds but the trustees determine a museum's policy.

Recently, however, there have been suggestions that the current government may be seeking to influence some of the museums' management decisions. It seems that the funding department has insisted on having an assessor present at trustees' meetings and the Museums and Galleries Commission has drawn attention to the "uncertainty and imprecision surrounding the relationship between Government and Trustees, and the degree of control that is appropriate" (Museums and Galleries Commission, *The National Museums* 1988, 20–21). Recent events at the Victoria & Albert Museum, involving both restructuring and the forced retirement of senior curatorial staff, are open to an interpretation that there has been government activity behind the scenes (through the sudden availability of redundancy money) and, no doubt, the change was facilitated by the current board of trustees. When a question to this effect was asked in Parliament, government intervention was, however, denied. Unlike most other national museums, the Victoria & Albert only achieved trustee status under the National Heritage Act of 1983, with the result that all serving trustees have been appointed by Prime Minister Thatcher who tended to appoint more business people than those with museum experience or interest in the collections.

10.4.2   Income Sources and Expenditure Allocation

The measures taken by present government with the intention of reducing the national museums' dependence on state funding present the boards of trustees with new decisions:

1. Since only a proportion of operating costs will in future be met by government subsidy, increasing attention will need to be devoted to income generation. However, the accompanying change to grant-in-aid brings a

reward, as such income will, in general, no longer be appropriated by the government.

2. The change in funding base also means that museums' responsibilities for their resources have been increased: the most important new responsibility is that in future all national museums will themselves deal with the care and maintenance of their buildings. At present the freehold will continue to be held by the Crown, but it is the government's intention that eventually it will pass to the trustees.

3. Grant-in-aid will now be announced for a three-year period: this will enable museums to plan ahead but may bring problems when inflation exceeds anticipated levels.

Unfortunately there is little published information on the earned income of national and local authority museums. The bulk of their income comes from government; other sources include admission fees, trading income (from museum shops, snackbars, and publications) and donations. Figures for the seven major English national art museums for 1986–87 indicate that the amounts raised from these other sources may vary considerably by museums, as can be seen in table 10.9. There are no charges for admission to the main museums in London, but there are charges at branch museums; the remaining income raised under this heading comes from admission charges for exhibitions. The British Museum, National Gallery, Tate, and Victoria & Albert have all set up trading companies, and the income from these is not included in the total. The National Portrait Gallery, which earns a considerable amount from publications—likely to approach £1 million in the current financial year—is considering following suit.

Local authority museums also rely heavily on grants from local government. Earned income has risen from £4.6 million in 1979–80 to £12.4 million in 1986–87 for English museums, providing about 16 percent of total income.

All museums have to strike a balance in satisfying two types of customers: the general public, seeking entertainment and instruction, and scholars. Underlying the change in government policy is the feeling that museums have not been sufficiently responsive to the demands of the general public, and they are being urged to make their collections more attractive and more accessible by presenting them in a more inviting way and by using loans and traveling exhibitions. Such changes can only be achieved, given budget constraints, at a cost to other activities. Whilst all museums face the need to decide the balance to be struck, not all will make similar decisions—since collections, and hence their visitors, differ. For example, the Victoria & Albert, though holding a larger collection of paintings than the National Gallery, is predominantly dedicated to design; it has traditionally emphasized its educative role, but its National Art Library remains closed for one day a week due to insufficient funds.

Within a tight budget and faced with increasing commitments, trade-offs have to be decided in terms of the services to be provided. Much of a mu-

Table 10.9   Income Sources—Major English National Art Museums and English Local Authority Museums

	British Museum[a]	National Gallery	NMG Merseyside	National Portrait Gallery	Tate	Victoria & Albert Museum	Wallace	Average	Local Authority England
Total Income (£ thousands)	16,470.0	7,336.7	11,020.9	2,727.3	6,327.7	13,102.5	975.4	57,960.5	79,900.0
Government grants	81.7%	93.5%	93.6%	66.5%	91.4%	84.1%	92.9%	86.5%	84.5%
Fees and charges	2.3	0.0	3.0	4.4	0.3	0.3	0.0	1.5	6.3
Admission fees	1.1	0.0	2.7	0.0	2.8	0.0	0.0	1.1	0.0
Trading	0.0	2.5	0.0	15.1	0.0	6.0	7.1	2.5	3.5
Trust	0.0	1.4	0.0	0.0	0.0	0.0	0.0	0.2	0.0
Sponsorship	0.7	0.0	0.5	1.7	4.3	0.0	0.0	0.8	0.0
Donations[b]	10.9	2.1	0.0	9.4	0.1	5.2	0.0	5.0	0.0
Other	3.4	0.5	0.2	2.9	1.1	4.3	0.0	2.3	5.8

Source: Museums and Galleries, *Accounts for Year Ending 31 March 1987* (1988, Cmnd. 522).
[a]Excluding exceptional "other income."
[b]Donations for acquisition funds.

seum's work is less immediately visible; the effects of cuts in resources devoted to scholarship, conservation, documentation and general management of the collections may only become apparent after some time. Museums are having to reassess not only how much time and effort should be spent in such activities but also how much should be devoted to fund-raising where it is not always immediately clear which course of action will achieve maximum returns.

Some limited information on how museums currently allocate their income between alternative functions can be gleaned from a recent survey. It seems that, on average, United Kingdom museums allocate their resources in remarkably similar proportions to American museums, as can be seen from table 10.10. Taken over all museums, curatorial functions receive about one-quarter of the budget. However, there are differences between the main groups of U.K. museums: national and university museums allocate a larger proportion of their budgets to curatorial, library, and security functions than do local authority and independent museums, while the proportion devoted to maintenance is relatively low (perhaps reflecting the fact that for many national museums this is handled by another government agency) as is that for administration. All three categories of museums devote only a small proportion to conservation (Lord, Lord and Nicks 1989).

As collections grow, so do the operating costs of maintaining them. Over and above the purchase cost, it has been estimated that the curatorial costs of acquisition, documentation conservation, restoration, and display or storage amount to 24 percent of a museum's operating costs. If the costs of general maintenance, administration, and security are also added, this rises to about 67 percent (Lord, Lord, and Nicks, xxiii).

10.4.3 Costs

As, in future, operating grants are likely to remain constant and may even decline, the national museums will have to contain costs and put increasing

Table 10.10   **Allocation of Expenditure by Function, United Kingdom and United States (in percentages)**

	U.K.	U.S.
Curatorial (including conservation)	24	27
Library	2	5
Security	14	15
Maintenance	18	18
Administration	19	18
Education	4	6
Display and other public activities	10	
Development		11
Other	9	

Source: Lord, Lord, and Nicks (1989), table 3.1.

efforts into generating income. Table 10.11 shows the operating grants received by national art museums for the period from 1979 to 1989. Bearing in mind that the figures for 1988–89 include additional funding for some of the responsibilities passed from the central funding departments to the museums under the new grant-in-aid system, we can see that in 1988, prior to the changes, most museums were at a higher level of real funding than in 1979.

National museums will be under pressure in almost all areas of expenditure: rising labor costs, heavy capital expenditure to maintain and modernize buildings, and rapidly increasing art market prices. We will now consider each of these categories in more detail.

Labor Costs

All museums face rising labor costs: as Baumol and Bowen have argued, this is inevitable when labor is the major component of operating cost and there are few possibilities for productivity gains (1966). National museums are particularly vulnerable as pay levels for their staff are determined by Civil Service pay settlements, which are negotiated by the government outside of museum control. Where wage increases are determined after the grant assessment of running costs (based on agreed staffing levels), museums may find themselves in financial difficulty. In 1986–87, National Gallery salaries took 81 percent of its operating grant and 77 percent of operating income; figures for the Tate were 86 percent and 76 percent, for the Victoria & Albert 83 percent and 71 percent; the British Museum's salaries bill equaled its entire operating grant.

Local authority museum expenditure on labor takes a smaller proportion of the total budget, averaging slightly over 50 percent, reflecting both lower staffing levels and, in general, lower wages. Little is known about universities: in many cases administrative costs are absorbed into university budgets. Curatorship of smaller collections is often handled by academic staff of the department responsible for the collection. The larger collections, faced with rising costs, have often had insufficient staff to maintain regular opening hours.

Some of the national museums are also foist with cumbersome departmental structures. This is particularly true of the Victoria & Albert Museum, which separated in 1983 from the Department of Education and Science. The new director wishes to restructure management to separate research from administrative matters, where administration would include curatorial activities. Apart from providing a more rational structure and achieving savings on staff costs, the plan is intended to give those staff interested in scholarly activities more time to devote to them. The proposal made headline news in the major newspapers for several weeks and has been commented on in most art journals. There has been adverse comment on the changes (not only from within Britain) but much of the criticism has been directed at the enforced resignations of senior staff, some of whom were not far from retirement, and the brutality with which the changes were enforced. The loss of expertise is

Table 10.11   Government Operating Grants to National Art Museums

	1979–80	1980–81	1981–82	1982–83	1983–84	1984–85	1985–86	1986–87	1987–88	1988–89
					£ Thousands at Current Prices					
British Museum	6,802	8,624	9,441	10,012	10,733	11,034	11,593	11,945	12,538	15,665
National Gallery	1,829	2,436	2,727	3,017	3,328	3,661	3,821	4,021	4,267	5,233
NGM Merseyside								9,395	8,664	9,470
National Portrait Gallery	952	1,183	1,279	1,396	1,447	1,556	1,467	1,504	1,589	1,996
Tate Gallery	2,067	2,670	2,887	3,163	3,299	3,553	3,829	3,967	4,682	6,300
Victoria & Albert Museum	4,584	6,040	6,589	7,181	7,865	8,906	9,525	9,878	10,535	12,900
Wallace Collection	414	617	656	759	781	822	876	906	939	1,149
England	16,648	21,570	23,579	25,528	27,453	29,532	31,111	41,616	43,214	52,713
National Galleries of Scotland	829	1,166	1,281	1,403	1,399	1,559	1,603	1,681	1,862	2,306
National Museums of Scotland	1,643	2,164	2,382	2,462	2,577	2,872	3,100	3,940	4,232	5,226
National Museum of Wales	3,244	4,017	4,553	4,882	5,122	5,634	6,061	6,419	5,661	5,803
Ulster Museum	1,150	1,421	1,650	1,745	1,800	1,897	2,027	2,108	2,247	2,291
Total, all art museums	23,514	30,338	33,445	36,020	38,351	41,494	43,902	55,764	57,216	68,339

£ Thousands at 1985 Prices[a]

British Museum	10,848	11,607	11,570	11,468	11,782	11,494	11,467	11,442	11,409	13,287
National Gallery	2,917	3,279	3,342	3,456	3,653	3,814	3,779	3,852	3,883	4,439
NGM Merseyside								8,999	7,884	8,032
National Portrait Gallery	1,518	1,592	1,567	1,599	1,588	1,621	1,451	1,441	1,446	1,693
Tate Gallery	3,297	3,594	3,538	3,623	3,621	3,701	3,787	3,800	4,260	5,344
Victoria & Albert Museum	7,311	8,129	8,075	8,226	8,633	9,277	9,421	9,462	9,586	10,941
Wallace Collection	660	830	804	869	857	856	866	868	854	975
England	26,552	29,031	28,896	29,242	30,135	30,763	30,773	39,862	39,321	44,710
National Galleries of Scotland	1,322	1,569	1,570	1,607	1,536	1,624	1,586	1,610	1,694	1,956
National Museums of Scotland	2,620	2,913	2,919	2,820	2,829	2,992	3,066	3,774	3,851	4,433
National Museum of Wales	5,174	5,406	5,580	5,592	5,622	5,869	5,995	6,148	5,151	4,922
Ulster Museum	1,834	1,913	2,022	1,999	1,976	1,976	2,005	2,019	2,045	1,943
Total, all art museums	37,502	40,832	40,987	41,260	42,098	43,223	43,424	53,414	52,062	57,964

Notes: With the exception of the Ulster Museum and NGM Merseyside, operating grants exclude funds for buildings.

All figures are for outturn expenditure except 1987–88 figures which are forecast outturn, and 1988–89 figures which are provisional.

With the exception of the National Museum of Wales, the figures for 1988–89 include additional funding for responsibilities previously borne on central departments' votes.

[a]Deflated by GDP deflator.

bound to make it difficult for the museum to provide the government with expert advice in some fields.

Staff in the national art museums have increased by about 33 percent over the period 1974–87 as shown in table 10.12 (top panel), but, as can be seen from the lower panel of the table, not all posts were filled in 1987. There have been occasions when shortage of wardens has meant that for security reasons some galleries and even whole museums have had to be closed to the public for varying periods.[11]

One solution to high labor costs is to take on volunteer workers, and most museums, and particularly local authority or independent museums, make use of volunteers. Surveys suggest that such workers are mainly used to help with documentation of collections and, to a lesser extent, with sales, information, and guiding (Mattingly 1984; Lord, Lord, and Nicks 1989). Many museums have also made use of government temporary employment schemes. Trainees from the Manpower Services Commission have been used to assist with documentation, but this scheme is now being replaced by other training programs which seem less well adapted to museum needs, as trainees available under the new schemes lack basic skills.

The growth in numbers of museum staff, many of whom do not have specialist training, and the loss of skills as experienced workers retire, have led to the recognition of the need for a training program to develop key skills. Following the report of a working party on training needs, it has been agreed to set up a training consortium. Initial funding for the first five years will be provided by the Office of Arts and Libraries but, in due course, the museums will absorb an increasing share of the costs so that the consortium will eventually become self-financing.

Curatorial Management

There is little information on curatorial management in general. Recent reports do, however, provide some material on conservation aspects.

A government report has criticized the British Museum, the Tate, and the Victoria & Albert Museum for poor conservation and slow implementation of computerized inventories (National Audit Office 1988; see also Public Accounts Committee 1988). There has been some debate as to whether the picture is as uniformly dismal as this report suggests and whether the cause is poor management or insufficient funding. That there is a large backlog of conservation work in certain departments is not in debate: examples include problems caused by acid to nineteenth-century books and manuscripts, and ethnological collections, many of which are in a poor state. Whether, in all types of collections, there is a serious risk that objects will deteriorate beyond recall is

11. The director of the Victoria & Albert Museum reported that in the early 1980s the national and branch museums had to close one day a week, that up to 20 galleries were closed on any given day, and that, after 130 years, it had terminated its service to the regions (Education, Science and Arts Committee 1982, Strong, evidence to the committee).

Table 10.12   **National Art Museums—Staffing**

	Staff in Post[a]			
	1/4/74	1/4/77	1/4/84	1/4/87
British Museum	931	696	1,008	1,005
National Gallery	215	254	275	264
NGM Merseyside				551
National Portrait Gallery	89	96	105	105
Tate Gallery	224	240	304	326
Victoria & Albert Museum	646	670	667	665
Wallace Collection	68	74	77	76
England	2,173	2,302	2,346	2,992
National Galleries of Scotland	108	122	127	127
National Museums of Scotland	237	247	233	247
National Museum of Wales	293	387	407	416
Ulster Museum	132	147	155	157
Total, all art museums	2,943	3,205	3,358	3,939

(*continued*)

Table 10.12   (continued)

Staffing Complements, 1987

	Curatorial		Warders		Others		Total		Short-fall
	Complement	In Post	Complement	In Post	Complement	In Post	Complement	In Post	
British Museum	297	268	397	377	400	360	1,094	1,005	89
National Gallery	23	23	202	181	70	60	295	264	31
NGM Merseyside	43	41	243	235	285	275	571	551	20
National Portrait Gallery	25	25	62	62	18	18	105	105	0
Tate Gallery	85	73	187	187	87	87	359	326	33
Victoria & Albert Museum	158	152	188	188	347	331	693	665	28
Wallace Collection	13	13	56	56	7	7	76	76	0
England	644	595	1,335	1,259	1,214	1,138	3,193	2,992	201
National Galleries of Scotland	24	23	71	71	33	33	128	127	1
National Museums of Scotland	125	113	79	79	55	55	259	247	12
National Museum of Wales	b	109	b	191	b	116	b	416	0
Ulster Museum	43	41	69	66	57	50	169	157	12
Totals, all museums		881		1,666		1,342		3,939	226

Source: Museums and Galleries Commission, *The National Museums* (1988)—*top panel*, table 2; *bottom panel*, appendices.
[a]Including staff at branch museums.
[b]No complement fixed.

not clear. The reports lay the blame for deficiencies on curators; others accept neither the gloomy picture nor that curators have been neglectful. Evidence given to the investigating bodies by the directors of the British and Victoria & Albert Museums suggests (1) that there is a shortage of appropriately skilled conservators, (2) that even if staff were available, museums are not able to offer salaries to attract them as the demand by private institutions has increased rapidly in recent years, and (3) even if staff could be recruited, it might not be possible to provide adequate working space for them.

This discussion is linked to questions of research: for example, the National Gallery has a strong record of research into conservation techniques and, to the extent that such work is no longer funded under central grants-in-aid, this debate constitutes another strand in the argument about both the level of central government funding and its purpose. The Victoria & Albert Museum runs a course to train conservators, and it has been suggested that other national museums should provide similar programs.

A detailed survey of conservation in Scottish museums provides some indication of the nature of the problems experienced by nonnational museums. The 209 museums surveyed held a wide variety of collections, including fine and decorative art. About two-thirds had inventoried 50 percent or more of their permanent collections but one-fifth had no inventory at all. Just under half had catalogued over 50 percent of collections but only 12 percent had used a recognized system. Assessments of the state of collections varied: 75 percent of easel paintings had been assessed in the last five years, as had 78 percent of textiles. However only 45 percent of watercolors, drawings, and prints had been similarly assessed. The survey also reported a serious shortage of skilled conservators (Ramer 1989). While no similar survey had been done of English and Welsh regional museums, it seems likely that the picture would not be dissimilar to that in Scotland.

Help for conservation activities at regional level is provided through conservation grants which are available to English museums through the Museums and Galleries Commission which divides some half a million pounds a year between the Area Museum Councils (to supplement their basic grants), capital projects for conservation-related projects, and equipment grants made by the commission's conservation unit. In Wales and Scotland, similar help is provided by their respective museum councils.

Documentation backlogs appear to be a fairly widespread problem, though their size varies by institution and type of collection (Lord, Lord, and Nicks 1989). The introduction of computers has raised expectations about documentation levels but, as has already been mentioned, many museums lack the staff to undertake this work and rely on voluntary or trainee workers.

In general, the evidence suggests that, with duties expanding and becoming more varied, skilled staff are carrying heavier loads. In the smaller museums this means that staff may have to carry out a variety of duties, many of which may be administrative, so that they have little time to work with the collections.

Buildings

All museums, national and provincial, have serious and, in some cases, acute problems with buildings, both as regards space and maintenance. Many museums occupy adapted buildings though perhaps not so many are still to be found in "disused castles, gaols, chapels, crypts, mansions, cottages and lean-to sheds" as was the case when Miers surveyed provincial museums in the 1920s (1928). A good many occupy buildings which are reaching the end of their normal life and can be preserved only at increasingly heavy expense: a recent survey found that, of the museums in its sample, over half the buildings were more than 100 years old and that 57 percent of museums occupied listed buildings that would require special care (Lord, Lord, and Nicks 1989).

Building Maintenance and Repair. Up to 1987, the building work for most of the national museums was handled by the government Property Services Agency (PSA). This unsatisfactory arrangement has now been terminated, and in 1988 responsibility for the care of their buildings was passed to all national museums. Most of the national museums need substantial renovation in addition to the most basic repairs: it is reported in the press that the Tate and the National Gallery have had to place buckets to collect rainwater from leaking roofs in order to prevent damage to pictures. The British Museum has seven acres of roof to maintain, which may well make a dent in its building grant of £7.6 million. Quite apart from problems with basic fabric, many art museums, including the National Gallery, lack air conditioning in all galleries. These problems arise from years of neglect. Spending on building maintenance, at current prices, has risen from £17.2 million in 1978–79 to £27.6 million in 1987–88. Measured at constant prices, this represents a decrease of approximately £7 million. With the transfer of responsibility, a total of £39.1 million was allocated in 1988–89 which, at constant prices, represents only £1 million more than the sum spent by the PSA ten years ago. The Victoria & Albert alone claims that it needs £100 million to repair its buildings. Certainly the sums allocated by the government are insufficient, and huge sums of money will be needed if the Minister for the Arts is to realize his ambition of getting museum buildings into good shape by the year 2000.[12]

Quite apart from normal maintenance and repair, museums also have heavy costs in bringing their buildings up to national safety standards. With their change in status, museums are no longer protected by Crown Immunity and local authority fire inspectors adopt stricter fire and safety standards than the Property Services Agency. This work has to be put in hand immediately with the result that other urgent building work has been postponed. The combined

12. See the report of the minister's speech in *The Independent*, 20 September 1989.

bill for the British Museum, the National Gallery and the Victoria & Albert has been estimated at £14 million of which £4 million will be needed to strengthen the upper floor structure of the nineteenth century building which houses the British Museum.[13]

Display and Storage Space. In addition to basic repair and maintenance, many museums are in need of extra display, conservation, and storage space to accommodate expanding collections. Many national and provincial museums also lack temporary exhibition space. The government has indicated that it expects private money to fund such building costs, and some sponsorship and large donations have been received, notably by the National Gallery and the Tate.

With only about one-third of art collections being on display at any time (Lord, Lord, and Nicks 1989), satisfactory storage space is essential. A survey of Scottish local museums found that, in most cases, stores were cramped and generally lacked the necessary environmental recording and monitoring equipment. In some cases, the buildings required repair, and in many cases, objects were left uncovered on shelves. Of the collections of paintings that were inspected, five out of six had insufficient funds to install the necessary environmental controls, and the collections exhibited deterioration in varying degrees, due also to poorly trained staff and shortage of staff time (Ramer 1989).

One solution to both display and storage problems would be to start branch museums. The National Portrait Gallery has set up three such museums, and the NGM Merseyside includes a branch of the Tate. It has been hoped that private funding would permit the Victoria & Albert to show some of its wide collection of Asian objects in Bradford, a city with a large immigrant population, but so far nothing has been finalized. In Scotland there is currently debate about whether the large collections of paintings by Scottish artists would be better displayed in two branch museums or, as the director hopes, in a brand new building. Branch museums, while bringing the national collections to a wider public, are not without cost to run, and so far it has been difficult to attract donations for operating costs. Similarly, while donations may cover the building costs of new wings, as they have at the National Gallery and the Tate, they do not cover the running and maintenance costs.

Acquisitions

Centrally funded purchase grants to English museums have not been increased since 1985–86. This means that in real terms, where current values have been deflated by the gross domestic product (GDP) deflator, all English museums have experienced severe cuts, with the National Gallery most ad-

---

13. See the report in *The Observer,* 6 August 1989, which estimates that the total bill for all museums is likely to be £20 million.

versely affected as its grant is now just over half of what it was in 1979.[14] The Scottish and Welsh museums have not suffered in this way, coming as they do under a separate vote, and their grants have increased. Details are given in table 10.13.

The use of the GDP deflator to measure the real value of purchase grants can only give a rough indication of the real loss in purchasing power. Over this period, British art market prices have increased much more rapidly than prices in general: particularly steep have been increases in Impressionist and modern paintings, Chinese ceramics, and English furniture. Some idea of the impact on museums' purchasing power for paintings can be gained by looking at Sotheby's (£ sterling) Index, shown in table 10.14, though these figures should be used with caution. This index is compiled by Sotheby's on the basis of "estimated prices" in relation to a constant portfolio of sample items in different sectors of the auction market but variations in quality, irregular appearance of items at auctions, and uniqueness of the paintings mean that any such index is essentially an artificial construct.[15] Perhaps a more graphic illustration of the reduced value of purchase grants is the sale of Van Gogh's *Sunflowers* and Manet's *La Rue Mosnier aux Paveurs* for a total of £32,892,500, which is more than the annual purchase grants for all United Kingdom museums over the last two years (Museums and Galleries Commission, *The National Museums*, 1988).

In addition to the national museum purchase grants, there is a centrally funded local purchase grant which was £1.3 million in 1979–80 and has been frozen at £1,114,000 since 1985 so that, in real terms, its value has halved over this period. Local museums, public and independent, may apply for grants which may not exceed 50 percent of the purchase price, and the museums must find at least 25 percent of the price from their own resources. For many local museums this is impossible.[16]

The National Heritage Memorial Fund, established in 1980, provides a source of emergency help when objects of outstanding historic interest come on to the market and museums do not have sufficient funds to acquire them. Any museum or art gallery is eligible for a grant to supplement its own contribution, and during the first three years of operation, the fund distributed over £11 million; about £5.5 million went to museums and galleries in general, including nearly £3 million to national art museums (Museums and Galleries Commission 1988). In 1986–87, the British Museum received grants amounting to £1.006 million, about two-thirds of its annual purchase grant. Help from this source represents a form of last resort assistance, through which valuable items can be retained for the nation, but the fund cannot substitute for a viable annual purchase grant. Moreover, the fund's terms of reference

14. The National Gallery has benefitted from a large donation by J. Paul Getty.
15. See Myerscough (1986, 52). It should also be noted that Sotheby's produce two separate series, one denominated in United States dollars and the other, shown in table 10.14, in sterling.
16. Bristol Art Gallery had no purchase grant for 1988–89.

Table 10.13   Government Purchase Grants to National Art Museums

	1979–80	1980–81	1981–82	1982–83	1983–84	1984–85	1985–86	1986–87	1987–88	1988–89
£' Thousands at Current Prices										
British Museum	1,217	1,422	1,450	1,617	1,617	1,400	1,400	1,400	1,400	1,400
National Gallery	2,612	3,109	2,930	2,988	3,331	3,331	2,750	2,750	2,750	2,750
NGM Merseyside								750	750	750
National Portrait Gallery	244	291	272	278	310	310	310	310	310	310
Tate Gallery	1,570	1,888	1,794	1,830	2,041	2,041	1,815	1,815	1,815	1,815
Victoria & Albert Museum	950	1,130	1,160	1,184	1,320	1,320	1,145	1,145	1,145	1,145
England	6,593	7,840	7,606	7,897	8,619	8,402	7,420	8,170	8,170	8,170
National Galleries of Scotland	685	897	941	1,211	1,265	1,274	1,439	1,517	1,555	1,578
National Museums of Scotland	277	360	382	495	520	524	591	503	560	642
National Museum of Wales	598	778	877	955	1,014	1,065	1,108	1,141	1,170	1,199
Ulster Museum	150					30	45	135	136	167
Total, all art museums	8,303	9,875	9,806	10,558	11,418	11,295	10,603	11,466	11,591	11,758
£' Thousands at 1985 Prices[a]										
British Museum	1,941	1,914	1,777	1,852	1,775	1,458	1,385	1,341	1,274	1,184
National Gallery	4,166	4,184	3,591	3,423	3,656	3,470	2,720	2,634	2,502	2,332
NGM Merseyside								718	682	636
National Portrait Gallery	389	392	333	318	340	323	307	297	282	263
Tate Gallery	2,504	2,541	2,199	2,096	2,240	2,126	1,795	1,739	1,652	1,539
Victoria & Albert Museum	1,515	1,521	1,422	1,356	1,449	1,375	1,133	1,097	1,042	971
England	10,515	10,552	9,321	9,046	9,461	8,752	7,339	7,826	7,434	6,930
National Galleries of Scotland	1,093	1,207	1,153	1,387	1,389	1,327	1,423	1,453	1,415	1,338
National Museums of Scotland	442	485	468	567	571	546	585	482	510	545
National Museum of Wales	954	1,047	1,075	1,094	1,113	1,109	1,096	1,093	1,065	1,017
Ulster Museum	239					31	45	129	124	142
Total, all art museums	13,242	13,291	12,017	12,094	12,533	11,766	10,488	10,983	10,547	9,971

Source: Museum and Galleries Commission *The National Museums* (1988), table 4.

Notes: All figures are for outturn expenditure (excluding revotes) except 1987–88 figures which are forecast outturn and 1988–89 figures which are provisional. Victoria & Albert figures exclude local museum purchase grants. The Wallace Collection has no purchase grant.

[a]Deflated by GDP deflator.

Table 10.14   Sotheby's Art Index (£ Basis)

Category	1975	1976	1977	1978	1979	1980	1981	1982	1983	1984	1985	1986	1987	1988
Old Master paintings	100	111	142	192	233	248	195	207	252	349	375	384	447	516
Nineteenth-century European paintings	100	104	128	178	224	218	173	191	229	306	323	316	388	463
Impressionist art	100	113	124	148	182	200	234	266	347	440	482	547	847	1,399
Modern paintings	100	111	117	147	185	198	227	255	320	418	444	543	854	1,397
Aggregate index	100	117	138	180	226	246	236	257	314	411	426	457	601	838

Source: Sotheby's.

Notes: Figures are shown in absolute terms without making any allowance for inflation. The basis for the series is September 1975. The Aggregate Index is a weighted figure, achieved by applying the following weights to the individual constituent sectors: Old Master paintings 18, nineteenth-century European paintings 13, Impressionist art 19, modern paintings 11, continental ceramics 3, Chinese ceramics 11, English silver 5, continental silver 5, French and continental furniture 7, English furniture 8.

mean that it is more likely to benefit some museums than others: the Tate, with its emphasis on modern art and sculpture, cannot approach the fund for assistance.

The government freeze on purchase grants has been justified on the grounds that money must be switched into building grants, the rationale for this switch being that until museums have more and better accommodations, no further objects be acquired. The sum involved, approximately an extra £4 million for English national museums, is very small in terms of total museum expenditure. Moreover, in the period from 1985 to 1988 (when the freeze was first instituted), expenditure on buildings, through the Property Services Agency, actually declined from £30.1 million to £27.6 million. Nevertheless, the view that the state should not fund purchases is one held by many: the Bow Group, a Tory fringe group, has argued that no grant should be made from central funds and that all purchases should be privately financed.

Few figures are available on donations: we have seen that museums may receive works under the scheme in which they are accepted in lieu of tax and they may receive direct donations, though as table 10.9 illustrated, these may not amount to significant sums, even for national museums. The National Art Collections Fund (NACF), a charity founded in 1903, receives donations both in cash and kind which enables it to assist museums, whether state funded or independent. While it does admirable work, the funds at its disposal are small, as table 10.15 shows. Nevertheless, it provides an extremely useful supplementary source for regional museums which apply to the centrally funded Local Purchases Fund but are unable to find the whole 50 percent required to match any grants received from this source.

The purchase of modern art constitutes a particular problem. Prewar purchases were few, partly because of prevailing tastes and partly because purchase grants were small. Following a survey of 56 British public galleries, Alley noted that, apart from the Tate, no gallery had purchased an oil painting by Picasso, Matisse, Braque, or Rouault, and he doubted whether there was "a single painting or sculpture which can be said to occupy a key position in the development of twentieth century art" outside of the Tate (1961, 24). The Contemporary Art Society, founded in 1910, managed by astute purchases to make many magnificent donations to the Tate and other museums, but the museums themselves missed their chance to buy works by major artists when prices were low. Now that there is a large public demand for modern art, museums are unable to enter the market effectively. Early this year, the NACF launched an appeal for donations to set up a modern art fund but, even if successful, it will be some time before its effect will be noticeable. If museums have to rely increasingly on private donations collections will suffer, as it is unlikely that donations will be sufficient to enable them to acquire new work by the new generations of artists unless significant tax concessions are made. And it is not only museums' collections of modern art that would suffer: collections of decorative art and design, such as that of the Victoria &

Table 10.15   National Art Collection Fund—Grants and Income (£)

	Grants Authorized	Income	Legacies	Subscriptions	Donations	Investment Income
1979	180,685	558,796	188,866	73,911	48,444	247,575
1980	289,608	1,178,303	192,617	84,519	52,534	289,837
1981	288,561	863,663	435,591	96,709	76,615	254,748
1982	274,267	841,139	380,087	89,818	58,054	313,180
1983	511,516	1,199,329	635,593	103,996	96,329	363,411
1984	1,669,436	833,345	116,154	110,495	211,881	394,815
1985	958,200	1,287,243	448,866	146,122	148,675	543,580
1986	960,184	2,363,488	1,326,558	157,878	217,909	508,742
1987	1,261,953	2,397,600	1,039,847	198,070	333,641	539,901
1988	1,432,467	3,132,604	930,778	223,052	539,589	1,121,996

Source: National Art Collection Fund accounts.

Albert, would be diminished and their value reduced if they were to become frozen at their current levels.

It has been said that "a museum which ceases to collect is a dead museum."[17] Many of the smaller museums already cannot afford purchases; with frozen purchase grants and rising art market prices, national museums might find themselves in a similar state.

Disposals

As a large proportion of art collections is not on display, as storage space is often cramped, and as museums are short of purchase funds, disposal might seem a logical solution. Up until now disposal has only been hinted at through guarded suggestions that the government would favor sales both as a means of "rationalizing" collections and in order to raise funds. Some trustees do not have the power to sell and have consistently declared that they do not want it; new trustees might be appointed who would be less reluctant. Others have the necessary powers and have formulated disposal policies though, in most cases, they have not implemented them, exceptions being one or two universities. It is not clear whether these include art museums.

Certainly most museums have acquired items, often through donations and bequests, which they relegate to store as they do not match the standard of objects on display. These might nevertheless be valued by other museums or, through sale, could help augment limited purchase funds. The Victoria & Albert holds many duplicates, acquired to fulfill an early educational obligation to provide loans and traveling exhibitions to the regions. This service has now been discontinued due to shortage of funds and, if there were any question of disposing of such duplicates, it seems likely that the regional museums would

17. The director of the British Museum made this reply to the question whether he would agree with the view that "further acquisitions are today the least important thing" (Education, Science and Arts Committee 1982).

expect to have the right to receive them as donations before sale is considered.[18]

Arguments against sales include the view that suitable items for sale are not numerous, that they are unlikely to raise much money, that tastes change and pictures and art objects currently out of favour may well experience a revival in future times, that collections are meant to be representative rather than selective, and that sales will tend to discourage potential beneficiaries. All would agree that disposal should be undertaken only after careful consideration of the object's merits and under expert advice.[19]

10.5 Admission Charges

Faced with the need for additional income, most art museums have increased their trading activities. Many already had shops and have now refurbished these and their snackbars. Publications also provide a useful source of income.

At present, none of the national art museums charges for admission to the main collection. Some local authority museums have been charging for some time. It seems likely that the introduction of charges depends not only on the type of museums but also on size, charges seldom being a feasible option for the small collection.[20] The introduction of charges at national museums would not be without precedent: both the National Gallery and the Victoria & Albert charged for admission on a few days in the week until 1939, and in 1974 charges were imposed at all national museums for three months until the charges were abolished following a change in government.

A summary of the main arguments for and against charges would fall under the following headings:

In favor of admission charge
1. Equity within the arts sector. The visual arts should not be treated more favourably than the performing arts; the large direct subsidy which enables museums to provide free entry is obtained at the expense of other arts.[21]
2. Distribution. Subsidies are paid for by all taxpayers, but the benefits are enjoyed by visitors who form a small proportion of the population and many of whom could afford to pay entry charges.

18. The Victoria & Albert trustees have the power to dispose of duplicates but so far have not indicated that they intend to sell any items from the collection.
19. For the case in favor of disposals, see Montias (1976). He also suggests that all donations involving tax concessions should be put up for auction, leaving the benefitting museum either to bid for the object or to accept the sale proceeds (less auction fees). Where purchase grants are small, this would probably result in many of the more desirable objects leaving Britain.
20. See evidence by the director of Norwich Museum to the Education, Science and Arts Committee (1982); also *National Art Collections Fund Magazine* (Christmas 1987):24.
21. See Blaug (1976b). He assumes that if museums were to charge, the money released would be transferred to the performing arts, an assumption unlikely to hold at the present time.

3. Expediency. Faced with rising costs and the government's determination to cut public spending, museums have no option but to raise income through charges, in addition to other means. With rising real incomes and greater leisure time, visitors are unlikely to be deterred by charges, providing special arrangements are made for those who cannot pay (Cossons 1987).

Counter-arguments

1. Economic. Once the government has decided to provide a museum, charges are only necessary as a rationing device if there is overcrowding. Where there is no congestion, the marginal costs of admitting an additional visitor are zero (Robbins 1971).
2. Betrayal of benefactors. Many bequests were received on the understanding that access would be free of charge.[22]
3. Equality of opportunity. Charging will deter low-income individuals, especially the young and the old. This argument is often merged with that stressing externalities arising from the educational role of museums.
4. Pragmatic. Recognizing the expediency argument above, it is nevertheless probable that the net revenue to be gained from charges will be relatively small. Charges will reduce attendance, thus depressing trading receipts, and will impose additional costs through the need to install manned ticket machines and turnstiles, possibly generating queues at the entrance. Concessionary rates for students, the young, and the old will tend to increase these costs. Moreover value added tax would have to be paid on any revenue raised through charges.[23]

It is this pragmatic argument that seems to have carried the day with national art museums. The main questions that arise are whether the museums' fears about the effect of charges on attendance are justified, which visitors would be deterred, and how such charges would affect the pattern of visits. Surveys of museum visitors can provide us with some information on these matters.

As can be seen from table 10.16, attendance at the major art museums has traced a somewhat uneven pattern over recent years. Figures for attendance at local authority museum are more difficult to obtain, but estimates for 1984–85 and 1986–87 are given in table 10.17. A recent survey, which combined a national poll with surveys of visitors to 12 museums in various parts of the United Kingdom, suggests that museum visiting is a popular activity.[24] It found that 44 percent of the adult population had visited a museum in the last

22. For example, the bequest by Sir Hans Sloane, on which the British Museum was founded (Rankine 1987).
23. See article by Rankine (1987).
24. Five of the museums were art museums or museums with substantial art collections; they included two national museums.

Table 10.16   Attendances—National Art Museums (in thousands)

	1978	1979	1980	1981	1982	1983	1984	1985	1986	1987
England										
British Museum	4,034	4,100	3,880	2,869	2,966	3,079	3,467	4,142	3,897	4,008
National Gallery	2,300	2,738	2,618	2,738	2,633	2,897	2,937	3,157	3,182	3,567
NGM Merseyside									1,163	1,329
National Portrait Gallery	400	400	400	500	524	468	581	516	625	591
Tate Gallery	1,081	1,141	1,331	895	1,230	1,283	1,278	996	1,153	1,742
Victoria & Albert Museum	1,937	1,992	1,724	1,711	2,058	2,221	2,079	2,067	1,431	1,399
Wallace Collection	145	128	160	139	142	177	178	179	171	168
Scotland, Wales and Northern Ireland										
National Galleries of Scotland	388	442	421	437	426	442	469	538	530	524
National Museums of Scotland	700	744	768	721	730	765	724	751	701	817
National Museum of Wales	700	700	700	700	700	700	800	800	800	1,039
Ulster Museum	214	195	227	209	201	271	255	291	318	277
Total art galleries and museums	11,899	12,580	12,229	10,919	11,610	12,303	12,768	13,437	13,971	15,461

Source: Museums and Galleries Commission, *The National Museums* (1988), table 1.

Notes: National figures include branch museum attendance (Tate Gallery from 1981 onwards). National Museums of Scotland figures include attendance for Scottish United Services Museum from 1987.

Table 10.17   Estimated Attendance—Local Authority Museums and Art Galleries, England and Wales (in thousands)

	1984–85	1986–87
London	302	331
Metropolitan	3,744	4,680
Nonmetropolitan	8,046	8,521
Wales	383	447
Total	12,475	13,979

Source: Chartered Institute of Public Finance and Accountancy, *Leisure and Recreation Statistics.*
Note: Local authority figures are estimated from surveys.

two years; this compares with 35 percent who had visited historic houses and 25 percent visiting art exhibitions (other than those in museums). Of those who visited museums, about one-half had paid three or more visits to museums in the previous year. The survey found that museum visitors tended to be young, single, and from the higher socioeconomic groups, and very few came for reasons connected with study or work (Touche Ross 1989).

Surveys of various national museums suggest that there are differences in the characteristics of visitors to different types of museum.[25] As can be seen from table 10.18 (top panel), these surveys confirm that a high proportion of museum visitors are young; this is particularly so in the case of the Science Museum where over half the visitors were under the age of 21. The peak age group for the National Portrait Gallery and the Victoria & Albert falls in the 21–30 group. The two art museums have a higher proportion of foreign visitors than do the Science and Railway Museums, and these visitors, as one would expect, tend to be somewhat older than British visitors. Other differences between the art and nonart museums are that visits in family groups are less likely at art museums—only about one-third visiting in this way—and a higher proportion of art museum visitors come alone. The Science and Railway Museums appear to be a more popular destination for school visits than is the Victoria & Albert: 19 percent of visitors to the Science Museum came with school parties compared with only 9 percent for the Victoria & Albert. It would seem that visitors to the Victoria & Albert are more likely to have visited other museums during the previous year; only 9 percent had not visited another museums during this period (compared with 16 percent of visitors to the Science Museum) while 55 percent had visited five museums or more in that time (33 percent for Science Museum visitors). In general, more of the visitors to the art museums have finished their full-time education at a later age—see Table 10.18 (lower panel). In this table, the first column for each

25. Material in this section is drawn from Harvey (1987), Heady (1984), and Smyth and Ayton (1985).

Table 10.18 **Museum Visitor Characteristics**

Age Distribution of Visitors to Various National Museums

Age Group	National Portrait Gallery (1985)	Victoria & Albert (1980)	National Maritime Museum (1984)	Science Museum (1980)	National Railway (1980)	United Kingdom Population (1984)
0–10	2%	6%	5%	19%	11%	13%
11–20	16	23	17	36	21	16
21–30	31	28	20	15	15	15
31–40	13	16	17	15	27	14
41–50	15	12	12	8	11	11
51–70	20	13	13[a]	6	15	21
70+	5	4	13[a]	1	1	10

Age at Which Full-time Education Was Completed

Finished Education at Age	General Population	Victoria & Albert		Science Museum		National Railway	
		Actual Visitors	Expected Visitors	Actual Visitors	Expected Visitors	Actual Visitors	Expected Visitors
16 or younger	79%	30%	75%	40%	75%	66%	76%
17–20	13	25	15	26	15	19	13
21 or older	8	45	10	34	10	15	11

Source: top panel—Harvey (1987) and Smyth and Ayton (1985); *bottom panel*—Heady (1984), table 2.8.

Note: bottom panel—figures for the general population are derived from the 1980 General Household Survey. Figures for expected visitors show what the distribution would be if the museum's visitors were typical of other British people of the same sex and age.

[a]Age groups 51–50 and 60 or over.

museum shows the distribution of ages at which its visitors finished their full-time education. The second column for each museum gives what that distribution would be if the museum's visitors were typical in this respect of other British people of the same sex and age (Heady 1984, 14–15). Table 10.19 shows that all the national museums draw the majority of their British visitors from the surrounding regions: for the four national museums in London, about 70 percent come from Greater London or the South East region. The National Railway Museum, a branch of the Science Museum which is located in York, has only about 10 percent of visitors from London and the South East, drawing people instead from the surrounding Northern and Midland areas.

Two surveys have attempted to analyze how visitors might respond to admission charges. The national survey, conducted by Touche Ross, found that about three-quarters of those surveyed would be prepared to pay for entrance, the average amount being £1.32. In their separate survey of museum visitors, Touche Ross found that while the average price for all visitors was somewhat higher (£1.78), there was considerable variation within this sample, depending on whether the person questioned had been visiting a museum where charges were paid or not. Those who had visited museums which were free (as were the majority of art museums in the sample) would on average have been willing to pay £1, while the figure for those questioned after visits to charging museums was £2 or more.[26] The survey also found that both the national and the museum polls suggested that respondents considered the government should be the principle source of finance for museums with local authorities as runners up (Touche Ross 1989).

A survey of visitors to the National Portrait Gallery, conducted in 1985, is of particular interest as, unlike the Touche Ross survey which covered a variety of types of museums, it provides an insight into the views of visitors to art museums. It suggests that if a charge of £1 were introduced, attendance would fall by about one-third, the decrease being uniform over all age groups. However, the fall would be greater for British visitors than it would for foreign: 45 percent of British visitors (who make up two-thirds of all visitors) would not have been willing to pay the suggested charge, as against 22 percent of foreign visitors. As might be expected, visitors from higher socioeconomic groups were more willing to pay a fee than were those from lower ones. People making a single visit were the least deterred, but 64 percent of frequent visitors and 43 percent of returning visitors would not have paid. Rather surprisingly, family visitors were most willing to pay the fee, but the survey noted that the family composition rarely included small children (Harvey 1987).

Surveys are, of course, unreliable guides as to what people would do if faced with a charge. It is instructive, therefore, to examine what happened

26. Possibly reflecting the fee that they had paid as of the museums surveyed, half charged with the average amount being £2.65.

Table 10.19 Regional Distribution of National Museum Visitors

Region	National Portrait Gallery	Victoria & Albert Museum	National Maritime Museum	Science Museum	National Railway Museum	United Kingdom Population, 1981
Greater London	44%	59%	51%	37%	4%	12%
Rest of Southeast	29	20	24	30	7	18
Yorkshire and Humberside	3	2	2	5	30	9
North and Northwest	5	4	5	6	25	17
Midlands and East Anglia	8	8	10	12	23	19
Wales and Southwest	7	5	7	10	4	13
Scotland	4	2	2	2	7	9
Northern Ireland	1	0	0	0	0	3

Sources: Harvey (1987); Heady (1984).

when two nonart national museums introduced charges. The National Maritime Museum, which brought in admission fees in 1986, experienced a fall in attendance of about one-third in the first year. In the following year, the latest year for which figures are available, visits have started to rise and were only about 25 percent down compared with the last year when admission was free. The Natural History Museum introduced charges in 1987 and attendance fell by 50 percent in that year. Both museums have sought to draw in visitors through mounting special exhibitions, but expenditure on building work has meant that the Natural History Museum has recently had to postpone proposed exhibition plans. The Victoria & Albert does not charge for entrance but, since 1985, has operated an aggressive donation policy, suggesting an amount of £2; this has resulted in a 30 percent fall in attendance which has continued and shows no signs of being reversed. Such figures suggest that the 33 percent fall indicated by the survey of National Portrait Gallery visitors may well be accurate, at least in the initial years following the introduction of charges.

The survey evidence thus suggests that a significant proportion of visitors to national art museums would not be willing to pay for visits, or if willing to pay, would be willing to pay a figure of slightly less than £2 at most. Entrance charges would change the composition of visitors: a higher proportion would come from abroad, and there would be fewer regular or returning visits. This latter effect might be mitigated by season tickets, but it has to be recognized that many visitors do not live within easy reach of the national museums.

If entrance fees are not introduced, it might nevertheless be worthwhile putting efforts into collecting donations from visitors. The Victoria & Albert's experience is probably not representative of the likely outcome: survey evidence indicates that the suggested donation of £2 per person is too high. Moreover, it would seem sensible that, where an amount is suggested, an upper limit for family contributions should be mentioned. One advantage of a visitor donation policy is that it rarely requires much expenditure to implement and, moreover, donations do not attract VAT. Elkan (1986) has suggested that museums might do well to study how some cathedrals operate visitor donation schemes, making use of friends and volunteers. Museums are beginning to promote friend groups, offering inducements such as friends' evenings, private views, lectures, members rooms, and so on. Other arts associations, such as those for the performing arts, are doing the same, and clearly they are often appealing to overlapping groups of people.

The failure of art museums to attract as large a proportion of young people as do other museums suggests that there is a need to develop displays which place a stronger emphasis on the entertainment aspect of any visit, while still maintaining the education element. Surveys suggest that people want both education and entertainment, but to attract the young and the less educated, a greater stress on the entertainment side might be needed. It seems also that museums need to take more care over publicity (Touche Ross 1989).

10.6 Export Rules

Concern over the export of many works of art was the main reason for establishing the Reviewing Committee on the Export of Works of Art in 1952. The United Kingdom was one of the first countries to operate a system of export licensing, the main purpose of which is to allow time for a public museum or gallery to raise the necessary purchase money. If an application for an export license is opposed by the expert advisers from the national collections, the matter is referred to the reviewing committee, which assesses the application, endeavoring to strike a balance between maintaining the national interest and ensuring that private individuals and firms obtain a fair market price. In agreeing upon a fair market price the committee takes expert advice, including that offered by the applicant's valuer; this price has included commission but generally no other charges. However, following representations, the practice is currently being reviewed.

Export licenses are needed for: (1) photographic positives and negatives produced more than 60 years before date of exportation and valued at £200 or more per item; and (2) any other good manufactured or produced more than 50 years before the date of exportation. Most categories of antiques and collector's items, produced 50 years or more ago can be exported if the value per article is less than £20,000 (£30,000 in the case of paintings), except for certain textiles, arms and armor, representations of British historical personages valued at £16,000, documents, manuscripts and archives, and articles recovered from the soil. In its most recent report, the committee has recommended that these values be raised and reviewed annually. While it is clearly sensible to have a lower limit on the value, even at the current level of £16,000, many small items possibly of interest to regional museums are exported without such museums' having a chance to bid for them.

Relatively few applications for export licenses are referred to the reviewing committee in any one year. The number of cases, the number of licenses suspended, and the total value licensed are shown in table 10.20. Both numbers and value can vary widely from year to year, which is hardly surprising given the unique nature of most art objects, and it is interesting to compare the total value of objects licensed with art exports. Figures for imports and exports are shown in table 10.21, and it will be noted that the value of licensed exports is only a small proportion of the total. Both export and import values have risen over the ten-year period covered, and, in the last few years, exports have exceeded imports.

The committee can impose a "temporary stop" to allow time (generally six months) for raising the purchase money by public appeal and other means, or it can impose an "indefinite stop." This latter course is relatively infrequent and is only done when the applicant refuses a valid offer by a public institution which has raised the necessary money. When an indefinite stop is imposed,

Table 10.20 Export of Works of Art from the United Kingdom—Applications for Licenses Referred to the Reviewing Committee on the Export of Works of Art

Year	Total No. of Cases Considered (1)	No. Where Export License Suspended (2)	No. of Works Retained (3)	No. of Works Licensed (5)	Total Value Licensed (6)	% Licenses Granted (7)
1977–78	28	20	12	8	£ 1,008,484	40
1978–79	33	23	21	2	108,900	9
1979–80	16	11	7	4	512,817	36
1980–81	15	12	8	4	5,215,588	33
1981–82	10	9	7	2	418,500	22
1982–83	16	14	9	5	4,033,312	36
1983–84	47	29	19	10	2,821,010	34
1984–85	43	30	12	18	23,591,786	60
1985–86	51	44	25	19	10,672,378	43
1986–87	26	15	8	7	34,434,922	47
1987–88	32	24	12	12	8,308,570	50

Source: Reviewing Committee on the Export of Works of Art, *Annual Reports.*

Table 10.21 **United Kingdom Exports and Imports of Works of Art**

| Year | Paintings, Drawings, etc. | | Other Items | Total Value (£ thousand) |
	No. of Items	Value (£ thousand)	Value (£ thousand)	
Exports				
1978–79	97,024	144,105	166,707	310,812
1979–80	74,550	131,017	205,164	336,181
1980–81	60,989	113,173	141,783	254,956
1981–82	101,241	150,780	192,811	343,591
1982–83	81,820	219,823	239,381	459,204
1983–84	76,831	225,883	320,001	545,884
1984–85	101,560	363,023	372,714	735,737
1985–86	111,889	399,016	398,990	798,006
1986–87	161,863	587,795	424,290	1,012,085
1987–88	211,923	771,939	514,737	1,286,676
Imports				
1978–79	140,752	134,087	105,634	239,721
1979–80	192,460	189,659	153,148	342,807
1980–81	116,247	162,994	98,851	261,845
1981–82	161,650	186,153	188,627	374,780
1982–83	198,147	301,224	157,135	458,359
1983–84	298,629	226,448	189,334	415,782
1984–85	332,465	383,969	254,499	638,468
1985–86	579,587	354,867	273,257	628,124
1986–87	623,436	636,908	285,760	922,668
1987–88	705,707	692,076	365,562	1,057,638

Source: Reviewing Committee on the Export of Works of Art, *Annual Reports.*

Note: The figures for 1980–82 are incomplete, due to industrial action at the government computer center. The figures for 1980–81 cover 8 months ending February 1981, while those for 1981–82 cover 10 months from September 1981.

the committee has stated that no further appeal would be heard until ten years after the original hearing. However, it appears that the Secretary of State for Trade and Industry (who has the statutory responsibility for export licensing) cannot refuse to consider an application, and the reviewing committee has called for legislation to give it this right, so far without effect, in order to prevent abuse of the system.[27]

In reaching a decision to grant a temporary stop, the committee applies what are termed the "Waverley criteria." These are: (1) Is the object so closely connected with our history and national life that its departure would be a misfortune? (2) Is it of outstanding aesthetic importance? and (3) Is it of outstanding significance for the study of some particular branch of art, learning, or history?

27. As of 30 June 1986, there were 19 indefinite stops still in force, the earliest dating from 1957 and the latest two having been imposed in 1986.

When the committee was set up, it was assumed that the imposition of a temporary stop would result in every effort being made to raise purchase funds. Reduced purchase grants and today's high prices mean that often no such attempt is made. The committee therefore has announced that if, after a month or two, no appeal is forthcoming the license will be granted.

In recent years the need for additional operating funds has led to the breakup of privately held collections. This has suggested to the committee that a further criterion be added to cover collections such as these.[28] The matter has been referred to a working party and its report has not yet been published. It was recommended, however, that any new controls should be used sparingly and would cover relatively few collections. The committee explicitly stated that a new criterion was not intended to cover "country house collections built up over many generations or collections formed within the last fifty years" (Reviewing Committee on Export of Works of Art, *Annual Report* 1986, Cmnd. 44).

Until fairly recently, the age limit was 100 years, and reducing this to 50 years brings a wider range of objects within the remit of the system. However, even this limit raises problems where modern art is concerned as, for example, work by Henry Moore would not come under the licensing requirement. This can create difficulties for the Tate and other institutions interested in acquiring modern work.

10.7 Conclusion

Subsidies from government provide the main income for British public museums at national and regional levels, and it is clear that direct subsidies will have to continue. As long as tax concessions remain small, relatively little income is likely to be generated from donations, leaving museums to raise income in other ways to cover any residual gap between subsidies and rising expenditure. The recent change from votes to grant-in-aid represents an improvement, as the new system provides incentives to museums to respond to their consumers. However, the advantages of the new system will be jeopardized if, at the outset, museum initiatives are stifled because all energies have to be devoted to keeping buildings from crumbling about the collections. The amount of money that will be needed to put the buildings in good order and to satisfy safety requirements is so great that museums are not likely to be able to raise sufficient funds by their own efforts. If funds were made available to resolve these problems, museums could transfer their attention to efforts to raise income to supplement subsidies.

28. Collections that have broken up include two university collections (the George Brown Ethnological Collection, Newcastle University; and the John Rylands Library Sale, Manchester University) as well as the private Spencer collection of paintings. Although the George Brown collection comprised over 300 items, only 19 fell under the export rules, and the bulk of the collection was sold before the reviewing committee could express any view.

A thriving art market may benefit the economy, but for museums it constitutes a problem. With dwindling purchase grants and, as a consequence, increasingly frequent appeals to the National Heritage Memorial Fund and the public, it is impossible for museums to implement rational acquisition plans. One consequence of this is to diminish the relevance of the regulations covering the export of items of art: suspensions granted have to be rapidly withdrawn as it becomes apparent that there is no chance of funds being raised to retain the object in the United Kingdom.

If it is accepted that museums should continue to be subsidized, the size and choice of subsidy will continue to be matters for debate. The advantage of relying extensively on indirect subsidies through tax concessions, as is done in the United States, is that the amount of subsidy is determined by consumers. However, if there are significant education externalities, these contributions might require supplementing from government funds. Disadvantages include distortions to taxpayer behavior and fluctuating income experienced by museums as a result of changes in government tax policy. Direct subsidies leave museums more immediately vulnerable to changes in governments and their policies: spending on museums represents only a very small fraction of total public expenditure but for the museums any cuts in subsidy create problems when curatorial costs are increasing. As Don Fullerton has pointed out (see chap. 8 this volume), government can direct these grants to fund those activities it wishes to foster; this may or may not be desirable depending on whether it leads the government to intervene directly in art policy and, if so, what form such intervention may take.

Arguments advanced by economists to justify such subsidy have been examined in Fullerton's paper but provide no comprehensive answer as to the rationale for intervention, or the form it should take, or its size. Educational externalities provided the earliest justification for British government involvement at both central and local levels, and educational arguments continue to be used to counter proposals to introduce admission charges. Other defenses of subsidy have focused on the contribution of the arts to the U.K. economy. A recent study by John Myerscough estimates that museums as a whole have a turnover of some £224 million and are substantial employers while at the same time generating jobs in other industries. Their importance in the tourist trade has been appreciated for some time but Myerscough also shows that the arts provide community benefits by attracting new business to the regions and by revitalizing decaying inner urban areas. The fine arts are also a source of ideas, expertise, and training for areas of applied arts such as fashion, architecture, design, printing, and photography while the art trade, visual arts, and crafts, contribute about £743 million to invisible earnings (Myerscough 1988).

Studies, such as Myerscough's, provide a counter-argument to the view that museums constitute a drain on the economy, but there is a risk in relying too strongly on such arguments to justify state subsidies. The contribution that art museums make cannot be assessed in purely market terms: their collections are part of our heritage and help form our culture but, if all are to benefit, museums must reach out to the public and take an active part in its continuing education. Scitovsky considers that "the only valid argument for Government aid to the arts is that it is a means of educating the public's taste, and that the public would benefit from a more educated taste" (1976, 64). If he is right, then arts are a merit good and as such cannot be assessed using economic arguments. Where museums play an important role in the formation of tastes, the search for an economic rationale for aid to the arts may be a pointless exercise. John Maynard Keynes (1936), who took a deep interest in both the visual and the performing arts, deplored the "utilitarian and economic" view of the arts, which he thought was widely held at that time. Perhaps we, too, should consider whether everything has to be justified in economic terms.

References

Alley, Ronald. 1961. The Representation of Twentieth Century Foreign Art in British Public Galleries. *Museums Journal* 61(1):21–29.

Baumol, William J., & William G. Bowen. 1966. *Performing Arts—The Economic Dilemma*. New York: Basic Books.

Blaug, Mark, ed. 1976a. *The Economics of the Arts*. London: Martin Robertson.

———. 1976b. Rationalising Social Expenditure—The Arts. In *Public Expenditure: Allocation between Competing ends*, ed. M. Posner. Cambridge: Cambridge University Press.

Commission of the European Communities. 1989. *The Public Administration and the Funding of Culture in the European Community*. Luxembourg.

Cossons, N. 1987. Museum Funding—A Pragmatic Approach. *National Art Collections Fund Magazine* (Christmas):21–22.

Education, Science and Arts Committee. 1981. *Third Report: Interim Report on Works of Art: Their Retention in Britain and their Acquisition by Public Bodies*. HC 275, sess. 1981–82. London: HMSO.

———. 1982. *Eighth Report: Public and private funding of the Arts. Vols. 1, 2, and 3*. HC 49, sess. 1981–82. London: HMSO.

———. 1984. *First Report: The Effect of the Abolition of the GLC and Metropolitan Counties upon Support for the Arts. Vols. 1 and 2*. HC 264, sess. 1983–84. London: HMSO.

———. 1986. *First Report: Revised Financing Arrangements for the National Museums and Galleries*. HC 417, sess. 1985–86. London: HMSO.

Elkan, W. 1986. Collecting for Galleries and Museums. *National Westminster Bank Quarterly Review* (February):26–36.

Great Britain Department of Education and Science. 1973. *Provincial Museums and Galleries* (The Wright Report). London: HMSO.

H. M. Treasury. *The Government's Expenditure Plans*. Cmnd. paper. London: HMSO.

———. 1982. *Observations by the Government on the Third Report, Session 1980–81, of the Education, Science and Arts Committee on the Retention of Works of Art in Britain and Their Acquisition for the Nation*. Cmnd. 8538. London: HMSO.

Harris, John S. 1970. *Government Patronage of the Arts in Great Britain*. Chicago: University of Chicago Press.

Harvey, B. 1987. *Visiting the National Portrait Gallery*. Office of Population Censuses and Surveys, Social Survey Division. London: HMSO.

Heady, P. 1984. *Visiting Museums: A Report of a Survey of Visitors to the Victoria & Albert, Science and National Railway Museums for the Office of Arts and Libraries*. Office of Population Censuses and Surveys, Social Survey Division. London: HMSO.

Keynes, J. M. 1936. Art and the State. *The Listener* (26 August):371–74.

Lord, B., G. D. Lord, and J. Nicks. 1989. *The Cost of Collecting: Collection Management in UK Museums*. London: HMSO.

Markham, S. F. 1938. *A Report on the Museums and Art Galleries of the British Isles (other than the National Museums) to the Carnegie United Kingdom Trust*. Edinburgh: Carnegie United Kingdom Trust.

Mattingly, J. 1984. *Volunteers in Museums and Galleries*. Berkhamsted: The Volunteer Centre.

Miers, Henry. 1928. *A Report on the Public Museums of the British Isles (other than the National Museums) to the Carnegie United Kingdom Trustees*. Edinburgh: Carnegie United Kingdom Trust.

Minihan, Janet. 1977. *The Nationalization of Culture*. London: Hamish Hamilton.

Montias, J. M. 1976. Are Art Museums Betraying the Public's Trust? In *The Economics of the Arts*. See Blaug (1976a).

Museums and Galleries Commission. 1984. *Eleventh Report 1978–1983*. London: HMSO.

———. 1984 to 1988. *Annual Reports*. London: Museums and Galleries Commission.

———. 1987. *Museum Professional Training and Career Structure*. Report by a Working Party. London: HMSO.

———. 1988. *The National Museums*. London: HMSO.

Museums Association. 1987. *Museums UK: A Summary Report of the Findings of the Museums Database Project*. London: Museums Association.

Myerscough, John, ed. 1984. *Funding the Arts in Europe*. PSI Studies in European Politics, no. 8. London: Policy Studies Institute.

Myerscough, John. 1986. *Facts about the Arts 2*. PSI Report no. 653. London: Policy Studies Institute.

———. 1988. *The Economic Importance of the Arts in Britain*. PSI Report no. 672. London: Policy Studies Institute.

National Audit Office. 1988. *Management of the Collections of the English National Museums and Galleries*. Report by the Comptroller and Auditor General. HC 347, sess. 1987–88. London: HMSO.

Nissel, Muriel. 1983. *Facts about the Arts*. PSI Report no. 615. London: Policy Studies Institute.

Office of Arts and Libraries. 1983. *Observations by the Government on the Eighth Report, Session 1981–82, of the Education, Science and Arts Committee on the Public and Private Funding of the Arts*. Cmnd. 9127. London: HMSO.

Public Accounts Committee. 1987. *Fifteenth Report: Sponsorship of Non-Departmental Public Bodies*. HC, sess. 1986–87. London: HMSO.

———. 1988. *First Report: Management of the Collections of the English National Museums and Galleries*. HC 28, 1988–89. London: HMSO.

Ramer, B. 1989. *A Conservation Survey of Museum Collections in Scotland*. Scottish Museums Council, London: HMSO.

Rankine, Jean. 1987. Museum Charges. *National Art Collections Fund Magazine* (Christmas):23.

Reviewing Committee on Export of Works of Art. *Annual Reports*. Cmnd. paper. London: HMSO.

Ridley, F. F. 1987. Tradition, Change and Crisis in Great Britain. In *The Patron State: Government and the Arts in Europe, North America and Japan*, ed. M. C. Cummings, Jr. and R. S. Katz. New York: Oxford University Press.

Robbins, L. 1971. Unsettled Questions in the Political Economy of the Arts. *The Three Bank Review* (September):3–19.

Royal Commission on National Museums and Galleries. 1928. *Interim Report*. Cmd. 3192. London: HMSO.

———. 1929. *Final Report. Part 1*. Cmd. 3401. London: HMSO.

———. 1930. *Final Report. Part 2*. Cmd. 3463. London: HMSO.

Scitovsky, Tibor. 1976. What's Wrong with the Arts Is What's Wrong with Society. In *The Economics of the Arts*. See Blaug (1976a).

Smyth, M., and B. Ayton. 1985. *Visiting the National Maritime Museum: A Report of a Survey of Visitors*. Office of Population Censuses and Surveys, Social Survey Division. London: HMSO.

Standing Commission on Museums and Galleries. 1963. Survey of Provincial Museums and Galleries. London: HMSO.

———. 1977. *Report on University Museums*. London: HMSO.

Touche Ross. 1988. *Report on the Impact of Tax Incentives on Fund Raising*. London: Touche Ross Management Consultants.

———. 1989. *Museum Funding and Services—The Visitor's Perspective*. London: Touche Ross Management Consultants.

11   Marketing of Art Museums

Robert C. Blattberg and Cynthia J. Broderick

11.1 Introduction

Art museums have relied heavily on benefactors for donations of works of arts. With the changing tax laws, these donations have declined precipitously. The number of donated works in 1988 was approximately 37 percent of the 1986 level (Glueck 1989). At the same time that the number of donated works of arts is declining, the cost of acquisition is increasing rapidly. This is exacerbated by (1) a devaluation of the dollar, making it easier for Europeans and Japanese to enter the United States art market and bid up the prices of major works (Cox 1987) and (2) the improved efficiency of the art market (Lee 1988). Based on the declining donations of art works and the increasing cost of acquiring new works, museums will need to rely more heavily on sources of revenues such as membership fees, government subsidies, corporate gifts, and attendance to enhance their collection.

To counteract current trends, museums must reevaluate their marketing strategy. This paper applies marketing concepts to assist museums select the appropriate target audiences and to determine what products to "produce" for these different and diffuse target audiences. The focal points of this article will be the product and the customer. Other elements of marketing, such as pricing and advertising, are of secondary importance relative to determining how to modify the product. Art museums, if they want to increase attendance, must become more creative in how they appeal to new audiences. The difficult problem is how to avoid losing the museum's current "customer," whose interests often conflict with those of a more diverse audience, and at the same time appeal to a new, diverse audience.

One example is provided by the Field Museum of Chicago, which has refocused its museum. The management of the museum stated:

To reach the public . . . , exhibits and programs will need to be

- Adaptable to the changing needs of the public
- Interesting and useful to people with different backgrounds and levels of interest in the subject matter
- Useful as resource centers for the serious student, hobbyist, and collector, who seek a more comprehensive treatment of the subject or theme
- Able to give an overview of subjects and themes to millions of people (Field Museum 1986, 16–17).

To meet these diverse and often conflicting requirements, the Field Museum organized its public space into three different but interrelated formats:

- 1. Informal, interactive exhibits and programs which will be accessible to virtually any visitor;
- 2. Major thematic exhibits, which will provide broad overviews of their subject and highlight the museums' collection; and
- 3. Study halls which will make available in-depth resources on specific subjects, for visitors seeking a more comprehensive picture of the subject matter and collections.

The Field Museum has addressed the critical issue: How can the product change so that the museum expands its reach without alienating current customers?

The remainder of the paper is organized as follows: section 11.2 briefly discusses what should be "optimized" by museums, section 11.3 reviews the prior literature on the marketing of art museums, section 11.4 discusses the major issue of who should be the target audience, section 11.5 addresses the importance of the general public to the museum's financial structure, section 11.6 looks at the competitive environment, sections 11.7, 11.8, and 11.9 discuss the product, section 11.10 discusses how museums should distribute their product, section 11.11 addresses the pricing of the product, section 11.12 considers organizational issues, and section 11.13 gives a brief summary of the paper.

11.2   What to "Optimize?"

One of the most difficult questions facing a marketer when thinking about the marketing of art museums is what to optimize. With for-profit firms, this question is easier since the goal is to maximize long-term profits or shareholders' wealth. What do museums optimize? Many believe that community interests, aesthetic values, and the preservation of the museum should be the goals (Ames 1988; DiMaggio 1985; Hancocks 1987; Skloot 1983). To further complicate the issue, museum curators, boards-of-directors, and benefactors focus on "quality." Their goal is to make the institution a "world class" museum through its collection and curatorial staff. If the museum is financially stable, these additional goals should be pursued.

To focus on marketing issues while trying to maximize multiple objectives is extremely difficult. The conflicts and trade-offs cannot easily be resolved. In the real world of art museums, directors, curators, and boards must make these decisions. If revenue-generating ideas conflict with critical organizational goals, then the decision maker can choose not to pursue them. For example, servicing low-income audiences is a potential source of revenues through government subsidies, while not servicing these groups will result in lower revenues because government agencies will reduce subsidies such as free rent or free land.

11.3   How Has Marketing Been Applied to Art Museums?

There are numerous articles in which marketing academics or practitioners have written about how art museums should apply marketing concepts (Hendon 1979; Mokwa, Dawson, and Prieve 1980; Yorke and Jones 1987). Most of the literature indicates that determining the appropriate customer segments and the marketing mix are of prime importance. The marketing mix contains six major elements:[1]

1. Pricing
2. Products and services to offer
3. Advertising and public relations
4. Sales promotions
5. Sales force
6. Channels of distribution (where the product is sold or viewed)

The following points represent a consensus from the published articles:

- Despite the "elitist" nature of the art museum audience, museums have a social responsibility to broaden their target audience to include less well-educated viewers in order to justify government subsidies. Thus, museums are forced to reconcile opposing desires in determining their mission or objectives (Cramer 1979; Hancocks 1987; Zolberg 1984).
- Pricing within museums is not well understood, and very few studies have been conducted to try to determine the price responsiveness of current or potential members to the public being charged general admission to museums. The studies that have been conducted show that there is a low price elasticity (Cameron and Abbey 1962; O'Hare 1975).
- Product discussion focuses on current visitors and special exhibits with very little attention paid to target markets or likely audiences. Ancillary purchases from the bookstore and the restaurant are also considered but only as a secondary activity (Beer 1987; Bowden 1986; Braverman 1988; Gardner 1986; Hood 1986).

---

1. McCarthy (1975) defines the marketing mix as the 4P's (Price, Place, Product, and Promotion). We prefer to separate advertising and the sales force as distinct elements of the marketing mix.

- The primary focus of many of the marketing articles is on advertising and the need to communicate a consistent message (Adams 1986; Fronville 1985; Shapiro 1973; Stone 1988).
- Several museums are exploring alternative channels of distribution such as satellite branches, traveling exhibits, and interactive exhibits within traditional museums (Keens 1986; Bunch 1988).

In summary, museums are aware of standard marketing techniques to market their products and services to their customers.

In spite of most museums' using some form of marketing, there are many problems with the current state of marketing in art museums. First, the curatorial staff, who are the "product designers" and "purchasing agents," do little research to understand what the customer wants. Instead they select or design exhibits which they feel the visitor *should see*. The marketing personnel are then supposed to convince the public that they should see these exhibits. The problem is analogous to an engineering-driven company which produces products the customer does not demand. Achieving a museum's full potential in the marketplace depends on the integrated effort of all departments to produce and deliver the museum's product.

Second, competition has not been well-delineated, and no attempt has been made to focus on how an art museum must "compete" in the marketplace. The full effects of competition have not been visible to art museums because of the special market niche which they fill and the effective entry barrier to would-be new entrants. Thus, art museums have been spared the reality of typical competition. However, the decreasing leisure time of Americans (Louis Harris and Associates 1988) puts pressure on people to economize their time. Museums must enlarge their perspective on competition to include the alternatives from which the potential visitor chooses.

Third, most of the marketing emphasis has been on fund-raising through membership drives and the advertising of exhibits, not on products. Marketing is merely a staff function designed to serve the "product designers." Marketing's responsibility is to "sell" the finished product, not to assist in producing the product.

Finally, marketing has a negative image because it is thought to be trying to "mass market" the museum, which the curatorial staff views negatively. Top management of most museums does not come from a marketing background and has little understanding of the importance of marketing or its likely impact on the museum (Raymond and Greyser 1978; Unterman and Davis 1982). Complicating this misconception is that, as museums become more and more pressed for funds, the costs of a marketing staff are visible and thus vulnerable to cost-cutting measures, while their benefits remain intangible. In most museums, marketing is not formally part of the organization but is often subsumed under development or public relations. Even when there is a marketing director, his or her role often conflicts with the curatorial staff.

11.4 Targeting the Customer

Art viewership is a complex interaction between the viewer and the work of art. It requires sophistication, knowledge, and a desire to learn and appreciate the object being viewed. Because art is an "acquired" taste, it has historically appealed to certain segments of the market who have devoted time and effort to appreciating art.[2] Thus, the audience for art museums has been heavily populated by upper-income, educated households. This can be contrasted to science museums and zoos, which attract families and middle-income households more representative of the population. The issue facing art museums is: should they expand their viewership to appeal to new segments not currently attending museums?

There are two distinct types of audiences that art museums can target. The first is the group of potential donors, who often becomes members and are more likely to become heavily involved in museum activities. This group is small, will generate far more revenue and profits to the museum, and appreciates the current types of exhibits the museum offers. It is relatively easier to serve this group than it is to serve the general public. In fact, museums generally focus only on this audience. The second type of audience is the general public, who attend museums to be entertained and to be educated. Few will ever become donors of works of arts nor will they become major financial benefactors. However, they occasionally become members and often spend money at the museum store and restaurant.

11.4.1 The Potential Donor

Before discussing the public or mass market as a potential audience, it is important to understand the potential donor. Alfred Sloan, in designing a marketing strategy for General Motors in the early twenties, developed an ingenious strategy in which he created the pyramid of General Motors cars. Sloan recognized that a fraction of the customers at the bottom of a pyramid of General Motors cars (Chevrolet) eventually become customers for the cars near the top of the pyramid (Cadillac and Buick) as their incomes increase. The same concept can be applied to the potential donor. This group begins with a much less sophisticated understanding and appreciation of art, and then through various experiences, decides either to maintain a moderate level of interest or to become involved in collecting, education, and public service to the art community.

Potential donors have similar demographics: they are well-educated, high-income corporate executives and professionals. To market successfully to this group, museums must design programs which offer benefits for being in-

2. There is a school of thought that differs with the concept that art requires "contextual" knowledge to be appreciated. Members of that school would argue that art has a universal aesthetic appeal which transcends knowledge about its time and place in history.

volved with art museums. These can range from enhancing their experiences traveling in other cities and countries, to increasing the social prestige of being a major donor to an art museum, to becoming educated about art.

The problem art museums face with respect to this group is time availability and interest. Time availability means that programs need to be developed which are both involving and meet the key benefits of this group. Interest is important because there are many alternatives available to these people, ranging from other cultural activities to social activities. Art museums must make a special effort to reach this group through the use of "missionary" selling approaches because they represent a large potential payoff.

11.4.2   The General Public

The general public is more difficult for art museums to target. For example, middle- and low-income families are much less likely to attend art museums, and so trying to determine what types of exhibits will appeal to them is difficult. A major concern in appealing to this group is balancing the entertainment and educational value of the exhibit. If the museum were to compromise the aesthetic value of the exhibit, the traditional product would deteriorate, resulting in a potential loss of support from the museum's core audience.

The general public can be split into several groups (1) families with children, (2) senior citizens, and (3) lower-income, disadvantaged families. The first segment is less educated and less sophisticated families who are willing to try to educate their children in the visual arts. The product is important to this group. For these people, the museum must be "involving" and facilitate their understanding of art through a variety of media such as films, video tapes, and special exhibits. One way to reach their children is through the schools. This group will not become long-term patrons, but they will spend money on leisure-time activities for which they perceive value. Museums can capture some percentage of their leisure expenditures with the appropriate product.

The second segment is senior citizens who are interested in leisure-time activities and have both disposable income and time. They may have limited understanding of art, but want to be educated about art and have the time to enjoy viewing art. Currently, museums are not well designed for senior citizens because they require too much walking and have very few amenities (such as bathrooms, benches, food and beverage shops) which facilitate visits (Hood 1983). Capturing this market will depend on increasing the physical convenience and not as much on time or location. Thus the ease of transport takes on unprecedented importance. This group will not likely be long-term benefactors or patrons but is a growing segment of the population who will spend disposable income on leisure-time activities.

The third segment is an audience that art museums have already recognized, economically disadvantaged children and lower-income, inner city families. They have limited potential to spend money, but they represent an important audience for justifying government subsidies. Art museums offer very few exhibits to appeal to this segment, though schools often offer special visits to museums for their students. Schools provide a good means to reach this group, since the group might be the least receptive to the typical museum environment. Offering events at the schools could also be considered part of the museum's social responsibility to reach out to the community. In the discussion of the museum's product, special ways to reach this audience will be discussed.

In summary, museums currently target one segment actively (patrons and benefactors) but need to consider expanding its reach. Most museums do not have aggressive programs trying to build future patrons and benefactors, however, because of the low initial revenue potential, the high cost, and the problems with mobility (they leave the market). Attempts to reach middle-income families are almost nonexistent; such families are not viewed as part of the museums' target audience, yet they spend significant amounts of money on leisure activities. Some programs exist for senior citizens, but museums are not well designed for this group.

11.5   How Important is the General Public as an Audience for Art Museums?

The last section indicated that the museum has multiple audiences it can serve. It identified the general public as one potential audience (as distinct from upper-income, college-educated potential patrons). Museums do not automatically reject this audience, but they do very little to placate them. The exhibits and general structure of the museum do little to attract this audience. There are many reasons for this, including (1) the fear of alienating the existing museum audience, (2) the public's general lack of understanding of art, (3) the cost of serving this group, and (4) their limited donations and the lower probability of their becoming members. As has been stated earlier there is also a fear that if this audience is served, it will alienate the existing museum donors because the types of exhibits required do not necessarily meet the museum's quality standards. Further, the "exclusivity" of the museum would be in jeopardy.

How important is this audience to the museum? The easiest way to answer this question is to look at revenues generated implicitly by this group. From the 1988 statistical survey of the Association of Art Museum Directors, statistics have been compiled on the subsidies this group implicitly represents to museums. The local, state, and federal subsidies equal about 22 percent of the total operating revenue of the museum.[3] Excluding federal subsidies reduces this number to 8 percent. Further, corporate grants to museums can also fall

---

3. Twenty-two percent represents a median value which reduces any skewness caused, for example, by purely public museums with very high federal subsidies.

under this category. They add another 5 percent to the total subsidies and grants given because the museum serves the general public. If one contrasts this to membership and attendance revenue, one sees that the latter category represents only 10 percent of the total operating revenue. The remainder of operating revenue is made up of large donations and revenue from the museum's endowment and bookstores, restaurants, and other museum shops.

If one analyzes the costs associated with revenues, government subsidies are very profitable—excluding the need to provide exhibits directed to the general public. In contrast, bookstores, shops, and restaurants barely break even. Membership fees also have a high cost associated with them because of low renewal rates. While government subsidies average 22 percent of operating revenue, most museums could not operate without these subsidies.

Given these facts, it is essential for museums to learn how to serve the general public. To deal with the conflict, museums might consider developing "two museums", one to serve the general public and one to serve the more sophisticated donors and members. The two groups have different interests and needs, and therefore, it is necessary to offer different products. An alternative would be for museums to reduce their dependence on these subsidies. This would mean that the museum would become a boutique, producing only exhibits targeted to a small but elite audience. Could a museum survive with this strategy? It is very difficult to answer this question. It depends upon whether the members, donors of works of art, and financial donors would contribute to this type of museum. Little or no research is available to answer this question. The museum board and its president, however, must address this issue if they are unwilling to serve the general public.

11.6   The Competitive Environment

Art museums compete with many different types of organizations for audiences, members, and benefactors (Stone 1988). These competitors can be grouped into several categories: (1) cultural institutions, (2) science museums, natural history museums, and zoos, (3) amusement parks, sporting events, and other leisure-time activities, (4) charities, and (5) educational institutions. Each of these offers different benefits to the donors, members, and attenders.

In looking at competitors, art museums must begin to assess the product each segment wants and then how effectively they can compete with these other types of organizations. Following are the types of benefits being offered by each organization:

- Charities offer social prestige and a sense of "contribution to human kind."
- Cultural institutions offer benefits similar to art museums but for different types of activities:
    -The symphony, opera, and theater offer regular performances.

-The choice for the "medium" not social or humanistic considerations, appears to be the major differentiating factor.

• Science museums, natural history museums, and zoos offer higher entertainment value for children than do art museums or the performing arts.

• Amusement parks and sporting events offer high entertainment value but lower educational or cultural benefits to the attender.

• Educational institutions can offer equivalent social prestige and humanistic goals, and they also offer the added benefit of contributing to the preservation of one's own educational institution.

The major audience for whom it is most difficult for art museums to compete is the general public, not the donor group. The public represents a large potential audience as evidenced by the larger attendance at science museums and zoos; art museums do not perceive these organizations to be competitive, yet they attract large audiences who represent revenue potential to art museums.

Competition for the potential donor segment is entirely different. The competitors offer the same type of benefits that art museums do, and therefore art museums must focus on how they can offer a differentiated product. Art museums must determine what they can offer the potential donor group that other cultural organizations cannot. These include special trips, special showings of exhibits, art education, and video and audio tapes for home viewing. Further, art museums can assist young collectors in understanding how collections are built, can teach them how to begin or expand a collection, and can offer special lectures by experts in art and collecting.

Currently, art museums are not organized to provide these benefits, though the development department is responsible for these activities. The question is: Does the development department simply ask this segment for money, or do they also try to provide benefits to the potential donor group? Commercial organizations frequently have market or segment managers who learn about the needs of their segment. Art museums rarely have someone responsible for analyzing and understanding a specific market segment.

11.7 Managing the Product Line

Museums face many problems which are similar to those of a fashion retailer: What is the breadth of the product line? How should the "buying process" be managed? How can a retailer or museum serve distinct and conflicting market segments?

11.7.1 Breadth of the Product Line

One of the critical issues retailers face is determining what "quality" or "fashion levels" to offer its customer. If the retailer offers too wide a product line, the consumer becomes confused about its positioning. Consider a retailer like Neiman Marcus. If they begin offering low-priced merchandise, will their

regular customers continue to buy at Neiman Marcus? Probably not. Therefore, they must determine how far down the quality spectrum they can go
without tarnishing their image.

This is also one of the critical issues facing art museums. If they make their
product too entertainment-oriented to appeal to a mass audience, what happens to their current customer base? Therefore, trying to be all things to all
people is unlikely to succeed. However, the other problem is too narrow a
product line. Boutique retailers can cater to a high fashion, couture customer
but their volume is very small. To reach larger audiences, it is necessary to
have a broader quality range than a boutique offers. Museums currently are
closer to boutiques, in that they want one quality designation. However, this
limits their primary audience to benefactors and members. The result is lower
attendance because of the limited target market.

For museums thinking about broadening the product line, quality is not
necessarily the key problem. Rather it is breadth of appeal. Twentieth-century
Japanese pottery may be of high quality but of very limited appeal. Thus, the
museum curators (buyers) can try to identify exhibits that have broader appeal
without greatly diminishing the image of the museum. Unfortunately, curators
(like buyers) would rather run exclusive boutiques than focus on how to expand audiences through shows which have high quality and yet appeal to
larger audiences. (An example of a successful show was the Vatican exhibit
shown in several cities, which reached new audiences and yet did not lower
quality.)

11.7.2   Profit Centers

Most corporations separate their businesses into profit centers. The purpose
of profit centers is to relate revenue to costs and determine which divisions or
product lines are profitable. It also creates an internal mechanism for allocat-
ing resources.

If art museum management separates the museum into two distinct entities,
it then becomes advantageous to create profit centers to determine which part
of the museum is being subsidized. The fear of using profit centers is that the
more popular, "lower quality" public museum will be profitable but the more
sophisticated, less attended "donor" museum will be unprofitable. Corporations have unprofitable product lines because they have synergy with other
product lines. For art museums to maintain their long-run viability, it will be
necessary to analyze individual divisions or entities to ensure they are contributing to the financial and aesthetic goals of the museum.

11.7.3   How Should the Buying Process Work?

Retailers have buyers who are responsible for identifying items to sell. Similarly, curators create shows or select shows to exhibit. Each buyer selects the
season's merchandise from a wide variety of suppliers. Curators do not have a
similar wholesale market. However, there is no reason why a wholesale mar-

ket could not exist for art exhibits. The difficult issue is compensating the creators of the shows for their efforts. It could be accomplished through viewership fees and revenue sharing.

If there were a for-profit market created for exhibits, then the developers of the exhibits as well as the curators would be focusing on viewership and target audiences as well as potential revenue opportunities. Just as in fashion, it would not pay the curator to deviate from the accepted image of the museum. However, there would be greater emphasis on viewership, target audiences, and the ability to share costs across museums.

Curators would need to be both experts in a specific period of art and also highly knowledgeable about the customer. Currently, curators only need to be experts in art. Thus, there is very little focus on the general needs of the customer. Only if profit becomes increasingly important to museums will the buying process change.

11.7.4   How Can Museums Serve Two Distinct Audiences?

As has been stated throughout this paper, the primary problem is serving two highly distinct audiences. How do retailers and other organizations solve this problem? The answer is to create separate entities each with a distinct focus on a specific market segment. For example, Dayton-Hudson has Dayton's in Minneapolis, which is a premium quality department store, and Target, which is a mass merchandiser. By having separate organizations focusing on different target market segments and offering distinct fashion designation, they are able to serve these two segments. Other organizations do the same thing. Holiday Corporation has Crown Plazas which serve the high end of the hotel market and Hampton Inns which serve the lower-to-middle segment. They are located in separate cities and have different missions.

Can museums divide their audiences and serve them separately? The answer is yes. The Field Museum in Chicago has divided itself into a public museum whose charter is to serve the mass market and a museum with a research staff who are responsible for students and researchers of natural history. By dividing responsibilities, they allow each organization to focus on its specific mission. An art museum can also divide itself into two separate functions: (1) the mass marketing museum which is designed to appeal to the public at large, and (2) the boutique museum which is aimed at the donor and potential donor. By separating roles, the museum can serve both audiences.

Does marketing to two separate audiences pose problems to the current organization? Clearly, the part of the organization that will need to change is the curatorial staff. They will need to be restructured into two separate organizations. A public exhibit staff will need to be developed to focus on involving, high quality exhibits that educate as well as entertain the visitor. Special exhibition space will need to be devoted to these types of exhibits, and a wing or special building devoted to the public museum.

The cost of the public museum can be covered from the public funds as well as corporate gifts. The donors can fund the "high-fashion" museum. Special blockbuster exhibits can appeal to both groups and the revenue can be allocated accordingly. Since government funding as well as corporate donations can be used for the public museum, it will be easier for these organizations to justify their subsidies or grants.

In summary, it is possible for museums to approach their multiple audiences just as a retailer who serves segmented markets does. They can offer separate product lines to these segments. The result will be the broadening of the appeal of art museums without diminishing the quality of the product or alienating its existing audience.

11.8   The Product—A Major Dilemma

It is our contention that the product is the motivating factor that determines whether someone visits the museum. For example, to compete for the broad audience of middle-income families with children, it is necessary to develop alternative exhibits which are less sophisticated and which have an amusement component with subtle educational elements. Junior children's museums provide this type of product—but only for very young children.

Science museums effectively attract a large visitorship. Their exhibits are more interactive and more involving than art museums. People receive audio and sensory stimulation as well as visual. There is always a great deal of activity to attract the visitor's attention. Children, in particular, enjoy attending these museums.

The dilemma art museums face is threefold:

1. Redesigning the product to cater to this audience, which might offend its existing customer base. This potential problem requires coordination to protect the existing customer base;
2. Selecting the types of exhibits that will appeal to this audience; and
3. Generating enough revenue and attendance to justify product modification to meet their needs.

Comparing the audience demographics of science museums with art museums shows that science museums capture a large percentage of the middle-income family audience. Science museums have approximately three times the attendance of art museums. In Chicago, if the Art Institute could capture 10 percent of the audience of the Museum of Science and Industry, its attendance would increase 25 percent, and it would generate $2,000,000 in revenue from admission plus $6 per person in shop and food revenue which is an additional $2,400,000 in revenue, or approximately 10 percent of operating costs.

Modern technology, particularly computer and video technology, can be used to enhance exhibits by allowing visitors to explore their visual experience in greater detail. In an article entitled "Recipe for an Interactive Art Gallery," David Phillips cites several examples of interactive exhibits (1988). On a grand scale, the Tate Gallery accompanied a Paint and Painting exhibition with two tents full of art materials and equipment used by some 700 to 1000 adults daily. The Manchester City Art Gallery had a similar but more modest event associated with a watercolor show. Leicestershire Museums provided another type of exhibit in 1986 when they devised a pair of boxes full of objects similar to those found in particular paintings on exhibit. The boxes were wired to permit experimentation with lighting effects. In addition, the Colour Museum in Bradford lets visitors change appearances by switching on and off different kinds of artificial light. Yet another example is the use of kaleidoscopes to permit the manipulation of patterns. The creation of patterns can be shown with such simple equipment as a bowl of water and used motor oil or a continuous sheet of soap, water, and glycerine. Certainly alternatives abound, but what is noteworthy is the small cost and the spectacular response from museum visitors both from an entertainment and educational perspective. These exhibits demonstrate that artistic principles such as perspective, color, and light can be communicated successfully in a museum setting. Involvement is important, and few art museums have exhibits which allow the viewer to interact.

Another deterring characteristic of art museums is that they are foreboding and difficult for the neophyte viewer to peruse (Hood 1983). The general public is often unfamiliar and thus not comfortable with art museums. People are unsure about what they are supposed to do and how often they are supposed to attend. They need to be educated as to what to expect from museums. First-time visitors would also benefit from a suggested path through the museum. Places to sit or stop and have a drink make the experience much easier, particularly for families or senior citizens. Simple changes like better signs, maps, and information would make it easier to learn where the exhibits are and other information about the exhibits.

In summary, for museums to attract larger nonblockbuster audiences, it becomes important to address the issue of involving exhibits. Computer and video technology offers art museums an opportunity to make this possible.

11.9   Blockbusters: Museums' Promotional Tool

Most museums live and die on the basis of special exhibits which generate large viewership, called blockbusters, and would prefer some relief from the pressure of having to generate such exhibits frequently. The reason is that blockbusters have an adverse effect on staffing, organizational requirements, and normal attendance. Unfortunately, blockbusters represent a high percentage of museum traffic, and therefore it is almost impossible to eliminate them.

Blockbusters are analogous to sales offered by retailers. Retailers use sales to attract new customers. Once the customer is in the store, it is hoped that he or she will purchase additional items. Thus, sales generate traffic. Other departments in the store can then make additional profits. Most museums understand this strategy. They sell related merchandise (books, posters, and reproductions) to visitors of major exhibits. Membership also increases because becoming a member is a way to guarantee one's admission to very successful exhibits.

Most retailers would like to reduce their dependence on sales. Unfortunately, the customer has consistently voted (through his or her purchase patterns) in favor of sales. Similarly, it would be extremely difficult for art museums to eliminate blockbusters.

One goal of retailers' sales is to attract new types of customers. Very few exhibits are designed to attract new types of audiences. Notable exceptions were the Vatican and King Tut exhibits. (Robbins and Robbins 1979). These exhibits brought an audience with different demographics from the audience that attends the standard exhibits run by museums. The curatorial staff, however, rarely is interested in this type of exhibit. Very little time is devoted to creating exhibits that would expand the audience because these exhibits are not thought to be of the quality of more sophisticated exhibits such as Picasso or Renoir.

Typically, blockbuster exhibits are intended to

1. Attract new types of visitors to the museum;
2. Increase the museum's revenues;
3. Provide benefits (e.g. special showings) for members of the museum; and
4. Increase membership.

While museums, like retailers, would like to eliminate the blockbuster, it is improbable this will occur. Museums can redirect their thinking to address how blockbusters can be used to meet financial and viewership goals.

11.10   Where Should Museums Distribute Their Product?

Traditionally, museums use their primary location (the museum) for visitors' access to exhibits or their collection. However, there is a trend to create alternative sites where the visitors can view exhibits. This is similar to retailers' offering different locations to make it easier for customers to shop at their stores. In assessing this strategy, many of the same issues retailers consider in site selection are relevant to art museums.

The first and most important question is: Can a new location make a profit? For an art museum this means analyzing attendance, revenue potential, costs, and ancillary benefits such as increasing the attendance at the main museum because individuals become aware of the exhibits through branch locations. Often it may be possible to arrange for another organization to house the museum branch and cover most of the costs because they receive benefits from having the museum branch in their area. In selecting locations for museums the issues are (1) the number of people visiting the location, (2) the demographics of the area, (3) the cost of the space, (4) logistics, and (5) cannibalization of visitors to existing locations.

In New York City several museums have used remote sites to reach new audiences and to increase attendance. The Metropolitan has a branch at The Cloisters in Fort Tryon Park in Manhattan. The Whitney has several locations in New York (The Federal Reserve Plaza and the Equitable Tower) and one in Stamford, Connecticut.

To reach different market segments and to broaden its audience, art museums will require creativity in where and how they use remote outlets. Banks can serve as a model. Their outlets range from the main bank (often in the central business district) to ATMs (Automated Teller Machines). They recognize the need to offer numerous locations to make it convenient for their customers to use the bank. For example, art museums could develop special electronic kiosks in malls in which there are video presentations of special exhibits. The Louvre in Paris uses a subway station to display some of its art and to interest visitors. These remote shows could serve to interest as well as inform the public of new and exciting exhibits at the museum. Art museums, just like other retailers, can become creative in their use of different types of outlets to reach their customer. There is no reason that museums are limited to their current exhibition space.

11.11   Pricing

To most art museums, pricing is a mystery. There are many difficult and complex questions that need to be answered. In analyzing pricing it is easiest if it is separated into two types (1) general admission fees and (2) membership fees.

11.11.1   Admission Fees

Most museums grapple with the question of the correct admission fee to charge. There are many issues related to admission fees that the art museum management and boards must consider. The first issue is whether to charge an admission fee at all. This depends upon the funding of the art museum. Some, because it violates a municipal or county charter, do not charge an admission fee. To overcome this problem, many museums use a recommended donation or contribution which is similar to an admission fee. However, it is voluntary and therefore does not violate the museum's charter.

If admission fees are allowed in the charter of the museum or do not require governmental approval (or do not substitute for governmental subsidies), most museums charge some form of admission fee. The question then arises: How much? This is a standard microeconomic question which is extremely difficult to answer.

In theory, one simply looks at the demand curve and then determines the optimal price based on the formula marginal revenue equals marginal cost. The problem, as is obvious, is that estimating the demand curve is almost impossible for museums. Time-series data on attendance and admission prices is almost nonexistent. Even if data were available, there is very little variation in price over long periods of time making it difficult (or impossible) to estimate price elasticities. This is also a common problem in the for-profit sector, where very few firms know the shape of their demand curve.

Nagle (1987) tries to assist managers by offering some simple rules to show when the demand curve is more sensitive to price increases and when it is less sensitive.

1. *When there are close substitutes, the market is more price sensitive.* For art museums, the degree to which there are close substitutes depends upon the market segment being analyzed. For individuals committed to art viewership as a leisure-time activity, there are few substitutes. Collectors fit into this segment. However, "middle America" is more price sensitive because there are many available substitutes. These range from other types of museums (some of which are free), to the zoo, to other leisure time activities. For other target groups such as young professionals, the number of available substitutes is large but the price of admission to an art museum is relatively low (usually lower than a movie). This group is not likely to perceive pricing as a barrier. Thus, the only major group that will be price sensitive is the group museums target least, middle America. Therefore, admission fees could be close to those of other art museums or similar cultural events.

2. *When the expenditure is a significant percentage of total income, the customer is more price sensitive.* For this reason, durable goods are price sensitive. For most visitors, the price of admission is a relatively low expenditure. However, for larger families, senior citizens, or students, this may be a more important consideration. It makes sense to offer special discounts to senior citizens and students, as most museums do.

3. *The higher the admission fee is as a proportion of the total expenditure, the more price sensitive is the customer.* For tourists who have spent hundreds of dollars traveling to a city, the expenditure on a museum may be a small percentage of their total vacation expenditure. Thus, museums in tourist areas such as New York, San Francisco, Los Angeles, and Washington, D.C. may be able to charge higher prices than museums in cities which are not major tourist destinations. The ratio of tourists to local patrons should influence price sensitivity. The higher the local patronage, the more price sensitive will be the average museum visitor. Museums reduce the conflict concerning an entry fee since the local community has the alternative of low-price membership.

In summary, it is difficult to determine how price sensitive the visitors will be using historical sales and price records. However, because of the lack of available data, some rules of thumb have been given which should help in thinking about price sensitivity.

There are other pricing strategies that can be used by museums. First, it is possible to use some form of quantity discounting. Possibilities include offering a discount on the next visit, offering a package of X tickets for the price of Y, or giving the frequent visitor an annual pass. Another commonly used pricing technique is bundling. Ski resorts offer a combination of hotel, air fare and lift tickets at a rate far below the combination of the three purchased individually. Art museums can use this form of pricing to create museum weekends in which several events (related to the visual arts) can be bundled with hotel and air fares. For example, the Art Institute of Chicago could find available hotel space, arrange with an airline to discount air tickets, and offer special evening events at the Art Institute which could actually be priced at $50 to $100. The package would appeal to certain segments, and through special discounts would be advantageous to the museum visitor. Thus, there are many creative ways to price museum attendance.

11.11.2   Membership

Membership pricing is easier to evaluate because direct mail is used to solicit new members and to renew current members. The Museum of Science and Industry in Chicago set up a direct mail test to determine how price sensitive potential new members were. They sent 10 percent of the people they were soliciting a higher membership fee, and they sent the remainder the regular (or control) price. Through this form of testing, they were able to determine that charging the potential new member a higher membership fee did not decrease the response rate enough to reduce total revenue. Thus, they were able to increase their membership fees.

The same strategy applies to the renewal of existing members. Some percentage of the membership file can be mailed a higher price and compared to those receiving the regular membership price. If this is successful, then at the next period the membership price can be increased.

11.11.3   Relationship between Membership and Admission Fees

Because members often receive lower (or free) admission to the museum, frequent users will become members to reduce their admission fees. Thus, membership is a form of bundled admission fees and heavy users become members in order to purchase the fixed-price package.

Based on several interviews, it appears that museums that have admission fees have more members. Because of the small sample and the difficulty in equating museum types, this finding should serve only as an hypothesis. If this result holds after more detailed statistical analyses, however, it would imply that admission fees are an important factor in creating larger membership.

11.11.4   Should Museums Try to Generate Traffic Using Promotions?

Most retailers use promotions to generate traffic. These range from events (e.g., back-to-school sales) to price discounts (e.g., rebates offered by automobile dealers). Museums use special exhibits, which are similar to promotions. However, there are very few other types of promotions. Thus, when there is no special exhibit, attendance suffers. Museums live from special exhibit to special exhibit.

Promotions can be thought of as special inducements to generate traffic. Grocery retailers run weekly specials which are designed to give the customer a reason to shop each week. Other retailers offer special prices only available when the customer is in the store. Can museums generate promotions which give individuals incentives to visit the museum more frequently and to feel that if they attend something special will occur? The answer is yes, but it requires creativity. Contests could be offered which appeal to specific segments of the market. For example, naming all the Impressionist works of art at the Art Institute of Chicago could lead to a prize such as a free poster of an Impressionist painting. The problem has been that art museums have not been creative in offering promotions, nor does art museum management perceive promotions as acceptable. However, promotions can be tasteful and create excitement for those attending the museum.

11.12   The Marketing Organization

The changes considered in this paper would require museums to think about how their marketing and curatorial organization will need to change. First, curators must have a similar role to that of a buyer in a retail establishment. This means that the curator must not only manage a collection but must begin to understand the audience. This audience must be consistent with the overall objectives of the museum.

Second, the purpose of marketing is to understand the customer and then be an integral part of the organization in using this understanding to design exhibits and programs. It would make sense for the museum to create market managers who are responsible for understanding certain segments. Thus, there is a market manager for the general public, a manager for potential donors, a manager for collectors and major donors, and a manager for members. Some of these roles can be combined, so that staffing costs will not be too high. It is important for the museum to structure itself around customer needs, not the product as is currently being done. It makes no sense to have a manager for eighteenth-century European art because the customers do not organize themselves along these lines. This archaic organizational structure is related to internal expertise, not external needs.

Third, if the museum is going to separate its functions between the public museum and the donor museum, then it will be necessary to divide the staff so that they clearly understand their mission and goals. Curators can serve as consultants to the public museum in assisting the marketing and exhibition staff in understanding what to exhibit. However, a staff dedicated to the public museum is needed, otherwise it will simply become an extension of the current museum and will not devote its activity to serving the general public.

11.13   Summary

This article has focused on the key dilemma art museums face: having two separate and distinct audiences. It has used analogies from retailing and other types of business to discuss how these audiences can be served. The possibilities discussed include

1. Separating the museum into two distinct parts so that each suborganization can serve the needs of its constituency effectively;
2. Creating market managers who are responsible for understanding the needs of these two distinct segments;
3. Redesigning the product so that the general public is given a product that meets their needs (more involving and more entertaining) while at the same time serving the other audience which likes and appreciates more sophisticated art exhibits;
4. Requiring the curatorial staff to think more the way retail buyers do, who not only worry about the quality of the merchandise but also about the appeal of the product to each segment; and
5. Creating profit centers to analyze and manage the two distinct museums just as companies manage different products

References

Adams, Donald G., and John Boatright. 1986. *The Selling of the Museum 1986* (April), 16–21.
Ames, Peter J. 1988. A Challenge to Modern Museum Management: Reconciling Mission and Market. *Museum Studies Journal* (Spring/Summer):10–14.
Beer, Valorie. 1987. Great Expectations: Do Museums Know What Visitors Are Doing? *Curator* (September):206–15.
Bigley, James D. 1987. Marketing in Museums: Background and Theoretical Foundations. *Museum Studies Journal* (Fall/Winter):14–21.
Bowden, Christopher. 1986. Marketing a Rediscovery: Renior at the Boston Museum of Fine Arts. *Museum News* (August):40–45.
Braverman, Benjamin E. 1988. Empowering Visitors: Focus Group Interviews for Art Museums. *Curator* (March):43–52.
Bunch, S. et al. 1988. Do Traveling Exhibits Influence Museum Attendance? *Curator* (June):131–36.
Cameron, Duncan F., and David S. Abbey. 1962. Museum Audience Research: The Effect of an Admission Fee. *Museum News* 41, no. 3:25–28.

Cramer, Ted. 1979. Marketing the Museum. *Museum News* (January/February).

Cox, Meg. 1987. Spring Finds Art Market Vigorous but Some Paint a Gloomy Future. *Wall Street Journal,* 19 May 1987, 33.

DiMaggio, Paul J. 1985. When the "Profit" is Quality: Cultural Institutions in the Marketplace. *Museum News* (June):28–35.

Field Museum. 1986. *Field Museum of Natural History Bulletin,* pp. 16–17. Chicago: Field Museum of Natural History.

Fronville, Claire. 1985. Marketing for Museums: For-Profit Techniques in the Non-Profit World. *Curator* (September):169–82.

Gardner, Toni. 1986. Learning From Listening: Museums Improve Their Effectiveness through Visitor Studies. *Museum News* (February).

Glueck, Grace. 1989. Gifts to Museums Fall Sharply after Changes in the Tax Code. *The New York Times,* 7 May, 1.

Hancocks, A. 1987. Museum Exhibition as a Tool for Social Awareness. *Curator* (September):181–92.

Hendon, William S. 1979. *Analyzing an Art Museum.* New York: Praeger.

Hood, Marilyn. 1983. Staying Away: Why People Choose Not to Visit Museums. *Museum News,* (April):50–57.

———. 1986. Getting Started in Audience Research. *Museum News* (February):25–31.

Keens, William. 1986. Serving up Culture: The Whitney and Its Branch Museums. *Museum News* (April):22–28.

Lee, Susan. 1988. Greed Is Not Just for Profit. *Forbes,* 18 April 1988, 65–70.

Louis Harris and Associates. 1988. *Americans and the Arts V.* N. Manchester, Indiana: Heckman Bindery Inc.

McCarthy, Jerome E. 1975. *Basic Marketing: A Managerial Approach.* Homewood, Ill.: Richard D. Irwin, Inc.

Mokwa, Michael P., William M. Dawson, and E. Arthur Prieve, eds. 1980. *Marketing the Arts.* New York: Praeger.

Nagle, Thomas T. 1987. *The Strategy and Tactics of Pricing.* Englewood Cliffs, N.J.: Prentice-Hall.

O'Hare, Michael. 1975. Why Do People Go to Museums? The Effect of Prices and Hours on Museum Utilization. *Museum* 27 (3):134–46.

Phillips, David. 1988. Recipe for an Interactive Art Gallery. *The International Journal of Museum Management and Curatorship* (July):243–52.

Raymond, Thomas J. C., and Stephen A. Greyser. 1978. The Business of Managing the Arts. *Harvard Business Reiview* (July – August) 123–32.

Robbins, J. E., and Robbins, S. S. 1979. Segmentation for "Fine Arts" Marketing: Is King Tut Classless as Well as Ageless? In *Educators Conference Proceedings,* ed. N. Beckwith, et al. Chicago, Ill.: American Marketing Association.

Shapiro, Benson P. 1973. Marketing for Nonprofit Organizations. *Harvard Business Review* (September–October):123–32.

Skloot, Edward. 1983. Should Not-for-Profits Go into Business? *Harvard Business Review* (January–February):20–25.

Stone, Denise Lauzier. 1988. The Use of Advertising to Attract the Museum Public. *Curator.* (June):123–30.

Yorke, David, and P. R. Jones. 1987. Museums and Marketing Techniques. *Management Decisions* 25 (1):25–32.

Unterman, Israel, and Richard Hart Davis. 1982. The Strategy Gap in Not-for-Profits. *Harvard Business Review* (May–June):30–40.

Zolberg, Vera L. 1984. American Art Museum: Sanctuary or Free-for-All? *Social Forces* 63 (December).

Biographies

Alberta Arthurs is director for Arts and Humanities at the Rockefeller Foundation. Previously, she was president and professor of English at Chatham College and, before that, a dean at Harvard and Radcliffe Colleges. She has also taught at Rutgers and Tufts, and is currently chairman of the Independent Committee on Arts Policy.

Robert C. Blattberg is the Polk Brothers Distinguished Professor in Retailing at the Kellogg Graduate School of Management, Northwestern University. At the time of this conference, he was the Charles H. Kellstadt Professor of Marketing and Director of the Center for Marketing Information Technology in the Graduate School of Business, University of Chicago, where he had been a faculty member since 1969.

Edgar Peters Bowron is the Andrew W. Mellon Senior Consultative Curator at the National Gallery of Art. From 1985 to 1990, he was the Elizabeth and John Moors Cabot Director at the Harvard University Art Museums.

Cynthia J. Broderick is a marketing consultant at Kestnbaum & Company, formerly a division of Andersen Consulting. She holds an MBA from the University of Chicago and an M.S. in Operations Research from Stanford.

J. Carter Brown has been director of the National Gallery of Art since 1969. He received graduate degrees from the Harvard Business School and New York University's Institute of Fine Arts. He is a trustee of the American Academy in Rome, Corning Museum of Glass, The Henry Francis Du Pont Winterthur Museum, John F. Kennedy Center for the Performing Arts, National Geographic Society, Storm King Art Center, and the World Monuments Fund. He is a member of the International Committee for the History of Art, and, reappointed by President Bush in 1989, he continues as chairman of the Commission of Fine Arts.

Jay E. Cantor has been Senior Vice President and Director of Museum Services for Christie, Manson & Woods International since 1989 and was previously the head of American Paintings from 1978 to 1988.

Geoffrey Carliner is executive director of the National Bureau of Economic Research. Prior to coming to the NBER, he was a senior staff economist at the Council of Economic Advisers working on labor issues and international trade policy.

347

Rosemary Clarke is a lecturer in the Department of Economics, University of Birmingham, England.

Charles T. Clotfelter is professor of public policy studies and economics at Duke University and serves as director of Duke's Center for the Study of Philanthropy and Voluntarism. He is a research associate of the NBER.

Anne d'Harnoncourt has been the director of the Philadelphia Museum of Art since 1982. From 1971 to 1982, she served as curator of the museum's department of twentieth-century art, organizing such exhibitions as the retrospective of Marcel Duchamp (1973), "Eight Artists" (1980), and "John Cage: Scores and Prints" (1981).

Paul J. DiMaggio is associate professor of sociology at Yale University, where he also holds appointments in the School of Organization and Management and Institution for Social and Policy Studies. A former executive director of Yale's Program on Non-Profit Organizations, he has served on the Connecticut Commission on the Arts and is a 1990 fellow of the John Simon Guggenheim Memorial Foundation.

Douglas W. Elmendorf is an assistant professor of economics at Harvard University.

Bruce H. Evans is director of the Dayton Art Institute. He is a past-president of the Association of Art Museum Directors and has been responsible for the salary and statistical surveys of the art museum field that the association has conducted since 1982.

Ross W. Farrar is the executive director of Palmer & Dodge, Attorneys, and an overseer of the Museum of Fine Arts, Boston. Previously, he was the deputy director of the Museum of Fine Arts, Boston.

Martin Feldstein is the George F. Baker Professor of Economics at Harvard University and president and chief executive officer of the National Bureau of Economic Research. He was chairman of the Council of Economic Advisers from 1982 through 1984.

Don Fullerton is professor of economics at the University of Virginia and a Research Associate of the NBER. He was Deputy Assistant Secretary of the Treasury for Tax Analysis from 1985 to 1987 and a Senior Olin Fellow at the NBER from 1988 to 1989.

Millicent Hall Gaudieri is the executive director of the Association of Art Museum Directors. She is an ex officio member of the Board of the American Arts Alliance and has served on boards of a number of nonprofit organizations.

Sir John Hale is emeritus professor of history at University College in London and has been chairman of the trustees of the London National Gallery and a trustee of the Victoria and Albert Museum. He is now a trustee of the British Museum and a member of the Museums and Galleries Commission.

Gail Harrity is the assistant director for finance and administration of the Solomon R. Guggenheim Museum. Prior to joining the Guggenheim in 1989, she held several positions at the Metropolitan Museum of Art during the years 1982 through 1989, including the positions of special assistant to the president and assistant treasurer, and chief of budget, planning, and government relations.

Ashton Hawkins is executive vice president and counsel to the trustees of The Metropolitan Museum of Art.

Anne Hawley became director of the Isabella Stewart Gardner Museum in Boston in September 1989. Prior to that she led the Massachusetts Council on the Arts and Humanities, the commonwealth's cultural agency.

Roger G. Kennedy is the director of the National Museum of American History of the Smithsonian Institution. He was previously vice president for finance and senior financial officer and vice president for arts of the Ford Foundation. He is an author and lecturer and has served as a financial consultant to several foundations.

Thomas Krens is director of the Solomon R. Guggenheim Museum and concurrently serves as adjunct professor of art history at Williams College. He is also chairman of the Massachusetts Museum of Contemporary Art Commission (MASS MoCA).

William H. Luers has been president of the Metropolitan Museum of Art since 1986. During his previous 30 years as an American foreign service officer, he served as ambassador to Venezuela and Czechoslovakia. He is on the boards of several U.S. corporations, is a trustee of the Rockefeller Brothers Fund, and is a member of the Council on Foreign Relations.

Richard E. Oldenburg is director of The Museum of Modern Art, New York, a post he has held since 1972. He has also served as chairman of the Museum Policy Board of the National Endowment for the Arts, as chairman of the Modern Art Committee of the International Council of Museums, and as president of the Association of Art Museum Directors.

Andrew Oliver is director of the museum program at the National Endowment for the Arts. Previously, he was director of the Textile Museum in Washington, D.C. and associate curator of Greek and Roman art at the Metropolitan Museum of Art.

Harry S. Parker III is the director of the Fine Arts Museums of San Francisco and was formerly director of the Dallas Museum of Art.

Marilyn Perry is president of the Samuel H. Kress Foundation. She serves as chairman of the World Monuments Fund, and chairman of the program committee of the National Building Museum.

Richard N. Rosett is presently dean of the College of Business, Rochester Institute of Technology. Previously, he was professor of economics, Washington University.

Neil Rudenstine is president of Harvard University. At the time of this conference, he was executive vice-president of the Andrew W. Mellon Foundation in New York.

Scott J. Schaefer has been the vice president, director of Museum Services, and expert in Fine Art for Sotheby's since 1988. Previously, he was the curator of European painting and sculpture at the Los Angeles County Museum of Art from 1980 to 1987.

Martin Shubik has been the Seymour H. Knox Professor of Mathematical Institutional Economics at Yale University since 1975.

Theodore E. Stebbins, Jr. is John Moors Cabot Curator of American Paintings at the Museum of Fine Arts, Boston. He was formerly curator at the Yale University Art Gallery, and associate professor of art history and American studies at Yale.

Peter C. Sutton is Baker Curator of European Paintings at the Museum of Fine Arts, Boston. A Northern Baroque specialist, he has organized international loan exhibitions on Dutch painting.

Peter Temin is professor of economics at the Massachusetts Institute of Technology and a research associate of the NBER. He currently is chairman of the MIT Department of Economics.

Julia Brown Turrell is the director of the Des Moines Art Center, Des Moines, Iowa, and a trustee of the Association of Art Museum Directors. She was previously senior curator, Museum of Contemporary Art, Los Angeles.

John Walsh is director of the J. Paul Getty Museum in Los Angeles. He taught at Columbia University, was a curator of paintings at the Metropolitan Museum and Museum of Fine Arts, Boston, and served as president of the Association of Art Museum Directors in 1989–90.

Harold M. Williams has been president and chief executive officer of the J. Paul Getty Trust since 1981. From 1977 to 1981, he was chairman of the United States Securities and Exchange Commission. From 1970 to 1977, he was dean and professor of management at the Graduate School of Management at the University of California, Los Angeles, and prior thereto, chairman of the board of Norton Simon, Inc. He is a member of the Council on Foreign Relations, the Committee for Economic Development, The National Humanities Center, and a Regent of the University of California.

James N. Wood has been the director of The Art Institute of Chicago since 1980. His previous museum posts were at the Metropolitan Museum of Art in New York; the Albright-Knox Art Gallery in Buffalo; and the St. Louis Art Museum, of which he was director from 1975 to 1980.

Participants

Alberta Arthurs
Director for Arts and Humanities
The Rockefeller Foundation
1133 Avenue of the Americas
New York, NY 10036

Robert C. Blattberg
Kellogg Graduate School of
    Management
Leverone Hall
Northwestern University
Evanston, IL 60208–2008

Edgar Peters Bowron
Andrew W. Mellon Senior Consultative
    Curator
National Gallery of Art
6th and Constitution Avenue, NW
Washington, DC 20565

Cynthia J. Broderick
Kestnbaum & Company
55 West Wacker Drive, Suite 1210
Chicago, IL 60601–1612

J. Carter Brown
Director
National Gallery of Art
4th Street and Constitution Avenue, NW
Washington, DC 20565

Jay E. Cantor
Senior Vice President and Director of
    Museum Services
Christie, Manson & Woods International
502 Park Avenue
New York, NY 10022

Geoffrey Carliner
Executive Director
National Bureau of Economic Research
1050 Massachusetts Avenue
Cambridge, MA 02138

Rosemary Clarke
Department of Economics
University of Birmingham
Edgbaston
Birmingham, B15 2TT, U.K.

Charles T. Clotfelter
Institute of Policy Sciences and Public
    Affairs
Duke University
Box 4875 Duke Station
Durham, NC 27706

Anne d'Harnoncourt
Director
The Philadelphia Museum of Art
P.O. Box 7646
Philadelphia, PA 19101

Paul J. DiMaggio
Sociology Department
Yale University
140 Prospect Street
1965 Yale Station
New Haven, CT 06520

Douglas W. Elmendorf
Department of Economics
Harvard University
Cambridge, MA 02138

Bruce H. Evans
Director
Dayton Art Institute
P.O. Box 941
Dayton, OH 45401

Ross W. Farrar
Executive Director
Palmer & Dodge
One Beacon Street
Boston, MA 02108

Martin Feldstein
President and Chief Executive Officer
National Bureau of Economic Research
1050 Massachusetts Avenue
Cambridge, MA 02138

Don Fullerton
Department of Economics
Rouss Hall
University of Virginia
Charlottesville, VA 22901

Millicent Hall Gaudieri
Executive Director
Association of Art Museum Directors
41 East 65th Street
New York, NY 10021

Sir John Hale
26 Montpelier Row
Twickenham
Middlesex, TW1 2NQ, U.K.

Gail Harrity
Assistant Director for Finance and
    Administration
Solomon R. Guggenheim Museum
1071 Fifth Avenue
New York, NY 10128

Ashton Hawkins
Executive Vice President
The Metropolitan Museum of Art
Fifth Avenue and 82nd Street
New York, NY 10028

Anne Hawley
Director
Isabella Stewart Gardner Museum
2 Palace Road
Boston, MA 02115

Roger G. Kennedy
Director
National Museum of American History
Smithsonian Institution
Washington, DC 20560

Thomas Krens
Director
Solomon R. Guggenheim Museum
1071 Fifth Avenue
New York, NY 10128

William H. Luers
President
The Metropolitan Museum of Art
Fifth Avenue and 82nd Street
New York, NY 10028

Richard E. Oldenburg
Director
The Museum of Modern Art
11 West 53rd Street
New York, NY 10019

Andrew Oliver
Director, Museum Program
National Endowment for the Arts
1100 Pennsylvania Avenue, NW,
    Rm 624
Washington, DC 20506

Harry S. Parker III
Director
The Fine Arts Museums of San
    Francisco
Lincoln Park
San Francisco, CA 94121

Marilyn Perry
President
Samuel H. Kress Foundation
174 East 80th Street
New York, NY 10021

Richard N. Rosett
Dean, College of Business Rochester
    Institute of Technology
One Lomb Drive
Rochester, NY 14623–0887

Neil Rudenstine
President
Harvard University
Massachusetts Hall 1
Cambridge, MA 02138

Scott J. Schaefer
Vice President and Director of Museum
 Services
Sotheby's
1334 York Avenue
New York, NY 10021

Martin Shubik
Department of Economics
Yale University
1972 Yale Station
New Haven, CT 06520

Theodore E. Stebbins, Jr.
John Moors Cabot Curator of American
 Painting
Museum of Fine Arts, Boston
465 Huntington Avenue
Boston, MA 02115

Peter C. Sutton
Baker Curator of European Paintings
Museum of Fine Arts, Boston
465 Huntington Avenue
Boston, MA 02115

Peter Temin
Department of Economics
Massachusetts Institute of Technology
E52–274
Cambridge, MA 02139

Julia Brown Turrell
Director
Des Moines Art Center
4700 Grand Avenue
Greenwood Park
Des Moines, IA 50312

John Walsh
Director
J. Paul Getty Museum
P.O. Box 2112
Santa Monica, CA 90406

Harold M. Williams
President and Chief Executive Officer
J. Paul Getty Trust
1875 Century Park East, Suite 2300
Los Angeles, CA 90067

James N. Wood
Director
The Art Institute of Chicago
Michigan Avenue and Adams Street
Chicago, IL 60603

Name Index

Abbey, David S., 329
Abbing, Hans, 240n9
Adams, Donald G., 330
Ames, Peter J., 328
Andrews, William T., 196
Annenberg, Walter, 26, 72
Anthoine, Robert, 210
Arffman, Kathleen, 69
Arthur Andersen, 206n7, 227n29
Arthurs, Alberta, 59, 88, 104
Association of Art Museum Directors
    (AAMD), 253n43, 262n55
Austen-Smith, David, 240n9
Ayton, B., 314n25

Bailey, Anne Lowrey, 246n27
Banfield, Edward C., 199, 239n4, 241, 243–
    44, 245n22, 254, 264n59
Barthold, Thomas, 228
Baumol, William J., 200n3, 297
Beer, Valorie, 329
Berman, Ronald, 243, 245
Bernheim, B. Douglas, 227
Bethell, Tom, 242
Biddle, Livingston, 240n8
Blattberg, Robert C., 57, 59
Blaug, Mark, 311n21
Boskin, Michael, 228
Bowden, Christopher, 329
Bowen, William, 200n3, 297
Braverman, Benjamin E., 329
Brown, J. Carter, 60, 105
Brown, Paula, 41n5, 43n7

Buchanan, James, 239
Buckley, William F., 243
Bullard, Katherine, 183
Bunch, S., 330
Burt, N., 190

Cameron, Duncan F., 329
Cantor, Jay E., 31, 32
Carliner, Geoffrey, 87–88
Carter, Malcolm N., 244n20, 245n22, 253,
    260nn48,49, 261nn51,52,53
Casals, Pablo, 126
Clark, Kenneth, 53
Clarke, Rosemary, 33, 203
Clotfelter, Charles T., 30, 201, 205–6, 212–
    13, 215n20, 217, 219, 222–23, 225–28,
    230–31, 261n50
Coleman, Lawrence V., 47n16, 183, 185,
    188
Commerce Clearing House, 206n7, 217n23
Copeland, John, 219n25
Cossons, N., 275, 312
Cox, Meg, 327
Cramer, Ted, 329
Cummings, Milton C., 204, 245n24

Dana, John Cotton, 47
David, Robert, 247n32
Davis, Richard H., 330
Dawson, William M., 329
de Montebello, Philippe, 66, 69
d'Harnoncourt, Anne, 59
Dillon, Douglas, 71

Subject Index